Table of Contents

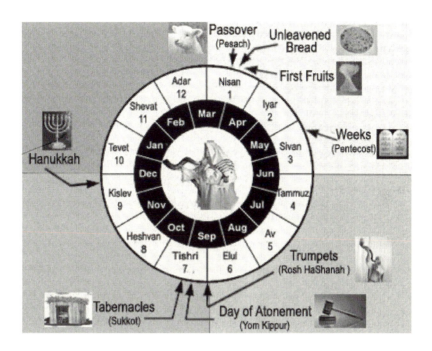

Introduction

The 7 Feasts of a Highly Effective God explores in detail the hidden meanings behind these sacred days. Leviticus 23 contains all 7 Feasts. Hanukkah, the Feast of Dedication (John 10), came later in Bible history. We see the 7 Feasts, also known as Holy Convocations, listed in the order of Passover, Unleavened Bread, First Fruits, Weeks, Trumpets, Day of Atonement and Tabernacles. They are listed in chronological order as they first occurred in the Bible. Moses experienced the first four upon leaving Egypt.

We will soon discover that the virgin conception of Jesus occurred on Hanukkah, nine months later Jesus was born on Trumpets (2 day Feast, also known as one long day of 48 hours), Eight days later He

1

was Circumcised on the Day of Atonement, He dwelt/tabernacled amongst us without sin for 33 years for Tabernacles, He was then our Passover Lamb, then in the Tomb for Unleavened Bread i.e. without sin, He was Resurrected on First Fruits, appeared to many during the 49 Days of the Feast of Weeks, then we have Pentecost, Day 50, Freedom Day, a Jubilee Day in a Jubilee Year. The chains of sin and death are both broken!!!

We weren't left as orphans, He sent the Helper, the Holy Spirit the day after He completed His 7 Feast Work. The 7 Feast Work of Jesus equals our Eternal 7th Day Sabbath Rest, His Work=our Eternal Rest. Remember the Manna from Heaven in Exodus 16? Twice as much Manna from Heaven was given on Friday, the sixth day, so the people of God could have their 7th Day Sabbath Rest. Jesus, the Manna from Heaven i.e. Bread of Life, was crucified on Friday, the sixth day, so the people of God could have Eternal Sabbath Rest. This is the true meaning of the Sabbath Commandment; it has nothing to do with which day you go to "church" on. Interestingly that when you use the Hebrew lunar calendar that was used in Bible times, since Passover is always on Nisan 14, and always a Saturday, the Messiah was crucified on Friday the 13th. Remember in the Old Testament the 7th Day was a Day of Rest. The 7th Year was also a Year of Rest. The land was not farmed in the 7th Year. Imagine having the whole year off, because God provided all you needed in the sixth year, the "Good Friday" year. We will be using the NASB translation throughout this book. The Bible will be in Times New Roman font. Commentary is in Calibri font. (Note: the Kindle e-book might not appear in two fonts.)

If you have been preaching the full Gospel, then you are already familiar with the 7 Feasts, you just didn't realize it. A good foundational statement for this book is: The Old Testament is Jesus concealed, the New Testament is Jesus revealed. Chapter one will cover the 7 Feasts within Luke chapters 1-3. Then we will study chapter by chapter through John, Acts, and Hebrews from the 7 Feasts perspective. We will always begin with the Bible chapter, then the commentary following. The actual full Bible chapters are within this book; I want the emphasis to be on His Word, and also this alleviates jumping back and forth between the Bible and this book. Many times when Bible references are inserted, many times people do not actually look them up. Below is Leviticus 23.

The LORD spoke again to Moses, saying, 2 "Speak to the sons of Israel and say to them, 'The LORD'S appointed times which you shall proclaim as holy convocations—My appointed times are these:

3 'For six days work may be done, but on the seventh day there is a sabbath of complete rest, a holy convocation. You shall not do any work; it is a sabbath to the LORD in all your dwellings.

4 'These are the appointed times of the LORD, holy convocations which you shall proclaim at the times appointed for them. 5 In the first month, on the fourteenth day of the month [a]at twilight is the LORD'S Passover. 6 Then on the fifteenth day of the same month there is the Feast of Unleavened Bread to the LORD; for seven days you shall eat unleavened bread. 7 On the first day you shall have a holy convocation; you shall not do any laborious work. 8 But for seven days you shall present an offering by fire to the LORD. On the seventh day is a holy convocation; you shall not do any laborious work.'"

9 Then the LORD spoke to Moses, saying, 10 "Speak to the sons of Israel and say to them, 'When you enter the land which I am going to give to you and reap its harvest, then you shall bring in the sheaf of the first fruits of your harvest to the priest. 11 He shall wave the sheaf before the LORD for you to be accepted; on the day after the sabbath the priest shall wave it. 12 Now on the day when you wave the sheaf, you shall offer a male lamb one year old without defect for a burnt offering to the LORD. 13 Its grain offering shall then be two-tenths *of an ephah* of fine flour mixed with oil, an offering by fire to

3

the LORD *for* a soothing aroma, with its drink offering, a fourth of a [b]hin of wine. [14] Until this same day, until you have brought in the offering of your God, you shall eat neither bread nor roasted grain nor new growth. It is to be a perpetual statute throughout your generations in all your dwelling places.

[15] 'You shall also count for yourselves from the day after the sabbath, from the day when you brought in the sheaf of the wave offering; there shall be seven complete sabbaths. [16] You shall count fifty days to the day after the seventh sabbath; then you shall present a new grain offering to the LORD. [17] You shall bring in from your dwelling places two *loaves* of bread for a wave offering, made of two-tenths *of an* [c]*ephah*; they shall be of a fine flour, baked with leaven as first fruits to the LORD. [18] Along with the bread you shall present seven one year old male lambs without defect, and a bull of the herd and two rams; they are to be a burnt offering to the LORD, with their grain offering and their drink offerings, an offering by fire of a soothing aroma to the LORD. [19] You shall also offer one male goat for a sin offering and two male lambs one year old for a sacrifice of peace offerings. [20] The priest shall then wave them with the bread of the first fruits for a wave offering with two lambs before the LORD; they are to be holy to the LORD for the priest. [21] On this same day you shall make a proclamation as well; you are to have a holy convocation. You shall do no laborious work. It is to be a perpetual statute in all your dwelling places throughout your generations.

[22] 'When you reap the harvest of your land, moreover, you shall not reap to the very corners of your field nor gather the gleaning of your harvest; you are to leave them for the needy and the alien. I am the LORD your God.'"

[23] Again the LORD spoke to Moses, saying, [24] "Speak to the sons of Israel, saying, 'In the seventh month on the first of the month you shall have a [d]rest, a reminder by blowing *of trumpets*, a holy convocation. [25] You shall not do any laborious work, but you shall present an offering by fire to the LORD.'"

The Day of Atonement

26 The LORD spoke to Moses, saying, 27 "On exactly the tenth day of this seventh month is the day of atonement; it shall be a holy convocation for you, and you shall humble your souls and present an offering by fire to the LORD. 28 You shall not do any work on this same day, for it is a day of atonement, to make atonement on your behalf before the LORD your God. 29 If there is any [e]person who will not humble himself on this same day, he shall be cut off from his people. 30 As for any person who does any work on this same day, that person I will destroy from among his people. 31 You shall do no work at all. It is to be a perpetual statute throughout your generations in all your dwelling places. 32 It is to be a sabbath of complete rest to you, and you shall humble your souls; on the ninth of the month at evening, from evening until evening you shall keep your sabbath."

33 Again the LORD spoke to Moses, saying, 34 "Speak to the sons of Israel, saying, 'On the fifteenth of this seventh month is the Feast of Booths for seven days to the LORD. 35 On the first day is a holy convocation; you shall do no laborious work of any kind. 36 For seven days you shall present an offering by fire to the LORD. On the eighth day you shall have a holy convocation and present an offering by fire to the LORD; it is an assembly. You shall do no laborious work.

37 'These are the appointed times of the LORD which you shall proclaim as holy convocations, to present offerings by fire to the LORD—burnt offerings and grain offerings, sacrifices and drink offerings, *each* day's matter on its own day— 38 besides *those of* the sabbaths of the LORD, and besides your gifts and besides all your [f]votive and freewill offerings, which you give to the LORD.

39 'On exactly the fifteenth day of the seventh month, when you have gathered in the crops of the land, you shall celebrate the feast of the LORD for seven days, with a [g]rest on the first day and a [h]rest on the eighth day. 40 Now on the first day you shall take for yourselves the [i]foliage of beautiful trees, palm branches and boughs of leafy trees and willows of the brook, and you shall rejoice before the LORD your

God for seven days. [41] You shall thus celebrate it *as* a feast to the LORD for seven days in the year. It *shall be* a perpetual statute throughout your generations; you shall celebrate it in the seventh month. [42] You shall [j]live in booths for seven days; all the native-born in Israel shall [k]live in booths, [43] so that your generations may know that I had the sons of Israel live in booths when I brought them out from the land of Egypt. I am the LORD your God.'" [44] So Moses declared to the sons of Israel the appointed times of the LORD. (Leviticus 23)
https://www.biblegateway.com/passage/?search=Leviticus+23&version=NASB

Chapter 1: Luke 1-3

Luke 1 New American Standard Bible (NASB)

Introduction

1 Inasmuch as many have undertaken to compile an account of the things [a]accomplished among us, [2] just as they were handed down to us by those who from the beginning [b]were eyewitnesses and [c]servants of the [d]word, [3] it seemed fitting for me as well, having [e]investigated everything carefully from the beginning, to write *it* out for you in consecutive order, most excellent Theophilus; [4] so that you may know the exact truth about the things you have been [f]taught.

Birth of John the Baptist Foretold

5 In the days of Herod, king of Judea, there was a priest named [g]Zacharias, of the division of [h]Abijah; and he had a wife [i]from the daughters of Aaron, and her name was Elizabeth. 6 They were both righteous in the sight of God, walking blamelessly in all the commandments and requirements of the Lord. 7 But they had no child, because Elizabeth was barren, and they were both advanced in [j]years.

8 Now it happened *that* while he was performing his priestly service before God in the *appointed* order of his division, 9 according to the custom of the priestly office, he was chosen by lot to enter the temple of the Lord and burn incense. 10 And the whole multitude of the people were in prayer outside at the hour of the incense offering. 11 And an angel of the Lord appeared to him, standing to the right of the altar of incense. 12 Zacharias was troubled when he saw *the angel*, and fear [k]gripped him. 13 But the angel said to him, "Do not be afraid, Zacharias, for your petition has been heard, and your wife Elizabeth will bear you a son, and you will [l]give him the name John. 14 You will have joy and gladness, and many will rejoice at his birth. 15 For he will be great in the sight of the Lord; and he will drink no wine or liquor, and he will be filled with the Holy Spirit [m]while yet in his mother's womb. 16 And he will turn many of the sons of Israel back to the Lord their God. 17 It is he who will go *as a forerunner* before Him in the spirit and power of Elijah, TO TURN THE HEARTS OF THE FATHERS BACK TO THE CHILDREN, and the disobedient to the attitude of the righteous, so as to make ready a people prepared for the Lord."

18 Zacharias said to the angel, "How will I know this *for certain*? For I am an old man and my wife is advanced in [n]years." 19 The angel answered and said to him, "I am Gabriel, who [o]stands in the presence of God, and I have been sent to speak to you and to bring you this good news. 20 And behold, you shall be silent and unable to speak until the day when these things take place, because you did not believe my words, which will be fulfilled in their proper time."

21 The people were waiting for Zacharias, and were wondering at his delay in the temple. 22 But when he came out, he was unable to speak to them; and they realized that he had seen a vision in the temple;

and he kept [p]making signs to them, and remained mute. 23 When the days of his priestly service were ended, he went back home.

24 After these days Elizabeth his wife became pregnant, and she [q]kept herself in seclusion for five months, saying, 25 "This is the way the Lord has dealt with me in the days when He looked *with favor* upon *me*, to take away my disgrace among men."

Jesus' Birth Foretold

26 Now in the sixth month the angel Gabriel was sent from God to a city in Galilee called Nazareth, 27 to a virgin [r]engaged to a man whose name was Joseph, of the [s]descendants of David; and the virgin's name was [t]Mary. 28 And coming in, he said to her, "Greetings, [u]favored one! The Lord [v]*is* with you." 29 But she was very perplexed at *this* statement, and kept pondering what kind of salutation this was. 30 The angel said to her, "Do not be afraid, Mary; for you have found favor with God. 31 And behold, you will conceive in your womb and bear a son, and you shall name Him Jesus. 32 He will be great and will be called the Son of the Most High; and the Lord God will give Him the throne of His father David; 33 and He will reign over the house of Jacob forever, and His kingdom will have no end." 34 Mary said to the angel, "How [w]can this be, since I [x]am a virgin?" 35 The angel answered and said to her, "The Holy Spirit will come upon you, and the power of the Most High will overshadow you; and for that reason the [y]holy Child shall be called the Son of God. 36 And behold, even your relative Elizabeth has also conceived a son in her old age; and [z]she who was called barren is now in her sixth month. 37 For [aa]nothing will be impossible with God." 38 And Mary said, "Behold, the [ab]bondslave of the Lord; may it be done to me according to your word." And the angel departed from her.

Mary Visits Elizabeth

39 Now [ac]at this time Mary arose and went in a hurry to the hill country, to a city of Judah, 40 and entered the house of Zacharias and greeted Elizabeth. 41 When Elizabeth heard Mary's greeting, the

baby leaped in her womb; and Elizabeth was filled with the Holy Spirit. [42] And she cried out with a loud voice and said, "Blessed *are* you among women, and blessed *is* the fruit of your womb! [43] And [ad]how has it *happened* to me, that the mother of my Lord would come to me? [44] For behold, when the sound of your greeting reached my ears, the baby leaped in my womb for joy. [45] And blessed *is* she who [ae]believed that there would be a fulfillment of what had been spoken to her [af]by the Lord."

The Magnificat

[46] And Mary said:

"My soul [ag]exalts the Lord,
[47] And my spirit has rejoiced in God my Savior.
[48] "For He has had regard for the humble state of His [ah]bondslave;
For behold, from this time on all generations will count me blessed.
[49] "For the Mighty One has done great things for me;
And holy is His name.
[50] "AND HIS MERCY IS [ai]UPON GENERATION AFTER GENERATION
TOWARD THOSE WHO FEAR HIM.
[51] "He has done [aj]mighty deeds with His arm;
He has scattered *those who were* proud in the [ak]thoughts of their heart.
[52] "He has brought down rulers from *their* thrones,
And has exalted those who were humble.
[53] "HE HAS FILLED THE HUNGRY WITH GOOD THINGS;
And sent away the rich empty-handed.
[54] "He has given help to Israel His servant,
[al]In remembrance of His mercy,
[55] As He spoke to our fathers,
To Abraham and his [am]descendants forever."

[56] And Mary stayed with her about three months, and *then* returned to her home.

John Is Born

[57] Now the time [an]had come for Elizabeth to give birth, and she gave birth to a son. [58] Her neighbors and her relatives heard that the Lord had [ao]displayed His great mercy toward her; and they were rejoicing with her.

[59] And it happened that on the eighth day they came to circumcise the child, and they were going to call him Zacharias, [ap]after his father. [60] But his mother answered and said, "No indeed; but he shall be called John." [61] And they said to her, "There is no one among your relatives who is called by that name." [62] And they made signs to his father, as to what he wanted him called. [63] And he asked for a tablet and wrote as follows, "His name is John." And they were all astonished. [64] And at once his mouth was opened and his tongue *loosed*, and he *began* to speak in praise of God. [65] Fear came on all those living around them; and all these matters were being talked about in all the hill country of Judea. [66] All who heard them kept them in mind, saying, "What then will this child *turn out to* be?" For the hand of the Lord was certainly with him.

Zacharias's Prophecy

[67] And his father Zacharias was filled with the Holy Spirit, and prophesied, saying:

[68] "Blessed *be* the Lord God of Israel,
For He has visited us and accomplished redemption for His people,
[69] And has raised up a horn of salvation for us
In the house of David His servant—
[70] As He spoke by the mouth of His holy prophets from of old—
[71] [aq]Salvation FROM OUR ENEMIES,
And FROM THE HAND OF ALL WHO HATE US;
[72] To show mercy toward our fathers,
And to remember His holy covenant,
[73] The oath which He swore to Abraham our father,
[74] To grant us that we, being rescued from the hand of our enemies,
Might serve Him without fear,
[75] In holiness and righteousness before Him all our days.
[76] "And you, child, will be called the prophet of the Most High;

For you will go on BEFORE THE LORD TO PREPARE HIS WAYS;
[77] To give to His people *the* knowledge of salvation
[ar]By the forgiveness of their sins,
[78] Because of the tender mercy of our God,
With which the Sunrise from on high will visit us,
[79] TO SHINE UPON THOSE WHO SIT IN DARKNESS AND THE SHADOW OF
DEATH,
To guide our feet into the way of peace."

[80] And the child continued to grow and to become strong in spirit, and he lived in the deserts until the day of his public appearance to Israel.

Luke 2 New American Standard Bible (NASB)

Jesus' Birth in Bethlehem

2 Now in those days a decree went out from Caesar Augustus, that a census be taken of all [a]the inhabited earth. [2] [b]This was the first census taken while [c]Quirinius was governor of Syria. [3] And everyone was on his way to register for the census, each to his own city. [4] Joseph also went up from Galilee, from the city of Nazareth, to Judea, to the city of David which is called Bethlehem, because he was of the house and family of David, [5] in order to register along with Mary, who was engaged to him, and was with child. [6] While they were there, the days were completed for her to give birth. [7] And she gave birth to her firstborn son; and she wrapped Him in cloths, and laid Him in a [d]manger, because there was no room for them in the inn.

[8] In the same region there were *some* shepherds staying out in the fields and keeping watch over their flock by night. [9] And an angel of the Lord suddenly stood before them, and the glory of the Lord shone around them; and they were terribly frightened. [10] But the angel said to them, "Do not be afraid; for behold, I bring you good news of great joy which will be for all the people; [11] for today in the

city of David there has been born for you a Savior, who is [e]Christ the Lord. [12] This *will be* a sign for you: you will find a baby wrapped in cloths and lying in a [f]manger." [13] And suddenly there appeared with the angel a multitude of the heavenly host praising God and saying,

[14] "Glory to God in the highest,
And on earth peace among men [g]with whom He is pleased."

[15] When the angels had gone away from them into heaven, the shepherds *began* saying to one another, "Let us go straight to Bethlehem then, and see this thing that has happened which the Lord has made known to us." [16] So they came in a hurry and found their way to Mary and Joseph, and the baby as He lay in the [h]manger. [17] When they had seen this, they made known the statement which had been told them about this Child. [18] And all who heard it wondered at the things which were told them by the shepherds. [19] But Mary treasured all these things, pondering them in her heart. [20] The shepherds went back, glorifying and praising God for all that they had heard and seen, just as had been told them.

Jesus Presented at the Temple

[21] And when eight days had passed, [i]before His circumcision, His name was *then* called Jesus, the name given by the angel before He was conceived in the womb.

[22] And when the days for their purification according to the law of Moses were completed, they brought Him up to Jerusalem to present Him to the Lord [23] (as it is written in the Law of the Lord, "EVERY *firstborn* MALE THAT OPENS THE WOMB SHALL BE CALLED HOLY TO THE LORD"), [24] and to offer a sacrifice according to what was said in the Law of the Lord, "A PAIR OF TURTLEDOVES OR TWO YOUNG PIGEONS."

[25] And there was a man in Jerusalem whose name was Simeon; and this man was righteous and devout, looking for the consolation of Israel; and the Holy Spirit was upon him. [26] And it had been revealed

to him by the Holy Spirit that he would not see death before he had seen the Lord's [j]Christ. 27 And he came in the Spirit into the temple; and when the parents brought in the child Jesus, [k]to carry out for Him the custom of the Law, 28 then he took Him into his arms, and blessed God, and said,

29 "Now Lord, You are releasing Your bond-servant to depart in peace,
According to Your word;
30 For my eyes have seen Your salvation,
31 Which You have prepared in the presence of all peoples,
32 A LIGHT [l]OF REVELATION TO THE GENTILES,
And the glory of Your people Israel."

33 And His father and mother were amazed at the things which were being said about Him. 34 And Simeon blessed them and said to Mary His mother, "Behold, this *Child* is appointed for the fall and [m]rise of many in Israel, and for a sign to be opposed— 35 and a sword will pierce even your own soul—to the end that thoughts from many hearts may be revealed."

36 And there was a prophetess, [n]Anna the daughter of Phanuel, of the tribe of Asher. She was advanced in [o]years and had lived with *her* husband seven years after her [p]marriage, 37 and then as a widow to the age of eighty-four. She never left the temple, serving night and day with fastings and prayers. 38 At that very [q]moment she came up and *began* giving thanks to God, and continued to speak of Him to all those who were looking for the redemption of Jerusalem.

Return to Nazareth

39 When they had performed everything according to the Law of the Lord, they returned to Galilee, to their own city of Nazareth. 40 The Child continued to grow and become strong, [r]increasing in wisdom; and the grace of God was upon Him.

Visit to Jerusalem

[41] Now His parents went to Jerusalem every year at the Feast of the Passover. [42] And when He became twelve, they went up *there* according to the custom of the Feast; [43] and as they were returning, after spending the full number of days, the boy Jesus stayed behind in Jerusalem. But His parents were unaware of it, [44] but supposed Him to be in the caravan, and went a day's journey; and they *began* looking for Him among their relatives and acquaintances. [45] When they did not find Him, they returned to Jerusalem looking for Him. [46] Then, after three days they found Him in the temple, sitting in the midst of the teachers, both listening to them and asking them questions. [47] And all who heard Him were amazed at His understanding and His answers. [48] When they saw Him, they were astonished; and His mother said to Him, "[s]Son, why have You treated us this way? Behold, Your father and I [t]have been anxiously looking for You." [49] And He said to them, "Why is it that you were looking for Me? Did you not know that I had to be in My Father's [u]*house*?" [50] But they did not understand the statement which He [v]had made to them. [51] And He went down with them and came to Nazareth, and He continued in subjection to them; and His mother treasured all *these* [w]things in her heart.

[52] And Jesus kept increasing in wisdom and [x]stature, and in favor with God and men.

Luke 3 New American Standard Bible (NASB)

John the Baptist Preaches

3 Now in the fifteenth year of the reign of Tiberius Caesar, when Pontius Pilate was governor of Judea, and Herod was tetrarch of Galilee, and his brother Philip was tetrarch of the region of Ituraea and Trachonitis, and Lysanias was tetrarch of Abilene, [2] in the high priesthood of Annas and Caiaphas, the word of God came to John, the son of Zacharias, in the wilderness. [3] And he came into all the district around the Jordan, preaching a baptism of repentance for the

forgiveness of sins; ⁴ as it is written in the book of the words of Isaiah the prophet,

"THE VOICE OF ONE CRYING IN THE WILDERNESS,
'MAKE READY THE WAY OF THE LORD,
MAKE HIS PATHS STRAIGHT.
⁵ 'EVERY RAVINE WILL BE FILLED,
AND EVERY MOUNTAIN AND HILL WILL BE [a]BROUGHT LOW;
THE CROOKED WILL BECOME STRAIGHT,
AND THE ROUGH ROADS SMOOTH;
⁶ AND ALL [b]FLESH WILL SEE THE SALVATION OF GOD.'"

⁷ So he *began* saying to the crowds who were going out to be baptized by him, "You brood of vipers, who warned you to flee from the wrath to come? ⁸ Therefore bear fruits in keeping with repentance, and do not begin to say [c]to yourselves, 'We have Abraham for our father,' for I say to you that from these stones God is able to raise up children to Abraham. ⁹ Indeed the axe is already laid at the root of the trees; so every tree that does not bear good fruit is cut down and thrown into the fire."

¹⁰ And the crowds were questioning him, saying, "Then what shall we do?" ¹¹ And he would answer and say to them, "The man who has two tunics is to share with him who has none; and he who has food is to do likewise." ¹² And *some* tax collectors also came to be baptized, and they said to him, "Teacher, what shall we do?" ¹³ And he said to them, "[d]Collect no more than what you have been ordered to." ¹⁴ *Some* soldiers were questioning him, saying, "And *what about* us, what shall we do?" And he said to them, "Do not take money from anyone by force, or accuse *anyone* falsely, and be content with your wages."

¹⁵ Now while the people were in a state of expectation and all were [e]wondering in their hearts about John, as to whether he was [f]the Christ, ¹⁶ John answered and said to them all, "As for me, I baptize you with water; but One is coming who is mightier than I, and I am not fit to untie the thong of His sandals; He will baptize you [g]with the Holy Spirit and fire. ¹⁷ His winnowing fork is in His hand to

thoroughly clear His threshing floor, and to gather the wheat into His barn; but He will burn up the chaff with unquenchable fire."

[18] So with many other exhortations he preached the gospel to the people. [19] But when Herod the tetrarch was reprimanded by him because of Herodias, his brother's wife, and because of all the wicked things which Herod had done, [20] Herod also added this to them all: he locked John up in prison.

Jesus Is Baptized

[21] Now when all the people were baptized, Jesus was also baptized, and while He was praying, heaven was opened, [22] and the Holy Spirit descended upon Him in bodily form like a dove, and a voice came out of heaven, "You are My beloved Son, in You I am well-pleased."

Genealogy of Jesus

[23] When He began His ministry, Jesus Himself was about thirty years of age, being, [h]as was supposed, the son of Joseph, [i]the son of [j]Eli, [24] the son of Matthat, the son of Levi, the son of Melchi, the son of Jannai, the son of Joseph, [25] the son of Mattathias, the son of Amos, the son of Nahum, the son of [k]Hesli, the son of Naggai, [26] the son of Maath, the son of Mattathias, the son of Semein, the son of Josech, the son of Joda, [27] the son of Joanan, the son of Rhesa, the son of Zerubbabel, the son of [l]Shealtiel, the son of Neri, [28] the son of Melchi, the son of Addi, the son of Cosam, the son of Elmadam, the son of Er, [29] the son of [m]Joshua, the son of Eliezer, the son of Jorim, the son of Matthat, the son of Levi, [30] the son of Simeon, the son of [n]Judah, the son of Joseph, the son of Jonam, the son of Eliakim, [31] the son of Melea, the son of Menna, the son of Mattatha, the son of Nathan, the son of David, [32] the son of Jesse, the son of Obed, the son of Boaz, the son of [o]Salmon, the son of [p]Nahshon, [33] the son of Amminadab, the son of Admin, the son of [q]Ram, the son of Hezron, the son of Perez, the son of Judah, [34] the son of Jacob, the son of Isaac, the son of Abraham, the son of Terah, the son of Nahor, [35] the son of Serug, the son of [r]Reu, the son of Peleg, the son

of [s]Heber, the son of Shelah, [36] the son of Cainan, the son of Arphaxad, the son of Shem, the son of Noah, the son of Lamech, [37] the son of Methuselah, the son of Enoch, the son of Jared, the son of Mahalaleel, the son of Cainan, [38] the son of Enosh, the son of Seth, the son of Adam, the son of God.

We see in Luke 1 that Zacharias, the future father of John the Baptist, is serving in his priestly duty. He is chosen to burn incense and while he is burning incense he is visited by an angel of the Lord. He is told that he will have a son and that the name of his son will be John; he will be a forerunner, a type of Elijah, the prophet of the Most High. In Luke 1:23 his priestly service was ended and he went home. When does his priestly service period end? The clue is in Luke 1:5, he is of the priestly division of Abijah. In 1 Chronicles 24:1-19 we have the order of priestly service. He was of Abijah, the eighth timeslot, starting two weeks before Pentecost. So his first service would have ended after Pentecost, because in addition to their regular service periods all priests had to serve at the required three Feast Weeks; Tabernacles, Passover and Weeks. Below is a picture showing the Jewish year. So there are 24 divisions of priests listed in 1 Chronicles 24. Each division served two weeks per year, one week at a time (1 Chronicles 9:25). They served Sabbath to Sabbath (2 Chronicles 23:8). They also served the three required Feast Weeks for all Jewish males (Exodus 23, 34 and Deuteronomy 16). So 48 plus 3 equals 51, which equates to the Hebrew year of 51 weeks. The priestly time slots begin in Nisan, month 1 of the year. This enabled the high priest to prepare himself for over six full months, prior to entering the Holy of Holies on the 10th of the 7th Month, the Day of Atonement. Note that the Hebrew/Jewish New Year's Day is not Nisan 1, it is Tishri 1 (Exodus 34:22 and Leviticus 25:8-13). God chose to have the Head of the Year, the Beginning, on the first day of the 7th Month, Tishri. It is interesting that the Jews kept all Babylonian names for their months. But if you look at 1 Kings 8:2, we find the original Hebrew name for the 7th Month, Ethanim, meaning Gift of God. The Gift of God, Jesus Christ, the Messiah was born on New Year's Day. Note as well that Trumpets is a two day Feast (also known as one long day of 48 hours). Why? Because the entire year was based off of this day, in which a sliver of the moon was used to determine. So they had two days to be positive. Remember as well that every Sabbath, such as Passover, was on a Saturday. The moon and stars, along with Daniel's prophecy are how the magi came to Christ. With today's calendar, Gregorian etc., Passover and all other Holydays "float". Passover might be on a Wednesday one year and on a Thursday in another year. With the Hebrew Calendar, the days did not float. The calendar is based off of the moon, being called a lunar calendar. Once the Head of the Year was established at Tishri/Ethanim, the beginning of 7th Month, then all the Sabbaths fell into place. The midmonth Sabbath i.e. Saturday would be a full moon. There is a sect of Jews called the Karaite Jews who still adhere to this calendar. So to get the most detail from God's Word we have to use the calendar that they used.

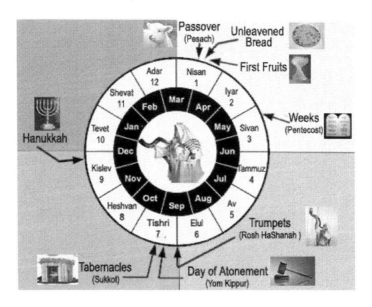

So once Zacharias returned home, his wife Elizabeth, became pregnant. For five months she hid herself. Then you have Mary, her relative, visiting her in her six month of pregnancy. This would be at Hanukkah. This is also the month that Mary would have conceived. This is interesting in that Mary lived in Nazareth and Elizabeth lived in the hill country of Judah. The trip would have been 80-100 miles. This is a neat point in that Mary conceived by the Holy Spirit, not by Joseph. Joseph was 80-100 miles away. Another awesome point is that Hanukkah is associated with light, the Holyday of the Light, Jesus being the Light of the world. Remember the Rainbow Covenant given to Noah? The Rainbow is Light in 7 Colors. So that puts John being born at the first month of the year, Nisan 1.

Six months pass and we have Mary giving birth to the Christ on the Feast of Trumpets, in the month of Tishri/Ethanim. On our calendar this would be the September/October timeframe. Jesus came in the fall for the fall of man. This is the First Trumpet. The Last Trumpet is the Rapture of the Church (1 Corinthians 15:52). The shepherds heard this Trumpet and were terrified (Luke 2:9). Would wolves, or even a bear or lion "terrify" shepherds? No, but thousands of angels blowing trumpets would. Note how humbly Jesus came into this world. His Trumpet birth announcement was to the lower class shepherds, and at night at that. He was born in a stable, not a palace.

Then on the eighth day, the Day of Atonement, Jesus is Circumcised. The Circumcision of Christ was in fulfillment of the Promise given to Abraham. Remember God told Abraham that through his loins all nations would be blessed. This is a really big deal in that all Hebrew males from Abraham on have been circumcised. Millions and millions of people circumcised to point to the coming Messiah. In Acts we learn that circumcision is no longer required, why? Because Christ fulfilled that Promise/Covenant made with Abraham. In Matthew 1, the Gospel that is directed to Jews, we see the genealogy from Abraham to Jesus. In Luke, the

Gospel directed to Greeks i.e. Gentiles, or better put to all nations, we have the genealogy all the way back to Adam, the first man. The Day of Atonement was the One Day a year that the High Priest could enter the Holy of Holies. The Holy of Holies was enclosed by the 12 inch thick Veil, eighty feet in height. We know that at the end of Jesus' 33 Years, while on the Cross, that this Veil was tore from Top to bottom, meaning God tore it, "it is finished". The Day of Atonement was for sin, to say that Jesus did not ultimately fulfill this Feast is just plain crazy.

We then go on to the Feast of Tabernacles. To tabernacle means to dwell in tents. We see Jesus "dwelling" in a human tent among men, growing up. In John 1:14, we read, "the Word became flesh and dwelt/tabernacled amongst us…." Even today temporary shelters are put up during the Tabernacles Feast Week (also called Booths or Sukkot). It is interesting that the covering of the temporary shelters are made up of palm branches. Remember the week before His Crucifixion that He rode over palm branches, this being a hidden message that He fulfilled this Feast and that His earthly Work was nearing its end.

We then have a Passover mentioned in Luke 2:41. So we have Passover, Unleavened Bread, and First Fruits being celebrated over their Jerusalem visit. Then we have Jesus "missing" for three days, being "found" on the third day. This is a foreshadow of His future death on Friday the 13th i.e. Good Friday (Passover is Saturday, Nisan 14), Jesus then being our Sabbath Passover Lamb, in the tomb at Unleavened Bread, and His Resurrection at First Fruits. Then in Luke 3:22 we have a picture of Pentecost, the Holy Spirit descending upon Him like a dove. Then Luke 3 ends with the genealogy of Christ. Christ is the Promised One, the Savior of the world, the 7 Feasts are all about Him. Will you dine with Him?

Behold, I stand at the door and knock; if anyone hears My voice and opens the door, I will come in to him and will dine with him, and he with Me. [21] He who overcomes, I will grant to him to sit down with Me on My throne, as I also overcame and sat down with My Father on His throne. [22] He who has an ear, let him hear what the Spirit says to the churches.'" (Revelation 3:20-22)

Hanukkah and the 7 Feast Gospel:

Hanukkah: Mary is overshadowed by the Holy Spirit, the virgin conception. Humility to the extreme, God the Creator, humbling Himself to a Single Cell, placed within the virgin Mary.

Trumpets: Nine months later Jesus, the Promised Messiah, was born, coming humbly into this world. We are to be humble. We are born again, a new birth announcement. This is the First Trumpet (the Last Trumpet is the Rapture). It is very important to note that in one of the most major Messianic prophecies found in Genesis 22, that when Abraham was about to sacrifice his son at the land of Moriah (Christ being crucified at Mount Moriah/Golgotha), that God stopped him and said that, "God will provide Himself a Sacrifice." Just then a Ram was there with His Head caught in the thorns, Crown of Thorns. The ONLY Feast/Holy Convocation that Ram's Horns are blown is during Trumpets. The other Feasts use silver trumpets. A very interesting fact is that although lambs are born in the spring, and some might say, well for God's Word to be perfect, the Lamb of God would have been born in the spring, but there is one species, called the Dorset sheep that are born year round. And awesomely enough the Dorset ram is where we get shofars from. Hebrew tradition says that the priests blew the left horn on one day and the right horn on the other day of Trumpets. Note as well that these two days are referred to as one long day (48 hours). Some believe the second day of Trumpets was added by the Prophets in 500 B.C., therefore not admissible in this view, but that does not matter because Hanukkah (starting around 165 B.C.) was added post Leviticus 23 as well. The Hebrews were to be "watchful" for the first coming of the Messiah, just like us today; we are to be "watchful" for His second coming. Note as well that the first Ten Days of the year, starting in the 7th Month, are known as the Ten Days of Awe, 10 Days of having a heart of repentance. A good practice is to reflect on the Ten Commandments during this time, one Commandment a day. We are guilty of breaking all Ten, but Jesus kept them all.

Atonement: The Covenant of Circumcision given to Abraham is fulfilled in Christ. Through the loins of Abraham all nations would be blessed. Jesus was brought to the Temple and circumcised on this Day. Jesus goes on to tabernacle amongst us for 33 years without sin. On Good Friday, when Jesus the Great High Priest said, "It is finished!" sin was atoned for, the Veil to the Holy of Holies was torn, from Top to bottom, God tore it. The Blood of Christ atones for our sin. We are forgiven, washed of our sin. Picture yourself in a bath tub; your sin is washed away. Don't lay in that dirty, putrid bath water. Let go of that sin, let it down the drain, let it flow off into the Jordan River into the Dead Sea. Later we will have more about the amazing Jordan River hidden meaning.

Tabernacles: Christ dwelt amongst us in a Human Tent. The Light came into the world and tabernacled amongst us. We are in the world but not of the world. We are to be the salt and light to the world. Salt heals, flavors, and preserves. Light exposes the darkness. During this Hebrew Feast people dwell in temporary shelters/tents made of palm branches. The week prior to Passover the people put palm branches on the ground for Jesus to ride over, Jesus having fulfilled this Feast.

Passover: Christ is our Perfect Passover Lamb, 33 years without sin. He died in our place. The angel of death passes over us because of this. By His Blood we are saved from sin, which ends with eternal death. hell was made for satan and his angels, not for us.

Unleavened Bread: He died for our sins and was buried in the tomb for three days and three nights as Jonah, Saturday, Sunday and Monday (Matthew 12:40). We are to be buried with Christ. We must die to self. Unleavened Bread, means without leaven, without sin. Jesus was sinless.

First Fruits (Easter): Jesus is the Resurrection and the Life, the First Fruits of all creation. He rose again. Easter is actually on a Tuesday. That's why God saw it was good twice on the Third Day (Tuesday) of Creation (Genesis 1:9-13). Some Orthodox Jews still get married on Tuesday because of the two goods in Genesis 1. First Fruits is also known as the "first day of the Week", meaning the first day of the week of the 7 Weeks of 7. First Fruits/Resurrection Day is Day 1 of the 49. Note as well that the Bible expresses Resurrection Day as the Third Day (Sunday 1, Monday 2, and Tuesday the Third Day). All three ways that the Bible expresses Resurrection Day lead to Tuesday. He not only conquered sin, but also death. We too, will rise again, at the Last Trumpet, the Rapture, unless of course we are alive at His return.

Weeks: Jesus appears to several witnesses over a period of 49 Days (7 weeks of 7 Days), being the 7th and last Feast of the 7 Feasts, giving proof to His conquering of not just sin, but sin and death. We then have Pentecost, which means the Fiftieth Day. This also occurred in the Fiftieth Year, the Year of Jubilee. The Year of Jubilee was the Year of Complete Freedom; any debts you owed were forgiven. Jesus was literally crucified in the Year of Jubilee. A major part of the Gospel that people are missing is that the Holy Spirit of

God now lives in us. We have the Helper, the Comforter within us. By faith, the Holy Spirit lives in our human tent or temple. It is interesting how the Apostle Paul was a tentmaker.

Our heart in essence is the new Holy of Holies. The deeper meaning of Jerusalem is that it is a picture of the believer's heart. Jesus took our sin upon Himself within the walls of Jerusalem, within the walls of our heart; He then took our sin outside of the walls of our heart, outside the walls of Jerusalem, to be Crucified at Golgotha, the Place of the Skull. We will see more on the Jerusalem/heart relationship later. Hanukkah and the 7 Feast Gospel is just that, the Full Gospel of Jesus. The Old Testament is Jesus concealed, the New Testament is Jesus revealed.

A special note, if you are asking yourself, what if the father of John the Baptist was told his wife would be pregnant at his second timeslot, then that would put Jesus being born at Passover. Which the shepherds would not have been in the field and Joseph himself would have had to be in Jerusalem for the mandatory Feast of Unleavened Bread, not in Bethlehem.

Also, some might say that when they use the Hebrew Lunar Calendar to count from Hanukkah to Trumpets they only get 38 weeks. A normal human pregnancy is 37 to 42 weeks. We throw around the term 9 months or 40 weeks, only because it is the average between 37 and 42, only four percent of humans are born at 40 weeks. So the Messiah being Born at 38 weeks is totally acceptable. There is a large group claiming that the Messiah was Born at Tabernacles, but remember this group also says that Christ has not yet fulfilled the Day of Atonement, which is the Only Day for the atonement of sin. To teach that Christ did not yet make atonement for sin is exactly what the enemy wants us to teach.

Note as well that I have a second book, also on Amazon, that journeys chapter by chapter through the Book of Revelation. The book takes a radically different view of Revelation compared to today's dominant, only 200 years old, dispensational view. The book is titled, *Revelation: Heart, Love and Marriage*. The book shows the deeper meaning of Revelation: the sinful heart of man, the Love of God in Christ Jesus, culminating in an Eternal Marriage made in Heaven.

Below is a wonderful Old Testament Scripture that echoes the 7 Feasts/Holy Convocations:

Then I will sprinkle clean water on you, and you will be clean; I will cleanse you from all your filthiness and from all your idols. [26] Moreover, I will give you a new heart and put a new spirit within you; and I will remove the heart of stone from your flesh and give you a heart of flesh. [27] I will put My Spirit within you and cause you to walk in My statutes, and you will be careful to observe My ordinances. (Ezekiel 36:25-27)

Chapter 2: The Gospel of John

John 1

In the beginning was the Word, and the Word was with God, and the Word was God. ² [a]He was in the beginning with God. ³ All things came into being through Him, and apart from Him nothing came into being that has come into being. ⁴ In Him was life, and the life was the Light of men. ⁵ The Light shines in the darkness, and the darkness did not [b]comprehend it.

⁶ There [c]came a man sent from God, whose name was John. ⁷ [d]He came [e]as a witness, to testify about the Light, so that all might believe through him. ⁸ [f]He was not the Light, but *he came* to testify about the Light.

⁹ There was the true Light [g]which, coming into the world, enlightens every man. ¹⁰ He was in the world, and the world was made through Him, and the world did not know Him. ¹¹ He came to His [h]own, and those who were His own did not receive Him. ¹² But as many as received Him, to them He gave the right to become children of God, *even* to those who believe in His name, ¹³ who were [i]born, not of [j]blood nor of the will of the flesh nor of the will of man, but of God.

¹⁴ And the Word became flesh, and [k]dwelt among us, and we saw His glory, glory as of [l]the only begotten from the Father, full of grace and truth. ¹⁵ John *testified about Him and cried out, saying, "This was He of whom I said, 'He who comes after me [m]has a higher rank than I, for He existed before me.'" ¹⁶ For of His fullness [n]we have all received, and [o]grace upon grace. ¹⁷ For the Law was given through Moses; grace and truth [p]were realized through Jesus Christ. ¹⁸ No one has seen God at any time; the only begotten God who is in the bosom of the Father, He has explained *Him.*

[19] This is the testimony of John, when the Jews sent to him priests and Levites from Jerusalem to ask him, "Who are you?" [20] And he confessed and did not deny, but confessed, "I am not [q]the Christ." [21] They asked him, "What then? Are you Elijah?" And he *said, "I am not." "Are you the Prophet?" And he answered, "No." [22] Then they said to him, "Who are you, so that we may give an answer to those who sent us? What do you say about yourself?" [23] He said, "I am A VOICE OF ONE CRYING IN THE WILDERNESS, 'MAKE STRAIGHT THE WAY OF THE LORD,' as Isaiah the prophet said."

[24] Now they had been sent from the Pharisees. [25] They asked him, and said to him, "Why then are you baptizing, if you are not the [r]Christ, nor Elijah, nor the Prophet?" [26] John answered them saying, "I baptize [s]in water, *but* among you stands One whom you do not know. [27] *It is* He who comes after me, the thong of whose sandal I am not worthy to untie." [28] These things took place in Bethany beyond the Jordan, where John was baptizing.

[29] The next day he *saw Jesus coming to him and *said, "Behold, the Lamb of God who takes away the sin of the world! [30] This is He on behalf of whom I said, 'After me comes a Man who [t]has a higher rank than I, for He existed before me.' [31] I did not recognize [u]Him, but so that He might be manifested to Israel, I came baptizing [v]in water." [32] John testified saying, "I have seen the Spirit descending as a dove out of heaven, and He remained upon Him. [33] I did not recognize [w]Him, but He who sent me to baptize [x]in water said to me, 'He upon whom you see the Spirit descending and remaining upon Him, this is the One who baptizes [y]in the Holy Spirit.' [34] I myself have seen, and have testified that this is the Son of God."

[35] Again the next day John was standing [z]with two of his disciples, [36] and he looked at Jesus as He walked, and *said, "Behold, the Lamb of God!" [37] The two disciples heard him speak, and they followed Jesus. [38] And Jesus turned and saw them following, and *said to them, "What do you seek?" They said to Him, "Rabbi (which translated means Teacher), where are You staying?" [39] He *said to them, "Come, and you will see." So they came and saw where He was staying; and they stayed with Him that day, for it was about the [aa]tenth hour. [40] One of the two who heard John *speak* and

27

followed Him, was Andrew, Simon Peter's brother. [41] He *found first his own brother Simon and *said to him, "We have found the Messiah" (which translated means [ab]Christ). [42] He brought him to Jesus. Jesus looked at him and said, "You are Simon the son of [ac]John; you shall be called Cephas" (which is translated [ad]Peter).

[43] The next day He purposed to go into Galilee, and He *found Philip. And Jesus *said to him, "Follow Me." [44] Now Philip was from Bethsaida, of the city of Andrew and Peter. [45] Philip *found Nathanael and *said to him, "We have found Him of whom Moses in the Law and *also* the Prophets wrote—Jesus of Nazareth, the son of Joseph." [46] Nathanael said to him, "Can any good thing come out of Nazareth?" Philip *said to him, "Come and see." [47] Jesus saw Nathanael coming to Him, and *said of him, "Behold, an Israelite indeed, in whom there is no deceit!" [48] Nathanael *said to Him, "How do You know me?" Jesus answered and said to him, "Before Philip called you, when you were under the fig tree, I saw you." [49] Nathanael answered Him, "Rabbi, You are the Son of God; You are the King of Israel." [50] Jesus answered and said to him, "Because I said to you that I saw you under the fig tree, do you believe? You will see greater things than these." [51] And He *said to him, "Truly, truly, I say to you, you will see the heavens opened and the angels of God ascending and descending on the Son of Man." (John 1) https://www.biblegateway.com/passage/?search=John+1&version=NASB

When we first became believers, someone may have suggested we read the book of John. It is said that John is the universal Gospel. Matthew is directed to "Jews", Mark to Romans, and Luke to Greeks. All four were written to the human heart, but knowing the audience can give us better understanding.

If we put verses one, fourteen, and seventeen together we get: "In the beginning was the Word, and the Word was with God, and the Word was God. And the Word became flesh, and dwelt among us, and we saw His glory, glory as of the only begotten from the Father, full of grace and truth. For the Law was given through Moses; grace and truth were realized through Jesus Christ." In Genesis 1, we have the creation account; God speaks the world into existence. Jesus was there, He is the Word that spoke the world into existence. Jesus is the Word that became flesh full of Grace and Truth.

The book of John was written, by inspiration of the Holy Spirit, by the disciple John. We have a different John, John the Baptist, introduced in verse six. John the Baptist was physically born six months before Jesus, yet in verse fifteen, John says Jesus existed before him. In Luke chapter one, you can take the name of the father of John the Baptist (he was a priest), go to 1 Chronicles 24, find out his priestly timeslot, then you can actually calculate that John the Baptist's mother, Elizabeth, was six months pregnant when the virgin Mary visited her. Oddly enough, or I should say perfectly enough, Jesus was conceived by the Holy Spirit during this visit. Perfectly enough, the virgin conception was on Hanukkah, the holiday celebrating the Light. We know that biologically light is so very essential for life. I remember during one of my annual physicals, the doctor said I wasn't getting enough sun; my doctor prescribed me vitamin D. Without the light we become pale and frail. Spiritually, the Light is also so very essential for Life. Jesus is the Light of the world.

We should point out the phrase in verse eighteen, "no one has seen God at any time". Then how can Jesus be God in the flesh if no one has ever seen God? I remember reading this verse and then calling my pastor on a payphone when I was stationed in Hawaii. Remember in the paragraph above, God Himself, puts Himself inside of the virgin Mary. The Creator of everything, humbles Himself, empties Himself of His glory, and enters Mary. So, the phrase no one has seen God means, no one has ever seen God in His full glory. In Philippians 2 and John 17, we learn about the emptying Himself of His glory and the reuniting Himself with the Father.

Have this attitude [e]in yourselves which was also in Christ Jesus, [6] who, although He existed in the form of God, did not regard equality with God a thing to be [f]grasped, [7] but [g]emptied Himself, taking the form of a bond-servant, *and* being made in the likeness of men. [8] Being found in appearance as a man, He humbled Himself by becoming obedient to the point of death, even death [h]on a cross. [9] For this reason also, God highly exalted Him, and bestowed on Him the name which is above every name, [10] so that at the name of Jesus EVERY KNEE WILL BOW, of those who are in heaven and on earth and under the earth, [11] and that every tongue will confess that Jesus Christ is Lord, to the glory of God the Father. (Philippians 2:5-11)

Jesus spoke these things; and lifting up His eyes to heaven, He said, "Father, the hour has come; glorify Your Son, that the Son may glorify You, [2] even as You gave Him authority over all flesh, that to [a]all whom You have given Him, He may give eternal life. [3] This is eternal life, that they may know You, the only true God, and Jesus Christ whom You have sent. [4] I glorified You on the earth, [b]having accomplished the work which You have given Me to do. [5] Now, Father, glorify Me together with Yourself, with the glory which I had with You before the world was. (John 17:1-5)

In verse twenty-eight we see John baptizing in "Bethany Beyond the Jordan". This is very significant. There were two Bethany's. Bethany means "house of fig". You can Biblically link the tree of knowledge of good and evil with the fig tree. Check out this video on the strangler fig tree: https://www.youtube.com/watch?v=UCUtpmwacoE One Bethany is near Jerusalem, the other is east of the Jordan River. The Jordan flows south into the Dead Sea. This is a beautiful picture of our sin being washed in the Jordan; our sin then flows south into the Dead Sea. Remember when the children of Israel came into the Promised Land? They literally as they came up, instead of going directly north to the Promised Land, went east, crossing the Jordan, then once everyone went east across the Jordan, they all crossed back over to the west side, the Jerusalem side. The Ark of the Covenant stayed on dry ground in the middle of the Jordan as the children crossed over and back. The water was pushed all the way back to the city of Adam. The Ark is a picture of the heart being washed, our sin being washed all the way back to the sin of Adam.

So when the people set out from their tents to cross the Jordan with the priests carrying the ark of the covenant before the people, [15] and when those who carried the ark came into the Jordan, and the feet of the priests carrying the ark were dipped in the edge of the water (for the Jordan overflows all its banks all the days of harvest), [16] the waters which were [d]flowing down from above stood *and* rose up in one heap, a great distance away at Adam, the city that is beside Zarethan; and those which were [e]flowing down toward the sea of the Arabah, the Salt Sea, were completely cut off. So the people crossed opposite Jericho. [17] And the priests who carried the ark of the covenant of the LORD stood firm on dry ground in the middle of the Jordan while all Israel crossed on dry ground, until all the nation had finished crossing the Jordan. (Joshua 3:14-17)

John the Baptist called Jesus the Lamb of God who takes away the sins of the world! Prior to God taking on human flesh and being sacrificed for our sin, unblemished lambs were sacrificed for sin.

knowing that you were not [r]redeemed with perishable things like silver or gold from your futile way of life inherited from your forefathers, [19] but with precious blood, as of a lamb unblemished and spotless, *the blood* of Christ. [20] For He was foreknown before the foundation of the world, but has appeared [s]in these last times for the sake of you ²¹ who through Him are believers in God, who raised Him from the dead and gave Him glory, so that your faith and hope are in God. (1 Peter 3:18-21)

Lastly, let's take a look at the names of the first few disciples: Andrew, Simon, Phillip, and Nathanael.

The name Andrew or Andreas derives from the familiar noun ανηρ (*aner*), meaning man.

The Greek name Simon is an adjusted version of the name Simeon, and that name comes from the common Hebrew verb שמע (*shama'*), meaning to hear.

The name Philippos consists of two elements. The first part comes from the adjective φιλος (*philos*), meaning friend or one who loves.

For a meaning of the name Nathanael, NOBSE Study Bible Name List reads **God Has Given**. Jones' Dictionary of Old Testament Proper Names doesn't treat this Greek name, but for the Hebrew equivalent Nathaniel Jones reads **Given Of God**.

http://www.abarim-publications.com/NaLi/A-MaleBig.html#.Vr825Jr2aUn

"Man has heard of the Friend Who loves given of God"

John 2

On the third day there was a wedding in Cana of Galilee, and the mother of Jesus was there; 2 and both Jesus and His disciples were invited to the wedding. 3 When the wine ran out, the mother of Jesus *said to Him, "They have no wine." 4 And Jesus *said to her, "Woman, [a]what does that have to do with us? My hour has not yet come." 5 His mother *said to the servants, "Whatever He says to you, do it." 6 Now there were six stone waterpots set there for the Jewish custom of purification, containing [b]twenty or thirty gallons each. 7 Jesus *said to them, "Fill the waterpots with water." So they filled them up to the brim. 8 And He *said to them, "Draw *some* out now and take it to the [c]headwaiter." So they took it *to him*. 9 When the headwaiter tasted the water which had become wine, and did not know where it came from (but the servants who had drawn the water knew), the headwaiter *called the bridegroom, 10 and *said to him, "Every man serves the good wine first, and when *the people* have [d]drunk freely, *then he serves* the poorer *wine; but* you have kept the good wine until now." 11 This beginning of *His* [e]signs Jesus did in Cana of Galilee, and manifested His glory, and His disciples believed in Him.

12 After this He went down to Capernaum, He and His mother and *His* brothers and His disciples; and they stayed there a few days.

13 The Passover of the Jews was near, and Jesus went up to Jerusalem. 14 And He found in the temple those who were selling oxen and sheep and doves, and the money changers seated *at their tables*. 15 And He made a scourge of cords, and drove *them* all out of the temple, with the sheep and the oxen; and He poured out the coins of the money changers and overturned their tables; 16 and to those who were selling the doves He said, "Take these things away; stop making My Father's house a [f]place of business." 17 His disciples remembered that it was written, "ZEAL FOR YOUR HOUSE WILL CONSUME ME." 18 The Jews then said to Him, "What sign do You show us [g]as your authority for doing these things?" 19 Jesus answered them, "Destroy this [h]temple, and in three days I will raise it up." 20 The Jews then said, "It took forty-six years to build this [i]temple, and will You raise it up in three days?" 21 But He was

speaking of the [i]temple of His body. 22 So when He was raised from the dead, His disciples remembered that He said this; and they believed the Scripture and the word which Jesus had spoken.

23 Now when He was in Jerusalem at the Passover, during the feast, many believed in His name, observing His signs which He was doing. 24 But Jesus, on His part, was not entrusting Himself to them, for He knew all men, 25 and because He did not need anyone to testify concerning man, for He Himself knew what was in man. (John 2)
https://www.biblegateway.com/passage/?search=John+2&version=NASB

Chapter two opens with "On the third day". Today many orthodox "Jews" still get married on the "Third Day" (Tuesday). We know this stems from the creation account in Genesis 1, where on the Third Day, God says, "it was good" twice.   The Third Day also relates to the Resurrection Day, in which also occurs twice, once already with Jesus, and another in the future with us.

Then God said, "Let the waters below the heavens be gathered into one place, and let the dry land appear"; and it was so. 10 God called the dry land earth, and the gathering of the waters He called seas; and God saw that it was good. 11 Then God said, "Let the earth sprout [j]vegetation, [k]plants yielding seed, *and* fruit trees on the earth bearing fruit after [l]their kind [m]with seed in them"; and it was so. 12 The earth brought forth [n]vegetation, [o]plants yielding seed after [p]their kind, and trees bearing fruit [q]with seed in them, after [r]their kind; and God saw that it was good. 13 There was evening and there was morning, a third day. (Genesis 1:9-13)

This is the first miracle that Jesus performs, turning water into wine. We know that in Exodus 7, when Moses touches the water with the "Staff" (picture of the Cross) that the water turns into "Blood" (picture of Jesus). Remember as well that this Staff was just previously turned into a serpent (sin). We are in Egypt, which is related to being "slaves to sin". We have "pharaoh's heart" mentioned as well. So we have the Gospel Message in Exodus 7.

Then the LORD said to Moses, "Pharaoh's heart is [g]stubborn; he refuses to let the people go. 15 Go to Pharaoh in the morning [h]as he is going out to the water, and station yourself to meet him on the bank of the Nile; and you shall take in your hand the staff that was turned into a serpent. 16 You shall say to him, 'The LORD, the God of the Hebrews, sent me to you, saying, "Let My people go, that they may serve Me in the wilderness. But behold, you have not listened until now." 17 Thus says the LORD, "By this you shall know that I am the LORD: behold, I will strike [i]the water that is in the Nile with the staff that is in my hand, and it will be turned to blood.

So with Moses, we have water turned into Blood (foretelling Jesus). With Jesus, we have Water turned into Wine (foretelling the Holy Spirit). It is interesting that during the "Jewish" Feast of Sukkot (Feast of Tabernacles) that the priest's mix water and wine during the ceremony. I believe the Feast of Tabernacles to represent Jesus dwelling amongst us in a Human Tabernacle. In John 1:14, the word "dwelt" means to tabernacle, "And the Word became flesh, and dwelt among us..." Another Feast, which I believe to be the 7th and last Feast, is the Feast of Weeks (7 times 7 days=49) This Feast ends with Pentecost (Day 50). During the Feast of Weeks, the harvest consists of olives and grapes. This is significant because olives are associated with oil for "Light" and grapes with "Wine", both being associated with the Holy Spirit. Remember the Holy Spirit was given on Pentecost, Day 50. Remember as well that every 50th Year, the Year of Jubilee, that all debts were forgiven. Jesus was crucified on a Jubilee Year.

Interesting as well is that in the entire book of John the mother of Jesus is never called Mary. Here she is called "woman". I believe this woman has a double meaning, besides referring to Mary, I believe it is referring to us, the bride, the church, and our future wedding at the Second Resurrection.

We also have the water being turned into wine in the waterpots. These waterpots were used in the "Purification" ceremony. We know from Numbers 19, that during the Purification Ceremony that the Red Heifer was brought outside the walls of Jerusalem (our sin put on the Red Heifer, then removed from within the walls of Jerusalem i.e. our heart) and slaughtered. The Red Heifer was then burned, and the ashes were mixed with water in these waterpots. When you study Numbers 19 you can't miss the many references to the Third (Resurrection) and Seventh day (Sabbath).

In John 1 we read that Jesus told Nathanael that He saw him under the fig tree. The fig tree is a picture of the tree of knowledge of good and evil. So we have Nathanael under the fig tree, a picture of being under the Law and sin. In John 21:2 we learn that Nathanael is from Cana of Galilee. So we have Nathanael (meaning Given of God) who was under the fig tree, now in his birth town, at a Wedding, with Water turned into Wine in Purification waterpots, i.e. a picture of being born again. In Galatians 3 we read "cursed is everyone who hangs on a Tree." Jesus takes the curse i.e. sin upon Himself. The curse of sin started at the tree of knowledge of good and evil.

Christ redeemed us from the curse of the Law, having become a curse for us—for it is written, "CURSED IS EVERYONE WHO HANGS ON A [v]TREE"— [14] in order that in Christ Jesus the blessing of Abraham might [w]come to the Gentiles, so that we would receive the promise of the Spirit through faith. (Galatians 3:13, 14)

In verse thirteen we are in Jerusalem in preparation for the Passover (which occurs on the 7th day, the Sabbath). So earlier we had the Third Day and now we have the Seventh Day. Again, note in Numbers 19 all the Third and Seventh day references. The Third and Seventh days correspond to Jesus saying, "I Am the Resurrection (3rd Day) and the Life (7th Day)." Jesus accomplished a perfect sinless life, becoming our Passover Lamb, rising on the Third Day, conquering sin and death. He is our Seventh Day, Eternal Life i.e. Sabbath Rest. Jesus accomplished the Sabbath Day work in our place. That's the real meaning behind the 4th Commandment, which Hebrews 4 so beautifully teaches us.

With cleansing the Temple, we know this to be a picture of Jesus cleansing our bodies of sin. We know the Ark of the Covenant (our heart) is within the Temple, behind the Veil. The high priest could only go behind the Veil into the Holy of Holies once a year. On the Cross, the 12 inch thick Veil tore from Top to Bottom (God tore it). Jesus Christ is the Final High Priest, the Great High Priest!

And lastly, notice on the Third Day, that Genesis 1 talks about "seeds". From biology, whether human, animal, vegetation etc. life comes from a seed being planted. Biologically life stems from a male and a female. Physically this is the basis of all life. Male plus male eventually will lead to death. Female plus female will eventually lead to death. Spiritually it is the same. God teaches us about spiritual eternal life through biological life. The Gospel Message of Jesus is the Seed being planted in our fertile heart that was prepared by the Holy Spirit. Spiritually we are the bride of Christ. Jesus Christ is the Bridegroom. Notice in the Bible, He is never just called the groom. Jesus is always called the Bridegroom, the bride and Groom in one word. We are One in the Spirit; We are One in the Lord!!!

Below are two links; one is a short awesome song and the other is a fig tree video (almost an hour long, but well worth it). There are a few different fig tree species. The most aggressive is the strangler fig. This one is the sycamore-fig; remember Zacchaeus climbed one in Jericho (walls of sin) in the book of Luke. Jesus curses a fig tree as well in the Gospels, now we know why. Also in Amos 7, we learn that Amos was a keeper of the fig. And the most obvious fig reference being the leaves that Adam and Eve clothed themselves with before God clothed them (Genesis 3:7).

https://www.youtube.com/watch?v=o7_wHi0PNHg

https://www.youtube.com/watch?v=xy86ak2fQJM

John 3

Now there was a man of the Pharisees, named Nicodemus, a ruler of the Jews; [2] this man came to Jesus by night and said to Him, "Rabbi, we know that You have come from God *as* a teacher; for no one can do these [a]signs that You do unless God is with him." [3] Jesus answered and said to him, "Truly, truly, I say to you, unless one is born [b]again he cannot see the kingdom of God."

[4] Nicodemus *said to Him, "How can a man be born when he is old? He cannot enter a second time into his mother's womb and be born, can he?" [5] Jesus answered, "Truly, truly, I say to you, unless one is born of water and the Spirit he cannot enter into the kingdom of God. [6] That which is born of the flesh is flesh, and that which is born of the Spirit is spirit. [7] Do not be amazed that I said to you, 'You must be born [c]again.' [8] The wind blows where it wishes and you hear the sound of it, but do not know where it comes from and where it is going; so is everyone who is born of the Spirit."

[9] Nicodemus said to Him, "How can these things be?" [10] Jesus answered and said to him, "Are you the teacher of Israel and do not understand these things? [11] Truly, truly, I say to you, we speak of what we know and testify of what we have seen, and you do not accept our testimony. [12] If I told you earthly things and you do not believe, how will you believe if I tell you heavenly things? [13] No one has ascended into heaven, but He who descended from heaven: the Son of Man. [14] As Moses lifted up the serpent in the wilderness, even so must the Son of Man be lifted up; [15] so that whoever [d]believes will in Him have eternal life.

[16] "For God so loved the world, that He gave His [e]only begotten Son, that whoever believes in Him shall not perish, but have eternal life. [17] For God did not send the Son into the world to judge the world, but that the world might be saved through Him. [18] He who believes in Him is not judged; he who does not believe has been judged already, because he has not believed in the name of the [f]only begotten Son of God. [19] This is the judgment, that the Light has come into the world, and men loved the darkness rather than the Light, for

their deeds were evil. [20] For everyone who does evil hates the Light, and does not come to the Light for fear that his deeds will be exposed. [21] But he who practices the truth comes to the Light, so that his deeds may be manifested as having been wrought in God."

[22] After these things Jesus and His disciples came into the land of Judea, and there He was spending time with them and baptizing. [23] John also was baptizing in Aenon near Salim, because there was much water there; and *people* were coming and were being baptized— [24] for John had not yet been thrown into prison.

[25] Therefore there arose a discussion on the part of John's disciples with a Jew about purification. [26] And they came to John and said to him, "Rabbi, He who was with you beyond the Jordan, to whom you have testified, behold, He is baptizing and all are coming to Him." [27] John answered and said, "A man can receive nothing unless it has been given him from heaven. [28] You yourselves [g]are my witnesses that I said, 'I am not the [h]Christ,' but, 'I have been sent ahead of Him.' [29] He who has the bride is the bridegroom; but the friend of the bridegroom, who stands and hears him, rejoices greatly because of the bridegroom's voice. So this joy of mine has been made full. [30] He must increase, but I must decrease.

[31] "He who comes from above is above all, he who is of the earth is from the earth and speaks of the earth. He who comes from heaven is above all. [32] What He has seen and heard, of that He testifies; and no one receives His testimony. [33] He who has received His testimony has set his seal to *this*, that God is true. [34] For He whom God has sent speaks the words of God; [i]for He gives the Spirit without measure. [35] The Father loves the Son and has given all things into His hand. [36] He who believes in the Son has eternal life; but he who does not [j]obey the Son will not see life, but the wrath of God abides on him."
(John 3)
https://www.biblegateway.com/passage/?search=John+3&version=NASB

Nicodemus is a Pharisee, which is one of the two main Jewish religious groups, the other being the Sadducees, both comprising the Sanhedrin. The Sanhedrin was the Jewish "ruling" class, although the Romans actually ruled. In the New Testament we hear a lot about the Pharisees and the Sadducees. Two major differences between them are that the Pharisees believe in angels and in the resurrection, the Sadducees do not, that's why they are "sad you see". The name Nicodemus is Greek; it means, "Victory for the people". Many Jews had Greek names during this era due to the Greeks occupying the area prior to the Roman occupation. We suspect Nicodemus does end up eventually becoming a believer. He and Joseph of Arimathea are the ones who ask for the Body of Christ, after His death on the Cross. He does address Jesus as Rabbi, which means Teacher. Nicodemus is drawn to Jesus, but he is very cautious, coming at night to see Him. Souly in the book of John do we see the many "truly, truly" statements made by Jesus. So when you see "truly, truly" pay close attention.

In John 3:5, Jesus says, ", "Truly, truly, I say to you, unless one is born of water and the Spirit he cannot enter into the kingdom of God." Two very awesome Scriptures that help us understand this "truly, truly" statement are found in Titus and Ezekiel. We are washed of our sin and empowered/filled by the Holy Spirit. The more emptied of ourselves, the more we are filled with His Spirit, hopefully to the point of overflowing unto others.

But when the kindness of God our Savior and *His* love for mankind appeared, [5] He saved us, not on the basis of deeds which we have done in righteousness, but according to His mercy, by the washing of regeneration and renewing by the Holy Spirit, [6] whom He poured out upon us richly through Jesus Christ our Savior, [7] so that being justified by His grace we would be made heirs [a]according to *the* hope of eternal life. (Titus 3:4-7)

Then I will sprinkle clean water on you, and you will be clean; I will cleanse you from all your filthiness and from all your idols.
[26] Moreover, I will give you a new heart and put a new spirit within you; and I will remove the heart of stone from your flesh and give you a heart of flesh. [27] I will put My Spirit within you and cause you

to walk in My statutes, and you will be careful to observe My ordinances. [28] You will live in the land that I gave to your forefathers; so you will be My people, and I will be your God. (Ezekiel 36:25-28)

In John 3:8 we read, "The wind blows where it wishes and you hear the sound of it, but do not know where it comes from and where it is going; so is everyone who is born of the Spirit." The Holy Spirit moves like the wind. We don't know which hearts God is currently preparing. We are tasked to plant and water Gospel Seeds. God puts people in our path, so pay attention. Also, we all believe in the wind, but none of us have ever seen the wind. When people ask, how can you believe in God, when you have never seen Him? Ask them, do you believe in the wind? They will say, "Yes." Then ask, but you can't see the wind, can you? They will say, "I can't see wind, but I can see the effects of the wind, it's measurable." As believers, our effects are being measured. That is how they will know we are Christians, by our love. Are we having a "love effect" on people around us? But remember works do not save us, but when we are saved we will work. "We love, because He first loved us." (1 John 4:19)

Remember, the Bible is not about "information". The Bible is about "transformation". Bible information/knowledge can puff up. "To know the Bible is good, but to know the Author is better." The information needs to make the eighteen inch journey from the brain to the heart for transformation. We know John is the "disciple whom Jesus loved"; he uses the word love much more often than anyone else in Scripture. David comes in second, "a man after God's own heart". David and John both understood that we love from the heart, from the inside out. John also talks a lot about "darkness". What we do in darkness "truly, truly" defines us. That's what the 3rd Commandment is really about. Taking the Lord's Name in vain has absolutely nothing to do with swearing. It has everything to do with putting on a fake front, a phony outer shell. Are we all "information", or are we "transformation"? Does our outward show match our inner flow? Does God's Holy Spirit flow through us from a pure "washed and overflowing" heart?

Note that the theme of being "washed" is seen very strongly in the Old Testament as well, especially with the river Jordan. Jordan means "descending", Jesus descended to wash us. Instead of going directly north into the Promised Land the children of Israel took time to go "beyond the Jordan" to be "washed", then they crossed back over to the Jerusalem side. Prior to the Exodus with Moses, in Genesis 50 after Jacob/Israel died in Egypt, Joseph travels back to the future Promised Land to bury his father. The Bible says he goes to Atad first; this city is on the east side of the Jordan, "Beyond the Jordan". Then they cross back over to the Jerusalem side to bury him. The name Atad means "thorn". Thorns are related to sin. Remember Paul's thorn in the flesh? Jesus Christ wore our Crown of Thorns. Note also the "threshing floor" reference below; remember Jesus will separate the wheat (believers) from the chaff (non-believers) at the threshing floor. Just because someone goes to "church" doesn't mean they are "wheat".

So Joseph went up to bury his father, and with him went up all the servants of Pharaoh, the elders of his household and all the elders of the land of Egypt, [8] and all the household of Joseph and his brothers and his father's household; they left only their little ones and their flocks and their herds in the land of Goshen. [9] There also went up with him both chariots and horsemen; and it was a very great company. [10] When they came to the [f]threshing floor of Atad, which is beyond the Jordan, they lamented there with a very great and [g]sorrowful lamentation; and he [h]observed seven days mourning for his father. [11] Now when the inhabitants of the land, the Canaanites, saw the mourning at [i]the threshing floor of Atad, they said, "This is a [j]grievous [k]mourning for the Egyptians." Therefore it was named [l]Abel-mizraim, which is beyond the Jordan. (Genesis 50:7-11)

John 3:14 refers to when Moses was instructed to put the serpent (picture of sin) on the Staff (picture of Cross), the people who looked to the Staff/serpent were healed from their sinful, venomous, deadly bites. Today, many ambulances have the snake (sin) and Staff (Cross) painted on them. Interesting as well is that Jesus came in the flesh during the Roman Empire, during the Bronze Age. Biblically, bronze signifies judgment. All humans will either be saved by the Cross or judged by the Cross.

Notice in John 3:23 that John the Baptist is now baptizing at Aenon near Salim, now on the west side of the Jordan, not "Beyond the Jordan" anymore. After baptizing Jesus, the "Beyond the Jordan" Scriptures are fulfilled. Aenon means springs or fountains. Salim means peace. You have a picture of first being washed (Jesus) in the Jordan, then you have a picture of the Holy Spirit with the fountain or spring. The Gihon Spring at Jerusalem is also a picture of the Holy Spirit. Remember in the Old Testament, when the people sinned, the Gihon Spring would not flow. The water supply to Jerusalem, the city of Peace, was cut off. Just like us, when we are in sin, God does not flow through us.   Interesting as well are the Water Gate and the Fountain Gate within the walls of Jerusalem, again a picture of being "washed and overflowing".

Lastly, below are the name definitions for John and Jesus, then Scripture from Ephesians 2, which beautifully speaks of grace (**G**od's **R**iches **A**t **C**hrist's **E**xpense) and saving faith:

For a meaning of the name John, NOBSE Study Bible Name List reads **Yahweh Has Been Gracious**, but for Johanan NOBSE reads **Yahweh Is Gracious**. Jones' Dictionary of Old Testament Proper Names does not treat John or Johanan separately and refers to the name Jehohanan, which Jones takes to mean **The Lord Graciously Gave**.

The name Jesus is the Greek transliteration of either the name יהושע (Joshua) or its shortened form (עושי) Jeshua, and consists of two elements. The first part is the appellative יה (Yah) = יהו (Yahu) = י (Yu), which in turn are abbreviated forms of the Tetragrammaton; the name of the Lord: YHWH, or Yahweh. The second element of the name Joshua/Jesus comes from the root-verb ישע (*yasha'*), meaning to save or deliver.

And you [a]were dead [b]in your trespasses and sins, 2 in which you
formerly walked according to the [c]course of this world, according
to the prince of the power of the air, of the spirit that is now working
in the sons of disobedience. 3 Among them we too all formerly lived
in the lusts of our flesh, [d]indulging the desires of the flesh and of
the [e]mind, and were by nature children of wrath, even as the rest.
4 But God, being rich in mercy, because of His great love with which
He loved us, 5 even when we were dead [f]in our transgressions, made
us alive together [g]with Christ (by grace you have been saved), 6 and
raised us up with Him, and seated us with Him in the heavenly
places in Christ Jesus, 7 so that in the ages to come He might show
the surpassing riches of His grace in kindness toward us in Christ
Jesus. 8 For by grace you have been saved through faith; and [h]that
not of yourselves, *it is* the gift of God; 9 not as a result of works, so
that no one may boast. 10 For we are His workmanship, created in
Christ Jesus for good works, which God prepared beforehand so that
we would walk in them. (Ephesians 2:1-10)

John 4

Therefore when the Lord knew that the Pharisees had heard that
Jesus was making and baptizing more disciples than John 2 (although
Jesus Himself was not baptizing, but His disciples were), 3 He left
Judea and went away again into Galilee. 4 And He had to pass
through Samaria. 5 So He *came to a city of Samaria called Sychar,
near the parcel of ground that Jacob gave to his son Joseph; 6 and
Jacob's well was there. So Jesus, being wearied from His journey,
was sitting thus by the well. It was about [a]the sixth hour.

7 There *came a woman of Samaria to draw water. Jesus *said to her,
"Give Me a drink." 8 For His disciples had gone away into the city to

buy food. [9] Therefore the Samaritan woman *said to Him, "How is it that You, being a Jew, ask me for a drink since I am a Samaritan woman?" (For Jews have no dealings with Samaritans.) [10] Jesus answered and said to her, "If you knew the gift of God, and who it is who says to you, 'Give Me a drink,' you would have asked Him, and He would have given you living water." [11] She *said to Him, "[b]Sir, You have nothing to draw with and the well is deep; where then do You get that living water? [12] You are not greater than our father Jacob, are You, who gave us the well, and drank of it himself and his sons and his cattle?" [13] Jesus answered and said to her, "Everyone who drinks of this water will thirst again; [14] but whoever drinks of the water that I will give him shall never thirst; but the water that I will give him will become in him a well of water springing up to eternal life."

[15] The woman *said to Him, "[c]Sir, give me this water, so I will not be thirsty nor come all the way here to draw." [16] He *said to her, "Go, call your husband and come here." [17] The woman answered and said, "I have no husband." Jesus *said to her, "You have correctly said, 'I have no husband'; [18] for you have had five husbands, and the one whom you now have is not your husband; this you have said truly." [19] The woman *said to Him, "[d]Sir, I perceive that You are a prophet. [20] Our fathers worshiped in this mountain, and you *people* say that in Jerusalem is the place where men ought to worship." [21] Jesus *said to her, "Woman, believe Me, an hour is coming when neither in this mountain nor in Jerusalem will you worship the Father. [22] You worship what you do not know; we worship what we know, for salvation is from the Jews. [23] But an hour is coming, and now is, when the true worshipers will worship the Father in spirit and truth; for such people the Father seeks to be His worshipers. [24] God is [e]spirit, and those who worship Him must worship in spirit and truth." [25] The woman *said to Him, "I know that Messiah is coming (He who is called Christ); when that One comes, He will declare all things to us." [26] Jesus *said to her, "I who speak to you am *He*."

[27] At this point His disciples came, and they were amazed that He had been speaking with a woman, yet no one said, "What do You seek?" or, "Why do You speak with her?" [28] So the woman left her

waterpot, and went into the city and *said to the men, ²⁹ "Come, see a man who told me all the things that I *have* done; this is not [f]the Christ, is it?" ³⁰ They went out of the city, and were coming to Him.

³¹ Meanwhile the disciples were urging Him, saying, "Rabbi, eat." ³² But He said to them, "I have food to eat that you do not know about." ³³ So the disciples were saying to one another, "No one brought Him *anything* to eat, did he?" ³⁴ Jesus *said to them, "My food is to do the will of Him who sent Me and to accomplish His work. ³⁵ Do you not say, 'There are yet four months, and *then* comes the harvest'? Behold, I say to you, lift up your eyes and look on the fields, that they are white for harvest. ³⁶ Already he who reaps is receiving wages and is gathering fruit for life eternal; so that he who sows and he who reaps may rejoice together. ³⁷ For in this *case* the saying is true, 'One sows and another reaps.' ³⁸ I sent you to reap that for which you have not labored; others have labored and you have entered into their labor."

³⁹ From that city many of the Samaritans believed in Him because of the word of the woman who testified, "He told me all the things that I *have* done." ⁴⁰ So when the Samaritans came to Jesus, they were asking Him to stay with them; and He stayed there two days. ⁴¹ Many more believed because of His word; ⁴² and they were saying to the woman, "It is no longer because of what you said that we believe, for we have heard for ourselves and know that this One is indeed the Savior of the world."

⁴³ After the two days He went forth from there into Galilee. ⁴⁴ For Jesus Himself testified that a prophet has no honor in his own country. ⁴⁵ So when He came to Galilee, the Galileans received Him, having seen all the things that He did in Jerusalem at the feast; for they themselves also went to the feast.

⁴⁶ Therefore He came again to Cana of Galilee where He had made the water wine. And there was a royal official whose son was sick at Capernaum. ⁴⁷ When he heard that Jesus had come out of Judea into Galilee, he went to Him and was imploring *Him* to come down and heal his son; for he was at the point of death. ⁴⁸ So Jesus said to him, "Unless you *people* see [g]signs and wonders, you *simply* will not

believe." [49] The royal official *said to Him, "[h]Sir, come down before my child dies." [50] Jesus *said to him, "Go; your son lives." The man believed the word that Jesus spoke to him and started off. [51] As he was now going down, *his* slaves met him, saying that his [i]son was living. [52] So he inquired of them the hour when he began to get better. Then they said to him, "Yesterday at the [j]seventh hour the fever left him." [53] So the father knew that *it was* at that hour in which Jesus said to him, "Your son lives"; and he himself believed and his whole household. [54] This is again a second [k]sign that Jesus performed when He had come out of Judea into Galilee. (John 4) https://www.biblegateway.com/passage/?search=John+4&version=NASB

To get an idea of the geography: picture the Mediterranean Sea to the left or west, picture the Jordan River to the east. At the top of the Jordan we have the Sea of Galilee. The Jordan runs south about 70 miles, dumping into the Dead Sea. So you have a water boundary to the east and west. Between these water boundaries are three main areas, the north is Galilee (containing Nazareth, Cana, Capernaum), then going south you have Samaria (containing Sychar), then further south you have Judea (containing Jerusalem, Jericho, Bethlehem).

Jesus and His disciples head north from Judea to Galilee. Although Samaria is sandwiched between Judea and Galilee, and the direct route being through Samaria, many Jews would walk around Samaria to make this trip. The Jews that did this were "outer shell" Jews. The "outer shell" Jews saw Samaritans as inferior because they were half Jew and half gentile. Jesus doesn't walk around. John 4:4 says, "And He had to pass through Samaria." Man looks at outer appearance, God looks at the heart (1 Samuel 16:7). Never judge by the outer shell. We are at the well, in the city of Samaria, called Sychar. The Hebrew name for Sychar is Shekar, which means drink or even strong drink. This area was Jacob's (later named

Israel). In the presence of Joseph, on his deathbed in Egypt, Israel gives the land to Joseph's two sons, Manasseh and Ephraim. Remember Joseph (picture of Christ) and Levi (picture of the Law) didn't get a land inheritance. So with Joseph and Levi removed, Manasseh (meaning forgiveness, to forget, picture of Jesus) and Ephraim (fruit, picture of the Holy Spirit) are inserted into the twelve. Later in Revelation 7 we do see Joseph and Levi reinstated (picture of Jesus fulfilling the Law). In Revelation 7, Dan (to judge) and Ephraim (fruit) are removed, probably signifying the Judgement Seat of Christ. So why did outer shell Jews not like Samaritans? Maybe Manasseh and Ephraim being half Egyptian had something to do with it. Joseph is a picture of Jesus. He was sent to Egypt to save the world from starvation/death. Forgiveness (Manasseh) and Fruit of the Spirit (Ephraim) are a result of the work of the Savior. We are washed and filled, hopefully overfilled, bearing His Fruit (Love, Joy, Peace, Patience, Kindness, Goodness, Faithfulness, Gentleness and Self-Control, Galatians 5). So we see Jesus and God's Holy Spirit all throughout the Scriptures.

This city, Sychar, meaning drink or strong drink has a well. Wells are holes dug down to an underground spring. So earlier in John we had the Jordan (Jesus) and now we have the Well/Spring (the Holy Spirit). Remember at Pentecost, after the outpouring of God's Holy Spirit, people thought that the disciples were drunk. Paul teaches us to not be drunk with wine, but be filled with the Holy Spirit (Ephesians 5:18). If you can handle drinking alcohol, and you don't drink too much, your heart does "become merry". That is in the physical world, in the spiritual world, we are not filled with earthly wine and spirits, but with the Holy Spirit. Physically we can have our blood alcohol content (BAC) levels measured. Spiritually, our blood Holy Spirit content levels (BHSC) can also be measured. "You know a tree by its fruit." (Matthew 7:16) For physical alcohol you take fruit, mash it, then you add yeast. You then put a check valve type lid on. The yeast eats the sugar, giving off carbon dioxide. The check valve lid allows carbon dioxide out. You do not want oxygen getting in. Ethanol alcohol (intoxicating alcohol) is created. Spiritually our hearts have the Fruit of the Spirit. Yeast (associated with sin in the Bible) comes in. This is the battle of the flesh vs. Spirit. Does the yeast move us toward God or toward our sinful flesh?

Something very interesting as well is that salt controls the growth of yeast. Christians are the salt of the earth. Interesting as well is that the human body needs salt, and a few more minerals to actually keep our heart beating. Those very same minerals needed for our bodies make up the Dead Sea. The shores of the Dead Sea are literally at the lowest elevation of any place on earth. I believe this is a teaching in humility. The Dead Sea is also 33% salt which enables people to float on top without even swimming. Our sin is washed in the Jordan, and dumped into the Dead Sea. Being forgiven, we are also to be humble. We are to be the salt of the earth. Salt is needed for a heartbeat, for food flavor, for food preservation, for infection etc. etc.

So it is noon (Jewish day starts at 6am) and Jesus is alone at the well. A woman comes with her "waterpot" (picture of heart) to draw water. Most women would come early morning or in the evening to draw water. Not this woman. She is a "sinner". She comes at the heat of the day to avoid others. Jesus talks to her and offers her Living Water, "a well of water springing up to eternal life". Notice Jesus first offers the Living Water. Then her sin is pointed out. We don't need to first "clean ourselves" up before coming to Christ. We first come to Him, and then God cleans us up. Our lives then become worship; worshipping in spirit and truth means we are now the temple of the Holy Spirit guided by His Truth, His Word, the Bible. At the end the woman says she believes the Messiah is coming. Jesus says, "I who speak to you am *He*." His disciples return and are surprised Jesus is talking to a woman. Today, especially in the Middle East, there is still a huge inequality between women and men. Not only does Jesus walk through Samaria, He stays two more days. So in this short period of time Jesus crushes racism and women inferiority. God is Awesome! After two more days of listening/hearing God's Word many believed, "for we have heard for ourselves and know that this One is indeed the Savior of the world." Remember faith comes by hearing, and hearing by the Word of Christ (Romans 10:17).

Back in verse twenty-eight we read, "So the woman left her waterpot, and went into the city and *said to the men…." The woman leaves her "waterpot" with Jesus. I believe the waterpot is a picture of the heart. She entrusts her heart to Jesus. In verse forty-six we are back in Cana. Remember John 2, the Wedding at Cana, Jesus turned Water into Wine in six Purification waterpots. In John 3 we learned that we are washed and then filled, hopefully overflowing. The Living Water is Jesus. The Wine is a picture of God's Holy Spirit.

In verse forty-eight we read, "Unless you *people* see [g]signs and wonders, you *simply* will not believe." This man, the royal official, was a Jew, probably on Herod's court. This Herod "ruled" up north in Galilee. Pilate (a Roman) ruled down south in Judea, where Jerusalem was. Remember during the trial of Jesus, that Herod was visiting Jerusalem. The father of this Herod, Herod the great, restored the Temple and killed all the children in Bethlehem around the birth of Christ. You see Jesus on more than one occasion, getting upset at the Jews for wanting signs and wonders. Remember the Jews were the people group that the Word of God came through. True "inner" "heart" Jews would share the Light, the Word of God. Not only did many not share the Word, their hearts became stone waterpots. They actually became heart hardened to the Word. The Word wasn't good enough, they needed signs and wonders. So in general, many Jews wanted signs and wonders, the gentiles were good with the Word. But remember, God has always looked at the heart. From His view a true "Jew" is an inner heart "Jew". You can get lost in the book of Romans, easily thinking that God puts Jews above gentiles, that gentiles were plan B. That is not so. Here are two beautiful Scriptures from Romans blowing that teaching out of the water!!! I believe that Paul himself struggled with this Jew/gentile issue. I personally believe this was his thorn in the flesh (Romans 7).

For he is not a Jew who is one outwardly, nor is circumcision that which is outward in the flesh. ²⁹ But he is a Jew who is one inwardly; and circumcision is that which is of the heart, by the Spirit, not by the letter; and his praise is not from men, but from God. (Romans 2:28)

But what does it say? "THE WORD IS NEAR YOU, IN YOUR MOUTH AND IN YOUR HEART"—that is, the word of faith which we are preaching, ⁹ [e]that if you confess with your mouth Jesus *as* Lord, and believe in your heart that God raised Him from the dead, you will be saved; ¹⁰ for with the heart a person believes, [f]resulting in righteousness, and with the mouth he confesses, [g]resulting in salvation. ¹¹ For the Scripture says, "WHOEVER BELIEVES IN HIM WILL NOT BE [h]DISAPPOINTED." ¹² For there is no distinction between Jew and Greek; for the same *Lord* is Lord of all, abounding in riches for all who call on Him; ¹³ for "WHOEVER WILL CALL ON THE NAME OF THE LORD WILL BE SAVED."

¹⁴ How then will they call on Him in whom they have not believed? How will they believe in Him whom they have not heard? And how will they hear without a preacher? ¹⁵ How will they preach unless they are sent? Just as it is written, "HOW BEAUTIFUL ARE THE FEET OF THOSE WHO [i]BRING GOOD NEWS OF GOOD THINGS!"

[16] However, they did not all heed the [i]good news; for Isaiah says, "LORD, WHO HAS BELIEVED OUR REPORT?" [17] So faith *comes* from hearing, and hearing by the word [k]of Christ. (Romans 10:8-17)

John 5

After these things there was a feast of the Jews, and Jesus went up to Jerusalem.

[2] Now there is in Jerusalem by the sheep *gate* a pool, which is called in [a]Hebrew [b]Bethesda, having five porticoes. [3] In these lay a multitude of those who were sick, blind, lame, and withered, [[c]waiting for the moving of the waters; [4] for an angel of the Lord went down at certain seasons into the pool and stirred up the water; whoever then first, after the stirring up of the water, stepped in was made well from whatever disease with which he was afflicted.] [5] A man was there who had been [d]ill for thirty-eight years. [6] When Jesus saw him lying *there*, and knew that he had already been a long time *in that condition*, He *said to him, "Do you wish to get well?" [7] The sick man answered Him, "Sir, I have no man to put me into the pool when the water is stirred up, but while I am coming, another steps down before me." [8] Jesus *said to him, "Get up, pick up your pallet and walk." [9] Immediately the man became well, and picked up his pallet and *began* to walk.

Now it was the Sabbath on that day. [10] So the Jews were saying to the man who was cured, "It is the Sabbath, and it is not permissible for you to carry your pallet." [11] But he answered them, "He who made me well was the one who said to me, 'Pick up your pallet and walk.'" [12] They asked him, "Who is the man who said to you, 'Pick up *your pallet* and walk'?" [13] But the man who was healed did not know who it was, for Jesus had slipped away while there was a crowd in *that* place. [14] Afterward Jesus *found him in the temple and said to him, "Behold, you have become well; do not sin anymore, so that nothing worse happens to you." [15] The man went away, and told the Jews that it was Jesus who had made him well. [16] For this reason the Jews were persecuting Jesus, because He was doing these things on the Sabbath. [17] But He answered them, "My Father is working until now, and I Myself am working."

[18] For this reason therefore the Jews were seeking all the more to kill Him, because He not only was breaking the Sabbath, but also was calling God His own Father, making Himself equal with God.

[19] Therefore Jesus answered and was saying to them, "Truly, truly, I say to you, the Son can do nothing of Himself, unless *it is* something He sees the Father doing; for whatever [e]the Father does, these things the Son also does in like manner. [20] For the Father loves the Son, and shows Him all things that He Himself is doing; and *the Father* will show Him greater works than these, so that you will marvel. [21] For just as the Father raises the dead and gives them life, even so the Son also gives life to whom He wishes. [22] For not even the Father judges anyone, but He has given all judgment to the Son, [23] so that all will honor the Son even as they honor the Father. He who does not honor the Son does not honor the Father who sent Him.

[24] "Truly, truly, I say to you, he who hears My word, and believes Him who sent Me, has eternal life, and does not come into judgment, but has passed out of death into life.

[25] Truly, truly, I say to you, an hour is coming and now is, when the dead will hear the voice of the Son of God, and those who hear will live. [26] For just as the Father has life in Himself, even so He gave to the Son also to have life in Himself; [27] and He gave Him authority to execute judgment, because He is [f]*the* Son of Man. [28] Do not marvel at this; for an hour is coming, in which all who are in the tombs will hear His voice, [29] and will come forth; those who did the good *deeds* to a resurrection of life, those who committed the evil *deeds* to a resurrection of judgment.

³⁰ "I can do nothing on My own initiative. As I hear, I judge; and My judgment is just, because I do not seek My own will, but the will of Him who sent Me.

³¹ "If I *alone* testify about Myself, My testimony is not [g]true. ³² There is another who testifies of Me, and I know that the testimony which He gives about Me is true.

³³ You have sent to John, and he has testified to the truth. ³⁴ But the testimony which I receive is not from man, but I say these things so that you may be saved. ³⁵ He was the lamp that was burning and was shining and you were willing to rejoice for [h]a while in his light.

³⁶ But the testimony which I have is greater than *the testimony of* John; for the works which the Father has given Me to accomplish— the very works that I do—testify about Me, that the Father has sent Me.

³⁷ And the Father who sent Me, He has testified of Me. You have neither heard His voice at any time nor seen His form. ³⁸ You do not have His word abiding in you, for you do not believe Him whom He sent.

³⁹ [i]You search the Scriptures because you think that in them you have eternal life; it is these that testify about Me; ⁴⁰ and you are unwilling to come to Me so that you may have life. ⁴¹ I do not receive glory from men; ⁴² but I know you, that you do not have the love of God in yourselves. ⁴³ I have come in My Father's name, and you do not receive Me; if another comes in his own name, you will receive him. ⁴⁴ How can you believe, when you receive [j]glory from one another and you do not seek the [k]glory that is from the *one and only* God? ⁴⁵ Do not think that I will accuse you before the Father; the one who accuses you is Moses, in whom you have set your hope. ⁴⁶ For if you believed Moses, you would believe Me, for he wrote about Me. ⁴⁷ But if you do not believe his writings, how will you believe My words?" (John 5)
https://www.biblegateway.com/passage/?search=John+5&version=N
ASB

There were three times a year that all Jewish males had to attend Feasts in Jerusalem. The first was the Feast of Tabernacles (aka Booths or Ingathering). Trumpets and Atonement are attached and precede the Feast of Tabernacles. The second was called The Feast of Unleavened Bread, which includes Passover, Unleavened Bread and First Fruits. The third was called the Feast of Weeks (aka Harvest), which concluded with Pentecost. So within these three timeframes you have: Trumpets, Atonement, Tabernacles, Passover, Unleavened Bread, First Fruits, and Weeks.

"Three times a year you shall celebrate a feast to Me. [15] You shall observe the Feast of Unleavened Bread; for seven days you are to eat unleavened bread, as I commanded you, at the appointed time in the month Abib, for in it you came out of Egypt. And [m]none shall appear before Me empty-handed. [16] Also *you shall observe* the Feast of the Harvest *of* the first fruits of your labors *from* what you sow in the field; also the Feast of the Ingathering at the end of the year when you gather in *the fruit of* your labors from the field. [17] Three times a year all your males shall appear before the Lord [n]GOD. (Exodus 23:14-17)

"Three times in a year all your males shall appear before the Lord your God in the place which He chooses, at the Feast of Unleavened Bread and at the Feast of Weeks and at the Feast of Booths, and they shall not appear before the Lord empty-handed. [17] Every man [i]shall give as he is able, according to the blessing of the Lord your God which He has given you. (Deuteronomy 16:16, 17)

In verse one we are in Jerusalem during one of these Feast times. Jerusalem is packed with Jews from all over. Some travelled great distances these three times a year. So you have a picture of their whole year really being planned around these Seven Feasts.

We see the issue of working on the Sabbath come up here. We see this many times in Scripture with Jesus. The Fourth Commandment talks about the Seventh Day, Sabbath Rest.

"Remember the sabbath day, to keep it holy. [9] Six days you shall labor and do all your work, [10] but the seventh day is a sabbath of the LORD your God; *in it* you shall not do any work, you or your son or your daughter, your male or your female servant or your cattle or your sojourner who [c]stays with you. [11] For in six days the LORD made the heavens and the earth, the sea and all that is in them, and rested on the seventh day; therefore the LORD blessed the sabbath day and made it holy. (Exodus 20:8-11)

'Observe the sabbath day to keep it holy, as the Lord your God commanded you. [13] Six days you shall labor and do all your work, [14] but the seventh day is a sabbath of the Lord your God; *in it* you shall not do any work, you or your son or your daughter or your male servant or your female servant or your ox or your donkey or any of your cattle or your sojourner who [k]stays with you, so that your male servant and your female servant may rest as well as you. [15] You shall remember that you were a slave in the land of Egypt, and the Lord your God brought you out of there by a mighty hand and by an outstretched arm; therefore the Lord your God commanded you to observe the sabbath day. (Deuteronomy 5:12-15)

Not only was the Seventh Day important, but every Seventh Year was important as well. Jews were to keep the weekly and Seventh Year Sabbath. So picture that, no farming the Seventh Year. God would provide enough in the previous six to enable a Seventh Year Rest. God actually kept track of all the Seventh Years that the Jews did not take off. The Jewish years of exiled captivity actually match the number of Sabbath Years that they did not trust God to provide. Remember as well that after Seven times Seven Years, we have a 50th Jubilee Year. All debts owed were forgiven in the Jubilee Year. Jesus was crucified in a Jubilee Year.

So what does the Sabbath Commandment actually mean? We can get some insight from Hebrews 4 and Mark 2.

Therefore, let us fear if, while a promise remains of entering His rest, any one of you may seem to have come short of it. [2] For indeed we have had good news preached to us, just as they also; but the word [a]they heard did not profit them, because [b]it was not united by faith in those who heard. ³ For we who have believed enter that rest, just as He has said,

"AS I SWORE IN MY WRATH,
THEY SHALL NOT ENTER MY REST,"

although His works were finished from the foundation of the world. ⁴ For He has said somewhere concerning the seventh *day*: "AND GOD RESTED ON THE SEVENTH DAY FROM ALL HIS WORKS"; ⁵ and again in this *passage*, "THEY SHALL NOT ENTER MY REST." ⁶ Therefore, since it remains for some to enter it, and those who formerly had good news preached to them failed to enter because of disobedience, ⁷ He again fixes a certain day, "Today," saying [c]through David after so long a time just as has been said before,

"TODAY IF YOU HEAR HIS VOICE,
DO NOT HARDEN YOUR HEARTS."

⁸ For if [d]Joshua had given them rest, He would not have spoken of another day after that. ⁹ So there remains a Sabbath rest for the people of God. ¹⁰ For the one who has entered His rest has himself also rested from his works, as God did from His. ¹¹ Therefore let us be diligent to enter that rest, so that no one will fall, through *following* the same example of disobedience. ¹² For the word of God is living and active and sharper than any two-edged sword, and piercing as far as the division of soul and spirit, of both joints and marrow, and able to judge the thoughts and intentions of the heart. ¹³ And there is no creature hidden from His sight, but all things are open and laid bare to the eyes of Him with whom we have to do.

¹⁴ Therefore, since we have a great high priest who has passed through the heavens, Jesus the Son of God, let us hold fast our confession. ¹⁵ For we do not have a high priest who cannot sympathize with our weaknesses, but One who has been tempted in all things as *we are, yet* without sin. ¹⁶ Therefore let us draw near with confidence to the throne of grace, so that we may receive mercy and find grace to help in time of need. (Hebrews 4)

And it happened that He was passing through the grainfields on the Sabbath, and His disciples began to make their way along while picking the heads *of grain*. [24] The Pharisees were saying to Him, "Look, why are they doing what is not lawful on the Sabbath?" [25] And He *said to them, "Have you never read what David did when he was in need and he and his companions became hungry; [26] how he entered the house of God in the time of Abiathar *the* high priest, and ate the [o]consecrated bread, which is not lawful for *anyone* to eat except the priests, and he also gave it to those who were with him?" [27] Jesus said to them, "The Sabbath came into being [q]for man, and not man [r]for the Sabbath. [28] So the Son of Man is Lord even of the Sabbath." (Mark 2:23-28)

We are to trust in the Sabbath work of Jesus. Jesus, God Himself, accomplished the work for us. All the "Seven" references in the Bible point to Jesus. Jesus is our Seventh Day Eternal Sabbath Rest. We can't work our way to Heaven. Jesus works our Way to Heaven. The Fourth Commandment is actually the Gospel Message. It is not about going to "church" on Saturday of Sunday.

"Come to Me, all [z]who are weary and heavy-laden, and I will give you rest. [29] Take My yoke upon you and learn from Me, for I am gentle and humble in heart, and YOU WILL FIND REST FOR YOUR SOULS. [30] For My yoke is [aa]easy and My burden is light." (Matthew 11:28-30)

Jesus spoke these things; and lifting up His eyes to heaven, He said, "Father, the hour has come; glorify Your Son, that the Son may glorify You, [2] even as You gave Him authority over all flesh, that to [a]all whom You have given Him, He may give eternal life. [3] This is eternal life, that they may know You, the only true God, and Jesus Christ whom You have sent. [4] I glorified You on the earth, [b]having accomplished the work which You have given Me to do. [5] Now, Father, glorify Me together with Yourself, with the glory which I had with You before the world was. (John 17:1-5)

"The Sabbath came into Being for man"

"Having accomplished the work which You have given Me to do"

"you will find Rest for your souls"

"For we who have believed enter that Rest"

John 6

After these things Jesus went away to the other side of the Sea of Galilee (or Tiberias). [2] A large crowd followed Him, because they saw the [a]signs which He was performing on those who were sick. [3] Then Jesus went up on the mountain, and there He sat down with His disciples. [4] Now the Passover, the feast of the Jews, was near. [5] Therefore Jesus, lifting up His eyes and seeing that a large crowd was coming to Him, *said to Philip, "Where are we to buy bread, so that these may eat?" [6] This He was saying to test him, for He Himself knew what He was intending to do. [7] Philip answered Him, "Two hundred [b]denarii worth of bread is not sufficient for them, for everyone to receive a little." [8] One of His disciples, Andrew, Simon Peter's brother, *said to Him, [9] "There is a lad here who has five barley loaves and two fish, but what are these for so many people?" [10] Jesus said, "Have the people [c]sit down." Now there was much grass in the place. So the men [d]sat down, in number about five thousand. [11] Jesus then took the loaves, and having given thanks, He distributed to those who were seated; likewise also of the fish as much as they wanted. [12] When they were filled, He *said to His disciples, "Gather up the leftover fragments so that nothing will be lost." [13] So they gathered them up, and filled twelve baskets with fragments from the five barley loaves which were left over by those who had eaten. [14] Therefore when the people saw the [e]sign which He had performed, they said, "This is truly the Prophet who is to come into the world."

[15] So Jesus, perceiving that they were [f]intending to come and take Him by force to make Him king, withdrew again to the mountain by Himself alone.

[16] Now when evening came, His disciples went down to the sea, [17] and after getting into a boat, they *started to* cross the sea to Capernaum. It had already become dark, and Jesus had not yet come to them. [18] The sea *began* to be stirred up because a strong wind was blowing. [19] Then, when they had rowed about [g]three or four miles, they *saw Jesus walking on the sea and drawing near to the boat; and they were frightened. [20] But He *said to them, "It is I; [h]do not be afraid." [21] So they were willing to receive Him into the boat, and immediately the boat was at the land to which they were going.

[22] The next day the crowd that stood on the other side of the sea saw that there was no other small boat there, except one, and that Jesus had not entered with His disciples into the boat, but *that* His disciples had gone away alone. [23] There came other small boats from Tiberias near to the place where they ate the bread after the Lord had given thanks. [24] So when the crowd saw that Jesus was not there, nor His disciples, they themselves got into the small boats, and came to Capernaum seeking Jesus. [25] When they found Him on the other side of the sea, they said to Him, "Rabbi, when did You get here?"

[26] Jesus answered them and said, "Truly, truly, I say to you, you seek Me, not because you saw signs, but because you ate of the loaves and were filled. [27] Do not work for the food which perishes, but for the food which endures to eternal life, which the Son of Man will give to you, for on Him the Father, God, has set His seal."
[28] Therefore they said to Him, "What shall we do, so that we may work the works of God?" [29] Jesus answered and said to them, "This is the work of God, that you believe in Him whom He has sent."
[30] So they said to Him, "What then do You do for a sign, so that we may see, and believe You? What work do You perform? [31] Our fathers ate the manna in the wilderness; as it is written, 'HE GAVE

THEM BREAD OUT OF HEAVEN TO EAT.'" [32] Jesus then said to them, "Truly, truly, I say to you, it is not Moses who has given you the bread out of heaven, but it is My Father who gives you the true bread out of heaven. [33] For the bread of God is [i]that which comes down out of heaven, and gives life to the world." [34] Then they said to Him, "Lord, always give us this bread."

[35] Jesus said to them, "I am the bread of life; he who comes to Me will not hunger, and he who believes in Me will never thirst. [36] But I said to you that you have seen Me, and yet do not believe. [37] All that the Father gives Me will come to Me, and the one who comes to Me I will certainly not cast out. [38] For I have come down from heaven, not to do My own will, but the will of Him who sent Me. [39] This is the will of Him who sent Me, that of all that He has given Me I lose nothing, but raise it up on the last day. [40] For this is the will of My Father, that everyone who beholds the Son and believes in Him will have eternal life, and I Myself will raise him up on the last day."

[41] Therefore the Jews were grumbling about Him, because He said, "I am the bread that came down out of heaven." [42] They were saying, "Is not this Jesus, the son of Joseph, whose father and mother we know? How does He now say, 'I have come down out of heaven'?" [43] Jesus answered and said to them, "Do not grumble among yourselves. [44] No one can come to Me unless the Father who sent Me draws him; and I will raise him up on the last day. [45] It is written in the prophets, 'AND THEY SHALL ALL BE TAUGHT OF GOD.' Everyone who has heard and learned from the Father, comes to Me. [46] Not that anyone has seen the Father, except the One who is from God; He has seen the Father. [47] Truly, truly, I say to you, he who believes has eternal life. [48] I am the bread of life. [49] Your fathers ate the manna in the wilderness, and they died. [50] This is the bread which comes down out of heaven, so that one may eat of it and not die. [51] I am the living bread that came down out of heaven; if anyone eats of this bread, he will live forever; and the bread also which I will give for the life of the world is My flesh."

[52] Then the Jews *began* to argue with one another, saying, "How can this man give us *His* flesh to eat?" [53] So Jesus said to them, "Truly, truly, I say to you, unless you eat the flesh of the Son of Man and

drink His blood, you have no life in yourselves. [54] He who eats My flesh and drinks My blood has eternal life, and I will raise him up on the last day. [55] For My flesh is true food, and My blood is true drink. [56] He who eats My flesh and drinks My blood abides in Me, and I in him. [57] As the living Father sent Me, and I live because of the Father, so he who eats Me, he also will live because of Me. [58] This is the bread which came down out of heaven; not as the fathers ate and died; he who eats this bread will live forever."

[59] These things He said in the synagogue as He taught in Capernaum.

[60] Therefore many of His disciples, when they heard *this* said, "This is a difficult statement; who can listen to it?" [61] But Jesus, conscious that His disciples grumbled at this, said to them, "Does this cause you to stumble? [62] *What* then if you see the Son of Man ascending to where He was before? [63] It is the Spirit who gives life; the flesh profits nothing; the words that I have spoken to you are spirit and are life. [64] But there are some of you who do not believe." For Jesus knew from the beginning who they were who did not believe, and who it was that would [j]betray Him. [65] And He was saying, "For this reason I have said to you, that no one can come to Me unless it has been granted him from the Father."

[66] As a result of this many of His disciples withdrew and were not walking with Him anymore. [67] So Jesus said to the twelve, "You do not want to go away also, do you?" [68] Simon Peter answered Him, "Lord, to whom shall we go? You have words of eternal life. [69] We have believed and have come to know that You are the Holy One of God." [70] Jesus answered them, "Did I Myself not choose you, the twelve, and *yet* one of you is a devil?" [71] Now He meant Judas *the son* of Simon Iscariot, for he, one of the twelve, [k]was going to betray Him. (John 6)
https://www.biblegateway.com/passage/?search=John+6&version=NASB

I will paste the Old Testament chapter about the Manna from Heaven below:

Then they set out from Elim, and all the congregation of the sons of Israel came to the wilderness of Sin, which is between Elim and Sinai, on the fifteenth day of the second month after their departure from the land of Egypt. ² The whole congregation of the sons of Israel grumbled against Moses and Aaron in the wilderness. ³ The sons of Israel said to them, "Would that we had died by the LORD's hand in the land of Egypt, when we sat by the pots of [a]meat, when we ate bread to the full; for you have brought us out into this wilderness to kill this whole assembly with hunger."

⁴ Then the LORD said to Moses, "Behold, I will rain bread from heaven for you; and the people shall go out and gather a day's portion every day, that I may test them, whether or not they will walk in My [b]instruction. ⁵ On the sixth day, when they prepare what they bring in, it will be twice as much as they gather daily." ⁶ So Moses and Aaron said to all the sons of Israel, "At evening [c]you will know that the LORD has brought you out of the land of Egypt; ⁷ and in the morning [d]you will see the glory of the LORD, for He hears your grumblings against the LORD; and what are we, that you grumble against us?"

⁸ Moses said, "*This will happen* when the LORD gives you [e]meat to eat in the evening, and bread to the full in the morning; for the LORD hears your grumblings which you grumble against Him. And what are we? Your grumblings are not against us but against the LORD."

⁹ Then Moses said to Aaron, "Say to all the congregation of the sons of Israel, 'Come near before the LORD, for He has heard your grumblings.'" ¹⁰ It came about as Aaron spoke to the whole congregation of the sons of Israel, that they [f]looked toward the wilderness, and behold, the glory of the LORD appeared in the cloud. ¹¹ And the LORD spoke to Moses, saying, ¹² "I have heard the grumblings of the sons of Israel; speak to them, saying, '[g]At twilight you shall eat [h]meat, and in the morning you shall be filled with bread; and you shall know that I am the LORD your God.'"

¹³ So it came about at evening that the quails came up and covered the camp, and in the morning there was a layer of dew around the camp. ¹⁴ When the layer of dew [i]evaporated, behold, on the

[i]surface of the wilderness there was a fine flake-like thing, fine as the frost on the ground. [15] When the sons of Israel saw *it*, they said to one another, "[k]What is it?" For they did not know what it was. And Moses said to them, "It is the bread which the LORD has given you to eat. [16] This is [l]what the LORD has commanded, 'Gather of it every man [m]as much as he should eat; you shall take [n]an omer apiece according to the number of persons each of you has in his tent.'"
[17] The sons of Israel did so, and *some* gathered much and *some* little. [18] When they measured it with an omer, he who had gathered much had no excess, and he who had gathered little had no lack; every man gathered [o]as much as he should eat. [19] Moses said to them, "Let no man leave any of it until morning." [20] But they did not listen to Moses, and some left part of it until morning, and it bred worms and became foul; and Moses was angry with them. [21] They gathered it morning by morning, every man [p]as much as he should eat; but when the sun grew hot, it would melt.

[22] Now on the sixth day they gathered twice as much bread, two omers for each one. When all the leaders of the congregation came and told Moses, [23] then he said to them, "This is what the LORD [q]meant: Tomorrow is a sabbath observance, a holy sabbath to the LORD. Bake what you will bake and boil what you will boil, and all that is left over [r]put aside to be kept until morning." [24] So they [s]put it aside until morning, as Moses had ordered, and it did not become foul nor was there any worm in it. [25] Moses said, "Eat it today, for today is a sabbath to the LORD; today you will not find it in the field. [26] Six days you shall gather it, but on the seventh day, *the* sabbath, there will be [t]none."

[27] It came about on the seventh day that some of the people went out to gather, but they found none. [28] Then the LORD said to Moses, "How long do you refuse to keep My commandments and My [u]instructions? [29] See, [v]the LORD has given you the sabbath; therefore He gives you bread for two days on the sixth day. Remain every man in his place; let no man go out of his place on the seventh day." [30] So the people rested on the seventh day.

[31] The house of Israel named it [w]manna, and it was like coriander seed, white, and its taste was like wafers with honey. [32] Then Moses

said, "This is [x]what the LORD has commanded, 'Let an omerful of it be kept throughout your generations, that they may see the bread that I fed you in the wilderness, when I brought you out of the land of Egypt.'" 33 Moses said to Aaron, "Take a jar and put an omerful of manna in it, and place it before the LORD to be kept throughout your generations." 34 As the LORD commanded Moses, so Aaron placed it before the Testimony, to be kept. 35 The sons of Israel ate the manna forty years, until they came to an inhabited land; they ate the manna until they came to the border of the land of Canaan. 36 (Now an omer is a tenth of an [y]ephah.) (Exodus 16)

Note that some of this Manna was placed into the Ark of the Covenant (picture of heart). Eventually there would be three items in the Ark: Golden Jar of Manna (picture of Jesus, the Bread of Life), The Ten Commandments (picture of the Law), and the Almond Budded Rod of Aaron (picture of the Cross). Hebrews 9 (New Testament) describes the contents and teaches us that the Ark has always been about Jesus. Very importantly above in verse 22, we see the people of God gathering twice as much Manna on Friday, which enabled them to have their Saturday, 7th Day Sabbath Rest. Jesus was crucified on Good Friday for our Eternal Sabbath Rest. Hebrews 4 beautifully shows Jesus as our Sabbath Rest.

Now even the first *covenant* had regulations of divine worship and the earthly sanctuary. 2 For there was a [a]tabernacle prepared, the [b]outer one, in which *were* the lampstand and the table and the [c]sacred bread; this is called the holy place. 3 Behind the second veil there was a [d]tabernacle which is called the Holy of Holies, 4 having a golden [e]altar of incense and the ark of the covenant covered on all sides with gold, in which was a golden jar holding the manna, and Aaron's rod which budded, and the tables of the covenant; 5 and above it *were* the cherubim of glory overshadowing the mercy seat; but of these things we cannot now speak in detail.

6 Now when these things have been so prepared, the priests are continually entering the [f]outer [g]tabernacle performing the divine worship, 7 but into the second, only the high priest *enters* once a year, not without *taking* blood, which he offers for himself and for

the [h]sins of the people committed in ignorance. [8] The Holy Spirit *is* signifying this, that the way into the holy place has not yet been disclosed while the [i]outer tabernacle is still standing, [9] which *is* a symbol for the present time. Accordingly both gifts and sacrifices are offered which cannot make the worshiper perfect in conscience, [10] since they *relate* only to food and drink and various washings, regulations for the [j]body imposed until a time of reformation.

[11] But when Christ appeared *as* a high priest of the good things [k]to come, *He entered* through the greater and more perfect [l]tabernacle, not made with hands, that is to say, not of this creation; [12] and not through the blood of goats and calves, but through His own blood, He entered the holy place once for all, [m]having obtained eternal redemption. [13] For if the blood of goats and bulls and the ashes of a heifer sprinkling those who have been defiled sanctify for the [n]cleansing of the flesh, [14] how much more will the blood of Christ, who through [o]the eternal Spirit offered Himself without blemish to God, cleanse [p]your conscience from dead works to serve the living God?

[15] For this reason He is the mediator of a new covenant, so that, since a death has taken place for the redemption of the transgressions that were *committed* under the first covenant, those who have been called may receive the promise of the eternal inheritance. [16] For where a [q]covenant is, there must of necessity [r]be the death of the one who made it. [17] For a [s]covenant is valid *only* when [t]men are dead, [u]for it is never in force while the one who made it lives. [18] Therefore even the first *covenant* was not inaugurated without blood. [19] For when every commandment had been spoken by Moses to all the people according to the Law, he took the blood of the calves and the goats, with water and scarlet wool and hyssop, and sprinkled both the book itself and all the people, [20] saying, "THIS IS THE BLOOD OF THE COVENANT WHICH GOD COMMANDED YOU." [21] And in the same way he sprinkled both the [v]tabernacle and all the vessels of the ministry with the blood. [22] And according to the [w]Law, *one may* almost *say*, all things are cleansed with blood, and without shedding of blood there is no forgiveness.

[23] Therefore it was necessary for the copies of the things in the heavens to be cleansed with these, but the heavenly things themselves with better sacrifices than these. [24] For Christ did not enter a holy place made with hands, a *mere* copy of the true one, but into heaven itself, now to appear in the presence of God for us; [25] nor was it that He would offer Himself often, as the high priest enters the holy place year by year with blood that is not his own. [26] Otherwise, He would have needed to suffer often since the foundation of the world; but now once at the consummation of the ages He has been manifested to put away sin [x]by the sacrifice of Himself. [27] And inasmuch as it is [y]appointed for men to die once and after this *comes* judgment, [28] so Christ also, having been offered once to bear the sins of many, will appear a second time for salvation without *reference to* sin, to those who eagerly await Him. (Hebrews 9)

The Verse directly above states, "to those who eagerly await Him." As we eagerly await His return we take Communion, as to remember what Christ did for us. I will paste two Communion Scriptures below:

When the hour had come, He reclined *at the table*, and the apostles with Him. [15] And He said to them, "I have earnestly desired to eat this Passover with you before I suffer; [16] for I say to you, I shall never again eat it until it is fulfilled in the kingdom of God." [17] And when He had taken a cup *and* given thanks, He said, "Take this and share it among yourselves; [18] for I say to you, I will not drink of the fruit of the vine from now on until the kingdom of God comes." [19] And when He had taken *some* bread *and* given thanks, He broke it and gave it to them, saying, "This is My body which is given for you; do this in remembrance of Me." [20] And in the same way *He took* the cup after they had eaten, saying, "This cup which is poured out for you is the new covenant in My blood. [21] But behold, the hand of the one betraying Me is with [c]Mine on the table. [22] For indeed, the Son of Man is going as it has been determined; but woe to that man by whom He is betrayed!" [23] And they began to discuss among themselves which one of them it might be who was going to do this thing. (Luke 22:14-23)

For I received from the Lord that which I also delivered to you, that the Lord Jesus in the night in which He was betrayed took bread; [24] and when He had given thanks, He broke it and said, "This is My body, which is for you; do this in remembrance of Me." [25] In the same way *He took* the cup also after supper, saying, "This cup is the new covenant in My blood; do this, as often as you drink *it*, in remembrance of Me." [26] For as often as you eat this bread and drink the cup, you proclaim the Lord's death until He comes. (1 Corinthians 11:23-26)

Jesus said to them, "I am the bread of life; he who comes to Me will not hunger, and he who believes in Me will never thirst.

John 7

After these things Jesus was walking in Galilee, for He was unwilling to walk in Judea because the Jews were seeking to kill Him. [2] Now the feast of the Jews, the Feast of Booths, was near. [3] Therefore His brothers said to Him, "Leave here and go into Judea, so that Your disciples also may see Your works which You are doing. [4] For no one does anything in secret [a]when he himself seeks to be *known* publicly. If You do these things, show Yourself to the world." [5] For not even His brothers were believing in Him. [6] So Jesus *said to them, "My time is not yet here, but your time is always opportune. [7] The world cannot hate you, but it hates Me because I testify of it, that its deeds are evil. [8] Go up to the feast yourselves; I do not go up to this feast because My time has not yet fully come." [9] Having said these things to them, He stayed in Galilee.

¹⁰ But when His brothers had gone up to the feast, then He Himself also went up, not publicly, but as if, in secret. ¹¹ So the Jews were seeking Him at the feast and were saying, "Where is He?" ¹² There was much grumbling among the crowds concerning Him; some were saying, "He is a good man"; others were saying, "No, on the contrary, He leads the people astray." ¹³ Yet no one was speaking openly of Him for fear of the Jews.

¹⁴ But when it was now the midst of the feast Jesus went up into the temple, and *began to* teach. ¹⁵ The Jews then were astonished, saying, "How has this man become learned, having never been educated?" ¹⁶ So Jesus answered them and said, "My teaching is not Mine, but His who sent Me. ¹⁷ If anyone is willing to do His will, he will know of the teaching, whether it is of God or *whether* I speak from Myself. ¹⁸ He who speaks from himself seeks his own glory; but He who is seeking the glory of the One who sent Him, He is true, and there is no unrighteousness in Him.

¹⁹ "Did not Moses give you the Law, and *yet* none of you carries out the Law? Why do you seek to kill Me?" ²⁰ The crowd answered, "You have a demon! Who seeks to kill You?" ²¹ Jesus answered them, "I did one [b]deed, and you all marvel. ²² For this reason Moses has given you circumcision (not because it is from Moses, but from the fathers), and on *the* Sabbath you circumcise a man. ²³ If a man receives circumcision on *the* Sabbath so that the Law of Moses will not be broken, are you angry with Me because I made an entire man well on *the* Sabbath? ²⁴ Do not judge according to appearance, but [c]judge with righteous judgment."

²⁵ So some of the people of Jerusalem were saying, "Is this not the man whom they are seeking to kill? ²⁶ Look, He is speaking publicly, and they are saying nothing to Him. The rulers do not really know that this is [d]the Christ, do they? ²⁷ However, we know where this man is from; but whenever the Christ may come, no one knows where He is from." ²⁸ Then Jesus cried out in the temple, teaching and saying, "You both know Me and know where I am from; and I have not come of Myself, but He who sent Me is true, whom you do not know. ²⁹ I know Him, because I am from Him, and He sent Me." ³⁰ So they were seeking to seize Him; and no man laid his hand on

Him, because His hour had not yet come. ³¹ But many of the crowd believed in Him; and they were saying, "When [e]the Christ comes, He will not perform more [f]signs than those which this man has, will He?"

³² The Pharisees heard the crowd muttering these things about Him, and the chief priests and the Pharisees sent officers to seize Him. ³³ Therefore Jesus said, "For a little while longer I am with you, then I go to Him who sent Me. ³⁴ You will seek Me, and will not find Me; and where I am, you cannot come." ³⁵ The Jews then said to one another, "Where does this man intend to go that we will not find Him? He is not intending to go to the Dispersion among the Greeks, and teach the Greeks, is He? ³⁶ What is this statement that He said, 'You will seek Me, and will not find Me; and where I am, you cannot come'?"

³⁷ Now on the last day, the great *day* of the feast, Jesus stood and cried out, saying, "[g]If anyone is thirsty, [h]let him come to Me and drink. ³⁸ He who believes in Me, as the Scripture said, 'From [i]his innermost being will flow rivers of living water.'" ³⁹ But this He spoke of the Spirit, whom those who believed in Him were to receive; for the Spirit was not yet *given*, because Jesus was not yet glorified.

⁴⁰ *Some* of the people therefore, when they heard these words, were saying, "This certainly is the Prophet." ⁴¹ Others were saying, "This is [j]the Christ." Still others were saying, "Surely [k]the Christ is not going to come from Galilee, is He? ⁴² Has not the Scripture said that the Christ comes from the descendants of David, and from Bethlehem, the village where David was?" ⁴³ So a division occurred in the crowd because of Him. ⁴⁴ Some of them wanted to seize Him, but no one laid hands on Him.

⁴⁵ The officers then came to the chief priests and Pharisees, and they said to them, "Why did you not bring Him?" ⁴⁶ The officers answered, "Never has a man spoken the way this man speaks." ⁴⁷ The Pharisees then answered them, "You have not also been led astray, have you? ⁴⁸ No one of the rulers or Pharisees has believed in Him, has he? ⁴⁹ But this crowd which does not know the Law is

accursed." [50] Nicodemus (he who came to Him before, being one of them) *said to them, [51] "Our Law does not judge a man unless it first hears from him and knows what he is doing, does it?" [52] They answered him, "You are not also from Galilee, are you? Search, and see that no prophet arises out of Galilee." [53] [1]Everyone went to his home. (John 7)
https://www.biblegateway.com/passage/?search=John+7&version=NASB

The Feast of Booths is also called the Feast of Tabernacles, Feast of Ingathering, or Sukkot. This is one of the three required attendance Feast times for all Jewish males. During these three timeframes you actually have all Seven Feasts. The Feast of Booths is just after the Jewish New Year's Day called Rosh Hashanah or Trumpets and the Day of Atonement, also called Yom Kippur. It is interesting how the first day of the Jewish year is the first day of the Seventh month (On a Roman calendar this would be late September). I believe Jesus was born on Trumpets. I do know many people say that the Feast of Trumpets is fulfilled in the future at the "Last Trumpet", but the Bible purposely says "Last Trumpet" in 1 Corinthians 15:52. I believe Jesus was born at the "First Trumpet". Remember the shepherds were terrified. Imagine thousands of angels blowing trumpets.

Shortly after Trumpets is the Day of Atonement (10th Day of the year), which coincides with the day that Jesus was circumcised. For modern day believers to say that the Day of Atonement has not yet been fulfilled, in my opinion, is madness. The Day of Atonement, Yom Kippur, was the one and only Day a year the High Priest could go behind the Veil into the Holy of Holies. Thirty-three years after the Christ Child was circumcised on the Day of Atonement, on the Cross He said, "It is finished." The twelve inch thick Veil to the Holy of Holies tore, from Top to bottom. The Veil was circumcised from around the Ark of the Covenant, the Ark representing the heart.

71

But he is a Jew who is one inwardly; and circumcision is that which is of the heart, by the Spirit, not by the letter; and his praise is not from men, but from God. (Romans 2:29)

Therefore, brethren, since we have confidence to enter the holy place by the blood of Jesus, [20] by a new and living way which He inaugurated for us through the veil, that is, His flesh, [21] and since *we have* a great priest over the house of God, [22] let us draw near with a [h]sincere heart in full assurance of faith, having our hearts sprinkled *clean* from an evil conscience and our bodies washed with pure water. [23] Let us hold fast the confession of our hope without wavering, for He who promised is faithful; [24] and let us consider how to stimulate one another to love and good deeds, [25] not forsaking our own assembling together, as is the habit of some, but encouraging *one another*; and all the more as you see the day drawing near. (Hebrews 10:19-25)

Then on the 15th day of the Seventh month you have the Feast of Booths. This Feast time included making temporary shelters out of palm branches. The deeper meaning of this Feast of Booths/Tabernacles is that God Himself took on a Human Tabernacle/ Temporary Shelter. John 1 says, Jesus "dwelt" amongst us, this "dwelt" means, "to tabernacle". A week preceding the Cross/Passover was "Palm Sunday". People placed palm branches on the ground for Jesus to ride over. This represented Jesus' Temporary Shelter/Human Body was about to be dismantled/crucified. Notice that Jesus gets on a colt (Matthew 21 uses the term "beast of burden") that has never been ridden. Jesus is riding on a "working" animal, meaning that He alone works our way to Heaven. No one, except the Christ, has or can ride this beast of burden.

When they had approached Jerusalem and had come to Bethphage, at the Mount of Olives, then Jesus sent two disciples, [2] saying to them, "Go into the village opposite you, and immediately you will find a donkey tied *there* and a colt with her; untie them and bring them to Me. [3] If anyone says anything to you, you shall say, 'The Lord has need of them,' and immediately he will send them." [4] This [a]took place to fulfill what was spoken through the prophet:

[5] "SAY TO THE DAUGHTER OF ZION,
'BEHOLD YOUR KING IS COMING TO YOU,
GENTLE, AND MOUNTED ON A DONKEY,
EVEN ON A COLT, THE FOAL OF A BEAST OF BURDEN.'"

[6] The disciples went and did just as Jesus had instructed them, [7] and brought the donkey and the colt, and laid their coats on them; and He sat on [b]the coats. [8] Most of the crowd spread their coats in the road, and others were cutting branches from the trees and spreading them in the road. [9] The crowds going ahead of Him, and those who followed, were shouting,

"Hosanna to the Son of David;
BLESSED IS HE WHO COMES IN THE NAME OF THE LORD;
Hosanna in the highest!" (Matthew 21:1-9)

When He approached Bethphage and Bethany, near the [n]mount that is called Olivet, He sent two of the disciples, [30] saying, "Go into the village ahead of *you*; there, as you enter, you will find a colt tied on which no one yet has ever sat; untie it and bring it *here*. [31] If anyone asks you, 'Why are you untying it?' you shall say, 'The Lord has need of it.'" [32] So those who were sent went away and found it just as He had told them. [33] As they were untying the colt, its [o]owners said to them, "Why are you untying the colt?" [34] They said, "The Lord has need of it." [35] They brought it to Jesus, and they threw their coats on the colt and put Jesus *on it*. [36] As He was going, they were spreading their coats on the road. [37] As soon as He was approaching, near the descent of the Mount of Olives, the whole crowd of the disciples began to praise God [p]joyfully with a loud voice for all the [q]miracles which they had seen, [38] shouting:

"Blessed is the King who comes in the name of the Lord; Peace in heaven and glory in the highest!" (Luke 19:29-38)

Notice in the Luke reference that two cities are mentioned. Bethphage means house of unripe figs. Bethany means house of ripe figs. The fig tree has a Biblical meaning of sin. Remember John the Baptist, in John 1, was baptizing at the Bethany "Beyond the Jordan", up until he baptized Jesus. I believe the tree of knowledge of good and evil was a fig tree. So you have a beautiful picture of Jesus being crucified for ALL sin, those sins that have already occurred (ripe figs) and those to occur in the future (unripe figs).

Verse five says His own brothers did not believe in Him. We can't knock His brothers for their unbelief. In fact, all of Jesus' disciples ran scared before the Cross/Passover, even Peter, one of the toughest disciples, wimped out to a young girl. But after Passover, Unleavened Bread, First Fruits and Weeks that all changed. After the Seventh Feast, the Feast of Weeks, 7 weeks of 7, at Day 50, called Pentecost, the Holy Spirit was given. Aside from John, every disciple died for their faith in Christ after they received the Holy Spirit. It is important to note that two of Jesus' half brothers, James and Jude, after receiving the Holy Spirit wrote the Books of James and Jude.

Notice in verse 37-39:

Now on the last day, the great *day* of the feast, Jesus stood and cried out, saying, "[g]If anyone is thirsty, [h]let him come to Me and drink. 38 He who believes in Me, as the Scripture said, 'From [i]his innermost being will flow rivers of living water.'" 39 But this He spoke of the Spirit, whom those who believed in Him were to receive; for the Spirit was not yet *given*, because Jesus was not yet glorified.

John 8

But Jesus went to the Mount of Olives. [2] Early in the morning He came again into the temple, and all the people were coming to Him; and He sat down and *began* to teach them. [3] The scribes and the Pharisees *brought a woman caught in adultery, and having set her in the center *of the court*, [4] they *said to Him, "Teacher, this woman has been caught in adultery, in the very act. [5] Now in the Law Moses commanded us to stone such women; what then do You say?" [6] They were saying this, testing Him, so that they might have grounds for accusing Him. But Jesus stooped down and with His finger wrote on the ground. [7] But when they persisted in asking Him, He straightened up, and said to them, "He who is without sin among you, let him *be the* first to throw a stone at her." [8] Again He stooped down and wrote on the ground. [9] When they heard it, they *began* to go out one by one, beginning with the older ones, and He was left alone, and the woman, where she was, in the center *of the court*. [10] Straightening up, Jesus said to her, "Woman, where are they? Did no one condemn you?" [11] She said, "No one, [a]Lord." And Jesus said, "I do not condemn you, either. Go. From now on sin no more."]

[12] Then Jesus again spoke to them, saying, "I am the Light of the world; he who follows Me will not walk in the darkness, but will have the Light of life." [13] So the Pharisees said to Him, "You are testifying about Yourself; Your testimony is not [b]true." [14] Jesus answered and said to them, "Even if I testify about Myself, My testimony is [c]true, for I know where I came from and where I am going; but you do not know where I come from or where I am going. [15] You judge [d]according to the flesh; I am not judging anyone. [16] But even if I do judge, My judgment is true; for I am not alone *in it*, but I and the Father who sent Me. [17] Even in your law it has been written that the testimony of two men is [e]true. [18] I am He who testifies about Myself, and the Father who sent Me testifies about Me." [19] So they were saying to Him, "Where is Your Father?" Jesus answered, "You know neither Me nor My Father; if you knew Me, you would know My Father also." [20] These words He spoke in the

treasury, as He taught in the temple; and no one seized Him, because His hour had not yet come.

21 Then He said again to them, "I go away, and you will seek Me, and will die in your sin; where I am going, you cannot come." 22 So the Jews were saying, "Surely He will not kill Himself, will He, since He says, 'Where I am going, you cannot come'?" 23 And He was saying to them, "You are from below, I am from above; you are of this world, I am not of this world. 24 Therefore I said to you that you will die in your sins; for unless you believe that [f]I am *He*, you will die in your sins." 25 So they were saying to Him, "Who are You?" Jesus said to them, "[g]What have I been saying to you *from* the beginning? 26 I have many things to speak and to judge concerning you, but He who sent Me is true; and the things which I heard from Him, these I speak to the world." 27 They did not realize that He had been speaking to them about the Father. 28 So Jesus said, "When you lift up the Son of Man, then you will know that [h]I am *He*, and I do nothing on My own initiative, but I speak these things as the Father taught Me. 29 And He who sent Me is with Me; He [i]has not left Me alone, for I always do the things that are pleasing to Him." 30 As He spoke these things, many came to believe in Him.

31 So Jesus was saying to those Jews who had believed Him, "If you continue in My word, *then* you are truly disciples of Mine; 32 and you will know the truth, and the truth will make you free." 33 They answered Him, "We are Abraham's descendants and have never yet been enslaved to anyone; how is it that You say, 'You will become free'?"

34 Jesus answered them, "Truly, truly, I say to you, everyone who commits sin is the slave of sin. 35 The slave does not remain in the house forever; the son does remain forever. 36 So if the Son makes you free, you will be free indeed. 37 I know that you are Abraham's descendants; yet you seek to kill Me, because My word [j]has no place in you. 38 I speak the things which I have seen [k]with *My* Father; therefore you also do the things which you heard from *your* father."

[39] They answered and said to Him, "Abraham is our father." Jesus *said to them, "If you are Abraham's children, do the deeds of Abraham. [40] But as it is, you are seeking to kill Me, a man who has told you the truth, which I heard from God; this Abraham did not do. [41] You are doing the deeds of your father." They said to Him, "We were not born of fornication; we have one Father: God." [42] Jesus said to them, "If God were your Father, you would love Me, for I proceeded forth and have come from God, for I have not even come on My own initiative, but [l]He sent Me. [43] Why do you not understand [m]what I am saying? *It is* because you cannot hear My word. [44] You are of *your* father the devil, and you want to do the desires of your father. He was a murderer from the beginning, and does not stand in the truth because there is no truth in him. Whenever he speaks [n]a lie, he speaks from his own *nature*, for he is a liar and the father of [o]lies. [45] But because I speak the truth, you do not believe Me. [46] Which one of you convicts Me of sin? If I speak truth, why do you not believe Me? [47] He who is of God hears the words of God; for this reason you do not hear *them*, because you are not of God."

[48] The Jews answered and said to Him, "Do we not say rightly that You are a Samaritan and have a demon?" [49] Jesus answered, "I do not have a demon; but I honor My Father, and you dishonor Me. [50] But I do not seek My glory; there is One who seeks and judges. [51] Truly, truly, I say to you, if anyone keeps My word he will never see death." [52] The Jews said to Him, "Now we know that You have a demon. Abraham died, and the prophets *also*; and You say, 'If anyone keeps My word, he will never taste of death.' [53] Surely You are not greater than our father Abraham, who died? The prophets died too; whom do You make Yourself out *to be*?" [54] Jesus answered, "If I glorify Myself, My glory is nothing; it is My Father who glorifies Me, of whom you say, 'He is our God'; [55] and you have not come to know Him, but I know Him; and if I say that I do not know Him, I will be a liar like you, but I do know Him and keep His word. [56] Your father Abraham rejoiced [p]to see My day, and he saw *it* and was glad." [57] So the Jews said to Him, "You are not yet fifty years old, and have You seen Abraham?" [58] Jesus said to them, "Truly, truly, I say to you, before Abraham [q]was born, I am." [59] Therefore they picked up stones to throw at Him, but Jesus [r]hid

Himself and went out of the temple. (John 8)
https://www.biblegateway.com/passage/?search=John+8&version=N
ASB

We start this chapter at the Mount of Olives. This is about two miles east of Jerusalem. The cities Bethphage (house of unripe fig/sin) and Bethany (house of ripe fig/sin) are located here. There is a huge fig/sin connection in the Bible. At one point in Scripture Jesus actually curses the fig tree (Mark 11 and Matthew 21). Note that just prior to cursing that fig tree/sin, that Jesus cleanses the Temple by driving out the buyers/sellers and money changers. We know that our body, once born again, becomes the Temple of the Holy Spirit. The Garden of Gethsemane (means oil press) is also in this area. Remember Jesus actually sweats blood (blood press/oil press) prior to the Cross in Gethsemane. This area is also where Martha (mastered), Mary (sin), and Lazarus (Holy Spirit) are from. Later Judas betrays Jesus here. Jesus also ascends into Heaven from here after the Feast of First Fruits (Resurrection) at the end of the Feast of Weeks (the over forty days Jesus appeared to many witnesses as proof of Resurrection).

Judas is a very interesting person. He is actually the buyer/seller/money changer for Jesus and the disciples. His name, Judas, is Greek, but in Hebrew it is Judah. As believers we are of Christ, the Tribe of Judah. The deeper meaning is that just as Judas, we also betray Christ. Technically, all humans, that want nothing to do with God, but wish to ignore Him, are in fact betraying Christ. People think that if they don't believe in God, then He doesn't exist. But remember we can't knock them; we were blind at one time as well. We can pray that the Holy Spirit prepare their hearts for the Good News that we are to present.

We have a woman caught in adultery, which is betrayal. Whenever you see a woman reference in Scripture, keep in mind that many times this can be a picture of the church, the bride of Christ. In this case, I believe it is, partly because you don't see a man mentioned, it takes two to commit adultery. The focus is on the woman, meaning the bride, meaning us, the church. The Seventh Commandment is "you shall not commit adultery." Up to this point in the Bible, people were stoned to death for breaking this Commandment. You see Jesus actually writing on the ground. Maybe He is writing out the Ten Commandments. Jesus says, "He who is without sin among you, let him *be the* first to throw a stone at her." Jesus continues to write, and then one by one, starting with the oldest, they all leave. Then Jesus says, "Woman, where are they? Did no one condemn you?" [11] She said, "No one, [a]Lord." And Jesus said, "I do not condemn you, either. Go. From now on sin no more."

Jesus goes on to say that He is the Light of the world. There was a festival added to the Jewish calendar when Herod the Great (under the Romans) took back Jerusalem from the Greeks. The festival is called Hanukkah/Chanukah/Feast of Dedication. Even today in Jerusalem, called the Festival of Lights, they still light up the Temple Mount during this celebration. Jews from all over the world still celebrate Hanukkah. The holiday is in the same month as Christmas, the month of Chislev/Kislev. Here is a neat thought, Herod finished the Temple, and dedicated it about the same time as Jesus was conceived by the Holy Spirit. This would explain Herod's deep anger, when the Magi, came and wanted to anoint the newborn King nine months later at Trumpets. Wow, we have God in the Flesh, in a Human Temple, during the same timeframe as the physical Temple was finished and rededicated. Luke 2 has the dedication of Jesus at the Temple on the Day of Atonement. Later

Jesus says, "Destroy this Temple and I will raise it up in three days."
So we have an obvious connection of the Body of Christ and the
Temple.

Jesus goes on to present the Gospel Message:

So Jesus said, "When you lift up the Son of Man, then you will know
that [h]I am *He*, and I do nothing on My own initiative, but I speak
these things as the Father taught Me. [29] And He who sent Me is with
Me; He [i]has not left Me alone, for I always do the things that are
pleasing to Him." [30] As He spoke these things, many came to believe
in Him. [31] So Jesus was saying to those Jews who had believed Him,
"If you continue in My word, *then* you are truly disciples of Mine;
[32] and you will know the truth, and the truth will make you free."
[33] They answered Him, "We are Abraham's descendants and have
never yet been enslaved to anyone; how is it that You say, 'You will
become free'?" [34] Jesus answered them, "Truly, truly, I say to you,
everyone who commits sin is the slave of sin. [35] The slave does not
remain in the house forever; the son does remain forever. [36] So if the
Son makes you free, you will be free indeed.

Jesus goes on to say:

Jesus said to them, "Truly, truly, I say to you, before Abraham [q]was
born, I am." [59] Therefore they picked up stones to throw at Him, but
Jesus [r]hid Himself and went out of the temple.

When Jesus used the term, "I AM", relating to Himself, the Jews
saw this as Him making Himself out to be God. There are actually
Seven "I AM" statements in John. The original statement is found in
Exodus 3. In conclusion, I will paste below a previous paper called
"I AM":

Then Moses said to God, "Behold, I am going to the sons of Israel, and I
will say to them, 'The God of your fathers has sent me to you.' Now they
may say to me, 'What is His name?' What shall I say to them?" [14] God said

80

to Moses, "[g]I AM WHO [h]I AM"; and He said, "Thus you shall say to the sons of Israel, '[i]I AM has sent me to you.'" (Exodus 3:13, 14)

Jesus said to them, "Truly, truly, I say to you, before Abraham [j]was born, I am." [59] Therefore they picked up stones to throw at Him, but Jesus [r]hid Himself and went out of the temple. (John 8:58, 59)

In John 8, Jesus equates Himself to the "I AM". Just as John is the only book of the Bible to contain the truly, truly statements, this book is also the only book to contain the "I AM" statements. In John, Jesus gives us the 7 "I AM"........'s.

Then Jesus again spoke to them, saying, "I am the Light of the world; he who follows Me will not walk in the darkness, but will have the Light of life." (John 8:12)

Jesus *said to him, "I am the way, and the truth, and the life; no one comes to the Father but through Me. (John 14:6)

So Jesus said to them again, "Truly, truly, I say to you, I am the door of the sheep. [8] All who came before Me are thieves and robbers, but the sheep did not hear them. [9] I am the door; if anyone enters through Me, he will be saved, and will go in and out and find pasture. (John 10:7-9)

"I am the good shepherd; the good shepherd lays down His life for the sheep. [12] He who is a hired hand, and not a shepherd, who is not the owner of the sheep, sees the wolf coming, and leaves the sheep and flees, and the wolf snatches them and scatters *them*. [13] *He flees* because he is a hired hand and is not concerned about the sheep. [14] I am the good shepherd, and I know My own and My own know Me, [15] even as the Father knows Me and I know the Father; and I lay down My life for the sheep. (John 10:11-15)

Jesus said to them, "I am the bread of life; he who comes to Me will not hunger, and he who believes in Me will never thirst. (John 6:35)

Jesus said to her, "I am the resurrection and the life; he who believes in Me will live even if he dies, [26] and everyone who lives and believes in Me will never die. Do you believe this?" [27] She *said to Him, "Yes, Lord; I have believed that You are [f]the Christ, the Son of God, *even* [g]He who comes into the world." (John 11:25-27)

"I am the true vine, and My Father is the vinedresser. [2] Every branch in Me that does not bear fruit, He takes away; and every *branch* that bears fruit, He [a]prunes it so that it may bear more fruit. [3] You are already [b]clean because of the word which I have spoken to you. [4] Abide in Me, and I in you. As the branch cannot bear fruit [c]of itself unless it abides in the vine, so neither *can* you unless you abide in Me. [5] I am the vine, you are the branches; he who abides in Me and I in him, he bears much fruit, for apart from Me you can do nothing. (John 15:1-5)

https://www.youtube.com/watch?v=w2Yh4exnBU0

https://www.youtube.com/watch?v=mMknfsWrzN8

John 9

As He passed by, He saw a man blind from birth. [2] And His disciples asked Him, "Rabbi, who sinned, this man or his parents, that he would be born blind?" [3] Jesus answered, "*It was* neither *that* this man sinned, nor his parents; but *it was* so that the works of God might be displayed in him. [4] We must work the works of Him who sent Me as long as it is day; night is coming when no one can work. [5] While I am in the world, I am the Light of the world." [6] When He had said this, He spat on the ground, and made clay of the spittle, and applied the clay to his eyes, [7] and said to him, "Go, wash in the pool of Siloam" (which is translated, Sent). So he went away and washed, and came *back* seeing. [8] Therefore the neighbors, and those who previously saw him as a beggar, were saying, "Is not this the one who used to sit and beg?" [9] Others were saying, "This is he," *still* others were saying, "No, but he is like him." [a]He kept saying, "I am the one." [10] So they were saying to him, "How then were your eyes opened?" [11] He answered, "The man who is called Jesus made clay, and anointed my eyes, and said to me, 'Go to Siloam and wash'; so I went away and washed, and I received sight." [12] They said to him, "Where is He?" He *said, "I do not know."

[13] They *brought to the Pharisees the man who was formerly blind. [14] Now it was a Sabbath on the day when Jesus made the clay and opened his eyes. [15] Then the Pharisees also were asking him again how he received his sight. And he said to them, "He applied clay to my eyes, and I washed, and I see." [16] Therefore some of the Pharisees were saying, "This man is not from God, because He does not keep the Sabbath." But others were saying, "How can a man who is a sinner perform such [b]signs?" And there was a division among them. [17] So they *said to the blind man again, "What do you say about Him, since He opened your eyes?" And he said, "He is a prophet."

[18] The Jews then did not believe *it* of him, that he had been blind and had received sight, until they called the parents of the very one who had received his sight, [19] and questioned them, saying, "Is this your son, who you say was born blind? Then how does he now see?" [20] His parents answered them and said, "We know that this is our son, and that he was born blind; [21] but how he now sees, we do not know; or who opened his eyes, we do not know. Ask him; he is of age, he will speak for himself." [22] His parents said this because they were afraid of the Jews; for the Jews had already agreed that if anyone confessed Him to be [c]Christ, he was to be put out of the synagogue. [23] For this reason his parents said, "He is of age; ask him."

[24] So a second time they called the man who had been blind, and said to him, "Give glory to God; we know that this man is a sinner." [25] He then answered, "Whether He is a sinner, I do not know; one thing I do know, that though I was blind, now I see." [26] So they said to him, "What did He do to you? How did He open your eyes?" [27] He answered them, "I told you already and you did not listen; why do you want to hear *it* again? You do not want to become His disciples too, do you?" [28] They reviled him and said, "You are His disciple, but we are disciples of Moses. [29] We know that God has spoken to

Moses, but as for this man, we do not know where He is from."
[30] The man answered and said to them, "Well, here is an amazing thing, that you do not know where He is from, and *yet* He opened my eyes. [31] We know that God does not hear sinners; but if anyone is God-fearing and does His will, He hears him. [32] [d]Since the beginning of time it has never been heard that anyone opened the eyes of a person born blind. [33] If this man were not from God, He could do nothing." [34] They answered him, "You were born entirely in sins, and are you teaching us?" So they put him out.

[35] Jesus heard that they had put him out, and finding him, He said, "Do you believe in the Son of Man?" [36] He answered, "Who is He, [e]Lord, that I may believe in Him?" [37] Jesus said to him, "You have both seen Him, and He is the one who is talking with you." [38] And he said, "Lord, I believe." And he worshiped Him. [39] And Jesus said, "For judgment I came into this world, so that those who do not see may see, and that those who see may become blind." [40] Those of the Pharisees who were with Him heard these things and said to Him, "We are not blind too, are we?" [41] Jesus said to them, "If you were blind, you would have no sin; but [f]since you say, 'We see,' your sin remains. (John 9)
https://www.biblegateway.com/passage/?search=John+9&version=NASB

Jesus first heals the man's physical blindness, and then He heals his spiritual blindness. The eyes of the man's heart are opened. But Jesus made clay and healed on the Sabbath so these Pharisees are not very happy. It is interesting to note that there are 7 Sabbath Day miracles recorded in the Gospels. These Pharisees do not understand the Sabbath Commandment. What happens within a person's heart determines if they will enter into His Sabbath Rest.

"Come to Me, all [z]who are weary and heavy-laden, and I will give you rest. [29] Take My yoke upon you and learn from Me, for I am gentle and humble in heart, and YOU WILL FIND REST FOR YOUR SOULS. [30] For My yoke is [aa]easy and My burden is light." (Matthew 11:28-30)

The man is told to go wash the clay off of his eyes in the Pool of Siloam. The Pool of Siloam, meaning Sent, originates from the Gihon Spring. Gihon means bursting forth. Without this spring next to Jerusalem the city would perish. This is a one of a kind spring; it is an intermittent, pulsing spring. Water is pumped into the heart of the city via a tunnel that was chiseled through solid rock. The Pool of Siloam was built to catch the water when the Gihon Spring pulsed. The Gihon Spring is a picture of Jesus, our Living Water from the Rock. The walls of Jerusalem represent the walls of our hearts. Remember Jesus took our sin upon Himself within the walls of our heart/Jerusalem. He then took our sin outside the walls and was crucified on Calvary. He conquered sin and death.

https://www.youtube.com/watch?v=Qxz7047yuCQ

John 10

"Truly, truly, I say to you, he who does not enter by the door into the fold of the sheep, but climbs up some other way, he is a thief and a robber. ² But he who enters by the door is a shepherd of the sheep. ³ To him the doorkeeper opens, and the sheep hear his voice, and he calls his own sheep by name and leads them out. ⁴ When he puts forth all his own, he goes ahead of them, and the sheep follow him because they know his voice. ⁵ A stranger they simply will not follow, but will flee from him, because they do not know the voice of strangers." ⁶ This figure of speech Jesus spoke to them, but they did not understand what those things were which He had been saying to them.

⁷ So Jesus said to them again, "Truly, truly, I say to you, I am the door of the sheep. ⁸ All who came before Me are thieves and robbers, but the sheep did not hear them. ⁹ I am the door; if anyone enters through Me, he will be saved, and will go in and out and find

pasture. ¹⁰ The thief comes only to steal and kill and destroy; I came that they may have life, and [a]have *it* abundantly.

¹¹ "I am the good shepherd; the good shepherd lays down His life for the sheep. ¹² He who is a hired hand, and not a shepherd, who is not the owner of the sheep, sees the wolf coming, and leaves the sheep and flees, and the wolf snatches them and scatters *them*. ¹³ *He flees* because he is a hired hand and is not concerned about the sheep. ¹⁴ I am the good shepherd, and I know My own and My own know Me, ¹⁵ even as the Father knows Me and I know the Father; and I lay down My life for the sheep. ¹⁶ I have other sheep, which are not of this fold; I must bring them also, and they will hear My voice; and they will become one flock *with* one shepherd. ¹⁷ For this reason the Father loves Me, because I lay down My life so that I may take it again. ¹⁸ No one has taken it away from Me, but I lay it down on My own initiative. I have authority to lay it down, and I have authority to take it up again. This commandment I received from My Father."

¹⁹ A division occurred again among the Jews because of these words. ²⁰ Many of them were saying, "He has a demon and is insane. Why do you listen to Him?" ²¹ Others were saying, "These are not the sayings of one demon-possessed. A demon cannot open the eyes of the blind, can he?"

²² At that time the Feast of the Dedication took place at Jerusalem; ²³ it was winter, and Jesus was walking in the temple in the portico of Solomon. ²⁴ The Jews then gathered around Him, and were saying to Him, "How long [b]will You keep us in suspense? If You are [c]the Christ, tell us plainly." ²⁵ Jesus answered them, "I told you, and you do not believe; the works that I do in My Father's name, these testify of Me. ²⁶ But you do not believe because you are not of My sheep. ²⁷ My sheep hear My voice, and I know them, and they follow Me; ²⁸ and I give eternal life to them, and they will never perish; and no one will snatch them out of My hand. ²⁹ [d]My Father, who has given *them* to Me, is greater than all; and no one is able to snatch *them* out of the Father's hand. ³⁰ I and the Father are [e]one."

³¹ The Jews picked up stones again to stone Him. ³² Jesus answered them, "I showed you many good works from the Father; for which of

them are you stoning Me?" ³³ The Jews answered Him, "For a good work we do not stone You, but for blasphemy; and because You, being a man, make Yourself out *to be* God." ³⁴ Jesus answered them, "Has it not been written in your Law, 'I SAID, YOU ARE GODS'? ³⁵ If he called them gods, to whom the word of God came (and the Scripture cannot be broken), ³⁶ do you say of Him, whom the Father sanctified and sent into the world, 'You are blaspheming,' because I said, 'I am the Son of God'? ³⁷ If I do not do the works of My Father, do not believe Me; ³⁸ but if I do them, though you do not believe Me, believe the works, so that you may [f]know and understand that the Father is in Me, and I in the Father." ³⁹ Therefore they were seeking again to seize Him, and He eluded their grasp.

⁴⁰ And He went away again beyond the Jordan to the place where John was first baptizing, and He was staying there. ⁴¹ Many came to Him and were saying, "While John performed no sign, yet everything John said about this man was true." ⁴² Many believed in Him there. (John 10)
https://www.biblegateway.com/passage/?search=John+10&version=NASB

The Sheep Gate is located at the northeast corner of the Jerusalem Gates. I believe this is the Gate that Jesus entered after being betrayed by Judas. The Garden of Gethsemane is on the northeast side of Jerusalem. In John 1 we read, "Behold, the Lamb of God who takes away the sin of the world!" We know Jesus was the Passover Lamb. Passover, Unleavened Bread and First Fruits are about conquering death. At the first Passover in Egypt, the Angel of Death passed over those that had the Blood on their doorposts and lintel (picture of Cross). The Day of Atonement was for sin. Jesus, being our unblemished Lamb of God, sinless for 33 (God in the Flesh) years, fulfilled the Day of Atonement as well. He conquered sin and death.

In Nehemiah 3:1 we see the Sheep Gate being the First Gate to be restored:

Then Eliashib the high priest arose with his brothers the priests and built the Sheep Gate; they consecrated it and hung its doors. They consecrated [a]the wall to the Tower of the Hundred *and* the Tower of Hananel.

Remember Nehemiah means repentance and comfort/consolation. Eliashib and Hananel mean:

For a meaning of the name Eliashib, NOBSE Study Bible Name List reads **God Will Restore**. Jones' Dictionary of Old Testament Proper Names proposes **Whom God Restore** or **Whom God Leads Back Again**. BDB Theological Dictionary has **God Restores**.

For a meaning of the name Hananel, NOBSE Study Bible Name List reads **God Has Been Gracious**. Jones' Dictionary of Old Testament Proper Names proposes **Graciously Given Of God**. And BDB Theological Dictionary has **El Is Gracious**.

Verse 4 says: When he puts forth all his own, he goes ahead of them, and the sheep follow him because they know his voice. (John 10:4)

So faith *comes* from hearing, and hearing by the word [k]of Christ. (Romans 10:17)

So we have an extremely strong Gospel Message associated with the Sheep Gate. The Jews start to divide over Jesus. The blind being restored etc. miracles come up (which there are many Old Testament prophesies regarding the Christ performing miracles, especially in Isaiah). They are in Jerusalem during the Feast of Dedication (Hanukkah/Chanukah) which is also known as the Holiday/Festival of the Light. In verse 24-25 they ask, "The Jews then gathered around Him, and were saying to Him, "How long [b]will You keep us in suspense? If You are [c]the Christ, tell us plainly." [25] Jesus answered them, "I told you, and you do not believe; the works that I do in My Father's name, these testify of Me.

I will paste some of Isaiah 35, and all of 53 below (written 400 years before God came in the Flesh):

[5] Then the eyes of the blind will be opened
And the ears of the deaf will be unstopped.
[6] Then the lame will leap like a deer,
And the tongue of the mute will shout for joy. (Isaiah 35:5, 6)

Who has believed our message?
And to whom has the arm of the LORD been revealed?
[2] For He grew up before Him like a tender [a]shoot,
And like a root out of parched ground;
He has no *stately* form or majesty
That we should look upon Him,
Nor appearance that we should [b]be attracted to Him.
[3] He was despised and forsaken of men,
A man of [c]sorrows and acquainted with [d]grief;
And like one from whom men hide their face
He was despised, and we did not esteem Him.

[4] Surely our [e]griefs He Himself bore,
And our [f]sorrows He carried;
Yet we ourselves esteemed Him stricken,
[g]Smitten of God, and afflicted.
[5] But He was [h]pierced through for our transgressions,
He was crushed for our iniquities;
The chastening for our [i]well-being *fell* upon Him,
And by His scourging we are healed.
[6] All of us like sheep have gone astray,
Each of us has turned to his own way;
But the LORD has caused the iniquity of us all
To [j]fall on Him.

[7] He was oppressed and He was afflicted,
Yet He did not open His mouth;

Like a lamb that is led to slaughter,
And like a sheep that is silent before its shearers,
So He did not open His mouth.
[8] By oppression and judgment He was taken away;
And as for His generation, who considered
That He was cut off out of the land of the [k]living
For the transgression of my people, to whom the stroke *was due*?
[9] His grave was assigned with wicked men,
Yet He was with a rich man in His death,
Because He had done no violence,
Nor was there any deceit in His mouth.

[10] But the LORD was pleased
To crush Him, [l]putting *Him* to grief;
If [m]He would render Himself *as* a guilt offering,
He will see *His* [n]offspring,
He will prolong *His* days,
And the [o]good pleasure of the LORD will prosper in His hand.
[11] As a result of the [p]anguish of His soul,
He will see [q]*it and* be satisfied;
By His knowledge the Righteous One,
My Servant, will justify the many,
As He will bear their iniquities.
[12] Therefore, I will allot Him a portion with the great,
And He will divide the booty with the strong;
Because He poured out [r]Himself to death,
And was numbered with the transgressors;
Yet He Himself bore the sin of many,
And interceded for the transgressors. (Isaiah 53)

John 10 ends with Jesus going "Beyond the Jordan", where John
first baptized. Remember the two Bethany's, House of Fig/Sin.
John preached repentance (turning from sin) at the "Bethany
Beyond the Jordan". The Jordan River represents our sin being
washed off, flowing south into the Dead Sea. Through Christ we are
washed of our sin. Something very interesting to also note is that
the "Upper Room" was probably in the Tower of Hananel (Grace),
which was adjoined to the Sheep Gate. Remember the "Upper

Room" was not only the place of the Last Supper (Communion Message), but also the place that the Holy Spirit was given on Pentecost.

When the day of Pentecost [a]had come, they were all together in one place. [2] And suddenly there came from heaven a noise like a violent rushing wind, and it filled the whole house where they were sitting. [3] And there appeared to them tongues as of fire [b]distributing themselves, and [c]they [d]rested on each one of them. [4] And they were all filled with the Holy Spirit and began to speak with other [e]tongues, as the Spirit was giving them [f]utterance. (Acts 2:1-4)

Peter *said* to them, "Repent, and each of you be baptized in the name of Jesus Christ for the forgiveness of your sins; and you will receive the gift of the Holy Spirit. [39] For the promise is for you and your children and for all who are far off, as many as the Lord our God will call to Himself." [40] And with many other words he solemnly testified and kept on exhorting them, saying, "[am]Be saved from this perverse generation!" [41] So then, those who had received his word were baptized; and that day there were added about three thousand [an]souls. [42] They were continually devoting themselves to the apostles' teaching and to fellowship, to the breaking of bread and [ao]to prayer. (Acts 2:38-42)

Remember Jesus told Peter after the Resurrection, just prior to Pentecost (Peter the one who denied Him three times, remember Judas denied Him once) to tend My lambs, shepherd My sheep, and to tend My sheep. Jesus at breakfast (His mercies are new every morning, Lamentations 3) gives Peter three reassurances for Peter's three denials. Forgiveness is a beautiful thing!!!

So when they had finished breakfast, Jesus *said to Simon Peter, "Simon, *son* of John, do you [f]love Me more than these?" He *said to Him, "Yes, Lord; You know that I [g]love You." He *said to him, "Tend My lambs." [16] He *said to him again a second time, "Simon, *son* of John, do you [h]love Me?" He *said to Him, "Yes, Lord; You know that I [i]love You." He *said to him, "Shepherd My sheep." [17] He *said to him the third time, "Simon, *son* of John, do you [j]love

Me?" Peter was grieved because He said to him the third time, "Do you [k]love Me?" And he said to Him, "Lord, You know all things; You know that I [l]love You." Jesus *said to him, "Tend My sheep. (John 21:15-17)

Behold, the Lamb of God Who takes away the sin of the world!

John 11

Now a certain man was sick, Lazarus of Bethany, the village of Mary and her sister Martha. [2] It was the Mary who anointed the Lord with ointment, and wiped His feet with her hair, whose brother Lazarus was sick. [3] So the sisters sent *word* to Him, saying, "Lord, behold, he whom You love is sick." [4] But when Jesus heard *this*, He said, "This sickness is not to end in death, but for the glory of God, so that the Son of God may be glorified by it." [5] Now Jesus loved Martha and her sister and Lazarus. [6] So when He heard that he was sick, He then stayed two days *longer* in the place where He was. [7] Then after this He *said to the disciples, "Let us go to Judea again." [8] The disciples *said to Him, "Rabbi, the Jews were just now seeking to stone You, and are You going there again?" [9] Jesus answered, "Are there not twelve hours in the day? If anyone walks in the day, he does not stumble, because he sees the light of this world. [10] But if anyone walks in the night, he stumbles, because the light is not in him." [11] This He said, and after that He *said to them, "Our friend Lazarus has fallen asleep; but I go, so that I may awaken him out of sleep." [12] The disciples then said to Him, "Lord, if he has fallen asleep, he will [a]recover." [13] Now Jesus had spoken of his death, but they thought that He was speaking of [b]literal sleep. [14] So Jesus then said to them plainly, "Lazarus is dead, [15] and I am glad for your sakes that I was not there, so that you may believe; but let us go to him." [16] Therefore Thomas, who is called [c]Didymus, said to *his* fellow disciples, "Let us also go, so that we may die with Him."

[17] So when Jesus came, He found that he had already been in the tomb four days. [18] Now Bethany was near Jerusalem, about [d]two miles off; [19] and many of the Jews had come to Martha and Mary, to console them concerning *their* brother. [20] Martha therefore, when she heard that Jesus was coming, went to meet Him, but Mary [e]stayed at the house. [21] Martha then said to Jesus, "Lord, if You had been here, my brother would not have died. [22] Even now I know that whatever You ask of God, God will give You." [23] Jesus *said to her, "Your brother will rise again." [24] Martha *said to Him, "I know that he will rise again in the resurrection on the last day." [25] Jesus said to her, "I am the resurrection and the life; he who believes in Me will live even if he dies, [26] and everyone who lives and believes in Me will never die. Do you believe this?" [27] She *said to Him, "Yes, Lord; I have believed that You are [f]the Christ, the Son of God, *even* [g]He who comes into the world."

[28] When she had said this, she went away and called Mary her sister, saying secretly, "The Teacher is here and is calling for you." [29] And when she heard it, she *got up quickly and was coming to Him.

[30] Now Jesus had not yet come into the village, but was still in the place where Martha met Him. [31] Then the Jews who were with her in the house, and consoling her, when they saw that Mary got up quickly and went out, they followed her, supposing that she was going to the tomb to weep there. [32] Therefore, when Mary came where Jesus was, she saw Him, and fell at His feet, saying to Him, "Lord, if You had been here, my brother would not have died." [33] When Jesus therefore saw her weeping, and the Jews who came with her *also* weeping, He was deeply moved in spirit and [h]was troubled, [34] and said, "Where have you laid him?" They *said to Him, "Lord, come and see." [35] Jesus wept. [36] So the Jews were saying, "See how He loved him!" [37] But some of them said, "Could not this man, who opened the eyes of the blind man, [i]have kept this man also from dying?"

[38] So Jesus, again being deeply moved within, *came to the tomb. Now it was a cave, and a stone was lying against it. [39] Jesus *said, "Remove the stone." Martha, the sister of the deceased, *said to Him, "Lord, by this time [j]there will be a stench, for he has been *dead* four days." [40] Jesus *said to her, "Did I not say to you that if you believe, you will see the glory of God?" [41] So they removed the stone. Then Jesus raised His eyes, and said, "Father, I thank You that You have heard Me. [42] I knew that You always hear Me; but because of the [k]people standing around I said it, so that they may believe that You sent Me." [43] When He had said these things, He cried out with a loud voice, "Lazarus, come forth." [44] The man who had died came forth, bound hand and foot with wrappings, and his face was wrapped around with a cloth. Jesus *said to them, "Unbind him, and let him go."

[45] Therefore many of the Jews who came to Mary, and saw what He had done, believed in Him. [46] But some of them went to the Pharisees and told them the things which Jesus had done.

[47] Therefore the chief priests and the Pharisees convened a council, and were saying, "What are we doing? For this man is performing many [l]signs. [48] If we let Him *go on* like this, all men will believe in Him, and the Romans will come and take away both our place and our nation." [49] But one of them, Caiaphas, who was high priest that year, said to them, "You know nothing at all, [50] nor do you take into account that it is expedient for you that one man die for the people, and that the whole nation not perish." [51] Now he did not say this [m]on his own initiative, but being high priest that year, he prophesied that Jesus was going to die for the nation, [52] and not for the nation only, but in order that He might also gather together into one the children of God who are scattered abroad. [53] So from that day on they planned together to kill Him.

[54] Therefore Jesus no longer continued to walk publicly among the Jews, but went away from there to the country near the wilderness, into a city called Ephraim; and there He stayed with the disciples.

[55] Now the Passover of the Jews was near, and many went up to Jerusalem out of the country before the Passover to purify

themselves. [56] So they were seeking for Jesus, and were saying to one another as they stood in the temple, "What do you think; that He will not come to the feast at all?" [57] Now the chief priests and the Pharisees had given orders that if anyone knew where He was, he was to report it, so that they might seize Him. (John 11) https://www.biblegateway.com/passage/?search=John+11&version=NASB

Below we have the name meanings for Martha, Mary, and Lazarus:

The name Martha means **Lady Boss, Mistress, Land Lady**.

For a meaning of the name Mary, NOBSE Study Bible Name List has "same as Miriam," and for Miriam it proposes **Obstinacy (Stubbornness)**. Jones' Dictionary of Old Testament Proper Names reads **Their Rebellion** for Miriam.

For a meaning of the name Lazarus, NOBSE Study Bible Name List reads the same as for the name Eleazar, namely **God Has Helped**. Spiros Zodhiates (The Complete Wordstudy Dictionary) translates Eleazar with My God Is Helper (which is rather the translation of the similar name Eliezer), and the name Lazarus with **Helped Of God**.

http://www.abarim-publications.com/Meaning/#.VqymrZr2aUm

With the name meaning of Martha, we can ask ourselves, who is the master of our house? Who is our land lady? Who is our lady boss? Don't be offended by the feminine connotation, remember we are the bride, or actually we are the cheating bride, the mistress. Sin is our master.

Mary is the sin, the rebellion, the leprosy, the uncleanness. Remember Miriam in the Old Testament when she rebelled, she turned leprous. We know the Red Heifer was for the unclean, the leprous.

Lazarus is the New Testament (Greek) version of the Old Testament (Hebrew) Eleazar, our Helper, the Holy Spirit.

So within John 11 we have the Gospel Message. The master of our heart is sin, but through the work of Jesus we are washed, and then filled (empowered) with the Holy Spirit. Notice in verse 5, "Now Jesus loved Martha and her sister and Lazarus", the Bible purposely leaves out the name of Mary (picture of sin, Jesus does not love sin, but He does love the sinner). Mary was aware of her sin, her master, but she repented at the feet of Christ, washing His feet with her hair, giving off a pleasing aroma with the myrrh. There is no better pleasing aroma to the Father than the aroma of repentance, turning to God, loving God.

Keep in mind also the timeline here. Jesus was in Jericho (heart walls of sin) when He got the news of Lazarus. Remember Martha, Mary, and Lazarus lived in Bethany (house of fig, house of sin). These were Jesus' very last days, after Bethany, He went to Jerusalem, to be crucified for us. So there we have another Gospel: Jericho (mastered by the walls, enslaved), Bethany (the sin), and Jerusalem; Jesus takes our sin within the walls of Jerusalem (walls of our heart) and was crucified outside the walls, removing our sin from our heart.

Remember also that there was another Bethany, "Bethany beyond the Jordon", where John baptized. This other Bethany was on the east side of the Jordan. That is yet another Gospel, John preached repentance. Our sin was washed in the Jordan, and then flowed south into the Dead Sea, the Sea of Forgetfulness, it never happened as far as God is concerned.

There is also a very strong connection of Moses, Miriam, and Aaron with Martha, Mary, and Lazarus. This helps us understand John 14:6, the way, the truth, and the life. Moses said to choose the way; Life or death is set before you. Do we choose Miriam the leprous, the unclean or the Jesus the Truth? Aaron is a picture of Christ the Great High Priest, the giver of Life. Notice in verse 20,

"Martha therefore, when she heard that Jesus was coming, went to meet Him, but Mary [e]stayed at the house." Mary (picture of sin) is still in the house, still in the heart.

In verses 25-29 we see Martha choosing Life and secretly (within her heart) she tells Mary (sin), the Teacher is calling for you: Jesus said to her, "I am the resurrection and the life; he who believes in Me will live even if he dies, 26 and everyone who lives and believes in Me will never die. Do you believe this?" 27 She *said to Him, "Yes, Lord; I have believed that You are [f]the Christ, the Son of God, *even* [g]He who comes into the world." 28 When she had said this, she went away and called Mary her sister, saying secretly, "The Teacher is here and is calling for you." 29 And when she heard it, she *got up quickly and was coming to Him.

Verses 43 and 44 say: When He had said these things, He cried out with a loud voice, "Lazarus, come forth." 44 The man who had died came forth, bound hand and foot with wrappings, and his face was wrapped around with a cloth. Jesus *said to them, "Unbind him, and let him go."

"Yes, Lord; I have believed that You are the Christ, the Son of God"

"The Teacher is here and is calling for you."

"Unbind him, and let him go."

https://www.youtube.com/watch?v=xnKhsTXoKCI

John 12

Jesus, therefore, six days before the Passover, came to Bethany where Lazarus was, whom Jesus had raised from the dead. ² So they made Him a supper there, and Martha was serving; but Lazarus was one of those reclining *at the table* with Him. ³ Mary then took a [a]pound of very costly perfume of pure nard, and anointed the feet of Jesus and wiped His feet with her hair; and the house was filled with the fragrance of the perfume. ⁴ But Judas Iscariot, one of His disciples, who was intending to [b]betray Him, *said, ⁵ "Why was this perfume not sold for [c]three hundred denarii and given to poor *people*?" ⁶ Now he said this, not because he was concerned about the poor, but because he was a thief, and as he had the money box, he used to pilfer what was put into it. ⁷ Therefore Jesus said, "Let her alone, so that she may keep [d]it for the day of My burial. ⁸ For you always have the poor with you, but you do not always have Me."

⁹ The large crowd of the Jews then learned that He was there; and they came, not for Jesus' sake only, but that they might also see Lazarus, whom He raised from the dead. ¹⁰ But the chief priests planned to put Lazarus to death also; ¹¹ because on account of him many of the Jews were going away and were believing in Jesus.

¹² On the next day the large crowd who had come to the feast, when they heard that Jesus was coming to Jerusalem, ¹³ took the branches of the palm trees and went out to meet Him, and *began* to shout, "Hosanna! BLESSED IS HE WHO COMES IN THE NAME OF THE LORD,

even the King of Israel." [14] Jesus, finding a young donkey, sat on it; as it is written, [15] "FEAR NOT, DAUGHTER OF ZION; BEHOLD, YOUR KING IS COMING, SEATED ON A DONKEY'S COLT." [16] These things His disciples did not understand at the first; but when Jesus was glorified, then they remembered that these things were written of Him, and that they had done these things to Him. [17] So the [e]people, who were with Him when He called Lazarus out of the tomb and raised him from the dead, continued to testify *about Him.* [18] For this reason also the [f]people went and met Him, because they heard that He had performed this [g]sign. [19] So the Pharisees said to one another, "You see that you are not doing any good; look, the world has gone after Him."

[20] Now there were some Greeks among those who were going up to worship at the feast; [21] these then came to Philip, who was from Bethsaida of Galilee, and *began to* ask him, saying, "Sir, we wish to see Jesus." [22] Philip *came and *told Andrew; Andrew and Philip *came and *told Jesus. [23] And Jesus *answered them, saying, "The hour has come for the Son of Man to be glorified. [24] Truly, truly, I say to you, unless a grain of wheat falls into the earth and dies, it remains alone; but if it dies, it bears much fruit. [25] He who loves his [h]life loses it, and he who hates his [i]life in this world will keep it to life eternal. [26] If anyone [j]serves Me, he must follow Me; and where I am, there My servant will be also; if anyone [k]serves Me, the Father will honor him.

[27] "Now My soul has become troubled; and what shall I say, 'Father, save Me from this hour'? But for this purpose I came to this hour. [28] Father, glorify Your name." Then a voice came out of heaven: "I have both glorified it, and will glorify it again." [29] So the crowd *of people* who stood by and heard it were saying that it had thundered; others were saying, "An angel has spoken to Him." [30] Jesus answered and said, "This voice has not come for My sake, but for your sakes. [31] Now judgment is upon this world; now the ruler of this world will be cast out. [32] And I, if I am lifted up from the earth, will draw all men to Myself." [33] But He was saying this to indicate the kind of death by which He was to die. [34] The crowd then answered Him, "We have heard out of the Law that [l]the Christ is to remain forever; and how can You say, 'The Son of Man must be lifted up'? Who is

this Son of Man?" ³⁵ So Jesus said to them, "For a little while longer the Light is among you. Walk while you have the Light, so that darkness will not overtake you; he who walks in the darkness does not know where he goes. ³⁶ While you have the Light, believe in the Light, so that you may become sons of Light."

These things Jesus spoke, and He went away and [m]hid Himself from them. ³⁷ But though He had performed so many [n]signs before them, *yet* they were not believing in Him. ³⁸ *This was* to fulfill the word of Isaiah the prophet which he spoke: "LORD, WHO HAS BELIEVED OUR REPORT? AND TO WHOM HAS THE ARM OF THE LORD BEEN REVEALED?" ³⁹ For this reason they could not believe, for Isaiah said again, ⁴⁰ "HE HAS BLINDED THEIR EYES AND HE HARDENED THEIR HEART, SO THAT THEY WOULD NOT SEE WITH THEIR EYES AND PERCEIVE WITH THEIR HEART, AND [o]BE CONVERTED AND I HEAL THEM." ⁴¹ These things Isaiah said because he saw His glory, and he spoke of Him. ⁴² Nevertheless many even of the rulers believed in Him, but because of the Pharisees they were not confessing *Him*, for fear that they would be [p]put out of the synagogue; ⁴³ for they loved the [q]approval of men rather than the [r]approval of God.

⁴⁴ And Jesus cried out and said, "He who believes in Me, does not believe in Me but in Him who sent Me. ⁴⁵ He who sees Me sees the One who sent Me. ⁴⁶ I have come *as* Light into the world, so that everyone who believes in Me will not remain in darkness. ⁴⁷ If anyone hears My sayings and does not keep them, I do not judge him; for I did not come to judge the world, but to save the world. ⁴⁸ He who rejects Me and does not receive My sayings, has one who judges him; the word I spoke is what will judge him at the last day. ⁴⁹ For I did not speak [s]on My own initiative, but the Father Himself who sent Me has given Me a commandment *as to* what to say and what to speak. ⁵⁰ I know that His commandment is eternal life; therefore the things I speak, I speak just as the Father has told Me." (John 12)
https://www.biblegateway.com/passage/?search=John+12&version=NASB

We are getting closer and closer to the Cross. Jesus recently raised Lazarus from the dead. Remember, the Resurrection was the main dividing point between the two main religious parties, the sadducees and the pharisees. The Resurrection is hugely important to our faith, Jesus conquered sin and death. Prior to Jesus resurrecting Lazarus, death had taken him away. If you look at the name meanings of Martha (mastered), Mary (sin), and Lazarus (death, prior to Jesus) you see the condition of the human race. We are mastered by sin and death. Jesus, God in the Flesh, conquered sin and death in our place.

In verse two, Martha is now serving Jesus. Lazarus (now with his name meaning "God has helped" being fulfilled) is at the table with Jesus. You then have Mary anointing the feet of Jesus with a pound of very costly perfume, pure nard. This very costly perfume is worth three hundred denarii, which is one year's wages. You might ask yourself, where did Mary get this costly perfume? Martha, Mary, and Lazarus are from Bethany, meaning house of fig/sin. They are poor. I believe this Lazarus is the same Lazarus in Luke's account of "the rich man and Lazarus". This would give more detail to Lazarus entering death, prior to Jesus raising him back to life. Prior to the Gospel Message, there were two parts of Hades, hell and Paradise/Bosom of Abraham. (In Ephesians 4:8, Jesus went to set the captives free, He told the thief on the Cross in Luke 23:43, "Today you will be with Me in Paradise", and in Matthew 27:52 many who had previously died are seen on their way to Heaven, these are those who took part in the First Resurrection.)

"Now there was a rich man, and he habitually dressed in purple and fine linen, joyously living in splendor every day. [20] And a poor man named Lazarus was laid at his gate, covered with sores, [21] and longing to be fed with the *crumbs* which were falling from the rich man's table; besides, even the dogs were coming and licking his sores. [22] Now the poor man died and was carried away by the angels to Abraham's bosom; and the rich man also died and was buried. [23] In Hades he lifted up his eyes, being in torment, and *saw Abraham far away and Lazarus in his bosom. [24] And he cried out and said, 'Father Abraham, have mercy on me, and send Lazarus so that he may dip the tip of his finger in water and cool off my tongue, for I am in agony in this flame.' [25] But Abraham said, 'Child, remember that during your life you received your good things, and likewise Lazarus bad things; but now he is being comforted here, and you are in agony. [26] And [r]besides all this, between us and you there is a great chasm fixed, so that those who wish to come over from here to you will not be able, and *that* none may cross over from there to us.' [27] And he said, 'Then I beg you, father, that you send him to my father's house— [28] for I have five brothers—in order that he may warn them, so that they will not also come to this place of torment.' [29] But Abraham *said, 'They have Moses and the Prophets; let them hear them.' [30] But he said, 'No, father Abraham, but if someone goes to them from the dead, they will repent!' [31] But he said to him, 'If they do not listen to Moses and the Prophets, they will not be persuaded even if someone rises from the dead.'" (Luke 16:19-31)

I believe Mary of Bethany to be Mary of Magdalene. Magdalene/Magdalena is about 70 miles away from Bethany. Magdalene was the main fish processing town on the Sea of Galilee. With no refrigeration, the fish were smoke or salt cured in Magdalene. I personally prefer to be "salt" cured for eternity. In Luke 7 we get some more insight to Mary. We see her called a sinner. She very well could have previously been a prostitute in the fishing town prior to following Jesus. At the beginning of Luke 8 we also see Mary as previously having seven evil spirits/demons.

Now one of the Pharisees was requesting Him to [aa]dine with him, and He entered the Pharisee's house and reclined *at the table*. [37] And there was a woman in the city who was a [ab]sinner; and when she

102

learned that He was reclining *at the table* in the Pharisee's house, she brought an alabaster vial of perfume, [38] and standing behind *Him* at His feet, weeping, she began to wet His feet with her tears, and kept wiping them with the hair of her head, and kissing His feet and anointing them with the perfume. [39] Now when the Pharisee who had invited Him saw this, he said to himself, "If this man were a prophet He would know who and what sort of person this woman is who is touching Him, that she is a [ac]sinner."

[40] And Jesus answered him, "Simon, I have something to say to you." And he [ad]replied, "Say it, Teacher." [41] "A moneylender had two debtors: one owed five hundred [ae]denarii, and the other fifty. [42] When they were unable to repay, he graciously forgave them both. So which of them will love him more?" [43] Simon answered and said, "I suppose the one whom he forgave more." And He said to him, "You have judged correctly." [44] Turning toward the woman, He said to Simon, "Do you see this woman? I entered your house; you gave Me no water for My feet, but she has wet My feet with her tears and wiped them with her hair. [45] You gave Me no kiss; but she, since the time I came in, has not ceased to kiss My feet. [46] You did not anoint My head with oil, but she anointed My feet with perfume. [47] For this reason I say to you, her sins, which are many, have been forgiven, for she loved much; but he who is forgiven little, loves little." [48] Then He said to her, "Your sins have been forgiven." [49] Those who were reclining *at the table* with Him began to say [af]to themselves, "Who is this *man* who even forgives sins?" [50] And He said to the woman, "Your faith has saved you; go in peace."

Soon afterwards, He *began* going around from one city and village to another, proclaiming and preaching the kingdom of God. The twelve were with Him, [2] and *also* some women who had been healed of evil spirits and sicknesses: Mary who was called Magdalene, from whom seven demons had gone out, [3] and Joanna the wife of Chuza, Herod's steward, and Susanna, and many others who were contributing to their support out of their private means. (Luke 7:36-8:3)

It is interesting that Mary Magdalene had seven demons cast out of her. I say this because in Proverbs 6 we have what has become known as the seven deadly sins. You could break down the seven deadly sins as: lust, gluttony, greed, sloth, wrath, envy, and pride. So this Mary, name meaning of sin, who actually had seven demons cast out, can be related to the seven deadly sins. The hidden meaning is that Christ died for all sin.

There are six things which the LORD hates,
Yes, seven which are an abomination [i]to Him:
[17] Haughty eyes, a lying tongue,
And hands that shed innocent blood,
[18] A heart that devises wicked plans,
Feet that run rapidly to evil,
[19] A false witness *who* utters lies,
And one who [i]spreads strife among brothers. (Proverbs 6:16-19)

So let's get back to the perfume question, how did Mary of Bethany/house of fig/sin i.e. Magdalene get an alabaster jar of perfume worth a year's wages? I believe Mary the mother of Jesus gave it to her to anoint her Son, Jesus the Christ, for His burial. I believe this to be one of the three gifts given to Mary the mother of Jesus at His birth, from the Magi. Remember Mary the mother of Jesus has been with her Son the whole way. Remember the first miracle at Cana? Mary the mother of Jesus was there, at the Cross, both Mary's were there, at the burial, both Mary's were there. In fact, the two Mary's were the first two who Jesus first appeared to after the Resurrection. Mary the mother of Jesus and Mary the "sinner" were both very special to our Lord and Savior. If you sinned less like Mary the mother of Jesus, she being like the debtor that owed fifty denarii, or if you sinned more, like Mary Magdalene, she being like the debtor that owed five hundred denarii, there is no partiality with God. He came for us all.

Now after the Sabbath, as it began to dawn toward the first *day* of the week, Mary Magdalene and the other Mary came to look at the grave. [2] And behold, a severe earthquake had occurred, for an angel of the Lord descended from heaven and came and rolled away the stone and sat upon it. [3] And his appearance was like lightning, and his clothing as white as snow. [4] The guards shook for fear of him and became like dead men. [5] The angel said to the women, "[a]Do not be afraid; for I know that you are looking for Jesus who has been crucified. [6] He is not here, for He has risen, just as He said. Come, see the place where He was lying. [7] Go quickly and tell His disciples that He has risen from the dead; and behold, He is going ahead of you into Galilee, there you will see Him; behold, I have told you."

[8] And they left the tomb quickly with fear and great joy and ran to report it to His disciples. [9] And behold, Jesus met them [b]and greeted them. And they came up and took hold of His feet and worshiped Him. [10] Then Jesus *said to them, "[c]Do not be afraid; go and take word to My brethren to leave for Galilee, and there they will see Me."

[11] Now while they were on their way, some of the guard came into the city and reported to the chief priests all that had happened. [12] And when they had assembled with the elders and consulted together, they gave a large sum of money to the soldiers, [13] and said, "You are to say, 'His disciples came by night and stole Him away while we were asleep.' [14] And if this should come to the governor's ears, we will win him over and [d]keep you out of trouble." [15] And they took the money and did as they had been instructed; and this story was widely spread among the Jews, *and is* to this day.

[16] But the eleven disciples proceeded to Galilee, to the mountain which Jesus had designated. [17] When they saw Him, they worshiped *Him*; but some were doubtful. [18] And Jesus came up and spoke to them, saying, "All authority has been given to Me in heaven and on earth. [19] [e]Go therefore and make disciples of all the nations, baptizing them in the name of the Father and the Son and the Holy Spirit, [20] teaching them to observe all that I commanded you; and lo, I am with you [f]always, even to the end of the age." (Mathew 28)

John 13

Now before the Feast of the Passover, Jesus knowing that His hour had come that He would depart out of this world to the Father, having loved His own who were in the world, He loved them [a]to the end. 2 During supper, the devil having already put into the heart of Judas Iscariot, *the son* of Simon, to betray Him, 3 *Jesus*, knowing that the Father had given all things into His hands, and that He had come forth from God and was going back to God, 4 *got up from supper, and *laid aside His garments; and taking a towel, He girded Himself.

5 Then He *poured water into the basin, and began to wash the disciples' feet and to wipe them with the towel with which He was girded. 6 So He *came to Simon Peter. He *said to Him, "Lord, do You wash my feet?" 7 Jesus answered and said to him, "What I do you do not realize now, but you will understand hereafter." 8 Peter *said to Him, "Never shall You wash my feet!" Jesus answered him, "If I do not wash you, you have no part with Me." 9 Simon Peter *said to Him, "Lord, *then wash* not only my feet, but also my hands and my head." 10 Jesus *said to him, "He who has bathed needs only to wash his feet, but is completely clean; and you are clean, but not all *of you*." 11 For He knew the one who was betraying Him; for this reason He said, "Not all of you are clean."

12 So when He had washed their feet, and taken His garments and reclined *at the table* again, He said to them, "Do you know what I have done to you? 13 You call Me Teacher and Lord; and [b]you are right, for *so* I am. 14 If I then, the Lord and the Teacher, washed your feet, you also ought to wash one another's feet. 15 For I gave you an example that you also should do as I did to you. 16 Truly, truly, I say to you, a slave is not greater than his master, nor *is* one who is sent greater than the one who sent him. 17 If you know these things, you are blessed if you do them. 18 I do not speak of all of you. I know the ones I have chosen; but *it is* that the Scripture may be fulfilled, 'He who eats My bread has lifted up his heel against Me.' 19 From

now on I am telling you before *it* comes to pass, so that when it does occur, you may believe that I am *He*. [20] Truly, truly, I say to you, he who receives whomever I send receives Me; and he who receives Me receives Him who sent Me."

[21] When Jesus had said this, He became troubled in spirit, and testified and said, "Truly, truly, I say to you, that one of you will [c]betray Me." [22] The disciples *began* looking at one another, at a loss *to know* of which one He was speaking. [23] There was reclining on Jesus' bosom one of His disciples, whom Jesus loved. [24] So Simon Peter *gestured to him, and *said to him, "Tell *us* who it is of whom He is speaking." [25] He, leaning back thus on Jesus' bosom, *said to Him, "Lord, who is it?" [26] Jesus then *answered, "That is the one for whom I shall dip the morsel and give it to him." So when He had dipped the morsel, He *took and *gave it to Judas, *the son* of Simon Iscariot. [27] After the morsel, Satan then entered into him. Therefore Jesus *said to him, "What you do, do quickly." [28] Now no one of those reclining *at the table* knew for what purpose He had said this to him. [29] For some were supposing, because Judas had the money box, that Jesus was saying to him, "Buy the things we have need of for the feast"; or else, that he should give something to the poor. [30] So after receiving the morsel he went out immediately; and it was night.

[31] Therefore when he had gone out, Jesus *said, "Now [d]is the Son of Man glorified, and God [e]is glorified in Him; [32] [f]if God is glorified in Him, God will also glorify Him in Himself, and will glorify Him immediately. [33] Little children, I am with you a little while longer. You will seek Me; and as I said to the Jews, now I also say to you, 'Where I am going, you cannot come.' [34] A new commandment I give to you, that you love one another, even as I have loved you, that you also love one another. [35] By this all men will know that you are My disciples, if you have love for one another."

[36] Simon Peter *said to Him, "Lord, where are You going?" Jesus answered, "Where I go, you cannot follow Me now; but you will follow later." [37] Peter *said to Him, "Lord, why can I not follow You right now? I will lay down my life for You." [38] Jesus *answered, "Will you lay down your life for Me? Truly, truly, I say to you, a

rooster will not crow until you deny Me three times. (John 13)
https://www.biblegateway.com/passage/?search=John+13&version=NASB

We are at the Last Supper. It is Thursday. We are in the Upper Room. The very next day, Good Friday, the Christ will be crucified for our sins. Jesus teaches the disciples about the Holy Spirit, the Helper, the Comforter, Who will be coming soon. Jesus teaches about the coming of the Holy Spirit in John 14-16. It is interesting that the disciples are again in this Upper Room, at the end of the last Feast, the Feast of Weeks, on Day 50, Jubilee Day, Freedom Day, which is Pentecost, when the Holy Spirit descends upon them in Acts 2.

We know people generally bash Judas, but I don't think we should. Yes, Judas betrayed our Lord, but we all betray Him. Judas did not have the privilege of having the Helper. The Holy Spirit had not yet been given. Remember Peter actually denied Jesus three times. To betray someone is one thing, but to deny that you even know them seems even deeper, three denials at that, two of them to little girls. The rooster crowed after Peter's third denial. Peter "chickened out" three times, and then the chicken crowed.

Judas only got thirty pieces of silver, not much money, but interestingly that was the price for a gored/pierced slave. We are the slaves to sin, but Christ paid the price, the thirty pieces actually redeemed us. Silver stands for redemption in the Bible. What if Judas hadn't betrayed the Christ? Judas did have extreme remorse. He actually either went into the Levite only area of the Temple, or he threw the money in there. (The Holy of Holies has the Ark the Covenant with the Mercy Seat; the High Priest could only enter once a year, on the Day of Atonement. Then there is the Holy Place, which has the Almond Lampstand, the Table of Showbread, and the Altar of Incense. Remember John the Baptist's dad was in the Holy Place when he received the news of he and his wife having a son named John. The Priests drew lots at their timeslot of service to get this duty.) Then we have the area in which the thirty pieces flew onto the floor. This area was for Levites only. There was a Bronze Altar and a Bronze Basin in this area. Remember in the Bible, bronze means judgement. John 13 has the only New Testament direct reference to a Basin/Laver. I will paste some of Exodus 12, the very first Passover below:

Then Moses called for all the elders of Israel and said to them, "[w]Go and take for yourselves [x]lambs according to your families, and slay the Passover *lamb.* [22] You shall take a bunch of hyssop and dip it in the blood which is in the basin, and [y]apply some of the blood that is in the basin to the lintel and the two doorposts; and none of you shall go outside the door of his house until morning. (Exodus 12:21, 22)

They did not have running water; the Basin was what they used for cleansing. They were "washed in the Blood". The Judgment Bowl, the Bronze Basin, contained the precious "Blood of the Lamb".   The lintel above and the doorposts on each side made a Cross. Notice below, the placement of the Bronze Basin/Laver, filled with "Living Water":

The LORD spoke to Moses, saying, [18] "You shall also make a laver of [x]bronze, with its base of bronze, for washing; and you shall put it between the tent of meeting and the altar, and you shall put water in it. (Exodus 30:17, 18)

For there is one God, *and* one mediator also between God and men, *the* man Christ Jesus, [6] who gave Himself as a ransom for all, the testimony [d]*given* at [e]the proper time. (1 Timothy 2:5, 6)

Therefore I urge you, brethren, by the mercies of God, to present your bodies a living and holy sacrifice, [a]acceptable to God, *which is* your [b]spiritual service of worship. [2] And do not be conformed to this [c]world, but be transformed by the renewing of your mind, so that you may [d]prove what the will of God is, that which is good and [e]acceptable and perfect. (Romans 12:1, 2)

Below in Exodus 21:32 we have the price for a gored (pierced) slave, thirty shekels of silver. Interesting how the Bible refers to male or female slaves, because we are all slaves to sin, all humans, male and female, but Jesus took our place:

If the ox gores a male or female slave, [ae]the owner shall give his *or her* master thirty shekels of silver, and the ox shall be stoned.

Notice the "ox" above. Below we see that the ox/bull was for the sin offering. Notice in the second reading that the kidneys and liver are removed and burned on the Altar. The rest of the bull/sin offering is taken outside the Camp (outside the heart). Remember the kidneys and liver are the organs that "cleanse the Blood".

Each day you shall offer a bull as a sin offering for atonement, and you shall [aa]purify the altar when you make atonement [ab]for it, and you shall anoint it to consecrate it. [37] For seven days you shall make atonement [ac]for the altar and consecrate it; then the altar shall be most holy, *and* whatever touches the altar shall be holy. (Exodus 29:36, 37)

Then the LORD spoke to Moses, saying, [2] "Speak to the sons of Israel, saying, 'If a person sins unintentionally in any of the [a]things which the LORD has commanded not to be done, and commits any of them, [3] if the anointed priest sins so as to bring guilt on the people, then let him offer to the LORD a [b]bull without defect as a sin offering for the sin he has [c]committed. [4] He shall bring the bull to the doorway of the tent of meeting before the LORD, and he shall lay his hand on the head of the bull and slay the bull before the LORD. [5] Then the anointed priest is to take some of the blood of the bull and bring it to the tent of meeting, [6] and the priest shall dip his finger in the blood and sprinkle some of the blood seven times before the LORD, in front of the veil of the sanctuary. [7] The priest shall also put some of the blood on the horns of the altar of fragrant incense which is before the LORD in the tent of meeting; and all the blood of the bull he shall pour out at the base of the altar of burnt offering which is at the doorway of the tent of meeting. [8] He shall remove from it all the fat of the bull of the sin offering: the fat that covers the entrails, and all the fat which is on the entrails, [9] and the two kidneys with the fat that is on them, which is on the loins, and the [d]lobe of the liver, which he shall remove with the kidneys [10] (just as it is removed from the ox of the sacrifice of peace offerings), and the priest is to offer them up in smoke on the altar of burnt offering. [11] But the hide of the bull and all its flesh with its head and its legs and its entrails and its refuse, [12] [e]that is, all *the rest of* the bull, he is to bring out to a clean place outside the camp where the [f]ashes are poured out, and burn it on wood with fire; where the [g]ashes are poured out it shall be burned. (Leviticus 4:1-12)

Also, note that Judas was so filled with remorse that he killed himself. He killed himself even before the Cross. Or you could actually truthfully even use the defense, since the devil entered Judas, "that the devil made me do it". Either way, lucifer, the prince of darkness, entered Judas. Judas didn't have a chance. He did not have God's Holy Spirit either.

Also Notice Jesus girds Himself. Remember the Armor of God. The first piece of Armor is "girded with the Loins of Truth". Many of the disciples already had faith (they believed) in their heart, the second piece of Armor is the Breastplate of Righteousness (heart). Jesus then cleans their feet, the third Armor, the Feet of the Gospel of Peace. I will paste Some of Ephesians 6 below. Remember the Armor is only activated with prayer. A huge point as well in the foot washing is that we are to humbly serve and love one another.

Finally, be strong in the Lord and in the strength of His might. [11] Put on the full armor of God, so that you will be able to stand firm against the schemes of the devil. [12] For our struggle is not against [e]flesh and blood, but against the rulers, against the powers, against the world forces of this darkness, against the spiritual *forces* of wickedness in the heavenly *places*. [13] Therefore, take up the full armor of God, so that you will be able to resist in the evil day, and having done everything, to stand firm. [14] Stand firm therefore, HAVING GIRDED YOUR LOINS WITH TRUTH, and HAVING PUT ON THE BREASTPLATE OF RIGHTEOUSNESS, [15] and having shod YOUR FEET WITH THE PREPARATION OF THE GOSPEL OF PEACE; [16] [f]in addition to all, taking up the shield of faith with which you will be able to extinguish all the flaming arrows of the evil *one*. [17] And take THE HELMET OF SALVATION, and the sword of the Spirit, which is the word of God.

[18] [g]With all prayer and petition [h]pray at all times in the Spirit, and with this in view, [i]be on the alert with all perseverance and petition for all the saints, [19] and *pray* on my behalf, that utterance may be given to me in the opening of my mouth, to make known with boldness the mystery of the gospel, [20] for which I am an ambassador in [j]chains; that [k]in *proclaiming* it I may speak boldly, as I ought to speak. (Ephesians 6:10-20)

The Scripture below shows the remorse of Judas:

Then when Judas, who had betrayed Him, saw that He had been condemned, he felt remorse and returned the thirty [a]pieces of silver to the chief priests and elders, [4] saying, "I have sinned by betraying innocent blood." But they said, "What is that to us? See *to that* yourself!" [5] And he threw the pieces of silver into the temple sanctuary and departed; and he went away and hanged himself. [6] The chief priests took the pieces of silver and said, "It is not lawful to put them into the temple treasury, since it is the price of blood." [7] And they conferred together and [b]with the money bought the Potter's Field as a burial place for strangers. [8] For this reason that field has been called the Field of Blood to this day. [9] Then that which was spoken through Jeremiah the prophet was fulfilled: "AND [c]THEY TOOK THE THIRTY PIECES OF SILVER, THE PRICE OF THE ONE WHOSE PRICE HAD BEEN SET by the sons of Israel; [10] AND [d]THEY GAVE THEM FOR THE POTTER'S FIELD, AS THE LORD DIRECTED ME." (Matthew 27:3-10)

"I have sinned by betraying innocent blood."

"It is not lawful to put them into the temple treasury, since it is the price of blood."

John 14

"Do not let your heart be troubled; [a]believe in God, believe also in Me. [2] In My Father's house are many dwelling places; if it were not so, I would have told you; for I go to prepare a place for you. [3] If I go and prepare a place for you, I will come again and receive you to Myself, that where I am, *there* you may be also. [4] And you know the way where I am going." [5] Thomas *said to Him, "Lord, we do not know where You are going, how do we know the way?" [6] Jesus *said to him, "I am the way, and the truth, and the life; no one comes to the Father but through Me.

[7] If you had known Me, you would have known My Father also; from now on you know Him, and have seen Him."

[8] Philip *said to Him, "Lord, show us the Father, and it is enough for us." [9] Jesus *said to him, "Have I been so long with you, and *yet* you have not come to know Me, Philip? He who has seen Me has seen the Father; how *can* you say, 'Show us the Father'? [10] Do you not believe that I am in the Father, and the Father is in Me? The words that I say to you I do not speak on My own initiative, but the Father abiding in Me does His works. [11] Believe Me that I am in the Father and the Father is in Me; otherwise believe because of the works themselves. [12] Truly, truly, I say to you, he who believes in Me, the works that I do, he will do also; and greater *works* than these he will do; because I go to the Father. [13] Whatever you ask in My name, that

will I do, so that the Father may be glorified in the Son. [14] If you ask Me anything in My name, I will do *it.*

[15] "If you love Me, you will keep My commandments.

[16] I will ask the Father, and He will give you another [b]Helper, that He may be with you forever; [17] *that is* the Spirit of truth, whom the world cannot receive, because it does not see Him or know Him, *but* you know Him because He abides with you and will be in you.

[18] "I will not leave you as orphans; I will come to you. [19] [c]After a little while the world will no longer see Me, but you *will* see Me; because I live, you will live also. [20] In that day you will know that I am in My Father, and you in Me, and I in you. [21] He who has My commandments and keeps them is the one who loves Me; and he who loves Me will be loved by My Father, and I will love him and will disclose Myself to him." [22] Judas (not Iscariot) *said to Him, "Lord, what then has happened that You are going to disclose Yourself to us and not to the world?" [23] Jesus answered and said to him, "If anyone loves Me, he will keep My word; and My Father will love him, and We will come to him and make Our abode with him. [24] He who does not love Me does not keep My words; and the word which you hear is not Mine, but the Father's who sent Me.

[25] "These things I have spoken to you while abiding with you. [26] But the Helper, the Holy Spirit, whom the Father will send in My name, He will teach you all things, and bring to your remembrance all that I said to you. [27] Peace I leave with you; My peace I give to you; not as the world gives do I give to you. Do not let your heart be troubled, nor let it be fearful. [28] You heard that I said to you, 'I go away, and I will come to you.' If you loved Me, you would have rejoiced because I go to the Father, for the Father is greater than I. [29] Now I have told you before it happens, so that when it happens, you may believe. [30] I will not speak much more with you, for the ruler of the world is coming, and he has nothing in Me; [31] but so that the world may know that I love the Father, [d]I do exactly as the Father commanded Me. Get up, let us go from here. (John 14)
https://www.biblegateway.com/passage/?search=John+14&version=NASB

114

We are still at the Last Supper. Judas Iscariot has left. There is more to learn from Judas. He is the only one, from the twelve disciples, from Judea (the name Jew is derived from Judah/Judea). His name Judas, in Hebrew, is Judah. So He is a Jew of Jews so to speak. The other eleven are from up north, above Samaria, from Galilee. Remember they had a Galilean accent. Judea contained Jerusalem. The sanhedrin (religious ruling council), was comprised of pharisees and sadducees and was based out of Jerusalem. Many times Jesus rebukes them for their pride. Most of them would not wash anyone's feet. They were big into social status/wealth. So Judas being in charge of the money bag was no mistake. The hidden lesson is that you can't serve God and wealth i.e. mammon (money/social status/religious status/pride).

"No one can serve two masters; for either he will hate the one and love the other, or he will be devoted to one and despise the other. You cannot serve God and [m]wealth. (Matthew 6:24)

Jesus let's His disciples know to not let their hearts be troubled. Most of them "believed" in their hearts. Thomas, the doubter, was a little slow. Their hearts heard the Word. Faith comes by hearing and hearing by the Word of Christ (Romans 10:17). Jesus confirms His Father's House, Heaven, the afterlife. Thomas asks, "... how do we know the way?" There are two ways a person can take:

There is a way *which seems* right to a man, but its end is the way of death. (Proverbs 14:12 and 16:25)

"I am the way, and the truth, and the life; no one comes to the Father but through Me. (John 14:6)

Jesus goes on to say: "If you love Me, you will keep My commandments....." What are His Commandments? Love God and love your neighbor as yourself.

But when the Pharisees heard that Jesus had silenced the Sadducees, they gathered themselves together. [35] One of them, [n]a lawyer, asked

Him *a question*, testing Him, [36] "Teacher, which is the great commandment in the Law?" [37] And He said to him, "'YOU SHALL LOVE THE LORD YOUR GOD WITH ALL YOUR HEART, AND WITH ALL YOUR SOUL, AND WITH ALL YOUR MIND.' [38] This is the great and [o]foremost commandment. [39] The second is like it, 'YOU SHALL LOVE YOUR NEIGHBOR AS YOURSELF.' [40] On these two commandments depend the whole Law and the Prophets." (Matthew 22:34-40)

In verse sixteen the Helper comes up. The Helper is the Holy Spirit. Many churches today avoid Scripture that teaches about the Holy Spirit. Three out of twenty-one chapters of John focus strongly on the Holy Spirit. So we cannot a "void" the Holy Spirit. Now many churches claim to be Spirit filled, but they are a circus. But let's not throw the baby out with the bathwater. We are "washed by the Word" (Ephesians 5:26), the Gospel Message of Christ. We are empowered by His Holy Spirit. We are washed and filled, hopefully overfilled, God's love flowing out from us onto others.

But when the kindness of God our Savior and *His* love for mankind appeared, [5] He saved us, not on the basis of deeds which we have done in righteousness, but according to His mercy, by the washing of regeneration and renewing by the Holy Spirit, [6] whom He poured out upon us richly through Jesus Christ our Savior, [7] so that being justified by His grace we would be made heirs [a]according to *the* hope of eternal life. (Titus 3:4-7)

Jesus answered, "Truly, truly, I say to you, unless one is born of water and the Spirit he cannot enter into the kingdom of God. (John 3:5)

Then I will sprinkle clean water on you, and you will be clean; I will cleanse you from all your filthiness and from all your idols. [26] Moreover, I will give you a new heart and put a new spirit within you; and I will remove the heart of stone from your flesh and give you a heart of flesh. [27] I will put My Spirit within you and cause you to walk in My statutes, and you will be careful to observe My ordinances. (Ezekiel 36:25-27)

John 15

"I am the true vine, and My Father is the vinedresser. [2] Every branch in Me that does not bear fruit, He takes away; and every *branch* that bears fruit, He [a]prunes it so that it may bear more fruit. [3] You are already [b]clean because of the word which I have spoken to you. [4] Abide in Me, and I in you. As the branch cannot bear fruit [c]of itself unless it abides in the vine, so neither *can* you unless you abide in Me. [5] I am the vine, you are the branches; he who abides in Me and I in him, he bears much fruit, for apart from Me you can do nothing. [6] If anyone does not abide in Me, he is thrown away as a branch and dries up; and they gather them, and cast them into the fire and they are burned. [7] If you abide in Me, and My words abide in you, ask whatever you wish, and it will be done for you. [8] My Father is glorified by this, that you bear much fruit, and *so* [d]prove to be My disciples. [9] Just as the Father has loved Me, I have also loved you; abide in My love. [10] If you keep My commandments, you will abide in My love; just as I have kept My Father's commandments and abide in His love. [11] These things I have spoken to you so that My joy may be in you, and *that* your joy may be made full.

[12] "This is My commandment, that you love one another, just as I have loved you. [13] Greater love has no one than this, that one lay down his life for his friends. [14] You are My friends if you do what I command you. [15] No longer do I call you slaves, for the slave does not know what his master is doing; but I have called you friends, for all things that I have heard from My Father I have made known to you. [16] You did not choose Me but I chose you, and appointed you that you would go and bear fruit, and *that* your fruit would remain, so that whatever you ask of the Father in My name He may give to you. [17] This I command you, that you love one another.

[18] "If the world hates you, [e]you know that it has hated Me before *it hated* you. [19] If you were of the world, the world would love its own; but because you are not of the world, but I chose you out of the world, because of this the world hates you. [20] Remember the word

that I said to you, 'A slave is not greater than his master.' If they persecuted Me, they will also persecute you; if they kept My word, they will keep yours also. [21] But all these things they will do to you for My name's sake, because they do not know the One who sent Me. [22] If I had not come and spoken to them, they would not have [f]sin, but now they have no excuse for their sin. [23] He who hates Me hates My Father also. [24] If I had not done among them the works which no one else did, they would not have [g]sin; but now they have both seen and hated Me and My Father as well. [25] But *they have done this* to fulfill the word that is written in their Law, 'THEY HATED ME WITHOUT A CAUSE.'

[26] "When the [h]Helper comes, whom I will send to you from the Father, *that is* the Spirit of truth who proceeds from the Father, He will testify about Me, [27] [i]and you *will* testify also, because you have been with Me from the beginning. (John 15)
https://www.biblegateway.com/passage/?search=John+15&version=NASB

The Last Supper has ended, the last verse of chapter fourteen says, "Get up, let us go from here." We get the next location in John 18:1, "When Jesus had spoken these words, He went forth with His disciples over the [a]ravine of the Kidron, where there was a garden, in which He entered [b]with His disciples." So we have Jesus and His disciples somewhere between the Upper Room and the Garden of Gethsemane for chapters 15-17. I believe the Upper Room to be the same Upper Room from Nehemiah 3:31, 32. This Upper Room was between the Sheep Gate and the Inspection Gate.

After him Malchijah, [q]one of the goldsmiths, carried out repairs as far as the house of the temple servants and of the merchants, in front of the [r]Inspection Gate and as far as the upper room of the corner. [32] Between the upper room of the corner and the Sheep Gate the goldsmiths and the merchants carried out repairs. (Nehemiah 3:31, 32)

So coming from the Upper Room, going south, you would pass right in front of the Temple Gate called Beautiful. I believe Jesus and His disciples entered the Temple Courtyard. It is interesting that this Gate called Beautiful leads into the Court of Women. Interesting as well is that the floorplan of this court is Cross shaped. Could this be a picture of us, "the beautiful bride of Christ?"

Going west from the Courtyard of Women you have the Nicanor Gate. According to the historian Josephus, in his writing, Antiquities 15.395 he describes this Gate:

395and over these, but under the crown-work, was spread out a golden vine, with its branches hanging down from a great height, the largeness and fine workmanship of which was a surprising sight to the spectators, to see what vast materials there were, and with what great skill the workmanship was done."

Only "Jewish" males could pass through the Nicanor Gate. Notice the golden vines and branches. Some clusters of golden grapes were said to be as large as a man. Below is a name definition of Nicanor:

The name Nicanor would literally mean **Man Of Victory**. For a meaning of the name Nicanor, NOBSE Study Bible Name List reads **Victorious** and Spiros Zodhiates (The Complete Wordstudy Dictionary) proposes **Conqueror**. http://www.abarim-publications.com/Meaning/Nicanor.html#.VvlzPpr2aUk

I believe Jesus and His disciples are on steps set before this Gate. Jesus is the "Man of Victory". Jesus will soon conquer sin and death, making Him the "Conqueror". The entire Bible, this Temple, all Seven Feasts, everything points to Jesus Christ. The term Jew was never supposed to be a race or religious term. A true Jew was one of the heart, a heart circumcision. The Promised Seed is Jesus Christ. True "heart Jews" were to share their faith. Which many did.

So in John 15 I believe we are on the steps in front of the Nicanor Gate. Jesus is giving a Gospel Message. The Vine is Jesus. Vines climb. Jesus is the "I AM" Vine that freely climbed the Cross in our place. The earth and all humans were and are created by Christ. We are all branches created by Christ, but not all are of Christ. When we are saved by Christ, we bear the Fruit of the Spirit. The Fruit is a result/proof of being saved. Without the Vine the branches die, because through the Vine comes the Living Water. Jesus being the Light is also necessary for our growth.

After the Seventh and Final Feast, called the Feast of Weeks, which is 7 weeks of 7, equaling 49 days, we end up back in the Upper Room on Day 50, Pentecost. Jesus sends His Helper, the Holy Spirit. We are now able to bear His Fruit.

But the fruit of the Spirit is love, joy, peace, patience, kindness, goodness, faithfulness, [23] gentleness, self-control; against such things there is no law. [24] Now those who [k]belong to Christ Jesus have crucified the flesh with its passions and desires. (Galatians 5:22-24)

In John 1, Colossians 1, and Hebrews 1 the Bible says that through Jesus the world was created. The point being is that Jesus, the Creator came for His entire creation. The audience is all humans ("...make disciples of all the nations,...Matthew 28:19)

In the beginning was the Word, and the Word was with God, and the Word was God. [2] [a]He was in the beginning with God. [3] All things came into being through Him, and apart from Him nothing came into being that has come into being. [4] In Him was life, and the life was the Light of men. [5] The Light shines in the darkness, and the darkness did not [b]comprehend it. (John 1:1-5) And the Word became flesh, and [k]dwelt among us, and we saw His glory, glory as of [l]the only begotten from the Father, full of grace and truth. (John 1:14) For the Law was given through Moses; grace and truth [p]were realized through Jesus Christ. (John 1:17)

For He rescued us from the [u]domain of darkness, and transferred us to the kingdom of [v]His beloved Son, [14] in whom we have redemption, the forgiveness of sins.[15] [w]He is the image of the invisible God, the firstborn of all creation. [16] For [x]by Him all things were created, *both* in the heavens and on earth, visible and invisible, whether thrones or dominions or rulers or authorities—all things have been created through Him and for Him. [17] He [y]is before all things, and in Him all things [z]hold together. [18] He is also head of the body, the church; and He is the beginning, the firstborn from the dead, so that He Himself will come to have first place in everything. [19] For [aa]it was the *Father's* good pleasure for all the [ab]fullness to dwell in Him, [20] and through Him to reconcile all things to Himself, having made peace through the blood of His cross; through Him, *I say*, whether things on earth or things in [ac]heaven. (Colossians 1:13-20)

John 16

"These things I have spoken to you so that you may be kept from stumbling. [2] [a]They will make you outcasts from the synagogue, but an hour is coming for everyone who kills you to think that he is offering service to God. [3] These things they will do because they have not known the Father or Me. [4] But these things I have spoken to you, so that when their hour comes, you [b]may remember that I told you of them. These things I did not say to you at the beginning, because I was with you.

[5] "But now I am going to Him who sent Me; and none of you asks Me, 'Where are You going?' [6] But because I have said these things to you, sorrow has filled your heart. [7] But I tell you the truth, it is to your advantage that I go away; for if I do not go away, the [c]Helper will not come to you; but if I go, I will send Him to you. [8] And He, when He comes, will convict the world concerning sin and righteousness and judgment; [9] concerning sin, because they do not believe in Me; [10] and concerning righteousness, because I go to the Father and you no longer see Me; [11] and concerning judgment, because the ruler of this world has been judged.

¹² "I have many more things to say to you, but you cannot bear *them* now. ¹³ But when He, the Spirit of truth, comes, He will guide you into all the truth; for He will not speak on His own initiative, but whatever He hears, He will speak; and He will disclose to you what is to come. ¹⁴ He will glorify Me, for He will take of Mine and will disclose *it* to you. ¹⁵ All things that the Father has are Mine; therefore I said that He takes of Mine and will disclose *it* to you.

¹⁶ "A little while, and you will no longer see Me; and again a little while, and you will see Me." ¹⁷ *Some* of His disciples then said to one another, "What is this thing He is telling us, 'A little while, and you will not see Me; and again a little while, and you will see Me'; and, 'because I go to the Father'?" ¹⁸ So they were saying, "What is this that He says, 'A little while'? We do not know what He is talking about." ¹⁹ Jesus knew that they wished to question Him, and He said to them, "Are you deliberating together about this, that I said, 'A little while, and you will not see Me, and again a little while, and you will see Me'? ²⁰ Truly, truly, I say to you, that you will weep and lament, but the world will rejoice; you will grieve, but your grief will be turned into joy. ²¹ Whenever a woman is in labor she has [d]pain, because her hour has come; but when she gives birth to the child, she no longer remembers the anguish because of the joy that a [e]child has been born into the world. ²² Therefore you too have grief now; but I will see you again, and your heart will rejoice, and no one *will* take your joy away from you.

²³ In that day you will not question Me about anything. Truly, truly, I say to you, if you ask the Father for anything in My name, He will give it to you. ²⁴ Until now you have asked for nothing in My name; ask and you will receive, so that your joy may be made full.

²⁵ "These things I have spoken to you in [f]figurative language; an hour is coming when I will no longer speak to you in [g]figurative language, but will tell you plainly of the Father. ²⁶ In that day you will ask in My name, and I do not say to you that I will request of the Father on your behalf; ²⁷ for the Father Himself loves you, because you have loved Me and have believed that I came forth from the Father. ²⁸ I came forth from the Father and have come into the world; I am leaving the world again and going to the Father."

²⁹ His disciples *said, "Lo, now You are speaking plainly and are not [h]using a figure of speech. ³⁰ Now we know that You know all things, and have no need for anyone to question You; by this we believe that You came from God." ³¹ Jesus answered them, "Do you now believe? ³² Behold, an hour is coming, and has *already* come, for you to be scattered, each to his own *home*, and to leave Me alone; and *yet* I am not alone, because the Father is with Me. ³³ These things I have spoken to you, so that in Me you may have peace. In the world you have tribulation, but take courage; I have overcome the world." (John 16)
https://www.biblegateway.com/passage/?search=John+16&version=NASB

Soon the disciples will be outcasts from the synagogue. Jesus read many times in the synagogue. Jesus said He Himself is the Fulfillment of Scripture in the synagogue. That was a hard pill to swallow for many. Remember in John 9, the parents of the man born blind, said ask their son, not them, for fear of getting kicked out of the synagogue. In John 12, we see another instance.

Nevertheless many even of the rulers believed in Him, but because of the Pharisees they were not confessing *Him*, for fear that they would be [p]put out of the synagogue; ⁴³ for they loved the [q]approval of men rather than the [r]approval of God. (John 12:42, 43)

You could boil this life down to two options, the approval (glory) of men or the approval (glory) of God. Do we choose the "world" system (mammon: pride i.e. glory of man, social status, love of money, "look how great I am", lust of the eyes, lust of the flesh, satan; the ruler of this sin system, haters of God etc.) or do we choose God (Love, Humility). Remember the Creator of all things, entered the world as a cell within the virgin Mary, Humility in the most extreme form. It is hard to fathom, 100% God, yet 100% Man. Some picture God with a huge ego; it isn't so, God "Embodies" Love and Humility through Jesus.

You might be asking, "Why did God even give us two options?" Love does not come by force, Love comes by choice. There were two trees that were center stage in the Garden of Eden: the tree of knowledge of good and evil and the Tree of Life. In the end of the Book of Revelation, the Last Book of the Bible, there is only One Tree that is center stage, The Tree of Life, choose Life.

Sadly, with choice come horrible outcomes. People can become the most wicked, dirtiest, evil scum of the world. In verse 33, above Jesus says to His disciples, which includes us, "In the world you have tribulation, but take courage; I have overcome the world." Our final "Sabbath Resting Place" i.e. Heaven is described in Revelation 21:

Then I saw a new heaven and a new earth; for the first heaven and the first earth passed away, and there is no longer *any* sea. [2] And I saw the holy city, new Jerusalem, coming down out of heaven from God, made ready as a bride adorned for her husband. [3] And I heard a loud voice from the throne, saying, "Behold, the tabernacle of God is among men, and He will [a]dwell among them, and they shall be His people, and God Himself will be among them[b], [4] and He will wipe away every tear from their eyes; and there will no longer be *any* death; there will no longer be *any* mourning, or crying, or pain; the first things have passed away."

[5] And He who sits on the throne said, "Behold, I am making all things new." And He *said, "Write, for these words are faithful and true." [6] Then He said to me, "[c]It is done. I am the Alpha and the Omega, the beginning and the end. I will give to the one who thirsts from the spring of the water of life without cost. [7] He who overcomes will inherit these things, and I will be his God and he will be My son. [8] But for the cowardly and [d]unbelieving and abominable and murderers and immoral persons and sorcerers and idolaters and all liars, their part *will be* in the lake that burns with fire and [e]brimstone, which is the second death." (Revelation 21:1-8)

In the beginning there is the Tree of Life, then Tent of Meeting in the wilderness, then the Temple, and finally to God Himself in the

Flesh, Jesus Christ, dwelling amongst us in a Human Tent/Temple. The synagogue/Temple pointed to Christ. The Veil to the Holy of Holies tore, from Top to bottom, God tore it. In 70 A.D. the Temple was destroyed. Now we are the Temple of the Holy Spirit because of the Work of Christ. Sin and righteousness and judgement; the "righteousness" makes the difference, are we Christ Righteous or are we self-righteous?

"For God so loved the world, that He gave His [e]only begotten Son, that whoever believes in Him shall not perish, but have eternal life. [17] For God did not send the Son into the world to judge the world, but that the world might be saved through Him. [18] He who believes in Him is not judged; he who does not believe has been judged already, because he has not believed in the name of the [f]only begotten Son of God. [19] This is the judgment, that the Light has come into the world, and men loved the darkness rather than the Light, for their deeds were evil. [20] For everyone who does evil hates the Light, and does not come to the Light for fear that his deeds will be exposed. [21] But he who practices the truth comes to the Light, so that his deeds may be manifested as having been wrought in God." (John 3:16-21)

Now judgment is upon this world; now the ruler of this world will be cast out. [32] And I, if I am lifted up from the earth, will draw all men to Myself." [33] But He was saying this to indicate the kind of death by which He was to die. (John 12:31-33)

Some people look at this life as God's laboratory experiment, a sort of "proving ground". We are like lab rats. Rats trapped in a cage. But think about it, we aren't trapped, God provided a way out. The song below talks about old Job from the Bible, it talks about being a rat in a cage, it even mentions Jesus, in the end the singer still had not yet come to believe in Christ. If we complain about being trapped, imagine God, the Creator, dwelling in a Human Tent, to the point of allowing His creation to make Him a bloody mess, to the point of death on a Cross.

https://www.youtube.com/watch?v=LSy8NWhykxw

Life isn't easy and yes there are way too many religious hypocrites, scumbag pastors etc. to count. We can't look to man, we must look to Jesus. Yes, it is true, there is no rest for the wicked, but there is "Rest in" the Prince of "Peace", Jesus Christ, in this life and the Life hereafter.

https://www.youtube.com/watch?v=wBgp5aDH23g

Jesus said if He be lifted up from the earth, that He would draw all men unto Him.

https://www.youtube.com/watch?v=WMJox5-K5jU

Remember He did not leave us as orphans; we can have His Holy Spirit dwelling within us, the Helper.

https://www.youtube.com/watch?v=2zEiiZi2DKk

John 17

Jesus spoke these things; and lifting up His eyes to heaven, He said, "Father, the hour has come; glorify Your Son, that the Son may glorify You, [2] even as You gave Him authority over all flesh, that to [a]all whom You have given Him, He may give eternal life. [3] This is eternal life, that they may know You, the only true God, and Jesus Christ whom You have sent. [4] I glorified You on the earth, [b]having accomplished the work which You have given Me to do. [5] Now, Father, glorify Me together with Yourself, with the glory which I had with You before the world was.

6 "I have manifested Your name to the men whom You gave Me out of the world; they were Yours and You gave them to Me, and they have kept Your word. 7 Now they have come to know that everything You have given Me is from You; 8 for the words which You gave Me I have given to them; and they received *them* and truly understood that I came forth from You, and they believed that You sent Me. 9 I ask on their behalf; I do not ask on behalf of the world, but of those whom You have given Me; for they are Yours; 10 and all things that are Mine are Yours, and Yours are Mine; and I have been glorified in them. 11 I am no longer in the world; and *yet* they themselves are in the world, and I come to You. Holy Father, keep them in Your name, *the name* which You have given Me, that they may be one even as We *are*. 12 While I was with them, I was keeping them in Your name which You have given Me; and I guarded them and not one of them perished but the [c]son of perdition, so that the Scripture would be fulfilled.

13 But now I come to You; and these things I speak in the world so that they may have My joy made full in themselves. 14 I have given them Your word; and the world has hated them, because they are not of the world, even as I am not of the world. 15 I do not ask You to take them out of the world, but to keep them [d]from [e]the evil *one*. 16 They are not of the world, even as I am not of the world. 17 Sanctify them in the truth; Your word is truth. 18 As You sent Me into the world, I also have sent them into the world. 19 For their sakes I sanctify Myself, that they themselves also may be sanctified in truth.

20 "I do not ask on behalf of these alone, but for those also who believe in Me through their word; 21 that they may all be one; even as You, Father, *are* in Me and I in You, that they also may be in Us, so that the world may [f]believe that You sent Me.

22 The glory which You have given Me I have given to them, that they may be one, just as We are one; 23 I in them and You in Me, that they may be perfected [g]in unity, so that the world may [h]know that You sent Me, and loved them, even as You have loved Me. 24 Father, I desire that they also, whom You have given Me, be with Me where

127

I am, so that they may see My glory which You have given Me, for You loved Me before the foundation of the world.

25 "O righteous Father, [i]although the world has not known You, yet I have known You; and these have known that You sent Me; 26 and I have made Your name known to them, and will make it known, so that the love with which You loved Me may be in them, and I in them." (John 17)
https://www.biblegateway.com/passage/?search=John+17&version=NASB

We are still in the Temple; it is still Thursday evening after the Last Supper. The Temple would usually be closed by now, but unlike most establishments, the Temple stayed open late on Holydays. Remember all "Jewish" males had to attend Three Feast times every year regardless of what country you lived in. This Feast was Passover. During these Three times (Tabernacles and Passover and Weeks) the Temple stayed open late and all priests were in Jerusalem. A priest served five weeks (His normal two, then the Three required) in the Temple every year.

This chapter is known as the High Priestly prayer. Jesus is the Ultimate and Final High Priest. We are in the Roman era of earth history, which oddly enough coincides with the bronze (judgement) age. Jesus via the Cross will either judge you or free you. The entire world (John 3:16) at this time is ruled by one government, the Romans. This was perfect timing being as they are famous for building our first road system. Roads were very useful for the spreading of the Gospel. Just prior to the Romans were the Greeks. They were famous for giving us the Olympics. Still to this day, one can win a bronze or silver or gold medal.

Looking into the Holy of Holies, we see everything in gold. Only the High Priest could enter this area, and only once a year. Remember the Ark of the Covenant, containing the sapphire Ten Commandments (dead blue heart) and the Almond Budded Rod of Aaron (Cross) and the Golden Jar of Manna (Jesus)? These are what were within the Ark in the Holy of Holies. We know Jesus won the Gold, He being our Great High Priest.

The area just prior to the Holy of Holies was known as the Holy Place. The Holy Place contained the Table of Showbread (Remember David ate this Bread) and the Almond Lampstand and the Altar of Incense. When the priests served they would draw lots to see who received Holy Place duty. John the Baptist's dad had this duty in Luke 1. Notice below in Matthew 27 that Judas (Judah in Hebrew) throws the silver into the Temple Sanctuary. I believe the silver (means redemption) went beyond the first area of the Bronze Wash Basin and Bronze Altar. Redemption went beyond Judgement.

Then when Judas, who had betrayed Him, saw that He had been condemned, he felt remorse and returned the thirty [a]pieces of silver to the chief priests and elders, ⁴ saying, "I have sinned by betraying innocent blood." But they said, "What is that to us? See *to that* yourself!" ⁵ And he threw the pieces of silver into the temple sanctuary and departed; and he went away and hanged himself. ⁶ The chief priests took the pieces of silver and said, "It is not lawful to put them into the temple treasury, since it is the price of blood." ⁷ And they conferred together and [b]with the money bought the Potter's Field as a burial place for strangers. ⁸ For this reason that field has been called the Field of Blood to this day. ⁹ Then that which was spoken through Jeremiah the prophet was fulfilled: "AND [c]THEY TOOK THE THIRTY PIECES OF SILVER, THE PRICE OF THE ONE WHOSE PRICE HAD BEEN SET by the sons of Israel; ¹⁰ AND [d]THEY GAVE THEM FOR THE POTTER'S FIELD, AS THE LORD DIRECTED ME." (Matthew 27:3-10)

The first area is the Court of Priests, which contained the Bronze Wash Basin and Bronze Altar. Biblically Gold is for a King, Silver is for Redemption, Bronze is for Judgement. The Three Magi gifts also coincide with the Three areas, Gold (Ark) and Frankincense (Altar of Incense) and Myrrh (Bronze (death/burial) Altar). Jesus achieved Gold.

Verse twelve mentions that Judas perished, which he did, he hung himself. In John 18:9 we read, "Of those whom You have given Me I lost not one." I personally believe Judas went to Paradise, the Bosom of Abraham, and that Jesus set him free after the Cross. This is nothing to argue about though.

In verse twenty-one we see "Us" mentioned. Remember in the Garden of Eden, "Let Us make man in Our image." "Us" speaks of the Trinity; the Father (Gold) and the Son (Bronze) and Holy Spirit (Silver), also coinciding with the Three Temple areas. After Jesus fulfilled the Seven Feasts, He said to wait in Jerusalem for the Holy Spirit. Our redemption came by the Holy Spirit, via the thirty pieces of silver, the price for a slave (slave to sin). We are not our own, we are now the Temple of the Holy Spirit. On Pentecost, Freedom Day, Jubilee Day, just after the Last Feast of Weeks (49 Days, "over forty days", Acts 1:3), we are given the Holy Spirit. Now we as believers in Christ will dwell forever in Heaven in the name of the Father and the Son and the Holy Spirit, "Us".

The first account I [a]composed, Theophilus, about all that Jesus began to do and teach, 2 until the day when He was taken up *to heaven*, after He had [b]by the Holy Spirit given orders to the apostles whom He had chosen. 3 To [c]these He also presented Himself alive after His suffering, by many convincing proofs, appearing to them over forty days and speaking of the things concerning the kingdom of God. 4 [d]Gathering them together, He commanded them not to leave Jerusalem, but to wait for [e]what the Father had promised, "Which," *He said*, "you heard of from Me; 5 for John baptized with water, but you will be baptized [f]with the Holy Spirit [g]not many days from now."

130

[6] So when they had come together, they were asking Him, saying, "Lord, is it at this time You are restoring the kingdom to Israel?" [7] He said to them, "It is not for you to know times or epochs which the Father has fixed by His own authority; [8] but you will receive power when the Holy Spirit has come upon you; and you shall be My witnesses both in Jerusalem, and in all Judea and Samaria, and even to the remotest part of the earth." (Acts 1:1-8)

Or do you not know that your body is a [k]temple of the Holy Spirit who is in you, whom you have from [l]God, and that you are not your own? [20] For you have been bought with a price: therefore glorify God in your body. (1 Corinthians 6:19, 20)

John 18

When Jesus had spoken these words, He went forth with His disciples over the [a]ravine of the Kidron, where there was a garden, in which He entered [b]with His disciples. [2] Now Judas also, who was [c]betraying Him, knew the place, for Jesus had often met there with His disciples. [3] Judas then, having received the *Roman* [d]cohort and officers from the chief priests and the Pharisees, *came there with lanterns and torches and weapons. [4] So Jesus, knowing all the things that were coming upon Him, went forth and *said to them, "Whom do you seek?" [5] They answered Him, "Jesus the Nazarene." He *said to them, "I am *He*." And Judas also, who was betraying Him, was standing with them. [6] So when He said to them, "I am *He*," they drew back and fell to the ground. [7] Therefore He again asked them, "Whom do you seek?" And they said, "Jesus the Nazarene." [8] Jesus answered, "I told you that I am *He*; so if you seek Me, let these go their way," [9] to fulfill the word which He spoke, "Of those whom You have given Me I lost not one." [10] Simon Peter then, having a sword, drew it and struck the high priest's slave, and cut off his right ear; and the slave's name was Malchus. [11] So Jesus said to Peter,

"Put the sword into the sheath; the cup which the Father has given Me, shall I not drink it?"

[12] So the *Roman* [e]cohort and the [f]commander and the officers of the Jews, arrested Jesus and bound Him, [13] and led Him to Annas first; for he was father-in-law of Caiaphas, who was high priest that year. [14] Now Caiaphas was the one who had advised the Jews that it was expedient for one man to die on behalf of the people.

[15] Simon Peter was following Jesus, and *so was* another disciple. Now that disciple was known to the high priest, and entered with Jesus into the court of the high priest, [16] but Peter was standing at the door outside. So the other disciple, who was known to the high priest, went out and spoke to the doorkeeper, and brought Peter in. [17] Then the slave-girl who kept the door *said to Peter, "You are not also *one* of this man's disciples, are you?" He *said, "I am not." [18] Now the slaves and the officers were standing *there*, having made a charcoal fire, for it was cold and they were warming themselves; and Peter was also with them, standing and warming himself.

[19] The high priest then questioned Jesus about His disciples, and about His teaching. [20] Jesus answered him, "I have spoken openly to the world; I always taught in [g]synagogues and in the temple, where all the Jews come together; and I spoke nothing in secret. [21] Why do you question Me? Question those who have heard what I spoke to them; they know what I said." [22] When He had said this, one of the officers standing nearby struck Jesus, saying, "Is that the way You answer the high priest?" [23] Jesus answered him, "If I have spoken wrongly, testify of the wrong; but if rightly, why do you strike Me?" [24] So Annas sent Him bound to Caiaphas the high priest.

[25] Now Simon Peter was standing and warming himself. So they said to him, "You are not also *one* of His disciples, are you?" He denied *it*, and said, "I am not." [26] One of the slaves of the high priest, being a relative of the one whose ear Peter cut off, *said, "Did I not see you in the garden with Him?" [27] Peter then denied *it* again, and immediately a rooster crowed.

²⁸ Then they *led Jesus from Caiaphas into the [h]Praetorium, and it was early; and they themselves did not enter into the [i]Praetorium so that they would not be defiled, but might eat the Passover.
²⁹ Therefore Pilate went out to them and *said, "What accusation do you bring against this Man?" ³⁰ They answered and said to him, "If this Man were not an evildoer, we would not have delivered Him to you." ³¹ So Pilate said to them, "Take Him yourselves, and judge Him according to your law." The Jews said to him, "We are not permitted to put anyone to death," ³² to fulfill the word of Jesus which He spoke, signifying by what kind of death He was about to die.

³³ Therefore Pilate entered again into the Praetorium, and summoned Jesus and said to Him, "Are You the King of the Jews?" ³⁴ Jesus answered, "Are you saying this [j]on your own initiative, or did others tell you about Me?" ³⁵ Pilate answered, "I am not a Jew, am I? Your own nation and the chief priests delivered You to me; what have You done?" ³⁶ Jesus answered, "My kingdom [k]is not of this world. If My kingdom were of this world, then My servants would be fighting so that I would not be handed over to the Jews; but as it is, My kingdom is not [l]of this realm." ³⁷ Therefore Pilate said to Him, "So You are a king?" Jesus answered, "You say *correctly* that I am a king. For this I have been born, and for this I have come into the world, to testify to the truth. Everyone who is of the truth hears My voice." ³⁸ Pilate *said to Him, "What is truth?"

And when he had said this, he went out again to the Jews and *said to them, "I find no guilt in Him. ³⁹ But you have a custom that I release someone [m]for you at the Passover; do you wish then that I release [n]for you the King of the Jews?" ⁴⁰ So they cried out again, saying, "Not this Man, but Barabbas." Now Barabbas was a robber. (John 18)
https://www.biblegateway.com/passage/?search=John+18&version=NASB

It is still Thursday, Jesus and His disciples go east from the Temple, crossing the ravine of the Kidron (means darkness/mourning). They end up in a garden. We know from the other Gospels, that this is the Garden of Gethsemane (means oil press). They really didn't need Judas to find Jesus, at least during the day, but taking Jesus during the day would have caused quite a stir. Judas knew where to find Jesus at night. Many times in Scripture Jesus, God in the Flesh, prays all night long, showing Him to be 100% Man, yet 100% God. Remember Him sleeping on the boat during a massive storm; you don't sleep through that unless you are physically exhausted.

We now see "Nazarene" used in John 18 and 19, why now? We saw "Nazareth" in John 1 twice; "Jesus of Nazareth" and "Can anything good come out of Nazareth?" Below is some info on the term Nazarene:

A Nazarene is one who comes from Nazareth. The word "Nazareth" is thought by some to refer to the word netzer (נֵ֫צֶר,) the "branch" or "sprout" of David mentioned in Isa. 11:1, 60:21 (though it might also come from the verb meaning to "guard" or "watch"). Since Nazareth was the name of the town (located in the north of Israel) where Yeshua lived, when the gospels say, "He shall be called a Nazarene," they are perhaps using wordplay. They are not by saying that Yeshua would be an "oath taker" (nazirite) but rather that He is the promised "Branch (netzer) of the LORD" (Isa. 11:1).
http://www.hebrew4christians.com/forum/viewtopic.php?f=151&t=2932

Notice how Nazarene is related to "guarding" or "watching". Remember the Budded Rod of Aaron? Remember the Almond Lampstand? "Almond" means to be watchful, to be ready. Today if you go on an Israel tour, and you go to Nazareth, you will discover that they are known for their Almond Trees.
http://www.nazarethvillage.com/new-at-the-village/listen-to-the-almond-tree/ I believe the Tree of Life in the Garden of Eden was

an Almond Tree. I believe the Tree of Life to be directly related to the Cross. Funny, almonds are physically the healthiest food for your heart. We are at the night just before the Cross.

We see Jesus saying, "I am He". Notice above that the "He" is written italicized. The Bible translators will sometimes add a word for clarification. To make us aware that they have added a word, it will be italicized. So without the He, we have more "I AM" references. When you study God's Word always pay attention to the italicized words, read without them as well, sometimes you will see major things.

We see Peter cutting the ear off of the slave to the high priest with a sword. Jesus is the True High Priest. We are slaves to sin. Faith comes by hearing (ear) and hearing by the Word of Christ (Romans 10:17). Hebrews 4:12 says the Word of God is a Sword. We "hear" through the ear to the heart. So you have a picture of Word (Sword) with the ear (faith comes by hearing) and a slave (slave to sin). In Luke we learn that Jesus healed the ear of Malchus. What does Malchus mean? Below we find the name means: "King, Counsellor, and Reigning" all being applicable to Jesus.

For a meaning of the name Malchus, NOBSE Study Bible Name List reads **King**. Spiros Zodhiates (The Complete Wordstudy Dictionary) appears to note that the noun is proposed to be pronounced as *melek*, whereas the name Malchus is spelled with an α (*alpha*), which might indicate that our name is a participle, drawn from the verb מלך (*malak*), meaning to be or become king, hence **Reigning**, or it's the Aramaic variant meaning **Counsellor**.
http://www.abarim-publications.com/Meaning/Malchus.html#.VwKbBZr2aUk

135

"Put the sword into the sheath; the cup which the Father has given Me, shall I not drink it?" The Sword is the Word, sheath, meaning close fitting covering, can be related to the heart. We see the "cup/cupbearer" many times is Scripture. Remember in Genesis, Joseph, while in "prison" in "Egypt" interprets the king's baker and the cupbearer's dreams? The baker (Bread of Life) gets hung. The cupbearer lives, the Blood of Christ is forever, Life is in the Blood. Blood is made in the bone, not one of Christ's bones was broken. Remember Joseph was betrayed for silver? Also remember the silver cup placed in Benjamin's sack? Joseph goes on to "save the world" from death/starvation. Joseph is one of the many, many Old Testament pictures of the Christ. Communion is all about the Body/Bread and Blood/Wine of Christ. Jesus is the Cupbearer to the Father.

Here is where Peter denies Christ three times. Day 50, Pentecost has not yet occurred. The Holy Spirit would not be given until Christ was back to the Father. The Christ fulfilled all three areas of the Temple, achieving Gold. He is the Real Great High Priest. Notice in verse 22, Annas is called high priest. Caiaphas is also called high priest. Annas was the high priest prior to Caiaphas. Caiaphas married the daughter of Annas. Regardless we know that neither one of them was the True High Priest. I personally think that John didn't know either one. In verse 16, John says, "So the other disciple, who was known to the high priest, went out and spoke to the doorkeeper, and brought Peter in." Remember John is a fisherman from up north in Galilee. I believe John is alluding to himself as knowing the High Priest, Jesus. Remember somehow John was the only disciple that was referred to as "the disciple that Jesus loved". Isn't that strange? If you search the Word Love in the Bible you will find that king David and John are the two that use the Word Love most often. Remember David was a man after God's own heart? David and John got it; it's all about the heart. Remember in Acts, even after the Holy Spirit was given, Peter still struggled with knowing this, eating at the table of the "Jewish" believers only, not mixing with gentile believers. "It's what's on the inside (heart) that counts."

Verse 14 shows that the high priest Caiaphas actually prophesies about Jesus: Now Caiaphas was the one who had advised the Jews that it was expedient for one man to die on behalf of the people. This was said by Caiaphas in John 11.

After Peter's third denial, we hear the rooster crow. It is now Good Friday morning. Roosters still crow every morning. God's mercies are new every morning. The two high priests are done and we are now before Pilate. Pilate's wife had a dream, in Matthew 27: While he was sitting on the judgment seat, his wife sent him *a message*, saying, "Have nothing to do with that righteous Man; for [g]last night I suffered greatly in a dream because of Him." I believe the Praetorium was at, or very near, the Inspection Gate. Jesus the Lamb of God was being inspected/judged. I believe they entered Jerusalem from the Garden of Gethsemane through the Sheep Gate. Both of these Gates are on the northeast side and are next to one another.   But Pilate says in verse 38: And when he had said this, he went out again to the Jews and *said to them, "I find no guilt in Him. Pilate inspected Jesus and found no guilt.

It is important to also note, to use extreme caution on your end time prophecy studying. Since Israel became a nation after World War II, a new end times prophecy has evolved. Jesus warns us in this chapter that His Kingdom is not of this world: Jesus answered, "My kingdom [k]is not of this world. If My kingdom were of this world, then My servants would be fighting so that I would not be handed over to the Jews; but as it is, My kingdom is not [l]of this realm." [37] Therefore Pilate said to Him, "So You are a king?" Jesus answered, "You say *correctly* that I am a king. For this I have been born, and for this I have come into the world, to testify to the truth. Everyone who is of the truth hears My voice." [38] Pilate *said to Him, "What is truth?" (John 18:36-38) We know Jesus is the Truth. In Romans 1:25 we have: For they exchanged the truth of God for [p]a lie, and worshiped and served the creature rather than the Creator, who is blessed [q]forever. Amen.

This chapter ends with a hidden picture of the Father and the Son: So they cried out again, saying, "Not this Man, but Barabbas." Now Barabbas was a robber. What does Barabbas mean? Anytime you see "Bar", it means "son". We are familiar with "Abba", meaning close Father or Dad. So we have Son of the Father. Barabbas was freed, "If the Son makes you free you will be free indeed." (John 8:36) What does the Son of the Father take back? Jesus conquers sin and death reclaiming us back from satan, the father of lies, sin, and death. Technically Jesus is not a robber/thief, because everyone/everything was His to begin with. Below are some Scriptures using the term "thief" in the context of the Second coming of Christ. The Almond Tree, meaning to be awake and watchful, is related to the Tree of Life. Jesus is coming back again, be watchful and ready!!!

But the day of the Lord will come like a thief, in which the heavens will pass away with a roar and the elements will be destroyed with intense heat, and the earth and [b]its works will be [c]burned up. (2 Peter 3:10)

Now as to the times and the epochs, brethren, you have no need of anything to be written to you. [2] For you yourselves know full well that the day of the Lord [a]will come just like a thief in the night. [3] While they are saying, "Peace and safety!" then [b]destruction [c]will come upon them suddenly like labor pains upon a woman with child, and they will not escape. [4] But you, brethren, are not in darkness, that the day would overtake you [d]like a thief; [5] for you are all sons of light and sons of day. We are not of night nor of darkness; [6] so then let us not sleep as [e]others do, but let us be alert and [f]sober. (1 Thessalonians 5:1-6)

So remember [b]what you have received and heard; and keep *it*, and repent. Therefore if you do not wake up, I will come like a thief, and you will not know at what hour I will come to you. (Revelation 3:3)

"Behold, I am coming like a thief. Blessed is the one who stays awake and keeps his clothes, so that he will not walk about naked and men will not see his shame." [16] And they gathered them together to the place which in Hebrew is called [j]Har-Magedon. (Revelation 16:15, 16)

So if the Son makes you free, you will be free indeed. (John 8:36)

John 19

Pilate then took Jesus and [a]scourged Him. [2] And the soldiers twisted together a crown of thorns and put it on His head, and put a purple robe on Him; [3] and they *began* to come up to Him and say, "Hail, King of the Jews!" and to give Him slaps *in the face*. [4] Pilate came out again and *said to them, "Behold, I am bringing Him out to you so that you may know that I find no guilt in Him." [5] Jesus then came out, wearing the crown of thorns and the purple robe. *Pilate* *said to them, "Behold, the Man!" [6] So when the chief priests and the officers saw Him, they cried out saying, "Crucify, crucify!" Pilate *said to them, "Take Him yourselves and crucify Him, for I find no guilt in Him." [7] The Jews answered him, "We have a law, and by that law He ought to die because He made Himself out *to be* the Son of God."

[8] Therefore when Pilate heard this statement, he was *even* more afraid; [9] and he entered into the [b]Praetorium again and *said to Jesus, "Where are You from?" But Jesus gave him no answer. [10] So

Pilate *said to Him, "You do not speak to me? Do You not know that I have authority to release You, and I have authority to crucify You?" [11] Jesus answered, "You would have no authority [c]over Me, unless it had been given you from above; for this reason he who delivered Me to you has *the* greater sin." [12] As a result of this Pilate [d]made efforts to release Him, but the Jews cried out saying, "If you release this Man, you are no friend of Caesar; everyone who makes himself out *to be* a king [e]opposes Caesar."

[13] Therefore when Pilate heard these words, he brought Jesus out, and sat down on the judgment seat at a place called [f]The Pavement, but in [g]Hebrew, Gabbatha. [14] Now it was the day of preparation for the Passover; it was about the [h]sixth hour. And he *said to the Jews, "Behold, your King!" [15] So they cried out, "Away with *Him*, away with *Him*, crucify Him!" Pilate *said to them, "Shall I crucify your King?" The chief priests answered, "We have no king but Caesar."

[16] So he then handed Him over to them to be crucified.

[17] They took Jesus, therefore, and He went out, [i]bearing His own cross, to the place called the Place of a Skull, which is called in [j]Hebrew, Golgotha. [18] There they crucified Him, and with Him two other men, one on either side, and Jesus in between. [19] Pilate also wrote an inscription and put it on the cross. It was written, "JESUS THE NAZARENE, THE KING OF THE JEWS." [20] Therefore many of the Jews read this inscription, for the place where Jesus was crucified was near the city; and it was written in [k]Hebrew, Latin *and* in Greek. [21] So the chief priests of the Jews were saying to Pilate, "Do not write, 'The King of the Jews'; but that He said, 'I am King of the Jews.'" [22] Pilate answered, "What I have written I have written."

[23] Then the soldiers, when they had crucified Jesus, took His outer garments and made four parts, a part to every soldier and *also* the [l]tunic; now the tunic was seamless, woven [m]in one piece. [24] So they said to one another, "Let us not tear it, but cast lots for it, *to decide* whose it shall be"; *this was* to fulfill the Scripture: "THEY DIVIDED MY OUTER GARMENTS AMONG THEM, AND FOR MY

CLOTHING THEY CAST [n]LOTS." [25] Therefore the soldiers did these things.

But standing by the cross of Jesus were His mother, and His mother's sister, Mary the *wife* of Clopas, and Mary Magdalene. [26] When Jesus then saw His mother, and the disciple whom He loved standing nearby, He *said to His mother, "Woman, behold, your son!" [27] Then He *said to the disciple, "Behold, your mother!" From that hour the disciple took her into his own *household*.

[28] After this, Jesus, knowing that all things had already been accomplished, to fulfill the Scripture, *said, "I am thirsty." [29] A jar full of sour wine was standing there; so they put a sponge full of the sour wine upon *a branch of* hyssop and brought it up to His mouth. [30] Therefore when Jesus had received the sour wine, He said, "It is finished!" And He bowed His head and gave up His spirit.

[31] Then the Jews, because it was the day of preparation, so that the bodies would not remain on the cross on the Sabbath ([o]for that Sabbath was a high day), asked Pilate that their legs might be broken, and *that* they might be taken away. [32] So the soldiers came, and broke the legs of the first man and of the other who was crucified with Him; [33] but coming to Jesus, when they saw that He was already dead, they did not break His legs. [34] But one of the soldiers pierced His side with a spear, and immediately blood and water came out. [35] And he who has seen has testified, and his testimony is true; and he knows that he is telling the truth, so that you also may believe. [36] For these things came to pass to fulfill the Scripture, "NOT A BONE OF HIM SHALL BE [p]BROKEN." [37] And again another Scripture says, "THEY SHALL LOOK ON HIM WHOM THEY PIERCED."

[38] After these things Joseph of Arimathea, being a disciple of Jesus, but a secret *one* for fear of the Jews, asked Pilate that he might take away the body of Jesus; and Pilate granted permission. So he came and took away His body. [39] Nicodemus, who had first come to Him by night, also came, bringing a [q]mixture of myrrh and aloes, about a hundred [r]pounds *weight*. [40] So they took the body of Jesus and bound it in linen wrappings with the spices, as is the burial custom of

the Jews. [41] Now in the place where He was crucified there was a garden, and in the garden a new tomb in which no one had yet been laid. [42] Therefore because of the Jewish day of preparation, since the tomb was nearby, they laid Jesus there. (John 19) https://www.biblegateway.com/passage/?search=John+19&version=NASB

The Book of Isaiah was written 400 years before Christ. Isaiah 53 perfectly describes God's Sacrifice for us. Notice "by His scourging we are healed."

Surely our [e]griefs He Himself bore,
And our [f]sorrows He carried;
Yet we ourselves esteemed Him stricken,
[g]Smitten of God, and afflicted.
[5] But He was [h]pierced through for our transgressions,
He was crushed for our iniquities;
The chastening for our [i]well-being *fell* upon Him,
And by His scourging we are healed.
[6] All of us like sheep have gone astray,
Each of us has turned to his own way;
But the Lord has caused the iniquity of us all
To [j]fall on Him. (Isaiah 53:4-6)

The Crown of Thorns can be traced back to Adam in the Garden of Eden, ""Both thorns and thistles it shall grow for you;"

Then to Adam He said, "Because you have listened to the voice of your wife, and have eaten from the tree about which I commanded you, saying, 'You shall not eat from it';

Cursed is the ground because of you;
In [f]toil you will eat of it
All the days of your life.
[18] "Both thorns and thistles it shall grow for you;
And you will eat the [g]plants of the field;
[19] By the sweat of your face
You will eat bread,

142

Till you return to the ground,
Because from it you were taken;
For you are dust,
And to dust you shall return." (Genesis 3:17-19)

Below in Luke 3 we have the genealogy of Jesus, the Son of God, all
the way back to Adam, the son of God. We can calculate the
Garden of Eden at approximately 4000 years before Christ.

When He began His ministry, Jesus Himself was about thirty years
of age, being, [h]as was supposed, the son of Joseph, [i]the son of
[j]Eli, 24 the son of Matthat, the son of Levi, the son of Melchi, the
son of Jannai, the son of Joseph, 25 the son of Mattathias, the son of
Amos, the son of Nahum, the son of [k]Hesli, the son of Naggai,
26 the son of Maath, the son of Mattathias, the son of Semein, the son
of Josech, the son of Joda, 27 the son of Joanan, the son of Rhesa, the
son of Zerubbabel, the son of [l]Shealtiel, the son of Neri, 28 the son
of Melchi, the son of Addi, the son of Cosam, the son of Elmadam,
the son of Er, 29 the son of [m]Joshua, the son of Eliezer, the son of
Jorim, the son of Matthat, the son of Levi, 30 the son of Simeon, the
son of [n]Judah, the son of Joseph, the son of Jonam, the son of
Eliakim, 31 the son of Melea, the son of Menna, the son of Mattatha,
the son of Nathan, the son of David, 32 the son of Jesse, the son of
Obed, the son of Boaz, the son of [o]Salmon, the son of [p]Nahshon,
33 the son of Amminadab, the son of Admin, the son of [q]Ram, the
son of Hezron, the son of Perez, the son of Judah, 34 the son of Jacob,
the son of Isaac, the son of Abraham, the son of Terah, the son of
Nahor, 35 the son of Serug, the son of [r]Reu, the son of Peleg, the son
of [s]Heber, the son of Shelah, 36 the son of Cainan, the son of
Arphaxad, the son of Shem, the son of Noah, the son of Lamech,
37 the son of Methuselah, the son of Enoch, the son of Jared, the son
of Mahalaleel, the son of Cainan, 38 the son of Enosh, the son of
Seth, the son of Adam, the son of God. (Luke 3:23-38)

They put a purple robe on Jesus. Purple was worn by kings. Back
then purple dye came from a special clam. Only a couple of drops
of purple dye could be harvested from each clam. These clams
were valuable because of this. The first European convert, Lydia

(means from the Almond Tree) from Thyatira (means Hill Graveyard) in Acts 16 was a seller of purple.

Pilate still says Jesus is innocent, "Pilate came out again and *said to them, "Behold, I am bringing Him out to you so that you may know that I find no guilt in Him." The people say, ""We have a law, and by that law He ought to die because He made Himself out *to be* the Son of God." The people are saying because of the Law, that Jesus should be crucified. Notice where Pilate is standing, [13] Therefore when Pilate heard these words, he brought Jesus out, and sat down on the judgment seat at a place called [f]The Pavement, but in [g]Hebrew, Gabbatha. This word Pavement is interesting; remember where the Law, the Ten Commandments were given? On Mount Sinai, the Sapphire Blue Ten Commandments were given.

Then Moses went up [e]with Aaron, Nadab and Abihu, and seventy of the elders of Israel, [10] and they saw the God of Israel; and under His feet [f]there appeared to be a pavement of sapphire, [g]as clear as the sky itself. [11] Yet He did not stretch out His hand against the nobles of the sons of Israel; and they saw God, and they ate and drank.

[12] Now the LORD said to Moses, "Come up to Me on the mountain and [h]remain there, and I will give you the stone tablets [i]with the law and the commandment which I have written for their instruction." [13] So Moses arose [j]with Joshua his [k]servant, and Moses went up to the mountain of God. (Exodus 24:9-13)

Pilate finds no fault in Him, but the people bring up Caesar, "We have no king but Caesar." At that point Pilate hands Jesus over to be crucified.

The walls of Jerusalem are a picture of the walls of our heart. Jesus, although innocent, took all of the world's sin upon Himself, within the walls of Jerusalem. He then took our sin outside the walls of Jerusalem, outside of our heart. In 2 Corinthians 5:21 we read: He made Him who knew no sin *to be* sin on our behalf, so that we might become the righteousness of God in Him.

144

It is interesting that there are three Mary's mentioned at the Cross, "But standing by the cross of Jesus were His mother, and His mother's sister, Mary the *wife* of Clopas, and Mary Magdalene." We also have John there with them. Below are the Mary and John name definitions. Notice "their rebellion", that's us.

For a meaning of the name Mary, NOBSE Study Bible Name List has "same as Miriam," and for Miriam it proposes **Obstinacy (Stubbornness)**. Jones' Dictionary of Old Testament Proper Names reads **Their Rebellion** for Miriam.

For a meaning of the name John, NOBSE Study Bible Name List reads **Yahweh Has Been Gracious**, but for Johanan NOBSE reads **Yahweh Is Gracious**. Jones' Dictionary of Old Testament Proper Names does not treat John or Johanan separately and refers to the name Jehohanan, which Jones takes to mean **The Lord Graciously Gave**.

http://www.abarim-publications.com/Meaning/#.VwanmJr2aUk

So with these name definitions you have a beautiful picture of "being saved from sin/rebellion by grace." The following is also very important: "Therefore when Jesus had received the sour wine, He said, "It is finished!" And He bowed His head and gave up His spirit. What is finished? We know from the other three Gospels that the Veil tore at this moment, from Top to bottom. God tore the Veil to the Holy of Holies; Jesus fulfilled the requirements of the Great High Priest. The Day of Atonement was fulfilled. Jesus is the Manna from Heaven on the Almond Budded Rod (Cross) perfectly fulfilling the Sapphire Blue Ten Commandments.

The legs of Jesus were not broken; the Blood is made in the bone marrow. His bones not broken are a picture of His Everlasting Blood. Notice also that when His side was pierced that Blood and Water flowed out. Remember the first area of Temple, the Water in the Bronze Basin and the Blood thrown against the Bronze Altar? Also the spear that pierced His side no doubt went into His kidney.

A normal kidney would have had blood and urine, He having Blood and Water is another picture of no impurities in Him, no sin. In the Old Testament the liver and kidneys were removed and placed on the Altar, but the body of the sin offering (Bull) was taken outside the walls of the Camp.   The liver and the kidney are the organs that clean the blood.

For if the blood of goats and bulls and the ashes of a heifer sprinkling those who have been defiled sanctify for the [n]cleansing of the flesh, [14] how much more will the blood of Christ, who through [o]the eternal Spirit offered Himself without blemish to God, cleanse [p]your conscience from dead works to serve the living God? (Hebrews 9:13, 14)

But the Lord has caused the iniquity of us all to fall on Him. Isaiah 53:6b

John 20

Now on the first *day* of the week Mary Magdalene *came early to the tomb, while it *was still dark, and *saw the stone *already* taken away from the tomb. [2] So she *ran and *came to Simon Peter and to the other disciple whom Jesus loved, and *said to them, "They have taken away the Lord out of the tomb, and we do not know where they have laid Him." [3] So Peter and the other disciple went forth, and they were going to the tomb. [4] The two were running together; and the other disciple ran ahead faster than Peter and came to the tomb first; [5] and stooping and looking in, he *saw the linen wrappings lying *there*; but he did not go in. [6] And so Simon Peter also *came, following him, and entered the tomb; and he *saw the linen wrappings lying *there*, [7] and the face-cloth which had been on His head, not lying with the linen wrappings, but rolled up in a place by itself. [8] So the other disciple who had first come to the tomb then also entered, and he saw and believed. [9] For as yet they did not understand the Scripture, that He must rise again from the dead. [10] So the disciples went away again to their own homes.

[11] But Mary was standing outside the tomb weeping; and so, as she wept, she stooped and looked into the tomb; [12] and she *saw two angels in white sitting, one at the head and one at the feet, where the body of Jesus had been lying. [13] And they *said to her, "Woman, why are you weeping?" She *said to them, "Because they have taken away my Lord, and I do not know where they have laid Him." [14] When she had said this, she turned around and *saw Jesus standing *there*, and did not know that it was Jesus. [15] Jesus *said to her, "Woman, why are you weeping? Whom are you seeking?" Supposing Him to be the gardener, she *said to Him, "Sir, if you have carried Him away, tell me where you have laid Him, and I will take Him away." [16] Jesus *said to her, "Mary!" She turned and *said to Him in [a]Hebrew, "Rabboni!" (which means, Teacher). [17] Jesus *said to her, "Stop clinging to Me, for I have not yet ascended to the Father; but go to My brethren and say to them, 'I ascend to My Father and your Father, and My God and your God.'" [18] Mary Magdalene *came, announcing to the disciples, "I have seen the Lord," and *that* He had said these things to her.

[19] So when it was evening on that day, the first *day* of the week, and when the doors were shut where the disciples were, for fear of the Jews, Jesus came and stood in their midst and *said to them, "[b]Peace *be* with you." [20] And when He had said this, He showed them both His hands and His side. The disciples then rejoiced when they saw the Lord. [21] So Jesus said to them again, "Peace *be* with you; as the Father has sent Me, I also send you." [22] And when He had said this, He breathed on them and *said to them, "Receive the Holy Spirit. [23] If you forgive the sins of any, *their sins* [c]have been

forgiven them; if you retain the *sins* of any, they have been retained."

²⁴ But Thomas, one of the twelve, called [d]Didymus, was not with them when Jesus came. ²⁵ So the other disciples were saying to him, "We have seen the Lord!" But he said to them, "Unless I see in His hands the imprint of the nails, and put my finger into the place of the nails, and put my hand into His side, I will not believe."

²⁶ [e]After eight days His disciples were again inside, and Thomas with them. Jesus *came, the doors having been [f]shut, and stood in their midst and said, "Peace *be* with you." ²⁷ Then He *said to Thomas, "Reach here with your finger, and see My hands; and reach here your hand and put it into My side; and do not be unbelieving, but believing." ²⁸ Thomas answered and said to Him, "My Lord and my God!" ²⁹ Jesus *said to him, "Because you have seen Me, have you believed? Blessed *are* they who did not see, and *yet* believed."

³⁰ Therefore many other [g]signs Jesus also performed in the presence of the disciples, which are not written in this book; ³¹ but these have been written so that you may believe that Jesus is [h]the Christ, the Son of God; and that believing you may have life in His name. (John 20)
https://www.biblegateway.com/passage/?search=John+20&version=NASB

We have previously studied the Three required Feasts that all "Jewish" males had to attend every year in Jerusalem. No matter which countries, or how far you lived, you came to Jerusalem Three times a year. The Three Feasts are Tabernacles and Unleavened Bread and Weeks. There are Seven Holy Convocations i.e. Seven Appointed Times, in Leviticus 23: Trumpets, the Day of Atonement, Tabernacles, Passover, Unleavened Bread, First Fruits, and Weeks. These Seven are known by many as the Seven Feasts, but if you speak to an orthodox Jew they might correct you, preferring Three Feasts with Seven Holy Convocations.

"Three times a year you shall celebrate a feast to Me. [15] You shall observe the Feast of Unleavened Bread; for seven days you are to eat unleavened bread, as I commanded you, at the appointed time in the month Abib, for in it you came out of Egypt. And [m]none shall appear before Me empty-handed. [16] Also *you shall observe* the Feast of the Harvest *of* the first fruits of your labors *from* what you sow in the field; also the Feast of the Ingathering at the end of the year when you gather in *the fruit of* your labors from the field. [17] Three times a year all your males shall appear before the Lord [n]GOD. (Exodus 23:14-17) (Also found in Exodus 34 and Deuteronomy 16)

New Year's Day, every year, was the First Day of the Seventh Month. This Day was called Trumpets, the Head of the Year. On our calendar this is September. The configuration of the sun, moon and stars were used to determine this Day. Then the entire Year was based off of this Day. This is precisely how the Magi came to Jerusalem to seek the New Born King. Herod, who just finished rebuilding the Temple, was not thrilled. Remember he murdered all the young male children that were under two in Bethlehem?

It is also very important to note that nine months prior to Trumpets is the Holyday of the Light, Hanukkah. Mary was overshadowed by the Holy Spirit on Hanukkah. So in a sense, evolutionists are sort of on the right trail, all Life did come from One Cell, when God emptied Himself of His Glory and entered mankind as One Cell, within the virgin Mary.

After Trumpets, we have the Day of Atonement. This was the One Day a year that the High Priest could enter the Holy of Holies, going behind the Veil. This Day coincides with the circumcision of Jesus. Jesus goes on to live 33 sinless years; He then circumcises the Veil from around the Ark of the Covenant. Which we know the Ark represents the Heart. The deeper meaning of circumcision is that of the heart.

For he is not a Jew who is one outwardly, nor is circumcision that which is outward in the flesh. [29] But he is a Jew who is one inwardly; and circumcision is that which is of the heart, by the Spirit, not by the letter; and his praise is not from men, but from God. (Romans 2:28, 29)

Shortly after the Day of Atonement, comes the required Feast of Tabernacles. This Feast is celebrated by dwelling in temporary shelters/tents made of palm branches. Tabernacles represents God in the Flesh dwelling in a Temporary Tent/Human Body amongst us. On Palm Sunday, prior to Passover, people laid palm branches on the ground and Jesus rode over them, signifying the fulfillment of this Feast.

Jesus was crucified on Good Friday. In John 19, Joseph of Arimathea and Nicodemus, took His Body down from the Cross and put Him into a Tomb before Friday evening, the start of Passover. Friday evening to Saturday evening is Passover. Then we have Saturday to Sunday and Sunday to Monday. Remember Jesus said He would be Three days and Three nights as was Jonah. It is interesting that the name Jonah means Dove. The Holy Spirit descended upon Jesus like a Dove (Also Noah and the Dove/Olive Branch: Holy Spirit connotations).

Then some of the scribes and Pharisees said to Him, "Teacher, we want to see a [ak]sign from You." [39] But He answered and said to them, "An evil and adulterous generation craves for a [al]sign; and *yet* no [am]sign will be given to it but the [an]sign of Jonah the prophet; [40] for just as JONAH WAS THREE DAYS AND THREE NIGHTS IN THE BELLY OF THE SEA MONSTER, so will the Son of Man be three days and three nights in the heart of the earth. [41] The men of Nineveh will stand up with this generation at the judgment, and will condemn it because they repented at the preaching of Jonah; and behold, something greater than Jonah is here. ⁴² *The* Queen of *the* South will rise up with this generation at the judgment and will condemn it, because she came from the ends of the earth to hear the wisdom of Solomon; and behold, something greater than Solomon is here. (Matthew 12:38-42)

We are now at Tuesday morning and Mary Magdalene is at the Tomb. Tuesday is First Fruits, also known as Resurrection Day or Easter. First Fruits starts within the Unleavened Bread Week. I will paste a link that shows a nice picture of this. I realize everyone places Easter on Sunday, but this was to suffice the original Roman holiday of the fertility god, hence the rabbits (multiply like rabbits). Just like Christmas is the supposed birth of Christ. December 25th was previously the Roman holiday of the sun god. Jesus was born in the fall (September) for the fall of man. Don't argue or divide over this. Just know that we are rightly dividing the Word of God. Know as well that Christ has already fulfilled all Seven Holy Convocations/Three Feast Times.

http://www.hebrew4christians.com/Holidays/Spring_Holidays/Unleavened_Bread/unleavened_bread.html

Now you know why all the Sevens and Threes are within the Red Heifer chapter, Numbers 19. I also believe God said "it was good" twice on Tuesday, the Third Day of creation, because there are two Resurrections, One already occurring on First Fruits, and the next at the Last Trumpet. The Third Day of creation was the Seed Day, I believe directly related to the Gospel Seed. Interesting as well, the age of Jesus was two Threes, 33. Women who give birth to a male child have 33 days of purification. The Salt Sea, which represents where our sin flows to after being washed in the Jordan River, is

33% salt. There are several 7 facts as well. One being that the earth's atmosphere is approximately 77% nitrogen (Nitrogen has an atomic number of 7, and is the element that keeps our atmosphere from instantaneous combustion, keeping our atmosphere at Rest, Jesus being our Seventh Day Sabbath Rest). Without nitrogen, the oxygen would instantly burn us all up with intense heat.

Then God said, "Let the waters below the heavens be gathered into one place, and let the dry land appear"; and it was so. [10] God called the dry land earth, and the gathering of the waters He called seas; and God saw that it was good. [11] Then God said, "Let the earth sprout [j]vegetation, [k]plants yielding seed, *and* fruit trees on the earth bearing fruit after [l]their kind [m]with seed in them"; and it was so. [12] The earth brought forth [n]vegetation, [o]plants yielding seed after [p]their kind, and trees bearing fruit [q]with seed in them, after [r]their kind; and God saw that it was good. [13] There was evening and there was morning, a third day. (Genesis 1:9-13)

But the day of the Lord will come like a thief, in which the heavens will pass away with a roar and the elements will be destroyed with intense heat, and the earth and [b]its works will be [c]burned up. (2 Peter 3:10)

So Tuesday morning, we are at First Fruits. First Fruits is also the first day of the first week of the Seven Weeks of Seven, which is the Feast of Weeks. The Feast of Weeks is 7 times 7, equaling 49 days (Remember the walls of Jericho fell after Seven times around on the Seventh Day). The Day following Weeks is Day 50, Pentecost, Freedom Day, the Day the Holy Spirit descended upon Jerusalem.

"Now on the first *day* of the week Mary Magdalene *came early to the tomb", so this phrase means the first day of the week of the Feast of Weeks which is First Fruits, which is Tuesday. Again, don't argue about this. But someone might throw in your face the

Matthew Jonah Scripture, and say, "How can Christ die on Friday and rise on Sunday morning?" That's only two nights. Remember also that "Jews" go from evening to evening for their days. So Passover was Friday night to Saturday night. That's why Joseph and Nicodemus had to hurry and get Him down from the Cross on Good Friday.

Notice in verse 26: "After eight days His disciples were again inside, and Thomas with them. Jesus *came, the doors having been [f]shut, and stood in their midst and said, "Peace *be* with you." The Feast of Unleavened Bread is Saturday to Saturday, eight days. The Tuesday within the Unleavened Bread Week starts the 49 Day countdown to Pentecost. Below we see that Jesus appeared to His disciples over forty days, remember the italicized words below, "a period of" were added. At the end of the forty-nine days, after the final Feast, the Feast of Weeks, Jesus went to the Right Hand of the Father, then sending the Holy Spirit of God, now available to all mankind, through the Gospel Message.

To [c]these He also presented Himself alive after His suffering, by many convincing proofs, appearing to them over *a period of* forty days and speaking of the things concerning the kingdom of God. 4 [d]Gathering them together, He commanded them not to leave Jerusalem, but to wait for [e]what the Father had promised, "Which," *He said,* "you heard of from Me; 5 for John baptized with water, but you will be baptized [f]with the Holy Spirit [g]not many days from now." (Acts 1:3-5)

But when the kindness of God our Savior and *His* love for mankind appeared, 5 He saved us, not on the basis of deeds which we have done in righteousness, but according to His mercy, by the washing of regeneration and renewing by the Holy Spirit, 6 whom He poured out upon us richly through Jesus Christ our Savior, 7 so that being

153

justified by His grace we would be made heirs [a]according to *the* hope of eternal life. (Titus 3:4-7)

Nicodemus *said to Him, "How can a man be born when he is old? He cannot enter a second time into his mother's womb and be born, can he?" ⁵ Jesus answered, "Truly, truly, I say to you, unless one is born of water and the Spirit he cannot enter into the kingdom of God. ⁶ That which is born of the flesh is flesh, and that which is born of the Spirit is spirit. ⁷ Do not be amazed that I said to you, 'You must be born [c]again.' ⁸ The wind blows where it wishes and you hear the sound of it, but do not know where it comes from and where it is going; so is everyone who is born of the Spirit." (John 3:4-8)

John 21

After these things Jesus [a]manifested Himself again to the disciples at the Sea of Tiberias, and He manifested *Himself* in this way. ² Simon Peter, and Thomas called [b]Didymus, and Nathanael of Cana in Galilee, and the *sons* of Zebedee, and two others of His disciples were together. ³ Simon Peter *said to them, "I am going fishing." They *said to him, "We will also come with you." They went out and got into the boat; and that night they caught nothing.

⁴ But when the day was now breaking, Jesus stood on the beach; yet the disciples did not know that it was Jesus. ⁵ So Jesus *said to them, "Children, you do not have [c]any fish, do you?" They answered Him, "No." ⁶ And He said to them, "Cast the net on the right-hand side of the boat and you will find *a catch*." So they cast, and then they were not able to haul it in because of the great number of fish. ⁷ Therefore that disciple whom Jesus loved *said to Peter, "It is the Lord." So when Simon Peter heard that it was the Lord, he put his outer garment on (for he was stripped *for work*), and threw himself into the sea. ⁸ But the other disciples came in the little boat, for they

were not far from the land, but about [d]one hundred yards away, dragging the net *full* of fish.

9 So when they got out on the land, they *saw a charcoal fire *already* laid and fish placed on it, and bread. 10 Jesus *said to them, "Bring some of the fish which you have now caught." 11 Simon Peter went up and drew the net to land, full of large fish, a hundred and fifty-three; and although there were so many, the net was not torn.

12 Jesus *said to them, "Come *and* have breakfast." None of the disciples ventured to question Him, "Who are You?" knowing that it was the Lord. 13 Jesus *came and *took the bread and *gave *it* to them, and the fish likewise. 14 This is now the third time that Jesus [c]was manifested to the disciples, after He was raised from the dead.

15 So when they had finished breakfast, Jesus *said to Simon Peter, "Simon, *son* of John, do you [f]love Me more than these?" He *said to Him, "Yes, Lord; You know that I [g]love You." He *said to him, "Tend My lambs." 16 He *said to him again a second time, "Simon, *son* of John, do you [h]love Me?" He *said to Him, "Yes, Lord; You know that I [i]love You." He *said to him, "Shepherd My sheep." 17 He *said to him the third time, "Simon, *son* of John, do you [j]love Me?" Peter was grieved because He said to him the third time, "Do you [k]love Me?" And he said to Him, "Lord, You know all things; You know that I [l]love You." Jesus *said to him, "Tend My sheep.

18 Truly, truly, I say to you, when you were younger, you used to gird yourself and walk wherever you wished; but when you grow old, you will stretch out your hands and someone else will gird you, and bring you where you do not wish to *go*." 19 Now this He said, signifying by what kind of death he would glorify God. And when He had spoken this, He *said to him, "Follow Me!"

20 Peter, turning around, *saw the disciple whom Jesus loved following *them*; the one who also had leaned back on His bosom at the supper and said, "Lord, who is the one who betrays You?" 21 So Peter seeing him *said to Jesus, "Lord, and what about this man?" 22 Jesus *said to him, "If I want him to remain until I come, what *is* *that* to you? You follow Me!" 23 Therefore this saying went out

among the brethren that that disciple would not die; yet Jesus did not say to him that he would not die, but *only*, "If I want him to remain until I come, what *is that* to you?"

[24] This is the disciple who is testifying to these things and wrote these things, and we know that his testimony is true.

[25] And there are also many other things which Jesus did, which if they *were written in detail, I suppose that even the world itself *would not contain the books that *would be written. (John 21) https://www.biblegateway.com/passage/?search=John+21&version=NASB

The Sea of Tiberias is more widely known in the Bible as the Sea of Galilee or Lake of Gennesaret. Why does John use the name Sea of Tiberias? John 6 mentions Tiberias for the city but here in John 21 we see it used for the Sea. The other Gospels do not use Tiberias. In history we learn that Tiberias was the last home to the sanhedrin, before they dissolved entirely. The sanhedrin were the 70 religious ruling council in Jerusalem (the supreme court of Jewish law). After the destruction of the Temple in Jerusalem in 70 AD, which is in Judea, they ultimately ended up going north through Samaria to Galilee, ending in Tiberias. I believe John is making the point that the law has been fulfilled through Christ, "it is finished." Most of the sanhedrin, at least publicly, thought they were in no need of a Savior. They were self-righteous, when they needed to be Christ-righteous. Here is a link with history and facts on Tiberias: http://www.chabad.org/special/israel/points_of_interest_cdo/aid/606244/jewish/Tiberias.htm

In verse two we have seven disciples mentioned. Five are named, two are not. The two unnamed could be a picture of you and I. Remember in the first chapter of John we had the names in an order that also made a sentence: "man has heard of the Friend Who loves given of God". Now in the last chapter of John we have another; we have Simon (Hearing) Peter (Stone), Thomas (Twin or Two), Nathanael (Given of God), James (from Jacob: supplanted), and John (Grace). So if you put them together in order you have: "Hear of the Stones (Stone Tablets/Ten Commandments) of Two that were Given of God, that were supplanted by Grace". To supplant means to supersede and or replace. The Law was superseded and replaced by Christ.

We are still within the 49 days of Weeks. Weeks is one of the three required Feasts. All Jewish males would be back in Jerusalem during the final week of Weeks. They were "free" to go "Home" after Pentecost, Day 50. So Peter decides to go fishing sometime after the required Unleavened Bread week, but before the last week of the Feast of Weeks. Peter and a few other disciples were already fishermen, prior to the call of Christ. Remember what Jesus said, "Follow Me, I will make you fishers of men." (Mark 1:17 and Matthew 4:19) Below in Luke 5 we see the first disciples being called.

Now it happened that while the crowd was pressing around Him and listening to the word of God, He was standing by the lake of Gennesaret; [2] and He saw two boats lying at the edge of the lake; but the fishermen had gotten out of them and were washing their nets. [3] And He got into one of the boats, which was Simon's, and asked him to put out a little way from the land. And He sat down and *began* teaching the [a]people from the boat. [4] When He had finished speaking, He said to Simon, "Put out into the deep water and let down your nets for a catch." [5] Simon answered and said, "Master, we worked hard all night and caught nothing, but [b]I will do as You say *and* let down the nets." [6] When they had done this, they enclosed a great quantity of fish, and their nets *began* to break; [7] so they signaled to their partners in the other boat for them to come and help them. And they came and filled both of the boats, so that they began to sink. [8] But when Simon Peter saw *that*, he fell down at Jesus' [c]feet, saying, "Go away from me Lord, for I am a sinful man!" [9] For amazement had seized him and all his companions because of the catch of fish which they had taken; [10] and so also *were* [d]James and John, sons of Zebedee, who were partners with Simon. And Jesus said to Simon, "Do not fear, from now on you will be catching men." [11] When they had brought their boats to land, they left everything and followed Him. (Luke 5:1-11)

Notice above that the nets tore. In John 21 the nets do not tear. Something to also note here; does your church net fish or bait fish? Do you net fish or bait fish when you present the Gospel? Don't bait people, and don't brag about your supposed fish count, because you yourself didn't catch anything. Notice in verse 11: Simon Peter went up and drew the net to land, full of large fish, a hundred and fifty-three; and although there were so many, the net was not torn. So what is the significance of 153? If you think I am a little nutty in some of these papers, try researching what others say about the 153! Seriously though, what does it mean? In context, we have to say it refers to "fishers of men", so the 153 are people who have believed in Christ up to this point in time. We know in Acts 1 that there were at least 120 believers prior to Pentecost.

At this time Peter stood up in the midst of the brethren (a gathering of about one hundred and twenty [r]persons was there together), and said, [16] "Brethren, the Scripture had to be fulfilled, which the Holy Spirit foretold by the mouth of David concerning Judas, who became a guide to those who arrested Jesus. [17] For he was counted among us and received his share in this ministry." (Acts 1:15-17)

What I actually did though, is go through Luke, Matthew, Mark, and John and count the people that were said or seemed to "believe", "have faith" in Jesus. These are the ones that were washed in the Word. After Pentecost, they would be washed and empowered. Many parts of Scripture repeat, so I only used the one instance. I

158

started with Luke, which there were about 117, about 16 in Matthew, 6 in Mark, and 9 in John. John also had two Scriptures that said "many" believed, and one that said "some Greeks". So not to overestimate, I counted only two each for the "many" and two for the "some". I ended up with 154. I did not count the 5,000 fed etc., because Jesus makes the point that they all came back just to get physically fed again, not spiritually fed. So what is awesome about this interpretation? It brings the Gospels all together; it unifies the Word of God.

So then we have Jesus at the shore, with a charcoal fire. Remember the charcoal fire that Peter was warming himself when he denied Christ the third time? Now we have Jesus reaffirming His Love for Peter. Three denials made obsolete with three affirmations. We see Jesus using the Word Agape for Love the first two times, then the third He uses phileo. Peter uses phileo love all three times. Eventually Peter does get it, just not totally yet.

God is also giving us the Gospel Message in a geography lesson as well. We learned in John 1 about how the Jordan represents the washing of our heart. The Ark of the Covenant is a picture of the heart. I will paste below two Old Testament Scriptures showing how travelers from Egypt would simply go north following the trade route parallel to the Mediterranean Sea to get to the "Jerusalem" i.e. "Promised Land" area. But in these two Old Testament Scriptures, they take a detour, crossing the Jordan, going "beyond the Jordan", then back to the Jerusalem side. Notice below the Jordan definition, this being a picture of Jesus Christ:

For a meaning of the name Jordan NOBSE Study Bible Name List reads **The Descender**. BDB Theological Dictionary and Jones' Dictionary of Old Testament Proper Names both propose **Descending**.
http://www.abarim-publications.com/Meaning/Jordan.html#.VwqEcZr2aUk

159

In the Old Testament when Joseph took his father Jacob/Israel from Egypt to be buried back home, he took a detour, going to a city called Atad (thorn), which was out of the way, being on the eastside of the Jordan (beyond the Jordan), then he went back west over the Jordan to bury his father on the Jerusalem side. Why?

There also went up with him both chariots and horsemen; and it was a very great company. [10] When they came to the [f]threshing floor of Atad, which is beyond the Jordan, they lamented there with a very great and [g]sorrowful lamentation; and he [h]observed seven days mourning for his father. [11] Now when the inhabitants of the land, the Canaanites, saw the mourning at [i]the threshing floor of Atad, they said, "This is a [j]grievous [k]mourning for the Egyptians." Therefore it was named [l]Abel-mizraim, which is beyond the Jordan.

[12] Thus his sons did for him as he had charged them; [13] for his sons carried him to the land of Canaan and buried him in the cave of the field of Machpelah before Mamre, which Abraham had bought along with the field for a [m]burial site from Ephron the Hittite. [14] After he had buried his father, Joseph returned to Egypt, he and his brothers, and all who had gone up with him to bury his father. (Genesis 50:9-14)

When the children of Israel came into the Promised Land, they also took a detour, going to the eastside of the Jordan, then back over. Remember the Ark of the Covenant (represents heart) stayed in the middle of the Jordan, while everyone went over to the eastside and then crossed back to the Jerusalem side. Remember the waters were pushed back to the city "Adam" (first sins of man).

So when the people set out from their tents to cross the Jordan with the priests carrying the ark of the covenant before the people, [15] and when those who carried the ark came into the Jordan, and the feet of the priests carrying the ark were dipped in the edge of the water (for the Jordan overflows all its banks all the days of harvest), [16] the waters which were [d]flowing down from above stood *and* rose up in one heap, a great distance away at Adam, the city that is beside

Zarethan; and those which were [c]flowing down toward the sea of the Arabah, the Salt Sea, were completely cut off. So the people crossed opposite Jericho. ¹⁷ And the priests who carried the ark of the covenant of the LORD stood firm on dry ground in the middle of the Jordan while all Israel crossed on dry ground, until all the nation had finished crossing the Jordan. (Joshua 3:14-17, continue to read Joshua 4 for further study)

In John 1, John the Baptist is initially baptizing at Bethany Beyond the Jordan, on the eastside of the Jordan. After he baptizes Jesus, John moves to the west side to the Aenon near Salim. We learned that there were two Bethany's. Bethany means "house of fig". We learned about the fig/sin relationship. Remember Martha, Mary, and Lazarus were from Bethany on the Jerusalem side.

Now they had been sent from the Pharisees. ²⁵ They asked him, and said to him, "Why then are you baptizing, if you are not the [r]Christ, nor Elijah, nor the Prophet?" ²⁶ John answered them saying, "I baptize [s]in water, *but* among you stands One whom you do not know. ²⁷ *It is* He who comes after me, the thong of whose sandal I am not worthy to untie." ²⁸ These things took place in Bethany beyond the Jordan, where John was baptizing. (John 1:24-28)

After these things Jesus and His disciples came into the land of Judea, and there He was spending time with them and baptizing. ²³ John also was baptizing in Aenon near Salim, because there was much water there; and *people* were coming and were being baptized— ²⁴ for John had not yet been thrown into prison. (John 3:22-24)

The Jordan River is between the Sea of Galilee and the Dead Sea (Salt Sea). The first disciples were called at the fishing town called Bethsaida. Bethsaida means "house of fish". Bethsaida is located north central on the Sea of Galilee, and is where the water enters the Sea of Galilee. The water source for the Sea of Galilee is Three Springs from Mount Hermon. The Three Springs could be a picture of the Trinity. They could also possibly be a picture of the Transfiguration, which occurred at Mount Hermon (Matthew 17,

161

Mark 6, and Luke 9). Mount Hermon has the highest elevation in all of Israel. The lowest elevation point in all of Israel, and actually the entire world, is the shores of the Dead Sea. Jesus makes them "fishers of men."

We learned that Mary Magdalene, who I believe was the sister to Martha and Lazarus, probably worked in Magdela. Magdela was the main fish processing town of Israel. They are historically famous for the "smoking" and "salt" preservation of fish. Remember there were no refrigerators back then. This is a picture of being preserved for eternity by "smoking" i.e. hell or by "salt" i.e. Heaven. The name Mary means "rebellion" i.e. sin. So you have a picture of sin (Mary) being tied directly to this town of two preservation choices.

Choosing to be salted, you have a picture of flowing south out of the Sea of Galilee into the Jordan. Our sin is washed and flows south into the Dead Sea. We are washed/forgiven of our sin. Another name for the Dead Sea is the Salt Sea. We are preserved for eternity in the Salt Sea.

"See, I have set before you today life and [t]prosperity, and death and [u]adversity; [16] in that I command you today to love the LORD your God, to walk in His ways and to keep His commandments and His statutes and His judgments, that you may live and multiply, and that the LORD your God may bless you in the land where you are entering to possess it. [17] But if your heart turns away and you will not obey, but are drawn away and worship other gods and serve them, [18] I declare to you today that you shall surely perish. You will not prolong *your* days in the land where you are crossing the Jordan to enter [v]and possess it. [19] I call heaven and earth to witness against you today, that I have set before you life and death, the blessing and the curse. So choose life in order that you may live, you and your [w]descendants, [20] by loving the LORD your God, by obeying His voice, and by holding fast to Him; for [x]this is your life and the length of your days, [y]that you may live in the land which the LORD swore to your fathers, to Abraham, Isaac, and Jacob, to give them." (Deuteronomy 30:15-20)

Be flavored, healed and preserved with Christ, the Promised Seed, which came through Abraham, Isaac, and Jacob. Remember the name Jerusalem is not a "jewish" word. Nobody knows the origins of the name. We just know it as the City Of Peace that will someday come down out of Heaven. This is the "Promised Land"!!! This is Amazing Grace!!!

Then I saw a new heaven and a new earth; for the first heaven and the first earth passed away, and there is no longer *any* sea. [2] And I saw the holy city, new Jerusalem, coming down out of heaven from God, made ready as a bride adorned for her husband. [3] And I heard a loud voice from the throne, saying, "Behold, the tabernacle of God is among men, and He will [a]dwell among them, and they shall be His people, and God Himself will be among them[b], [4] and He will wipe away every tear from their eyes; and there will no longer be *any* death; there will no longer be *any* mourning, or crying, or pain; the first things have passed away." (Revelation 21:1-4)

Smoked or Salted?

https://www.youtube.com/watch?v=rjXjkbODrro

163

Chapter 3: The Book of Acts

Acts 1

The first account I [a]composed, Theophilus, about all that Jesus began to do and teach, 2 until the day when He was taken up *to heaven*, after He had [b]by the Holy Spirit given orders to the apostles whom He had chosen. 3 To [c]these He also presented Himself alive after His suffering, by many convincing proofs, appearing to them over *a period of* forty days and speaking of the things concerning the kingdom of God. 4 [d]Gathering them together, He commanded them not to leave Jerusalem, but to wait for [e]what the Father had promised, "Which," *He said*, "you heard of from Me; 5 for John baptized with water, but you will be baptized [f]with the Holy Spirit [g]not many days from now."

6 So when they had come together, they were asking Him, saying, "Lord, is it at this time You are restoring the kingdom to Israel?" 7 He said to them, "It is not for you to know times or epochs which the Father has fixed by His own authority; 8 but you will receive power when the Holy Spirit has come upon you; and you shall be My witnesses both in Jerusalem, and in all Judea and Samaria, and even to the remotest part of the earth."

9 And after He had said these things, He was lifted up while they were looking on, and a cloud received Him out of their sight. 10 And as they were gazing intently into [h]the sky while He was going, behold, two men in white clothing stood beside them. 11 They also said, "Men of Galilee, why do you stand looking into [i]the sky? This Jesus, who has been taken up from you into heaven, will come in just the same way as you have watched Him go into heaven."

¹² Then they returned to Jerusalem from the [j]mount called [k]Olivet, which is near Jerusalem, a [l]Sabbath day's journey away. ¹³ When they had entered *the city*, they went up to the upper room where they were staying; that is, Peter and John and [m]James and Andrew, Philip and Thomas, Bartholomew and Matthew, [n]James *the son* of Alphaeus, and Simon the Zealot, and Judas *the* [o]*son* of [p]James. ¹⁴ These all with one mind were continually devoting themselves to prayer, along with *the* women, and Mary the mother of Jesus, and with His brothers.

¹⁵ [q]At this time Peter stood up in the midst of the brethren (a gathering of about one hundred and twenty [r]persons was there together), and said, ¹⁶ "Brethren, the Scripture had to be fulfilled, which the Holy Spirit foretold by the mouth of David concerning Judas, who became a guide to those who arrested Jesus. ¹⁷ For he was counted among us and received his share in this ministry." ¹⁸ (Now this man acquired a field with the price of his wickedness, and falling headlong, he burst open in the middle and all his intestines gushed out. ¹⁹ And it became known to all who were living in Jerusalem; so that in their own language that field was called Hakeldama, that is, Field of Blood.) ²⁰ "For it is written in the book of Psalms,

'LET HIS HOMESTEAD BE MADE DESOLATE,
AND LET NO ONE DWELL IN IT';

and,

'LET ANOTHER MAN TAKE HIS [s]OFFICE.'

²¹ Therefore it is necessary that of the men who have accompanied us all the time that the Lord Jesus went in and out [t]among us— ²² beginning [u]with the baptism of John until the day that He was taken up from us—one of these *must* become a witness with us of His resurrection." ²³ So they put forward two men, Joseph called Barsabbas (who was also called Justus), and Matthias. ²⁴ And they prayed and said, "You, Lord, who know the hearts of all men, show which one of these two You have chosen ²⁵ to [v]occupy this ministry and apostleship from which Judas turned aside to go to his own

place." ²⁶ And they ^[w]drew lots for them, and the lot fell ^[x]to Matthias; and he was ^[y]added to the eleven apostles. (Acts 1) https://www.biblegateway.com/passage/?search=Acts+1&version=NASB

The Book of Acts was inspired by the Holy Spirit through Luke. Both Luke and Acts are written to Theophilus. Theophilus means friend of God. We were once enemies due to sin resulting in death. Now these enemies, sin and death, are a footstool for Jesus. The verse below is quoted by Jesus in Matthew 22:44, Mark 12:36 and Luke 20:43. In the next chapter, Acts 2:35, we will see Peter also quoting this verse. We also see this verse in 1 Corinthians 15:25, Hebrews 1:13 and 10:13.

The LORD says to my Lord:
"Sit at My right hand
Until I make Your enemies a footstool for Your feet." (Psalm 110:1)

Now that we are no longer enemies, we are about to receive the gift of the Holy Spirit.

Peter *said* to them, "Repent, and each of you be baptized in the name of Jesus Christ for the forgiveness of your sins; and you will receive the gift of the Holy Spirit. (Acts 2:38)

Notice in Acts 1:3 that "a period of" is italicized. This means it was added to God's Word for clarification, but actually in this case, it should not have been added. This verse is speaking of Jesus appearing to His disciples during the Feast of Weeks, which was over forty days, 49 days. So without the added italicized words we have:

³ To ^[c]these He also presented Himself alive after His suffering, by many convincing proofs, appearing to them over forty days and speaking of the things concerning the kingdom of God.

There were three required Feasts every year that every Jewish male had to attend in Jerusalem. No matter where you lived in the world you had to attend these three. They were the Feasts of Tabernacles (aka Booths and Harvest), Unleavened Bread and Weeks (aka Ingathering and Shavuot). Strangers were also invited to these three Feasts. The day after the Feast of Weeks ended was Pentecost.

"Three times a year you shall celebrate a feast to Me. [15] You shall observe the Feast of Unleavened Bread; for seven days you are to eat unleavened bread, as I commanded you, at the appointed time in the month Abib, for in it you came out of Egypt. And [m]none shall appear before Me empty-handed. [16] Also *you shall observe* the Feast of the Harvest *of* the first fruits of your labors *from* what you sow in the field; also the Feast of the Ingathering at the end of the year when you gather in *the fruit of* your labors from the field. [17] Three times a year all your males shall appear before the Lord [n]GOD. (Exodus 23:14-17)

"Three times in a year all your males shall appear before the LORD your God in the place which He chooses, at the Feast of Unleavened Bread and at the Feast of Weeks and at the Feast of Booths, and they shall not appear before the LORD empty-handed. [17] Every man [i]shall give as he is able, according to the blessing of the LORD your God which He has given you. (Deuteronomy 16:16)

So you have a picture of Jerusalem being very crowded right now due to this required Feast of Weeks. People from all over the known world, from many countries are in Jerusalem. Remember Jerusalem is a picture of the heart of the world. Jesus took our sin upon Himself within the walls of Jerusalem, within the walls of our heart. He then took our sin outside the walls of Jerusalem, outside the walls of our heart and was crucified on Golgotha. Now with sin removed from our heart, we exchange our dead spirit for the Holy

Spirit. Beginning at the heart (Jerusalem), the Gospel Message (Blood of Christ) is being pumped out to the entire body (body of Christ).

[8] but you will receive power when the Holy Spirit has come upon you; and you shall be My witnesses both in Jerusalem, and in all Judea and Samaria, and even to the remotest part of the earth." (Acts 1:8)

We should also note that Jesus was crucified and resurrected in a Jubilee Year. The Deliver was to set us free in the Year of Jubilee aka the "Favorable Year of the Lord" (Isaiah 61). Just like the fiftieth year, Jubilee, was a Year of Freedom, the fiftieth day, Pentecost, was a Day of Freedom. I will paste some of Leviticus 25 below:

'You are also to count off seven sabbaths of years for yourself, seven times seven years, so that you have the time of the seven sabbaths of years, *namely*, forty-nine years. [9] You shall then sound a ram's horn abroad on the tenth day of the seventh month; on the day of atonement you shall sound a horn all through your land. [10] You shall thus consecrate the fiftieth year and proclaim [c]a release through the land to all its inhabitants. It shall be a jubilee for you, [d]and each of you shall return to his own property, [e]and each of you shall return to his family. [11] You shall have the fiftieth year as a jubilee; you shall not sow, nor reap its aftergrowth, nor gather in *from* its untrimmed vines. [12] For it is a jubilee; it shall be holy to you. You shall eat its crops out of the field. (Leviticus 25:8-12)

Jesus quotes from Isaiah 61 in Luke 4:

And Jesus returned to Galilee in the power of the Spirit, and news about Him spread through all the surrounding district. [15] And He *began* teaching in their synagogues and was praised by all.

[16] And He came to Nazareth, where He had been brought up; and as was His custom, He entered the synagogue on the Sabbath, and stood up to read. [17] And the [e]book of the prophet Isaiah was handed to Him. And He opened the [f]book and found the place where it was written,

[18] "THE SPIRIT OF THE LORD IS UPON ME,
BECAUSE HE ANOINTED ME TO PREACH THE GOSPEL TO THE POOR.
HE HAS SENT ME TO PROCLAIM RELEASE TO THE CAPTIVES,
AND RECOVERY OF SIGHT TO THE BLIND,
TO SET FREE THOSE WHO ARE OPPRESSED,
[19] TO PROCLAIM THE FAVORABLE YEAR OF THE LORD."

[20] And He closed the [g]book, gave it back to the attendant and sat down; and the eyes of all in the synagogue were fixed on Him. [21] And He began to say to them, "Today this Scripture has been fulfilled in your [h]hearing." (Luke 4:14-21)

So the disciples are in Jerusalem in the "Favorable Year of the Lord" aka a Jubilee Year, in the Upper room. Remember the Upper Room of the Corner (Jesus the Cornerstone) in the walls of Jerusalem in Nehemiah 3?

After him Malchijah, [q]one of the goldsmiths, carried out repairs as far as the house of the temple servants and of the merchants, in front of the [r]Inspection Gate and as far as the upper room of the corner. [32] Between the upper room of the corner and the Sheep Gate the goldsmiths and the merchants carried out repairs. (Nehemiah 3:31-32)

We pass inspection at the Inspection Gate because of the Lamb (Sheep Gate) of God Who takes away the sin of the world. So there are about 120 believers waiting in the Upper Room. The Seventh and Final Feast has been fulfilled by Jesus and Day 50 is right around the Corner. The disciples, being 11, need someone to replace Judas. It is interesting that Judas is the Greek version of Judah, and Jesus was from the tribe of Judah. Judas was also the only disciple from Judea. Jerusalem was in Judea. The other eleven disciples were from Galilee, which is north of Judea above Samaria. Judas hanging himself on a tree is found in Matthew 27. After he is bloated the rope breaks and as Acts 1:18 says, his intestines gush out.

Then when Judas, who had betrayed Him, saw that He had been condemned, he felt remorse and returned the thirty [a]pieces of silver to the chief priests and elders, ⁴ saying, "I have sinned by betraying innocent blood." But they said, "What is that to us? See *to that* yourself!" ⁵ And he threw the pieces of silver into the temple sanctuary and departed; and he went away and hanged himself. ⁶ The chief priests took the pieces of silver and said, "It is not lawful to put them into the temple treasury, since it is the price of blood." ⁷ And they conferred together and [b]with the money bought the Potter's Field as a burial place for strangers. ⁸ For this reason that field has been called the Field of Blood to this day. ⁹ Then that which was spoken through Jeremiah the prophet was fulfilled: "AND [c]THEY TOOK THE THIRTY PIECES OF SILVER, THE PRICE OF THE ONE WHOSE PRICE HAD BEEN SET by the sons of Israel; ¹⁰ AND [d]THEY GAVE THEM FOR THE POTTER'S FIELD, AS THE LORD DIRECTED ME." (Matthew 27:3-10)

Looking at Judas we quickly call him a betrayer, but don't we all betray Christ? Also satan himself entered Judas (Luke 22 and John 13). Judas did experience deep guilt and remorse for his sin. Remember the Law i.e. the Ten Commandments is written on the heart of every human, even if you have never read the Bible. We should mention that Peter denied Christ three times, even twice to young girls, but he did not experience the level of guilt and shame that Judas did. This guilt and shame from breaking the Law is the tutor to Christ. Judas is a picture of the tutor which leads us to

Christ. The silver (means redemption) used to buy the Field of Blood was the original Blood money.

But before faith came, we were kept in custody under the law, being shut up to the faith which was later to be revealed. ²⁴ Therefore the Law has become our tutor *to lead us* to Christ, so that we may be justified by faith. ²⁵ But now that faith has come, we are no longer under a [ai]tutor. ²⁶ For you are all sons of God through faith in Christ Jesus. ²⁷ For all of you who were baptized into Christ have clothed yourselves with Christ. ²⁸ There is neither Jew nor Greek, there is neither slave nor free man, there is [ai]neither male nor female; for you are all one in Christ Jesus. ²⁹ And if you [ak]belong to Christ, then you are Abraham's [al]descendants, heirs according to promise. (Galatians 3:23-29)

Notice the name of the replacement for Judas, being Matthias.

The name Matthias means **Gift Of The Lord**, or more specifically: **Gift Of Yah**. http://www.abarim-publications.com/Meaning/Matthias.html#.V78-WDBTGUk

The Gift is the Holy Spirit (Acts 2:38). Judas, a picture of the guilt and shame of sin, is washed away through Jesus Christ. The disciples "ran scared" prior to receiving the Holy Spirit. After the Holy Spirit came on Pentecost everything changed. They all boldly died for their faith after receiving the Holy Spirit, except for John, who tradition says there was an attempt to boil him to death, but he didn't die, so he was exiled to Patmos, where he wrote Revelation.

Peter *said* to them, "Repent, and each of you be baptized in the name of Jesus Christ for the

forgiveness of your sins; and you will receive the gift of the Holy Spirit. (Acts 2:38)

https://www.youtube.com/watch?v=GinLzE1zOa8

https://www.youtube.com/watch?v=wauFzMMenA0

Acts 2

When the day of Pentecost [a]had come, they were all together in one place. [2] And suddenly there came from heaven a noise like a violent rushing wind, and it filled the whole house where they were sitting. [3] And there appeared to them tongues as of fire [b]distributing themselves, and [c]they [d]rested on each one of them. [4] And they were all filled with the Holy Spirit and began to speak with other [e]tongues, as the Spirit was giving them [f]utterance.

[5] Now there were Jews living in Jerusalem, devout men from every nation under heaven. [6] And when this sound occurred, the crowd came together, and were bewildered because each one of them was hearing them speak in his own [g]language. [7] They were amazed and astonished, saying, "[h]Why, are not all these who are speaking Galileans? [8] And how is it that we each hear *them* in our own [i]language [j]to which we were born? [9] Parthians and Medes and Elamites, and residents of Mesopotamia, Judea and Cappadocia, Pontus and [k]Asia, [10] Phrygia and Pamphylia, Egypt and the districts of Libya around Cyrene, and [l]visitors from Rome, both Jews and [m]proselytes, [11] Cretans and Arabs—we hear them in our *own* tongues speaking of the mighty deeds of God." [12] And they all continued in amazement and great perplexity, saying to one another, "What does this mean?" [13] But others were mocking and saying, "They are full of [n]sweet wine."

14 But Peter, [o]taking his stand with the eleven, raised his voice and declared to them: "Men of Judea and all you who live in Jerusalem, let this be known to you and give heed to my words. 15 For these men are not drunk, as you suppose, for it is *only* the [p]third hour of the day; 16 but this is what was spoken of through the prophet Joel:

17 'AND IT SHALL BE IN THE LAST DAYS,' God says,
'THAT I WILL POUR FORTH OF MY SPIRIT ON ALL [q]MANKIND;
AND YOUR SONS AND YOUR DAUGHTERS SHALL PROPHESY,
AND YOUR YOUNG MEN SHALL SEE VISIONS,
AND YOUR OLD MEN SHALL DREAM DREAMS;
18 EVEN ON MY BONDSLAVES, BOTH MEN AND WOMEN,
I WILL IN THOSE DAYS POUR FORTH OF MY SPIRIT
And they shall prophesy.
19 'AND I WILL GRANT WONDERS IN THE SKY ABOVE
AND SIGNS ON THE EARTH BELOW,
BLOOD, AND FIRE, AND VAPOR OF SMOKE.
20 'THE SUN WILL BE TURNED INTO DARKNESS
AND THE MOON INTO BLOOD,
BEFORE THE GREAT AND GLORIOUS DAY OF THE LORD SHALL COME.
21 'AND IT SHALL BE THAT EVERYONE WHO CALLS ON THE NAME OF
THE LORD WILL BE SAVED.'

22 "Men of Israel, listen to these words: Jesus the Nazarene, a man [r]attested to you by God with [s]miracles and wonders and [t]signs which God performed through Him in your midst, just as you yourselves know— 23 this *Man*, delivered over by the predetermined plan and foreknowledge of God, you nailed to a cross by the hands of [u]godless men and put *Him* to death. 24 [v]But God raised Him up again, putting an end to the [w]agony of death, since it was impossible for Him to be held [x]in its power. 25 For David says of Him,

'I SAW THE LORD ALWAYS IN MY PRESENCE;
FOR HE IS AT MY RIGHT HAND, SO THAT I WILL NOT BE SHAKEN.
26 'THEREFORE MY HEART WAS GLAD AND MY TONGUE EXULTED;
MOREOVER MY FLESH ALSO WILL LIVE IN HOPE;
27 BECAUSE YOU WILL NOT ABANDON MY SOUL TO HADES,
NOR [y]ALLOW YOUR [z]HOLY ONE TO [aa]UNDERGO DECAY.

173

²⁸ 'YOU HAVE MADE KNOWN TO ME THE WAYS OF LIFE;
YOU WILL MAKE ME FULL OF GLADNESS WITH YOUR PRESENCE.'

²⁹ "[ab]Brethren, I may confidently say to you regarding the patriarch David that he both died and was buried, and his tomb is [ac]with us to this day. ³⁰ And so, because he was a prophet and knew that GOD HAD SWORN TO HIM WITH AN OATH TO SEAT *one* [ad]OF HIS DESCENDANTS ON HIS THRONE, ³¹ he looked ahead and spoke of the resurrection of [ae]the Christ, that HE WAS NEITHER ABANDONED TO HADES, NOR DID His flesh [af]SUFFER DECAY. ³² This Jesus God raised up again, to which we are all witnesses. ³³ Therefore having been exalted [ag]to the right hand of God, and having received from the Father the promise of the Holy Spirit, He has poured forth this which you both see and hear. ³⁴ For it was not David who ascended into [ah]heaven, but he himself says:

'THE LORD SAID TO MY LORD,
"SIT AT MY RIGHT HAND,
³⁵ UNTIL I MAKE YOUR ENEMIES A FOOTSTOOL FOR YOUR FEET."'

³⁶ Therefore let all the house of Israel know for certain that God has made Him both Lord and [ai]Christ—this Jesus whom you crucified."

³⁷ Now when they heard *this*, they were [aj]pierced to the heart, and said to Peter and the rest of the apostles, "[ak]Brethren, [al]what shall we do?" ³⁸ Peter *said* to them, "Repent, and each of you be baptized in the name of Jesus Christ for the forgiveness of your sins; and you will receive the gift of the Holy Spirit. ³⁹ For the promise is for you and your children and for all who are far off, as many as the Lord our God will call to Himself." ⁴⁰ And with many other words he solemnly testified and kept on exhorting them, saying, "[am]Be saved from this perverse generation!" ⁴¹ So then, those who had received his word were baptized; and that day there were added about three thousand [an]souls. ⁴² They were continually devoting themselves to the apostles' teaching and to fellowship, to the breaking of bread and [ao]to prayer.

⁴³ [ap]Everyone kept feeling a sense of awe; and many wonders and [aq]signs were taking place through the apostles. ⁴⁴ And all those who

had believed [ar]were together and had all things in common; [45] and they *began* selling their property and possessions and were sharing them with all, as anyone might have need. [46] Day by day continuing with one mind in the temple, and breaking bread [as]from house to house, they were taking their [at]meals together with gladness and [au]sincerity of heart, [47] praising God and having favor with all the people. And the Lord was adding [av]to their number day by day those who were being saved. (Acts 2)
https://www.biblegateway.com/passage/?search=Acts+2&version=NASB

We have 120 believers (Acts 1:15) waiting in Jerusalem for the Promise from the Father just as Jesus instructed them (Acts 1:4, 5). They are in the Upper Room of the Corner between the Inspection Gate and the Sheep Gate. Many visitors from all over the known world are in Jerusalem for this one of three required yearly Feasts, this being the Feast of Weeks. We are at Day 50, Pentecost, the day after the Feast of Weeks, 7 Weeks of 7. Resurrection Day was the Feast of First Fruits, which was Day 1 of the 49. Pentecost, the 50th Day is related to the Jubilee Year, the 50th Year, in which ALL debts were forgiven. If you were a slave, owed money, had lost your land etc., in the Jubilee Year, you would be forgiven everything. Through the Completed Work of Christ, we are forgiven all of our debts. We are debt free in Christ. We are now not only debt free, but now we are able to be filled with His Holy Spirit. You could call Pentecost, Repentecost, reminding us that while still in these bodies, sin will still try and crouch up on us. Unless we keep a repentant heart His Holy Spirit will not be poured out on us and through us. The Living Water stops and we are left with our water. Without flow, our water will grow stagnant, birthing "mosquitos" that carry viruses i.e. sin and suck the Blood (Life) right out of us.

The Gihon Spring is located directly adjacent to Jerusalem. We can understand the Holy Spirit by understanding this Spring. This is an intermittent Spring. Whenever Jerusalem, a picture of the heart, would be in sin, the flow of the Gihon would stop. The Gihon was the only Water Source for Jerusalem. I will paste some info about the Gihon Spring below.

The City of David was built on a hill of hard limestone, in which underground water created karstic caves. The Gihon Spring, the only source of water of the city, emerges in the Kidron Valley, east of the City of David. It is mentioned many times in the Bible, e.g., its location in the valley east of the city (II Chronicles 33:14); the anointing of Solomon as King of Israel (I Kings 1:35, 45). It made the founding of the City of David possible, and sustained its existence for thousands of years. The Hebrew name of the spring is derived from the verb meaning "to gush forth," reflecting the flow of the spring, which is not steady, but intermittent, its frequency varying with the seasons of the year and annual precipitation. It is a siphon-type karst spring fed by groundwater that accumulates in a subterranean cave. Each time that space fills to the brim, it empties at once through cracks in the rock and is siphoned to the surface. This natural feature made it necessary to accumulate water in a pool, to be available at times when the spring was not "gushing forth."

The spring emerged in a cave on the eastern slope of the City of David above the Kidron Valley, and from there water flowed into the valley, watering the terraced, agricultural plots on the slope of the City of David. This area is called in the Bible the "King's Garden" (II Kings 25:4; Jeremiah 52:7; Nehemiah 3:15). Today, the bed of the Kidron Valley is filled with 15 m. of erosion and debris, which have accumulated over the millennia. During the Second Temple period, a vault was built over the spring, to which one could descend via a long staircase. Water flowed from the spring along Hezekiah's Tunnel to the Siloam Pool, (John 9:7) which is located in the low, southern part of the Tyropoeon Valley, west of the City of David.
http://www.jewishvirtuallibrary.org/jsource/Archaeology/jer water.html

King Hezekiah is known for chiseling a tunnel through the Solid Rock from the Gihon Spring to the Pool of Siloam. I believe King Hezekiah to be a picture of Christ in the sense of it taking a lot of work to make that tunnel to the Pool of Siloam, likened to Christ doing all the Work necessary for us to get to Heaven. I personally believe Jesus literally walked directly above the underground tunnel as He carried our Cross. Interesting as well is that God "turns back time" for King Hezekiah (2 Kings 20:9 and Isaiah 38:8). Due to the Work of Christ, we get a new beginning, as though time were turned back for us. Here is a video link on Hezekiah's Tunnel and a Hezekiah name definition with link as well.

https://www.youtube.com/watch?v=RI3t80ZSg6M

For a meaning of the name Hezekiah, NOBSE Study Bible Name List reads **Yahweh Strengthens**. BDB Theological Dictionary has the similar **Yah Hath Strengthened** and **Yah Strengthens**, to account for the two different tenses this name comes in. Jones' Dictionary of Old Testament Proper Names reads **Strength Of The Lord**. http://www.abarim-publications.com/Meaning/Hezekiah.html#.V8cctTBTGUk

The Feast of Tabernacles has a Water Libation Ceremony using Water from the Pool of Siloam.

At the morning service on each of the seven days of the Feast of Tabernacles (Sukkot) a libation of water was made together with the pouring out of wine (Suk. iv. 1; Yoma 26b), the water being drawn from the Pool of Siloam in a golden ewer of the capacity of three logs. It was borne in solemn procession to the water-gate of the Temple, where the train halted while on the Shofar was blown "teḳi'ah, teru'ah, teḳi'ah." The procession then ascended the "kebesh," or slanting bridge to the altar, toward the left, where stood on the east side of the altar a silver bowl for the water and on the west another for the wine, both having snout-like openings, that in the vessel for the wine being somewhat the larger. Both libations were poured out

simultaneously (Suk. iv. 9).
http://www.jewishencyclopedia.com/articles/14794-water-drawing-feast-of

In John 7, while Jesus is at the Feast of Booths i.e. Tabernacles. He says this:

Now on the last day, the great *day* of the feast, Jesus stood and cried out, saying, "[g]If anyone is thirsty, [h]let him come to Me and drink. [38] He who believes in Me, as the Scripture said, 'From [i]his innermost being will flow rivers of living water.'" [39] But this He spoke of the Spirit, whom those who believed in Him were to receive; for the Spirit was not yet *given*, because Jesus was not yet glorified. (John 7:37-39)

We see the Pool of Siloam in John 9:

When He had said this, He spat on the ground, and made clay of the spittle, and applied the clay to his eyes, [7] and said to him, "Go, wash in the pool of Siloam" (which is translated, Sent). So he went away and washed, and came *back* seeing. [8] Therefore the neighbors, and those who previously saw him as a beggar, were saying, "Is not this the one who used to sit and beg?" [9] Others were saying, "This is he," *still* others were saying, "No, but he is like him." [a]He kept saying, "I am the one." [10] So they were saying to him, "How then were your eyes opened?" [11] He answered, "The man who is called Jesus made clay, and anointed my eyes, and said to me, 'Go to Siloam and wash'; so I went away and washed, and I received sight." (John 9:6-10)

We see that many come to Christ on Pentecost, growing from 120 to 3,000 that day. They hear the "hillbilly" Galileans praising God in their own language. This is the gift of tongues. Remember though, not everyone will get this gift. And yes, it is by far the most abused gift. Remember the body example in 1 Corinthians; imagine a human body made up entirely of tongues. Put emphasis on **ALL** the gifts for a healthy, non-stagnated water, church.

Now concerning spiritual *gifts*, brethren, I do not want you to be unaware. [2] You know that when you were pagans, *you were* led astray to the mute idols, however you were led. [3] Therefore I make known to you that no one speaking [a]by the Spirit of God says, "Jesus is [b]accursed"; and no one can say, "Jesus is Lord," except [c]by the Holy Spirit.

[4] Now there are varieties of gifts, but the same Spirit. [5] And there are varieties of ministries, and the same Lord. [6] There are varieties of effects, but the same God who works all things in all *persons*. [7] But to each one is given the manifestation of the Spirit for the common good. [8] For to one is given the word of wisdom through the Spirit, and to another the word of knowledge according to the same Spirit; [9] to another faith [d]by the same Spirit, and to another gifts of [e]healing [f]by the one Spirit, [10] and to another the [g]effecting of [h]miracles, and to another prophecy, and to another the [i]distinguishing of spirits, to another *various* kinds of tongues, and to another the interpretation of tongues. [11] But one and the same Spirit works all these things, distributing to each one individually just as He wills.

[12] For even as the body is one and *yet* has many members, and all the members of the body, though they are many, are one body, so also is Christ. [13] For [j]by one Spirit we were all baptized into one body, whether Jews or Greeks, whether slaves or free, and we were all made to drink of one Spirit.

[14] For the body is not one member, but many. [15] If the foot says, "Because I am not a hand, I am not *a part* of the body," it is not for this reason [k]any the less *a part* of the body. [16] And if the ear says, "Because I am not an eye, I am not *a part* of the body," it is not for this reason [l]any the less *a part* of the body. [17] If the whole body were an eye, where would the hearing be? If the whole were hearing, where would the sense of smell be? [18] But now God has placed the members, each one of them, in the body, just as He desired. [19] If they were all one member, where would the body be? [20] But now there are many members, but one body. [21] And the eye cannot say to the hand, "I have no need of you"; or again the head to the feet, "I have no need of you." [22] On the contrary, [m]it is much truer that the members

of the body which seem to be weaker are necessary; [23] and those *members* of the body which we [n]deem less honorable, [o]on these we bestow more abundant honor, and our less presentable members become much more presentable, [24] whereas our more presentable members have no need *of it*. But God has *so* composed the body, giving more abundant honor to that *member* which lacked, [25] so that there may be no [p]division in the body, but *that* the members may have the same care for one another. [26] And if one member suffers, all the members suffer with it; if *one* member is [q]honored, all the members rejoice with it.

[27] Now you are Christ's body, and individually members of it. [28] And God has [r]appointed in the church, first apostles, second prophets, third teachers, then [s]miracles, then gifts of healings, helps, administrations, *various* kinds of tongues. [29] All are not apostles, are they? All are not prophets, are they? All are not teachers, are they? All are not *workers of* [t]miracles, are they? [30] All do not have gifts of healings, do they? All do not speak with tongues, do they? All do not interpret, do they? [31] But earnestly desire the greater gifts.

And I show you a still more excellent way.

If I speak with the tongues of men and of angels, but do not have love, I have become a noisy gong or a clanging cymbal. [2] If I have *the gift of* prophecy, and know all mysteries and all knowledge; and if I have all faith, so as to remove mountains, but do not have love, I am nothing. [3] And if I give all my possessions to feed *the poor*, and if I surrender my body [a]to be burned, but do not have love, it profits me nothing.

[4] Love is patient, love is kind *and* is not jealous; love does not brag *and* is not arrogant, [5] does not act unbecomingly; it does not seek its own, is not provoked, does not take into account a wrong *suffered*, [6] does not rejoice in unrighteousness, but rejoices with the truth; [7] [b]bears all things, believes all things, hopes all things, endures all things.

[8] Love never fails; but if *there are gifts of* [c]prophecy, they will be done away; if *there are* tongues, they will cease; if *there is*

knowledge, it will be done away. [9] For we know in part and we prophesy in part; [10] but when the perfect comes, the partial will be done away. [11] When I was a child, I used to speak like a child, think like a child, reason like a child; when I [d]became a man, I did away with childish things. [12] For now we see in a mirror [e]dimly, but then face to face; now I know in part, but then I will know fully just as I also have been fully known. [13] But now faith, hope, love, abide these three; but the [f]greatest of these is love. (1 Corinthians 12-13)

Love is patient, love is kind *and* is not jealous; love does not brag *and* is not arrogant, [5] does not act unbecomingly; it does not seek its own, is not provoked, does not take into account a wrong *suffered*, [6] does not rejoice in unrighteousness, but rejoices with the truth; [7] bears all things, believes all things, hopes all things, endures all things. Love never fails;

Acts 3

Now Peter and John were going up to the temple at the [a]ninth *hour*, the hour of prayer. [2] And a man who had been lame from his mother's womb was being carried along, whom they used to set down every day at the gate of the temple which is called Beautiful, in order to beg [b]alms of those who were entering the temple. [3] When he saw Peter and John about to go into the temple, he *began* asking to receive alms. [4] But Peter, along with John, fixed his gaze on him and said, "Look at us!" [5] And he *began* to give them his attention, expecting to receive something from them. ⁶ But Peter said, "I do not possess silver and gold, but what I do have I give to you: In the name of Jesus Christ the Nazarene—walk!" ⁷ And seizing him by the right hand, he raised him up; and immediately his feet and his ankles were strengthened. ⁸ [c]With a leap he stood upright and *began* to walk; and he entered the temple with them, walking and leaping and praising God. ⁹ And all the people saw him walking and praising God; ¹⁰ and they were taking note of him as being the one who used to sit at the Beautiful Gate of the temple to *beg* alms, and they were filled with wonder and amazement at what had happened to him.

¹¹ While he was clinging to Peter and John, all the people ran together to them at the so-called [d]portico of Solomon, full of amazement. ¹² But when Peter saw *this*, he replied to the people, "Men of Israel, why are you amazed at this, or why do you gaze at us, as if by our own power or piety we had made him walk? ¹³ The God of Abraham, Isaac and Jacob, the God of our fathers, has glorified His [e]servant Jesus, *the one* whom you delivered and disowned in the presence of Pilate, when he had decided to release Him. ¹⁴ But you disowned the Holy and Righteous One and asked for a murderer to be granted to you, ¹⁵ but put to death the [f]Prince of life, *the one* whom God raised from the dead, *a fact* to which we are witnesses. ¹⁶ And on the basis of faith in His name, *it is* [g]the name of Jesus which has strengthened this man whom you see and know; and the faith which *comes* through Him has given him this perfect health in the presence of you all.

¹⁷ "And now, brethren, I know that you acted in ignorance, just as your rulers did also. ¹⁸ But the things which God announced beforehand by the mouth of all the prophets, that His [h]Christ would suffer, He has thus fulfilled. ¹⁹ Therefore repent and return, so that your sins may be wiped away, in order that times of refreshing may come from the presence of the Lord; ²⁰ and that He may send Jesus, the [i]Christ appointed for you, ²¹ whom heaven must receive until *the* [j]period of restoration of all things about which God spoke by the mouth of His holy prophets from ancient time. ²² Moses said, 'THE LORD GOD WILL RAISE UP FOR YOU A PROPHET [k]LIKE ME FROM YOUR BRETHREN; TO HIM YOU SHALL GIVE HEED to everything He says to

you. ²³ And it will be that every soul that does not heed that prophet shall be utterly destroyed from among the people.' ²⁴ And likewise, all the prophets who have spoken, from Samuel and *his* successors onward, also announced these days. ²⁵ It is you who are the sons of the prophets and of the covenant which God [l]made with your fathers, saying to Abraham, 'AND IN YOUR SEED ALL THE FAMILIES OF THE EARTH SHALL BE BLESSED.' ²⁶ For you first, God raised up His [m]Servant and sent Him to bless you by turning every one *of you* from your wicked ways." (Acts 3)
https://www.biblegateway.com/passage/?search=Acts+3&version=NASB

So we have Peter, meaning stone, and John, meaning grace going up to the temple to pray at the ninth hour. Remember Jesus was crucified at the third hour (9 a.m.), and then at the sixth hour (noon) darkness fell over the land, then at the ninth hour (3 p.m.) the Veil tore from Top to bottom when Jesus gave up His Spirit. In the Old Testament we see David and Daniel praying three times a day. The Old Testament sacrifices and offerings also correspond to these times. The Passover Lamb was sacrificed at the ninth hour.

Evening and morning and at noon, I will complain and murmur, And He will hear my voice. (Psalm 55:17)

Now when Daniel knew that the document was signed, he entered his house (now in his roof chamber he had windows open toward Jerusalem); and he continued kneeling on his knees three times a day, praying and giving thanks before his God, [h]as he had been doing previously. (Daniel 6:10)

These three times a day prayers, sacrifices and offerings point to the Crucifixion of Christ. When we come across one of these three times we should reflect on the Crucifixion. Similar to Communion, "do this in remembrance of Me". Today we are to pray without ceasing.

Rejoice always; [17] pray without ceasing; [18] in everything give thanks; for this is God's will for you in Christ Jesus. [19] Do not quench the Spirit; [20] do not despise prophetic [l]utterances. [21] But examine everything *carefully*; hold fast to that which is good; [22] abstain from every [m]form of evil. (1 Thessalonians 5:16-21)

The Gospel Message would begin at Jerusalem, then all Judea, then Samaria, then everywhere else.

but you will receive power when the Holy Spirit has come upon you; and you shall be My witnesses both in Jerusalem, and in all Judea and Samaria, and even to the remotest part of the earth." (Acts 1:8)

So Peter and John are still in Jerusalem. They are going to the Temple at the ninth hour. There is a forty year old man lame from birth at the Gate Beautiful. Remember this is the outer gate that led into the Court of the Women, which is a picture of the bride, being us, the church. We are the Beautiful Bride of Christ. Note as well that this man would have been there when Jesus passed by when He entered the Temple. Why wasn't he healed by Jesus back then? People had witnessed this lame man for forty years; the "works of God "would be evidence that Jesus sent His Holy Spirit. Everybody already knew that Jesus healed. Jesus gives us the answer after a healing found in John 9.

Jesus answered, "*It was* neither *that* this man sinned, nor his parents; but *it was* so that the works of God might be displayed in him. (John 9:3)

"The works of God might be displayed in him", who receives the glory? God or man? Due to this healing, many listened to the Gospel, which led to the church growing to 5,000 (Acts 4). Why don't we see many healings like this today? It is a shame when people that were supposedly healed at one of these modern day "healing ministries" is exposed later as not really being healed. These "healing ministries" will have a "man up on stage", he will claim to be god's anointed; he claims to wield the power of god like the force from the movie Star Wars. Glory goes to these men.

"Not everyone who says to Me, 'Lord, Lord,' will enter the kingdom of heaven, but he who does the will of My Father who is in heaven *will enter*. [22] Many will say to Me on that day, 'Lord, Lord, did we not prophesy in Your name, and in Your name cast out demons, and in Your name perform many [n]miracles?' [23] And then I will declare to them, 'I never knew you; DEPART FROM ME, YOU WHO PRACTICE LAWLESSNESS.' (Matthew 7:21-23)

Notice how Peter gives all glory and all credit to Jesus. Notice the praising of God.

But Peter said, "I do not possess silver and gold, but what I do have I give to you: In the name of Jesus Christ the Nazarene—walk!" [7] And seizing him by the right hand, he raised him up; and immediately his feet and his ankles were strengthened. [8] [c]With a leap he stood upright and *began* to walk; and he entered the temple with them, walking and leaping and praising God. [9] And all the people saw him walking and praising God; [10] and they were taking note of him as being the one who used to sit at the Beautiful Gate of the temple to *beg* alms, and they were filled with wonder and amazement at what had happened to him. (Acts 3:6-10)

"Men of Israel, why are you amazed at this, or why do you gaze at us, as if by our own power or piety we had made him walk? [13] The God of Abraham, Isaac and Jacob, the God of our fathers, has glorified His [e]servant Jesus, *the one* whom you delivered and disowned in the presence of Pilate, when he had decided to release Him. [14] But you disowned the Holy and Righteous One and asked for a murderer to be granted to you, [15] but put to death the [f]Prince of life, *the one* whom God raised from the dead, *a fact* to which we are witnesses. [16] And on the basis of faith in His name, *it is* [g]the name of Jesus which has strengthened this man whom you see and know; and the faith which *comes* through Him has given him this perfect health in the presence of you all. (Acts 3:12-16)

God still heals today. All glory must go to Him. Seek and pray that God would bless you with the gifts of healings, by the Power of the Holy Spirit, remember it is **not** you, but the Holy Spirit that flows through you. Remember sin stops His flow. Stagnant water breeds mosquitos, which can carry disease (picture of sin) and suck the Blood, the Life from you. You being filled with the Light will also attract mosquitos, put on the Armor of God, which is our sin repellent.

For to one is given the word of wisdom through the Spirit, and to another the word of knowledge according to the same Spirit; [9] to another faith [d]by the same Spirit, and to another gifts of [e]**healing** [f]by the one Spirit, [10] and to another the [g]effecting of [h]miracles, and to another prophecy, and to another the [i]distinguishing of spirits, to another *various* kinds of tongues, and to another the interpretation of tongues. [11] But one and the same Spirit works all these things, distributing to each one individually just as He wills. (1 Corinthians 12:8-11)

Now you are Christ's body, and individually members of it. [28] And God has [r]appointed in the church, first apostles, second prophets, third teachers, then [s]miracles, then gifts of **healings**, helps, administrations, *various* kinds of tongues. [29] All are not apostles, are they? All are not prophets, are they? All are not teachers, are they? All are not *workers of* [t]miracles, are they? [30] All do not have gifts of **healings**, do they? All do not speak with tongues, do they? All do not interpret, do they? [31] But earnestly desire the greater gifts. (1 Corinthians 12:27-31)

Stand firm therefore, HAVING GIRDED YOUR LOINS WITH TRUTH, and HAVING PUT ON THE BREASTPLATE OF RIGHTEOUSNESS, 15 and having shod YOUR FEET WITH THE PREPARATION OF THE GOSPEL OF PEACE; 16 [f]in addition to all, taking up the shield of faith with which you will be able to extinguish all the flaming arrows of the evil *one*. 17 And take THE HELMET OF SALVATION, and the sword of the Spirit, which is the word of God.

18 [g]With all prayer and petition [h]pray at all times in the Spirit, and with this in view, [i]be on the alert with all perseverance and petition for all the saints, 19 and *pray* on my behalf, that utterance may be given to me in the opening of my mouth, to make known with boldness the mystery of the gospel, 20 for which I am an ambassador in [j]chains; that [k]in *proclaiming* it I may speak boldly, as I ought to speak. (Ephesians 6:14-20)

Remember prayer activates the Armor of God. Always remember what Christ did for us at the third hour, at the sixth hour, and at the ninth hour.

It was the [i]**third hour** [j]when they crucified Him. 26 The inscription of the charge against Him [k]read, "THE KING OF THE JEWS."

27 They *crucified two robbers with Him, one on His right and one on His left. 28 [[l]And the Scripture was fulfilled which says, "And He was numbered with transgressors."] 29 Those passing by were [m]hurling abuse at Him, wagging their heads, and saying, "Ha! You who *are going to* destroy the temple and rebuild it in three days, 30 save Yourself, and come down from the cross!" 31 In the same way the chief priests also, along with the scribes, were mocking *Him* among themselves and saying, "He saved others; [n]He cannot save Himself. 32 Let *this* Christ, the King of Israel, now come down from the cross, so that we may see and believe!" Those who were crucified with Him were also insulting Him.

33 When the [o]**sixth hour** came, darkness [p]fell over the whole land until the [q]**ninth hour**. 34 At the **ninth hour** Jesus cried out with a

loud voice, "ELOI, ELOI, LAMA SABACHTHANI?" which is translated, "MY GOD, MY GOD, WHY HAVE YOU FORSAKEN ME?" [35] When some of the bystanders heard it, they *began* saying, "Behold, He is calling for Elijah." [36] Someone ran and filled a sponge with sour wine, put it on a reed, and gave Him a drink, saying, "[r]Let us see whether Elijah will come to take Him down." [37] And Jesus uttered a loud cry, and breathed His last. [38] And the veil of the temple was torn in two from top to bottom. [39] When the centurion, who was standing [s]right in front of Him, saw [t]the way He breathed His last, he said, "Truly this man was [u]the Son of God!" (Mark 15:25-39)

Acts 4

As they were speaking to the people, the priests and the captain of the temple *guard* and the Sadducees came up to them, [2] being greatly disturbed because they were teaching the people and proclaiming [a]in Jesus the resurrection from the dead. [3] And they laid hands on them and put them in jail until the next day, for it was already evening. [4] But many of those who had heard the [b]message believed; and the number of the men came to be about five thousand.

[5] On the next day, their rulers and elders and scribes were gathered together in Jerusalem; [6] and Annas the high priest *was there*, and Caiaphas and John and Alexander, and all who were of high-priestly descent. [7] When they had placed them in the center, they *began to* inquire, "By what power, or in what name, have you done this?" [8] Then Peter, [c]filled with the Holy Spirit, said to them, "[d]Rulers and elders of the people, [9] if we are [e]on trial today for a benefit done to a sick man, [f]as to how this man has been made well, [10] let it be known to all of you and to all the people of Israel, that [g]by the name of Jesus Christ the Nazarene, whom you crucified, whom God raised from the dead—[h]by [i]this *name* this man stands here before you in good health. [11] [j]He is the STONE WHICH WAS REJECTED by you, THE

BUILDERS, *but* WHICH BECAME THE CHIEF CORNER *stone.* [12] And there is salvation in no one else; for there is no other name under heaven that has been given among men by which we must be saved."

[13] Now as they observed the confidence of Peter and John and understood that they were uneducated and untrained men, they were amazed, and *began* to recognize them [k]as having been with Jesus. [14] And seeing the man who had been healed standing with them, they had nothing to say in reply. [15] But when they had ordered them to leave the [l]Council, they *began* to confer with one another, [16] saying, "What shall we do with these men? For the fact that a noteworthy [m]miracle has taken place through them is apparent to all who live in Jerusalem, and we cannot deny it. [17] But so that it will not spread any further among the people, let us warn them to speak no longer to any man in this name." [18] And when they had summoned them, they commanded them not to speak or teach at all [n]in the name of Jesus. [19] But Peter and John answered and said to them, "Whether it is right in the sight of God to give heed to you rather than to God, you be the judge; [20] for we cannot stop speaking about what we have seen and heard." [21] When they had threatened them further, they let them go (finding no basis on which to punish them) on account of the people, because they were all glorifying God for what had happened; [22] for the man was more than forty years old on whom this [o]miracle of healing had been performed.

[23] When they had been released, they went to their own *companions* and reported all that the chief priests and the elders had said to them. [24] And when they heard *this*, they lifted their voices to God with one accord and said, "O [p]Lord, it is You who MADE THE HEAVEN AND THE EARTH AND THE SEA, AND ALL THAT IS IN THEM, [25] who by the Holy Spirit, *through* the mouth of our father David Your servant, said,

'WHY DID THE [q]GENTILES RAGE,
AND THE PEOPLES DEVISE FUTILE THINGS?
[26] 'THE KINGS OF THE EARTH [r]TOOK THEIR STAND,
AND THE RULERS WERE GATHERED TOGETHER
AGAINST THE LORD AND AGAINST HIS [s]CHRIST.'

^{27} For truly in this city there were gathered together against Your holy [t]servant Jesus, whom You anointed, both Herod and Pontius Pilate, along with the [u]Gentiles and the peoples of Israel, ^{28} to do whatever Your hand and Your purpose predestined to occur. ^{29} And [v]now, Lord, take note of their threats, and grant that Your bond-servants may speak Your word with all confidence, ^{30} while You extend Your hand to heal, and [w]signs and wonders take place through the name of Your holy [x]servant Jesus." ^{31} And when they had prayed, the place where they had gathered together was shaken, and they were all filled with the Holy Spirit and *began* to speak the word of God with boldness.

^{32} And the [y]congregation of those who believed were of one heart and soul; and not one *of them* [z]claimed that anything belonging to him was his own, but all things were common property to them. ^{33} And with great power the apostles were giving testimony to the resurrection of the Lord Jesus, and abundant grace was upon them all. ^{34} For there was not a needy person among them, for all who were owners of land or houses would sell them and bring the [aa]proceeds of the sales ^{35} and lay them at the apostles' feet, and they would be distributed to each as any had need.

^{36} Now Joseph, a Levite of Cyprian birth, who was also called Barnabas by the apostles (which translated means Son of [ab]Encouragement), ^{37} and who owned a tract of land, sold it and brought the money and laid it at the apostles' feet. (Acts 4) https://www.biblegateway.com/passage/?search=Acts+4&version=NASB

In the previous chapter we saw the healing of a man born lame. The lame man was more than forty years old and had been sitting outside the Temple Gate named Beautiful for many years. Peter and John are giving glory to God for the healing and preaching the Good News of Christ. We see the Sadducees mentioned. The Sadducees are one of the main groups that comprised the Sanhedrin. The Sanhedrin was the Council i.e. the Rulers and elders of the people. The Sanhedrin was headquartered in Jerusalem.

This concept originated in the Old Testament, in Numbers 11. Moses is overwhelmed and spread thin amongst many faithless, ungrateful people. God tells Moses to appoint 70 people to assist him. In the New Testament, these 70, with the high priest, are called the Sanhedrin.

The LORD therefore said to Moses, "Gather for Me seventy men from the elders of Israel, whom you know to be the elders of the people and their officers and bring them to the tent of meeting, and let them take their stand there with you. [17] Then I will come down and speak with you there, and I will take of the Spirit who is upon you, and will put *Him* upon them; and they shall bear the burden of the people with you, so that you will not bear *it* all alone. (Numbers 11:16, 17)

Another large group that you see in Scripture is the Pharisees. They also have members in the Sanhedrin. We learn in the Bible that the Sadducees don't believe in the Resurrection. So with Peter and John preaching the Gospel, which includes the Resurrection, the Sadducees are not too happy about it. Here is an old joke to help remember the main difference between these two groups: How did the Sadducees get their name? Since they didn't believe in the Resurrection, that's why they're "sad you see". We get more info on these two groups in Acts 23:

But perceiving that one group were Sadducees and the other Pharisees, Paul *began* crying out in the [c]Council, "Brethren, I am a Pharisee, a son of Pharisees; I am on trial for the hope and resurrection of the dead!" [7] As he said this, there occurred a dissension between the Pharisees and Sadducees, and the assembly was divided. [8] For the Sadducees say that there is no resurrection, nor an angel, nor a spirit, but the Pharisees acknowledge them all. [9] And there occurred a great uproar; and some of the scribes of the Pharisaic party stood up and *began* to argue heatedly, saying, "We find nothing wrong with this man; suppose a spirit or an angel has spoken to him?" [10] And as a great dissension was developing, the [d]commander was afraid Paul would be torn to pieces by them and ordered the troops to go down and take him away from them by force, and bring him into the barracks. (Acts 23:6-10)

Acts 4 ends with the introduction of Joseph a Levite, of Cyprian birth. Later in Acts we will see the Gospel going out to Cyprus. The apostles also call him Barnabas, which is translated Son of Encouragement. Notice the little "ab" before the word Encouragement in Acts 4:36. In the footnotes that are listed below the chapter for "ab" we read: Or *Exhortation* or *Consolation*. Here is the actual link to the internet Bible chapter so you can see the footnotes.
https://www.biblegateway.com/passage/?search=Acts+4&version=NASB

So the name Barnabas actually means to encourage and exhort and console, which is the definition of the gift of prophecy. We find that definition in 1 Corinthians 14:3: "But one who prophesies speaks to men for edification and exhortation and consolation."

I first learned this definition as "to build, to stir and to cheer." When you usually think of prophecy you might think of someone telling the future. That can be one aspect of prophecy. In 1 Corinthians 14:1 we read, "Pursue love, yet desire earnestly spiritual *gifts*, but especially that you may prophesy." The gift of prophecy is extremely important to the Body of Christ. We need to build people up and stir people up and cheer people up.

Build Stir Cheer

Acts 5

But a man named Ananias, with his wife Sapphira, sold a piece of property, [2] and kept back *some* of the price for himself, with his wife's [a]full knowledge, and bringing a portion of it, he laid it at the apostles' feet. [3] But Peter said, "Ananias, why has Satan filled your heart to lie to the Holy Spirit and to keep back *some* of the price of the land? [4] While it remained *unsold*, did it not remain your own? And after it was sold, was it not [b]under your control? Why is it that you have [c]conceived this deed in your heart? You have not lied to men but to God." [5] And as he heard these words, Ananias fell down and breathed his last; and great fear came over all who heard of it. [6] The young men got up and covered him up, and after carrying him out, they buried him.

[7] Now there elapsed an interval of about three hours, and his wife came in, not knowing what had happened. [8] And Peter responded to her, "Tell me whether you sold the land [d]for such and such a price?" And she said, "Yes, [e]that was the price." [9] Then Peter *said* to her, "Why is it that you have agreed together to put the Spirit of the Lord to the test? Behold, the feet of those who have buried your husband are at the door, and they will carry you out *as well*." [10] And immediately she fell at his feet and breathed her last, and the young men came in and found her dead, and they carried her out and buried her beside her husband. [11] And great fear came over the whole church, and over all who heard of these things.

[12] [f]At the hands of the apostles many signs and wonders were taking place among the people; and they were all with one accord in Solomon's portico. [13] But none of the rest dared to associate with them; however, the people held them in high esteem. [14] And all the more believers in the Lord, multitudes of men and women, were constantly added to *their number*, [15] to such an extent that they even

carried the sick out into the streets and laid them on cots and pallets, so that when Peter came by at least his shadow might fall on any one of them. [16] Also the [g]people from the cities in the vicinity of Jerusalem were coming together, bringing people who were sick [h]or afflicted with unclean spirits, and they were all being healed.

[17] But the high priest rose up, along with all his associates (that is the sect of the Sadducees), and they were filled with jealousy. [18] They laid hands on the apostles and put them in a public jail. [19] But during the night an angel of the Lord opened the gates of the prison, and taking them out he said, [20] "Go, stand and [i]speak to the people in the temple [j]the whole message of this Life." [21] Upon hearing *this*, they entered into the temple about daybreak and *began* to teach.

Now when the high priest and his associates came, they called the [k]Council together, even all the Senate of the sons of Israel, and sent *orders* to the prison house for them to be brought. [22] But the officers who came did not find them in the prison; and they returned and reported back, [23] saying, "We found the prison house locked quite securely and the guards standing at the doors; but when we had opened up, we found no one inside." [24] Now when the captain of the temple *guard* and the chief priests heard these words, they were greatly perplexed about them as to what [l]would come of this. [25] But someone came and reported to them, "The men whom you put in prison are standing in the temple and teaching the people!" [26] Then the captain went along with the officers and *proceeded* to bring them *back* without violence (for they were afraid of the people, that they might be stoned).

[27] When they had brought them, they stood them [m]before the Council. The high priest questioned them, [28] saying, "We gave you strict orders not to continue teaching in this name, and [n]yet, you have filled Jerusalem with your teaching and intend to bring this man's blood upon us." [29] But Peter and the apostles answered, "We must obey God rather than men. [30] The God of our fathers raised up Jesus, [o]whom you had put to death by hanging Him on a [p]cross. [31] He is the one whom God exalted [q]to His right hand as a [r]Prince and a Savior, to grant repentance to Israel, and forgiveness of sins.

[32] And we are witnesses [s]of these things; and *so is* the Holy Spirit, whom God has given to those who obey Him."

[33] But when they heard this, they were cut [t]to the quick and intended to kill them. [34] But a Pharisee named Gamaliel, a teacher of the Law, respected by all the people, stood up in the Council and gave orders to put the men outside for a short time. [35] And he said to them, "Men of Israel, take care what you propose to do with these men. [36] For some time ago Theudas rose up, claiming to be somebody, and a group of about four hundred men joined up with him. [u]But he was killed, and all who [v]followed him were dispersed and came to nothing. [37] After this man, Judas of Galilee rose up in the days of the census and drew away *some* people after him; he too perished, and all those who [w]followed him were scattered. [38] So in the present case, I say to you, stay away from these men and let them alone, for if this plan or [x]action is of men, it will be overthrown; [39] but if it is of God, you will not be able to overthrow them; or else you may even be found fighting against God."

[40] They [y]took his advice; and after calling the apostles in, they flogged them and ordered them not to [z]speak in the name of Jesus, and *then* released them. [41] So they went on their way from the presence of the [aa]Council, rejoicing that they had been considered worthy to suffer shame for *His* name. [42] And every day, in the temple and [ab]from house to house, they [ac]kept right on teaching and [ad]preaching Jesus *as* the [ae]Christ. (Acts 5) https://www.biblegateway.com/passage/?search=Acts+5&version=N ASB

There are a couple acronyms that are very useful for studying God's Word. One is C.O.M.A., which means Context, Observation, Meaning, and Application. Another one that is similar is, O.I.A., which means Observation, Interpretation, and Application.

So at the end of chapter four we saw people selling their land etc. and giving the money to the apostles. We ended chapter four with Barnabas, who was a Levite from Cyprus, giving money from the land that he sold. Technically Levites were not to own land, but

195

somehow he had land. Remember we are in a Jubilee Year. In a Jubilee Year, every fiftieth year, all land debts, any and all debt, etc. was forgiven. So we are in Jerusalem, and many have land that they did not have the previous year. Believers are being kicked out of the synagogue left and right. The system that took care of the elderly, widows, single moms etc. was no longer accessible by believers. But perfect timing, we are in a Jubilee Year, just as Christ forgave all sin in this Year, all debts were also forgiven.

Now we have Ananias and Sapphira. Their lying to God, puts them both lying in a grave. The grave was probably in the Potter's Field, bought with Blood money, via Judas. A field with holes already pre-dug. The potter would dig until he found clay. When the clay ended in that hole, he went to the next. What is the interpretation? It is the third Commandment, taking the Lord's Name in vain. The ninth Commandment, lying, also comes into play. Taking the Lord's Name in vain, is the big one. Hey look at me, he didn't even bring his wife to share in the glory, look what I gave the church. He did not give from the heart, giving to glorify God, but to glorify himself. Three hours later, his wife also went along with it. Application is do not be an outer shell fake believer, do all from a completed heart in Christ.

Could there be a deeper meaning as well, with their name meanings? Remember our study of the Ten Commandments. We discovered that they weren't some crusty old stone tablets. They were beautiful sapphire stone Tablets. You can actually trace all written language back to the Tablets. Previously they used symbols, hieroglyphics etc. Sapphira comes from the word sapphire. Let's take a peek into the names Ananias and Sapphira:

Ananias: The high priest at the time of Paul's trial in Jerusalem (Acts 23:2).

At the time of Christ and Paul, the high priesthood was mostly a secular and economic affair, much as the papacy was in the middle ages, and mostly designed to direct money from the people towards the ruling elite. That was the part of Judaism which agreed most with the Romans, and it was also the part of it which was mostly opposed by the Jewish masses, and which ultimately sparked the great revolt of 66 AD. Josephus makes mention of a high priest Ananias (for several reasons probably not the same as the one who heard Paul) who was greatly loved by the citizens (that's the Roman nobility) because he was a "great hoarder up of money" (*Ant*.20.9.2).

The high priest Ananias who heard Paul, ordered him struck on the mouth after his first statement, and Paul reminded him in no small terms that this violated the Law (Deuteronomy 25:2). When someone reminded Paul that he shouldn't speak ill of the high priest, Paul submitted that he didn't know that he was either a high priest or a ruler of the people. This was obviously still part of Paul's previous observation that Ananias was a white-washed wall because (1) everybody knew who the high priest was, and (2) in case someone didn't know, the high priest came with an elaborate uniform. Paul basically stated that he didn't recognize the authority of the Sanhedrin. http://www.abarim-publications.com/Meaning/Ananias.html#.V-Gt7zAVCUk

The name Sapphira quite obviously is related to the name of the gem sapphire, which is a name that shows up in many ancient languages with remarkable consistency. In Greek it's called σαπφειρος (*sappheiros*), and in Hebrew it exists as ספיר (*sappir*). http://www.abarim-publications.com/Meaning/Sapphira.html#.V-GvQDAVCUk

So the deeper meaning is Ananias, being a false prophet (I personally believe to be thee false prophet) and Sapphira being a picture of the outer shell keeping of the Law. So they together are a picture of the Law and Prophets, the Two Witnesses, both now being buried with Christ, but as we know Christ rose, He Himself conquering sin and the death, He Himself fulfilling the Law and the Prophets. In John 15 we read, "Apart from Me you can do nothing." The point is, only with a heart from Christ, can one actually do things from the heart.

197

They laid hands on the apostles and put them in a public jail. [19] But during the night an angel of the Lord opened the gates of the prison, and taking them out he said, [20] "Go, stand and [i]speak to the people in the temple [i]the whole message of this Life." [21] Upon hearing *this*, they entered into the temple about daybreak and *began* to teach.

The Whole Message of this Life=

Jesus paid it all, all to Him I owe

https://www.youtube.com/watch?v=38EVco7eba0

Acts 6

Now [a]at this time while the disciples were increasing *in number*, a complaint arose on the part of the [b]Hellenistic *Jews* against the *native* Hebrews, because their widows were being overlooked in the daily serving *of food*. ² So the twelve summoned the [c]congregation of the disciples and said, "It is not desirable for us to neglect the word of God in order to serve tables. ³ Therefore, brethren, select from among you seven men of good reputation, full of the Spirit and of wisdom, whom we may put in charge of this task. ⁴ But we will devote ourselves to prayer and to the [d]ministry of the word." ⁵ The statement found approval with the whole [e]congregation; and they chose Stephen, a man full of faith and of the Holy Spirit, and Philip, Prochorus, Nicanor, Timon, Parmenas and [f]Nicolas, a [g]proselyte from Antioch. ⁶ And these they brought before the apostles; and after praying, they laid their hands on them.

⁷ The word of God kept on spreading; and the number of the disciples continued to increase greatly in Jerusalem, and a great many of the priests were becoming obedient to the faith.

⁸ And Stephen, full of grace and power, was performing great wonders and [h]signs among the people. ⁹ But some men from what was called the Synagogue of the Freedmen, *including* both Cyrenians and Alexandrians, and some from Cilicia and [i]Asia, rose up and argued with Stephen. ¹⁰ But they were unable to cope with the wisdom and the Spirit with which he was speaking. ¹¹ Then they secretly induced men to say, "We have heard him speak blasphemous words against Moses and *against* God." ¹² And they stirred up the people, the elders and the scribes, and they came up to him and dragged him away and brought him [j]before the [k]Council. ¹³ They put forward false witnesses who said, "This man incessantly speaks against this holy place and the Law; ¹⁴ for we have heard him

say that this Nazarene, Jesus, will destroy this place and alter the customs which Moses handed down to us." [15] And fixing their gaze on him, all who were sitting in the [l]Council saw his face like the face of an angel. (Acts 6)
https://www.biblegateway.com/passage/?search=Acts+6&version=NASB

So we are still in Jerusalem. Remember in the Gospel of John a couple times people were afraid to acknowledge Jesus for "fear of getting kicked out of the synagogue"? Here is one example from John 9: His parents said this because they were afraid of the Jews; for the Jews had already agreed that if anyone confessed Him to be Christ, he was to be put out of the synagogue. [23] For this reason his parents said, "He is of age; ask him." Another example can be found in John 12:42. So people are becoming believers and they are being booted out of the synagogue. Public aid was administered through the synagogue etc. So with public aid no longer available, we have widows' etc. needing food etc. Also believers were close knit (hearts actually knit together), meeting house to house. Funny how some of today's churches think they discovered some new thing with the modern huge success of small groups. We have some friction with the Hellenistic Jews and the Hebrew Jews. Remember prior to the Romans ruling, the Greeks ruled. So many Jews back then took on a lot of Greek culture etc., but some did not. The 12 disciples appoint 7 men to iron out the wrinkles.

Let's take a look at the name meanings of the seven. Nicanor jumps out at me. Remember the name of the Gate within the Temple area that led into the Inner Court (Bronze Basin and Altar)? That Gate was named Nicanor. This is the same word that the athletic apparel company Nike gets their name from.

Stephen: From the Greek name Στεφανος (Stephanos) meaning "crown". http://www.behindthename.com/name/stephen

Philip: The name Philippos consists of two elements. The first part comes from the adjective φιλος (philos), meaning friend or one who

200

loves. The second part comes from the familiar noun ιππος (*hippos*), meaning horse. http://www.abarim-publications.com/Meaning/Philip.html#.V-Y8-zAVCUk

Prochorus: The name Prochorus consists of two elements. The first one of these is the common prefix προ (*pro*), meaning before or prior. The second part of our name comes from the noun χορος (*choros*), meaning choir or dance. http://www.abarim-publications.com/Meaning/Prochorus.html#.V-Y98DAVCUk

Nicanor: The first part of our name comes from the noun νικη (*nike*), meaning victory. The second part of Nicandor and thus probably also of Nicanor, is the familiar noun ανδρος (*andros*), the genitive form of the word ανηρ (*aner*), meaning man. http://www.abarim-publications.com/Meaning/Nicanor.html#.V-Y-jzAVCUk

Timon: The name Timon comes from the noun τιμη (*time*), meaning honor, which in turn derives from the verb τιω (*tio*), meaning to honor or revere. http://www.abarim-publications.com/Meaning/Timon.html#.V-Y_MTAVCUk

Parmenas: The name Parmenas comes from the verb παραμενω (*parameno*), meaning to stay with or by someone's side. This word in turn consists of two parts, the first of which being the familiar particle παρα (*para*), meaning near. The second part of our name comes from the verb μενω (*meno*), meaning to remain or stay. http://www.abarim-publications.com/Meaning/Parmenas.html#.V-Y_pTAVCUk

Nicolas: The name Nicolas consists of two elements. The first part comes from the familiar noun νικη (*nike*), meaning victory. The second part of the name Nicolas comes from the noun λαος (*laos*), meaning (common) people. http://www.abarim-publications.com/Meaning/Nicolas.html#.V-ZANjAVCUk

Aside from Stephen and Philip, the other above five names are never again mentioned in the Bible. In short, the seven names could be saying something like: The Victory of the Man Jesus gives Victory for all people. I realize that not every name grouping in the Bible has some kind of meaning, but I believe this one does.

Note that these seven are full of the Holy Spirit. Note also that the twelve pray and lay hands on the seven. Notice in verse seven that many priests are coming to Christ. The disciples showed the priests how Christ was the Promised Messiah, the Promised Seed of Abraham. I am sure they showed them how Christ fulfilled the Seven Feasts, and how Christ is our Seventh Day Sabbath Rest. Christ did all the work for us; we can now and forever Sabbath Rest in Him. They showed how the Law and Prophets are fulfilled in Christ. They showed how the Temple and each and everything about it, pointed to Christ. The Veil to the Holy of Holies is now torn, from Top to bottom, meaning God Tore it. We are now the temple, the temple of the Holy Spirit. Jerusalem represents the heart of the earth. Jesus took our sin upon Himself within the walls of Jerusalem. They then led Him outside the walls of our heart, taking our sin outside of our heart, to the Cross. "It is finished", was spoken by our Lord just before He died. The earthly Temple had evolved into a "den of thieves". That era was now over. Believers are now the temple of the Holy Spirit.

We see a group of men called the Synagogue of the Freedman that are not too happy with Stephen. Remember there were three annual Feast Weeks held in Jerusalem, required by all Jewish males to attend, that "strangers" were also invited to (Deuteronomy 16). So the Jews did evangelize. The Synagogue of Freedman are from Northern Africa and Asia Minor. Picture Jerusalem in the middle, Asia Minor would be northwest, Northern Africa is southwest. They end up dragging Stephen to the Council i.e. the Sanhedrin, the 70 Sadducees, Pharisees etc. Remember the Sanhedrin convicted Jesus and gave Him over to Romans to be crucified. Stephen is before the Council having the "face of an angel". The next chapter we are about to get an over the top history of the Bible via Stephen.

Victory in Jesus

https://www.youtube.com/watch?v=D3xlq2L0hcs

Acts 7

The high priest said, "Are these things so?"

[2] And he said, "Hear me, brethren and fathers! The God of glory appeared to our father Abraham when he was in Mesopotamia, before he lived in [a]Haran, [3] and said to him, 'LEAVE YOUR COUNTRY AND YOUR RELATIVES, AND COME INTO THE LAND THAT I WILL SHOW YOU.' [4] Then he left the land of the Chaldeans and settled in [b]Haran. From there, after his father died, *God* had him move to this country in which you are now living. [5] But He gave him no inheritance in it, not even a foot of ground, and *yet*, even when he had no child, He promised that HE WOULD GIVE IT TO HIM AS A POSSESSION, AND TO HIS DESCENDANTS AFTER HIM. [6] But God spoke to this effect, that his DESCENDANTS WOULD BE ALIENS IN A FOREIGN LAND, AND THAT THEY WOULD [c]BE ENSLAVED AND MISTREATED FOR FOUR HUNDRED YEARS. [7] 'AND WHATEVER NATION TO WHICH THEY WILL BE IN BONDAGE I MYSELF WILL JUDGE,' said God, 'AND AFTER THAT THEY WILL COME OUT AND [d]SERVE ME IN THIS PLACE.' [8] And He gave him [e]the covenant of circumcision; and so *Abraham* became the father of Isaac, and circumcised him on the eighth day; and Isaac *became the father of* Jacob, and Jacob *of* the twelve patriarchs.

[9] "The patriarchs became jealous of Joseph and sold him into Egypt. *Yet* God was with him, [10] and rescued him from all his afflictions, and granted him favor and wisdom in the sight of Pharaoh, king of Egypt, and he made him governor over Egypt and all his household.

[11] "Now a famine came over all Egypt and Canaan, and great affliction *with it*, and our fathers [f]could find no food. [12] But when Jacob heard that there was grain in Egypt, he sent our fathers *there* the first time. [13] On the second *visit* Joseph [g]made himself known to his brothers, and Joseph's family was disclosed to Pharaoh. [14] Then Joseph sent *word* and invited Jacob his father and all his relatives to come to him, seventy-five [h]persons *in all*. [15] And Jacob went down to Egypt and *there* he and our fathers died. [16] *From there* they were removed to [i]Shechem and laid in the tomb which Abraham had purchased for a sum of money from the sons of [j]Hamor in [k]Shechem.

[17] "But as the time of the promise was approaching which God had assured to Abraham, the people increased and multiplied in Egypt, [18] until THERE AROSE ANOTHER KING OVER EGYPT WHO KNEW NOTHING ABOUT JOSEPH. [19] It was he who took shrewd advantage of our race and mistreated our fathers so that they would [l]expose their infants and they would not survive. [20] It was at this time that Moses was born; and he was lovely [m]in the sight of God, and he was nurtured three months in his father's home. [21] And after he had been set outside, Pharaoh's daughter [n]took him away and nurtured him as her own son. [22] Moses was educated in all the learning of the Egyptians, and he was a man of power in words and deeds. [23] But when he was approaching the age of forty, it entered his [o]mind to visit his brethren, the sons of Israel. [24] And when he saw one *of them* being treated unjustly, he defended him and took vengeance for the oppressed by striking down the Egyptian. [25] And he supposed that his brethren understood that God was granting them [p]deliverance [q]through him, but they did not understand. [26] On the following day he appeared to them as they were fighting together, and he tried to reconcile them in peace, saying, 'Men, you are brethren, why do you injure one another?' [27] But the one who was injuring his neighbor pushed him away, saying, 'WHO MADE YOU A RULER AND JUDGE OVER US? [28] YOU DO NOT MEAN TO KILL ME AS YOU KILLED THE

EGYPTIAN YESTERDAY, DO YOU?' [29] At this remark, MOSES FLED AND BECAME AN ALIEN IN THE LAND OF [r]MIDIAN, where he became the father of two sons.

[30] "After forty years had passed, AN ANGEL APPEARED TO HIM IN THE WILDERNESS OF MOUNT Sinai, IN THE FLAME OF A BURNING THORN BUSH. [31] When Moses saw it, he marveled at the sight; and as he approached to look *more* closely, there came the voice of the Lord: [32] 'I AM THE GOD OF YOUR FATHERS, THE GOD OF ABRAHAM AND ISAAC AND JACOB.' Moses shook with fear and would not venture to look. [33] BUT THE LORD SAID TO HIM, 'TAKE OFF THE SANDALS FROM YOUR FEET, FOR THE PLACE ON WHICH YOU ARE STANDING IS HOLY GROUND. [34] I HAVE CERTAINLY SEEN THE OPPRESSION OF MY PEOPLE IN EGYPT AND HAVE HEARD THEIR GROANS, AND I HAVE COME DOWN TO RESCUE THEM; [s]COME NOW, AND I WILL SEND YOU TO EGYPT.'

[35] "This Moses whom they disowned, saying, 'WHO MADE YOU A RULER AND A JUDGE?' is the one whom God [t]sent *to be* both a ruler and a deliverer with the [u]help of the angel who appeared to him in the thorn bush. [36] This man led them out, performing wonders and [v]signs in the land of Egypt and in the Red Sea and in the wilderness for forty years. [37] This is the Moses who said to the sons of Israel, 'GOD WILL RAISE UP FOR YOU A PROPHET [w]LIKE ME FROM YOUR BRETHREN.' [38] This is the one who was in the [x]congregation in the wilderness together with the angel who was speaking to him on Mount Sinai, and *who was* with our fathers; and he received living oracles to pass on to you. [39] Our fathers were unwilling to be obedient to him, but repudiated him and in their hearts turned back to Egypt, [40] SAYING TO AARON, 'MAKE FOR US GODS WHO WILL GO BEFORE US; FOR THIS MOSES WHO LED US OUT OF THE LAND OF EGYPT—WE DO NOT KNOW WHAT HAPPENED TO HIM.' [41] [y]At that time they made a [z]calf and brought a sacrifice to the idol, and were rejoicing in the works of their hands. [42] But God turned away and delivered them up to [aa]serve the [ab]host of heaven; as it is written in the book of the prophets, 'IT WAS NOT TO ME THAT YOU OFFERED VICTIMS AND SACRIFICES FORTY YEARS IN THE WILDERNESS, WAS IT, O HOUSE OF ISRAEL? [43] YOU ALSO TOOK ALONG THE TABERNACLE OF MOLOCH AND THE STAR OF THE GOD [ac]ROMPHA, THE IMAGES WHICH

YOU MADE TO WORSHIP. I ALSO WILL REMOVE YOU BEYOND
BABYLON.'

44 "Our fathers had the tabernacle of testimony in the wilderness, just
as He who spoke to Moses directed *him* to make it according to the
pattern which he had seen. 45 And having received it in their turn, our
fathers brought it in with [ad]Joshua upon dispossessing the [ae]nations
whom God drove out before our fathers, until the time of David.
46 *David* found favor in God's sight, and asked that he might find a
dwelling place for the [af]God of Jacob. 47 But it was Solomon who
built a house for Him. 48 However, the Most High does not dwell in
houses made by *human* hands; as the prophet says:

49 'HEAVEN IS MY THRONE,
AND EARTH IS THE FOOTSTOOL OF MY FEET;
WHAT KIND OF HOUSE WILL YOU BUILD FOR ME?' says the Lord,
'OR WHAT PLACE IS THERE FOR MY REPOSE?
50 'WAS IT NOT MY HAND WHICH MADE ALL THESE THINGS?'

51 "You men who are stiff-necked and uncircumcised in heart and
ears are always resisting the Holy Spirit; you are doing just as your
fathers did. 52 Which one of the prophets did your fathers not
persecute? They killed those who had previously announced the
coming of the Righteous One, whose betrayers and murderers you
have now become; 53 you who received the law as ordained by
angels, and *yet* did not keep it."

54 Now when they heard this, they were cut to the quick, and they
began gnashing their teeth at him. 55 But being full of the Holy
Spirit, he gazed intently into heaven and saw the glory of God, and
Jesus standing at the right hand of God; 56 and he said, "Behold, I see
the heavens opened up and the Son of Man standing at the right hand
of God." 57 But they cried out with a loud voice, and covered their
ears and rushed at him with one impulse. 58 When they had driven
him out of the city, they *began* stoning *him*; and the witnesses laid
aside their robes at the feet of a young man named Saul. 59 They
went on stoning Stephen as he called on *the Lord* and said, "Lord
Jesus, receive my spirit!" 60 Then falling on his knees, he cried out
with a loud voice, "Lord, do not hold this sin against them!" Having

said this, he [ag]fell asleep. (Acts 7)
https://www.biblegateway.com/passage/?search=Acts+7&version=N
ASB

This chapter opens with the high priest saying, "Are these things so?" So we have Stephen standing before the Sanhedrin, 70 men, plus the high priest. Below are the accusations which were made in the last chapter:

Then they secretly induced men to say, "We have heard him speak blasphemous words against Moses and *against* God." ¹² And they stirred up the people, the elders and the scribes, and they came up to him and dragged him away and brought him [j]before the [k]Council. ¹³ They put forward false witnesses who said, "This man incessantly speaks against this holy place and the Law; ¹⁴ for we have heard him say that this Nazarene, Jesus, will destroy this place and alter the customs which Moses handed down to us." ¹⁵ And fixing their gaze on him, all who were sitting in the [l]Council saw his face like the face of an angel. (Acts 6:11-15)

Stephen, by inspiration of the Holy Spirit, gives a detailed history from Abraham to Solomon. Solomon was about 1,000 years prior to Christ. Stephen actually ends his history with a quote from Isaiah 66:1, 2a, which is from the last chapter of Isaiah, written about 700 years before Christ. After the detailed history, Stephen says:

"You men who are stiff-necked and uncircumcised in heart and ears are always resisting the Holy Spirit; you are doing just as your fathers did. ⁵² Which one of the prophets did your fathers not persecute? They killed those who had previously announced the coming of the Righteous One, whose betrayers and murderers you have now become; ⁵³ you who received the law as ordained by angels, and *yet* did not keep it." (Acts 7:51-53)

This response did not go over very well, they then laid their robes at the feet of Saul, who later becomes the Apostle Paul, and they then stoned Stephen to death. Note that Stephen says that they are uncircumcised in heart.

For he is not a Jew who is one outwardly, nor is circumcision that which is outward in the flesh. [29] But he is a Jew who is one inwardly; and circumcision is that which is of the heart, by the Spirit, not by the letter; and his praise is not from men, but from God. (Romans 2:28)

Looking into the history we need to look at the big picture of eternity. Notice once Abraham is in the Jerusalem area, that he never owns any physical land. Remember in Revelation we saw New Jerusalem coming down out of Heaven. The Promised Land is in the future, it is Heaven coming down to earth. Stephen quotes from the first two verses of Isaiah 66. Below are the last verses from Isaiah 66, being the last chapter of Isaiah:

"For just as the new heavens and the new earth
Which I make will endure before Me," declares the LORD,
"So your offspring and your name will endure.
[23] "And it shall be from new moon to new moon
And from sabbath to sabbath,
All [m]mankind will come to bow down before Me," says the LORD.
[24] "Then they will go forth and look
On the corpses of the men
Who have [n]transgressed against Me.
For their worm will not die
And their fire will not be quenched;
And they will be an abhorrence to all [o]mankind." (Isaiah 66:22-24)

So we have the future New Heaven and new earth, along with the Lake of Fire. We see the children of Israel in slavery in Egypt for 400 years. Slavery in Egypt is a picture of our hearts in slavery to sin. Remember prior to Egypt that Jacob wrestled with God. Jacob was a shepherd. Jacob knew that when a sheep would go astray that he would dislocate the leg of the lamb. He would then carry the sheep on his shoulders. The lamb would grow fond of the Shepherd and never go astray again. Remember how the hip of Jacob of dislocated when he wrestled with God? Jacob learned and was shown a ladder to Heaven; He too saw the big picture. His name was then changed to Israel, which means to wrestle with God, a picture of a heart wrestling match. Within the nation of Israel there was always a remnant of heart believers, like Joshua and Caleb. One of my today's Bible chapter listening's (Joan Soft Bible App) was from Galatians 3.

You foolish Galatians, who has bewitched you, before whose eyes Jesus Christ was publicly portrayed *as* crucified? [2] This is the only thing I want to find out from you: did you receive the Spirit by the works of [b]the Law, or by [c]hearing with faith? [3] Are you so foolish? Having begun [d]by the Spirit, are you now [e]being perfected by the flesh? [4] Did you [f]suffer so many things in vain—if indeed it was in vain? [5] So then, does He who provides you with the Spirit and works [g]miracles among you, do it by the works of [h]the Law, or by [i]hearing with faith?

[6] [j]Even so Abraham BELIEVED GOD, AND IT WAS RECKONED TO HIM AS RIGHTEOUSNESS. [7] Therefore, [k]be sure that it is those who are of faith who are sons of Abraham. [8] The Scripture, foreseeing that God [l]would justify the [m]Gentiles by faith, preached the gospel beforehand to Abraham, *saying*, "ALL THE NATIONS WILL BE BLESSED IN YOU." [9] So then those who are of faith are blessed with [n]Abraham, the believer.

[10] For as many as are of the works of [o]the Law are under a curse; for it is written, "CURSED IS EVERYONE WHO DOES NOT ABIDE BY ALL THINGS WRITTEN IN THE BOOK OF THE LAW, TO PERFORM THEM." [11] Now that no one is justified [p]by [q]the Law before God is evident; for, "[r]THE RIGHTEOUS MAN SHALL LIVE BY FAITH." [12] [s]However, the Law is not [t]of faith; on the contrary, "HE WHO PRACTICES THEM SHALL LIVE [u]BY THEM." [13] Christ redeemed us from the curse of the Law, having become a curse for us—for it is written, "CURSED IS EVERYONE WHO HANGS ON A [v]TREE"— [14] in order that in Christ Jesus the blessing of Abraham might [w]come to the Gentiles, so that we would receive the promise of the Spirit through faith.

[15] Brethren, I speak [x]in terms of human relations: even though it is *only* a man's [y]covenant, yet when it has been ratified, no one sets it

aside or adds [z]conditions to it. [16] Now the promises were spoken to Abraham and to his seed. He does not say, "And to seeds," as *referring* to many, but *rather* to one, "And to your seed," that is, Christ. [17] What I am saying is this: the Law, which came four hundred and thirty years later, does not invalidate a covenant previously ratified by God, so as to nullify the promise. [18] For if the inheritance is [aa]based on law, it is no longer [ab]based on a promise; but God has granted it to Abraham by means of a promise.

[19] Why the Law then? It was added [ac]because of transgressions, having been ordained through angels by the [ad]agency of a mediator, until the seed would come to whom the promise had been made. [20] Now a mediator is not [ae]for one *party only*; whereas God is *only* one. [21] Is the Law then contrary to the promises of God? May it never be! For if a law had been given which was able to impart life, then righteousness [af]would indeed have been [ag]based on law. [22] But the Scripture has shut up [ah]everyone under sin, so that the promise by faith in Jesus Christ might be given to those who believe.

[23] But before faith came, we were kept in custody under the law, being shut up to the faith which was later to be revealed. [24] Therefore the Law has become our tutor *to lead us* to Christ, so that we may be justified by faith. [25] But now that faith has come, we are no longer under a [ai]tutor. [26] For you are all sons of God through faith in Christ Jesus. [27] For all of you who were baptized into Christ have clothed yourselves with Christ. [28] There is neither Jew nor Greek, there is neither slave nor free man, there is [aj]neither male nor female; for you are all one in Christ Jesus. [29] And if you [ak]belong to Christ, then you are Abraham's [al]descendants, heirs according to promise. (Galatians 3)

This physical earth is a proving ground,

But not for man, but for God.

God's Love is proven in Christ

Acts 8

Saul was in hearty agreement with putting him to death.

And on that day a great persecution [a]began against the church in Jerusalem, and they were all scattered throughout the regions of Judea and Samaria, except the apostles. ² *Some* devout men buried Stephen, and made loud lamentation over him. ³ But Saul *began* ravaging the church, entering house after house, and dragging off men and women, he would put them in prison.

⁴ Therefore, those who had been scattered went about [b]preaching the word. ⁵ Philip went down to the city of Samaria and *began* proclaiming [c]Christ to them. ⁶ The crowds with one accord were giving attention to what was said by Philip, as they heard and saw the [d]signs which he was performing. ⁷ For *in the case of* many who had unclean spirits, they were coming out *of them* shouting with a loud voice; and many who had been paralyzed and lame were healed. ⁸ So there was much rejoicing in that city.

⁹ Now there was a man named Simon, who formerly was practicing magic in the city and astonishing the people of Samaria, claiming to be someone great; ¹⁰ and they all, from smallest to greatest, were giving attention to him, saying, "This man is what is called the Great Power of God." ¹¹ And they were giving him attention because he had for a long time astonished them with his magic arts. ¹² But when they believed Philip preaching the good news about the kingdom of God and the name of Jesus Christ, they were being baptized, men and women alike. ¹³ Even Simon himself believed; and after being baptized, he continued on with Philip, and as he observed signs and great miracles taking place, he was constantly amazed.

[14] Now when the apostles in Jerusalem heard that Samaria had received the word of God, they sent them Peter and John, [15] who came down and prayed for them that they might receive the Holy Spirit. [16] For He had not yet fallen upon any of them; they had simply been baptized [e]in the name of the Lord Jesus. [17] Then they *began* laying their hands on them, and they were receiving the Holy Spirit. [18] Now when Simon saw that the Spirit was bestowed through the laying on of the apostles' hands, he offered them money, [19] saying, "Give this authority to me as well, so that everyone on whom I lay my hands may receive the Holy Spirit." [20] But Peter said to him, "May your silver perish with you, because you thought you could obtain the gift of God with money! [21] You have no part or portion in this [f]matter, for your heart is not right before God. [22] Therefore repent of this wickedness of yours, and pray the Lord that, if possible, the intention of your heart may be forgiven you. [23] For I see that you are in the gall of bitterness and in the [g]bondage of iniquity." [24] But Simon answered and said, "Pray to the Lord for me yourselves, so that nothing of what you have said may come upon me."

[25] So, when they had solemnly testified and spoken the word of the Lord, they started back to Jerusalem, and were preaching the gospel to many villages of the Samaritans.

[26] But an angel of the Lord spoke to Philip saying, "Get up and go south to the road that descends from Jerusalem to Gaza." ([h]This is a desert *road*.) [27] So he got up and went; and there was an Ethiopian eunuch, a court official of Candace, queen of the Ethiopians, who was in charge of all her treasure; and he had come to Jerusalem to worship, [28] and he was returning and sitting in his [i]chariot, and was reading the prophet Isaiah. [29] Then the Spirit said to Philip, "Go up and join this [i]chariot." [30] Philip ran up and heard him reading Isaiah the prophet, and said, "Do you understand what you are reading?" [31] And he said, "Well, how could I, unless someone guides me?" And he invited Philip to come up and sit with him. [32] Now the passage of Scripture which he was reading was this:

"HE WAS LED AS A SHEEP TO SLAUGHTER;
AND AS A LAMB BEFORE ITS SHEARER IS SILENT,

So HE DOES NOT OPEN HIS MOUTH.
33 "IN HUMILIATION HIS JUDGMENT WAS TAKEN AWAY;
WHO WILL [k]RELATE HIS [l]GENERATION?
FOR HIS LIFE IS REMOVED FROM THE EARTH."

34 The eunuch answered Philip and said, "Please *tell me*, of whom does the prophet say this? Of himself or of someone else?" 35 Then Philip opened his mouth, and beginning from this Scripture he preached Jesus to him. 36 As they went along the road they came to some water; and the eunuch *said, "Look! Water! What prevents me from being baptized?" 37 [[m]And Philip said, "If you believe with all your heart, you may." And he answered and said, "I believe that Jesus Christ is the Son of God."] 38 And he ordered the [n]chariot to stop; and they both went down into the water, Philip as well as the eunuch, and he baptized him. 39 When they came up out of the water, the Spirit of the Lord snatched Philip away; and the eunuch no longer saw him, [o]but went on his way rejoicing. 40 But Philip [p]found himself at [q]Azotus, and as he passed through he kept preaching the gospel to all the cities until he came to Caesarea. (Acts 8)
https://www.biblegateway.com/passage/?search=acts+8&version=N ASB

At the end of chapter 7 Stephen was stoned to death:

They went on stoning Stephen as he called on *the Lord* and said, "Lord Jesus, receive my spirit!" 60 Then falling on his knees, he cried out with a loud voice, "Lord, do not hold this sin against them!" Having said this, he [ag]fell asleep. (Acts 7:59, 60)

Acts 7:55 says that Stephen was full of the Holy Spirit. The question is **not**, how much of the Holy Spirit do you have? The question **is**, how much of you does the Holy Spirit have? Have you reached the end of yourself? Saul, later to be called Paul, heads up heavy persecution of the church. Many believers are scattered throughout Judea and Samaria. Jerusalem was in the region of Judea. Above Judea was Samaria. Above Samaria was Galilee. Remember only one disciple, that being Judas Iscariot, was from

Judea. The other eleven were from Galilee. Remember Samaritans were "half-breeds", and despised by outer shell Jews. Samaritans were half Jew and half gentile. Outer shell Jews would walk around Samaria to get to Galilee, adding several miles to their trip. How ignorant is this? Think about this, if you asked an outer shell Jew, who was your greatest king? They would probably say Solomon. Solomon was half Jew and half gentile! His mother was Bathsheba, the wife of Uriah the Hittite. Remember not all Israel is Israel. The best way I have found to distinguish is the use of outer shell Israel and heart Israel. As you read Scripture always notice the word heart. If you have time, read 2 Chronicles 6 and 7 (Solomon and the Temple). Remember David is a picture of Jesus. Remember Solomon is a picture of the Holy Spirit. Remember the Holy Spirit knit together the hearts of Jewish Heart Israel and gentile Heart Israel, Jews and gentiles, just like the parents of Solomon. So as we see all these new converts, whether they are from Judea, Samaria or Ethiopia (Africa), they are all heart Israel. Remember Jesus crushed this prejudice when He and His disciples walked straight through Samaria in John 4 with the "woman at the well". It is what's on the inside that counts (beats), your heart. It is absolutely no mistake that the biggest killer physically in this entire world, yes even countries without McDonalds, is heart disease. God uses the physical to teach us the spiritual. Notice what doctors do to many, many Americans with heart disease. They prescribe blood thinners. Spiritually the Blood of Jesus is a huge part of our Gospel. Without the shedding of Blood, there is no forgiveness of sins (Hebrews 9:22). What does today's church do to our Gospel? They water down the Blood, they thin out the Gospel.

A very, very good way to present the Gospel is through the 7 Feasts and Hanukah. This way you don't miss critical points. Today's Gospel many times only consists of the Passover. The virgin Mary conceived by the Holy Spirit on Hanukah, the Holyday of the Light. Imagine if you can, the Love and Humility of God Himself, emptying Himself of His Glory and entering as a single cell into the uterus of Mary. Nine months later Jesus is born of the virgin Mary on

Trumpets, the Jewish New Year's Day, being the first day of the Seventh Month. Eight days after Trumpets, a two day Feast, is the Day of Atonement, the Day our Lord was circumcised, this being the last required circumcision, all Jewish circumcisions were to point to the coming Messiah, the first Armor of God is the Loins of Truth, the genealogies in Luke 3 and Matthew 1, show this fulfillment. On the Cross, the Day of Atonement was ultimately fulfilled with the Veil to the Holy of Holies being circumcised. Remember the High Priest could only enter the Holy of Holies once a year, on the Day of Atonement. A few days later is the Feast of Tabernacles, showing how God Himself tabernacled amongst us, He dwelt amongst us. If you read the 2 Chronicles links below, notice you have these first three Feasts in 2 Chronicles 7. Then after dwelling as the Perfect God Man for 33 years, on Good Friday the 13th of Nisan, being month one of the Hebrew calendar, He is crucified, becoming our Passover Lamb, Friday evening begins the Jewish Saturday, He became the Lamb of God that takes away the sins of the world, then Jesus in the Tomb without sin fulfills the Feast of Unleavened Bread. Then after three days and three nights, our Lord and Savior conquers not only sin, but also death, rising from the dead on First Fruits, Resurrection Day, First Fruits being Day One of the 49 Days of the 7th and last, Feast of Weeks, during which time He showed Himself alive to many, then the very next Day is Pentecost, Day 50, the Day the Holy Spirit was given!!!

Isaiah 53, written 700 years before God became Flesh, and 2 Chronicles 6 & 7

https://www.biblegateway.com/passage/?search=isaiah+53&version=NASB

https://www.biblegateway.com/passage/?search=2%20Chronicles+6&version=NASB

https://www.biblegateway.com/passage/?search=2%20Chronicles+7&version=NASB

Acts 9

Now [a]Saul, still breathing [b]threats and murder against the disciples of the Lord, went to the high priest, [2] and asked for letters from him to the synagogues at Damascus, so that if he found any belonging to the Way, both men and women, he might bring them bound to Jerusalem. [3] As he was traveling, it happened that he was approaching Damascus, and suddenly a light from heaven flashed around him; [4] and he fell to the ground and heard a voice saying to him, "Saul, Saul, why are you persecuting Me?" [5] And he said, "Who are You, Lord?" And He *said*, "I am Jesus whom you are persecuting, [6] but get up and enter the city, and it will be told you what you must do." [7] The men who traveled with him stood speechless, hearing the [c]voice but seeing no one. [8] Saul got up from the ground, and though his eyes were open, he [d]could see nothing; and leading him by the hand, they brought him into Damascus. [9] And he was three days without sight, and neither ate nor drank.

[10] Now there was a disciple at Damascus named Ananias; and the Lord said to him in a vision, "Ananias." And he said, "Here I am, Lord." [11] And the Lord *said* to him, "Get up and go to the street called Straight, and inquire at the house of Judas for a man from Tarsus named Saul, for he is praying, [12] and he has seen [e]in a vision a man named Ananias come in and lay his hands on him, so that he might regain his sight." [13] But Ananias answered, "Lord, I have heard from many about this man, how much harm he did to Your [f]saints at Jerusalem; [14] and here he has authority from the chief priests to bind all who call on Your name." [15] But the Lord said to him, "Go, for he is a chosen [g]instrument of Mine, to bear My name before the Gentiles and kings and the sons of Israel; [16] for I will show him how much he must suffer for My name's sake." [17] So

Ananias departed and entered the house, and after laying his hands on him said, "Brother Saul, the Lord Jesus, who appeared to you on the road by which you were coming, has sent me so that you may regain your sight and be filled with the Holy Spirit." 18 And immediately there fell from his eyes something like scales, and he regained his sight, and he got up and was baptized; 19 and he took food and was strengthened.

Now for several days he was with the disciples who were at Damascus, 20 and immediately he *began* to proclaim Jesus in the synagogues, [h]saying, "He is the Son of God." 21 All those hearing him continued to be amazed, and were saying, "Is this not he who in Jerusalem destroyed those who called on this name, and *who* had come here for the purpose of bringing them bound before the chief priests?" 22 But Saul kept increasing in strength and confounding the Jews who lived at Damascus by proving that this *Jesus* is the [i]Christ.

23 When many days had elapsed, the Jews plotted together to do away with him, 24 but their plot became known to Saul. They were also watching the gates day and night so that they might put him to death; 25 but his disciples took him by night and let him down through *an opening in* the wall, lowering him in a large basket.

26 When he came to Jerusalem, he was trying to associate with the disciples; [j]but they were all afraid of him, not believing that he was a disciple. 27 But Barnabas took hold of him and brought him to the apostles and described to them how he had seen the Lord on the road, and that He had talked to him, and how at Damascus he had spoken out boldly in the name of Jesus. 28 And he was with them, [k]moving about freely in Jerusalem, speaking out boldly in the name of the Lord. 29 And he was talking and arguing with the [l]Hellenistic *Jews*; but they were attempting to put him to death. 30 But when the brethren learned *of it*, they brought him down to Caesarea and sent him away to Tarsus.

31 So the church throughout all Judea and Galilee and Samaria [m]enjoyed peace, being built up; and going on in the fear of the Lord and in the comfort of the Holy Spirit, it continued to increase.

³² Now as Peter was traveling through all *those regions*, he came down also to the [n]saints who lived at [o]Lydda. ³³ There he found a man named Aeneas, who had been bedridden eight years, for he was paralyzed. ³⁴ Peter said to him, "Aeneas, Jesus Christ heals you; get up and make your bed." Immediately he got up. ³⁵ And all who lived at [p]Lydda and Sharon saw him, and they turned to the Lord.

³⁶ Now in Joppa there was a disciple named Tabitha (which translated *in Greek* is called [q]Dorcas); this woman was abounding with deeds of kindness and charity which she continually did. ³⁷ And it happened [r]at that time that she fell sick and died; and when they had washed her body, they laid it in an upper room. ³⁸ Since Lydda was near Joppa, the disciples, having heard that Peter was there, sent two men to him, imploring him, "Do not delay in coming to us." ³⁹ So Peter arose and went with them. When he arrived, they brought him into the upper room; and all the widows stood beside him, weeping and showing all the [s]tunics and garments that Dorcas used to make while she was with them. ⁴⁰ But Peter sent them all out and knelt down and prayed, and turning to the body, he said, "Tabitha, arise." And she opened her eyes, and when she saw Peter, she sat up. ⁴¹ And he gave her his hand and raised her up; and calling the [t]saints and widows, he presented her alive. ⁴² It became known all over Joppa, and many believed in the Lord. ⁴³ And Peter stayed many days in Joppa with a tanner *named* Simon. (Acts 9)
https://www.biblegateway.com/passage/?search=acts+9&version=NASB

Saul name meaning: For a meaning of the name Shaul or Saul, NOBSE Study Bible Name List reads **Asked (of God)**, although God is not referred to in this name. BDB Theological Dictionary interprets our name Saul with **Asked (of YHWH)**. Jones' Dictionary of Old Testament Proper Names reads a more correct **Asked For**.
http://www.abarim-publications.com/Meaning/Saul.html#.V_VgdjAVCUk

Paul name meaning: The name Paulus means **Little** or **Small**.
http://www.abarim-publications.com/Meaning/Paul.html#.V_VhSTAVCUk

This chapter has the conversion of Saul. Some think that his name was changed to Paul in this chapter, but we see him still called Saul up until Acts 13:9. Note the street name Ananias was told to go to, to find Saul; Straight. Note that in the verse that Saul is first called Paul that there is a crooked vs. Straight relationship. The crooked i.e. the crook, the thief being the sinful flesh vs. the Straight i.e. the Spirit.

But Saul, who was also *known as* Paul, [a]filled with the Holy Spirit, fixed his gaze on him, [10] and said, "You who are full of all deceit and fraud, you son of the devil, you enemy of all righteousness, will you not cease to make crooked the straight ways of the Lord? (Acts 13:9, 10)

So what can we learn from this? I believe we are seeing what is depicted in Galatians 5, the battle between the flesh and the Spirit. In Romans 7:14-25 we see the battle firsthand. Within our hearts there are two at conflict with one another. The heart is the battleground. What we think and do in our hearts is everything. Many, many people have the fake outer shell down to a "t". They preach the "t", i.e. the Cross, but in their heart, they are severely losing the battle. When the heart rears its ugly face, many times many people have already paid the price, the individual and his or her loved ones suffer greatly. Know your enemy; don't forget the man or woman in the mirror.

Opponents:
https://www.biblegateway.com/passage/?search=Galatians+5&version=NASB

The Battle:
https://www.biblegateway.com/passage/?search=Romans+7%3A14-25&version=NASB

When you think of the name Saul, you might think of the first king of Israel. The people wanted a king. God did not prefer that, He was to be their King. As the name Saul means, the people "asked for" a king. The Saul in this chapter, Saul of Tarsus, and king Saul were both from the Tribe of Benjamin. Remember Saul was the outer appearance king. He was very handsome and head and shoulders above all other men. But yet at times he was full of God's Spirit.

He had a son whose name was Saul, a choice and handsome *man*, and there was not a more handsome person than he among the sons of Israel; from his shoulders and up he was taller than any of the people. (1 Samuel 9)

King Saul was anointed king at Gilgal (1 Samuel 11). Remember Gilgal was the place of the mass Circumcision of Israel just prior to entering the Promised Land (Joshua 5). Remember the deeper meaning of the Circumcision Covenant was to point to the future Christ. It was to signify the future Circumcision of the Heart, which Christ accomplished, the Veil tore, from Top to bottom, God tore it. After the Work of Christ, He sent His Holy Spirit, now we have a fighting chance; if we are humble, seek His face, and turn from the sinful flesh we will have victory (2 Chronicles 7:14). It is interesting that the very first king of Israel had a divided kingdom to deal with; a picture of a divided heart i.e. a picture of the flesh vs. the Spirit from the get go. King Saul never did unite the divided kingdom of Israel. Israel was a divided kingdom i.e. a divided heart. There was the Kingdom of Judah and the kingdom of Israel (aka Ephraim). King Saul is a picture of the flesh vs. the Spirit. At the end of Romans 7, we see the Solution to the sin problem, Jesus Christ.

King David was chosen by God, not by outer shell, but by the heart.

When they entered, he looked at Eliab and thought, "Surely the LORD'S anointed is before Him." [7] But the LORD said to Samuel, "Do not look at his appearance or at the height of his stature, because I have rejected him; for [b]God *sees* not as man sees, for man looks at the outward appearance, but the LORD looks at the heart." (1 Samuel 16:6, 7)

King David is a picture of the Christ. King David would unite Israel; the divided heart would become one. The name David means beloved. Remember the baptism of Christ, "This is my Beloved Son in Whom I am well pleased." Solomon is born to King David and Bathsheba. This is a picture of David, Heart Israel uniting with gentile Heart Israel, a picture of the future Groom (Jesus) and Bride (church). Until we are united for Eternity we are given the Holy Spirit. Solomon is a picture of the Holy Spirit. Solomon builds the Temple. This corresponds to us being the temple of the Holy Spirit. Solomon had the option of anything and everything. Solomon had freedom to choose. The lust of the flesh and the lust of the eyes and the boastful pride of life were at his disposal. With love (Love i.e. Christ) comes choice (Freedom i.e. the Holy Spirit). Solomon learned that the lust of the flesh and the lust of the eyes and the boastful pride of life is equated to vanity and vanity and vanity. Leading to "steal and to kill and to destroy." https://www.biblegateway.com/passage/?search=Ecclesiastes+1&version=NASB

So the Saul in this chapter is very similar to king Saul in that he has all the best outer shell qualities going for him, "confidence in the flesh".

Beware of the dogs, beware of the evil workers, beware of the [a]false circumcision; [3] for we are the *true* [b]circumcision, who worship in the Spirit of God and glory in Christ Jesus and put no confidence in the flesh, [4] although I myself might have confidence even in the flesh. If anyone else has a mind to put confidence in the flesh, I far more: [5] circumcised the eighth day, of the nation of Israel, of the tribe of Benjamin, a Hebrew of Hebrews; as to the Law, a Pharisee; [6] as to zeal, a persecutor of the church; as to the righteousness which is in the Law, found blameless. (Philippians 3:2-6)

Saul to Paul, humbled, getting knocked off his high horse (We don't know if Saul was actually on a physical horse, but either way he got humbled). Saul saw the Light and after Acts 13 is always called Paul, Paul meaning little or small i.e. humbled. Note: Damascus is about 150 miles north of Jerusalem. Damascus is in Syria.

We have a connection with both Saul's to the Tribe of Benjamin. Remember in the Old Testament, Joseph and Benjamin were the sons of Rachel. Rachel was the wife that Jacob (Israel) loved. The name Rachel means lamb. She was buried at Bethlehem. She died at the birth of Benjamin. Jesus would be the Lamb born at Bethlehem for the sins of the people, a picture of Benjamin (Judges 19-21). The Tribe of Benjamin was almost totally destroyed due to their horrible sin.   Remember the many pictures of Christ in Joseph. He saved the world from death/starvation. Remember the silver cup placed in the grain bag of Benjamin? In this chapter we see Saul at the house of "Judas". Remember how Judas betrayed Jesus for silver? So this Tribe of Benjamin connection can also be connected to a picture of a divided heart. Joseph is a picture of the inner Heart Christ and Benjamin the sinful flesh; another picture of the sinful flesh vs. the Spirit.

In the second part of this chapter we see Peter taking part in some awesome miracles. A lame man walks at the Name of Jesus and a dead woman is raised in the "Upper Room". Remember the Upper Room at Jerusalem, where the Holy Spirit was given. Her body (the church) was washed (Jesus) and she was given Life (the Holy Spirit). Jesus said you must be born of the Water and of the Spirit in John 3.

But when the kindness of God our Savior and *His* love for mankind appeared, [5] He saved us, not on the basis of deeds which we have done in righteousness, but according to His mercy, by the washing of regeneration and renewing by the Holy Spirit, [6] whom He poured out upon us richly through Jesus Christ our Savior, [7] so that being

222

justified by His grace we would be made heirs [a]according to *the* hope of eternal life. (Titus 3:4-7)

Remember even after Jesus changed Simon's name to Peter (Rock, Stone or even Pebble to stress Humility), that when Peter would "get in the flesh", Jesus would call him Simon. We have yet another flesh vs. the Spirit example. At the very end of this chapter we see Peter staying at the house of Simon the tanner. Simon means hearing. Faith comes by hearing. But remember there are two voices, the Voice of Truth and the voice of the sinful flesh.

https://www.youtube.com/watch?v=tcuiulwtpa4

Acts 10

Now *there was* a man at Caesarea named Cornelius, a centurion of what was called the Italian [a]cohort, 2 a devout man and one who feared God with all his household, and gave many [b]alms to the *Jewish* people and prayed to God continually. 3 About the [c]ninth hour of the day he clearly saw in a vision an angel of God who had *just* come in and said to him, "Cornelius!" 4 And fixing his gaze on him and being much alarmed, he said, "What is it, Lord?" And he said to him, "Your prayers and [d]alms have ascended as a memorial before God. 5 Now dispatch *some* men to Joppa and send for a man *named* Simon, who is also called Peter; 6 he is staying with a tanner *named* Simon, whose house is by the sea." 7 When the angel who was speaking to him had left, he summoned two of his [e]servants and a devout soldier of those who were his personal attendants, 8 and after he had explained everything to them, he sent them to Joppa.

9 On the next day, as they were on their way and approaching the city, Peter went up on the housetop about the [f]sixth hour to pray.

[10] But he became hungry and was desiring to eat; but while they were making preparations, he fell into a trance; [11] and he *saw the [g]sky opened up, and an [h]object like a great sheet coming down, lowered by four corners to the ground, [12] and there were in it all *kinds of* four-footed animals and [i]crawling creatures of the earth and birds of the [j]air. [13] A voice came to him, "Get up, Peter, [k]kill and eat!" [14] But Peter said, "By no means, Lord, for I have never eaten anything [l]unholy and unclean." [15] Again a voice *came* to him a second time, "What God has cleansed, no *longer* consider [m]unholy." [16] This happened three times, and immediately the [n]object was taken up into the [o]sky.

[17] Now while Peter was greatly perplexed in [p]mind as to what the vision which he had seen might be, behold, the men who had been sent by Cornelius, having asked directions for Simon's house, appeared at the gate; [18] and calling out, they were asking whether Simon, who was also called Peter, was staying there. [19] While Peter was reflecting on the vision, the Spirit said to him, "Behold, [q]three men are looking for you. [20] But get up, go downstairs and accompany them [r]without misgivings, for I have sent them Myself." [21] Peter went down to the men and said, "Behold, I am the one you are looking for; what is the reason for which you have come?" [22] They said, "Cornelius, a centurion, a righteous and God-fearing man well spoken of by the entire nation of the Jews, was *divinely* directed by a holy angel to send for you *to come* to his house and hear [s]a message from you." [23] So he invited them in and gave them lodging.

And on the next day he got up and went away with them, and some of the brethren from Joppa accompanied him. [24] On the following day he entered Caesarea. Now Cornelius was waiting for them and had called together his relatives and close friends. [25] When Peter entered, Cornelius met him, and fell at his feet and [t]worshiped *him*. [26] But Peter raised him up, saying, "Stand up; I too am *just* a man." [27] As he talked with him, he entered and *found many people assembled. [28] And he said to them, "You yourselves know how unlawful it is for a man who is a Jew to associate with a foreigner or to visit him; and *yet* God has shown me that I should not call any man [u]unholy or unclean. [29] That is why I came without even raising any objection when I was sent for. So I ask for what reason you have sent for me."

30 Cornelius said, "Four days ago to this hour, I was praying in my house during the [v]ninth hour; and behold, a man stood before me in shining garments, 31 and he *said, 'Cornelius, your prayer has been heard and your [w]alms have been remembered before God. 32 Therefore send to Joppa and invite Simon, who is also called Peter, to come to you; he is staying at the house of Simon *the* tanner by the sea.' 33 So I sent for you immediately, and you have [x]been kind enough to come. Now then, we are all here present before God to hear all that you have been commanded by the Lord."

34 Opening his mouth, Peter said:

"I most certainly understand *now* that God is not one to show partiality, 35 but in every nation the man who [y]fears Him and [z]does what is right is welcome to Him. 36 The word which He sent to the sons of Israel, preaching [aa]peace through Jesus Christ (He is Lord of all)— 37 you yourselves know the thing which took place throughout all Judea, starting from Galilee, after the baptism which John proclaimed. 38 [ab]*You know of* Jesus of Nazareth, how God anointed Him with the Holy Spirit and with power, [ac]and *how* He went about doing good and healing all who were oppressed by the devil, for God was with Him. 39 We are witnesses of all the things He did both in the [ad]land of the Jews and in Jerusalem. They also put Him to death by hanging Him on a [ae]cross. 40 God raised Him up on the third day and granted that He become visible, 41 not to all the people, but to witnesses who were chosen beforehand by God, *that is*, to us who ate and drank with Him after He arose from the dead. 42 And He ordered us to [af]preach to the people, and solemnly to testify that this is the One who has been appointed by God as Judge of the living and the dead. 43 Of Him all the prophets bear witness that through His name everyone who believes in Him receives forgiveness of sins."

44 While Peter was still speaking these words, the Holy Spirit fell upon all those who were listening to the [ag]message. 45 All the [ah]circumcised believers who came with Peter were amazed, because the gift of the Holy Spirit had been poured out on the Gentiles also.

⁴⁶ For they were hearing them speaking with tongues and exalting God. Then Peter answered, ⁴⁷ "Surely no one can refuse the water for these to be baptized who have received the Holy Spirit just as we *did*, can he?" ⁴⁸ And he ordered them to be baptized in the name of Jesus Christ. Then they asked him to stay on for a few days. (Acts 10) https://www.biblegateway.com/passage/?search=acts+10&version=NASB

This chapter opens with Cornelius, a gentile Roman soldier, being a centurion. A centurion was in charge of at least 100 soldiers or more. Cornelius is a devout man and in awe of God. Notice he is praying at the ninth hour. Remember the prayer/sacrifice times in the Old Testament. The times were the third, the sixth and the ninth hours. These times correspond to the Day of the Crucifixion (Mark 15). We see a ton of happenings in the Bible around these three times. Remember in the Old Testament how Daniel prayed three times a day facing Jerusalem during the captivity. Daniel knew freedom would come in Jerusalem (the Cross and Pentecost). We learned that Jerusalem is a picture of the world's heart. Jesus took our sin upon Himself within the walls of Jerusalem, within the walls of our heart, and then He removed our sin outside of the walls of our heart to Golgotha. When Jesus said in John 3 that you must be born of the Water and the Spirit, the removing of our sin was the Water. Titus 3:5 beautifully defines John 3:5.

We know that Jesus is the Centerpiece of the entire Bible. This chapter brings up dietary Laws. What can we learn from all these dietary Laws? How do these Laws point to the Christ? First off, Peter is a Jew, and he is staying at Simon the tanner's house by the sea. Now remember that many, many more dietary laws were added by the Jewish rabbis over the years. So let's stick to the Bible dietary Laws. A tanner worked with animals that were clean and unclean. So technically Peter, according to most Jews wouldn't be allowed to stay there. We are at Joppa. Joppa is on the sea, about 30 miles northwest of Jerusalem. Cornelius is another 30 miles further north on the sea at Caesarea. Simon means to hear, and he is a tanner. So we are about to hear the hidden Message of the unclean/Clean and unholy/Holy.

In Romans 1 we are taught that we can see God in nature. Observing nature we see that some animals eat only from the plant kingdom, being called herbivores. We see that some animals eat only from the animal kingdom, being called carnivores. If we look hard enough we see that there is yet one more group that eats from both kingdoms, they are called omnivores. The omnivores are the unclean in the Bible. For example camels, pigs, badgers, catfish, lobsters, shrimp; they all eat from both kingdoms. Man as well eats from both kingdoms. So what is God trying to teach us? We humans are also unclean, but Jesus washes us.

Then He *poured water into the basin, and began to wash the disciples' feet and to wipe them with the towel with which He was girded. 6 So He *came to Simon Peter. He *said to Him, "Lord, do You wash my feet?" 7 Jesus answered and said to him, "What I do you do not realize now, but you will understand hereafter." 8 Peter *said to Him, "Never shall You wash my feet!" Jesus answered him, "If I do not wash you, you have no part with Me." 9 Simon Peter *said to Him, "Lord, *then wash* not only my feet, but also my hands and my head." (John 13:5-9)

After Jesus called the crowd to Him, He said to them, "Hear and understand. 11 *It is* not what enters into the mouth *that* defiles the man, but what proceeds out of the mouth, this defiles the man."

12 Then the disciples *came and *said to Him, "Do You know that the Pharisees were [d]offended when they heard this statement?" 13 But He answered and said, "Every plant which My heavenly Father did not plant shall be uprooted. 14 Let them alone; they are blind guides [e]of the blind. And if a blind man guides a blind man, both will fall into a pit."

¹⁵ Peter ^[f]said to Him, "Explain the parable to us." ^{16 [g]}Jesus said, "Are you still lacking in understanding also? ¹⁷ Do you not understand that everything that goes into the mouth passes into the stomach, and is ^[h]eliminated? ¹⁸ But the things that proceed out of the mouth come from the heart, and those defile the man. ¹⁹ For out of the heart come evil thoughts, murders, adulteries, ^[i]fornications, thefts, false witness, slanders. ²⁰ These are the things which defile the man; but to eat with unwashed hands does not defile the man." (Matthew 15:10-20)

So when we see the terms unclean and unholy throughout Scripture these terms are in fact pointing to the Christ and the sending of His Holy Spirit on Pentecost, Washed and Filled. When we are Washed by Jesus, we go from unclean to Clean. When we submit to the Holy Spirit, walking by the Spirit, we go from unholy to Holy. When you come across Scriptures that seem to say that you can lose your salvation, take another look. The Work of Jesus is just that, the Work of Jesus, not our work. His Work equates to our Present and Eternal Sabbath Rest. If your heart is Washed you are Clean. The confusion comes into play with the unholy/Holy part. We can be saved, yet we can be constantly defeated in the battle within, the battle between the flesh and the Spirit. Remember it is not how much of the Holy Spirit that you have, **but** how much of you does the Holy Spirit have. **I don't have Him, He has me.**

He saved us, not on the basis of deeds which we have done in righteousness, but according to His mercy, by the washing of regeneration and renewing by the Holy Spirit, ⁶ whom He poured out upon us richly through Jesus Christ our Savior, ⁷ so that being justified by His grace we would be made heirs ^[a]according to *the* hope of eternal life. (Titus 3:5-7)

Jesus answered, "Truly, truly, I say to you, unless one is born of water and the Spirit he cannot enter into the kingdom of God. (John 3:5)

It is very interesting that there are 33 (age of Jesus at the Cross) verses in the New Testament that mention unclean:

It is very interesting as well that there are 7 (after the 7 Feasts,
Jesus sent the Holy Spirit) verses in the New Testament that
mention unholy:

I most certainly understand that God is not
one to show partiality, but in every nation the
man who is in awe of Him and does what is
right is welcome to Him. (Acts 10:34, 35)

Acts 11

Now the apostles and the brethren who were throughout Judea heard
that the Gentiles also had received the word of God. ² And when
Peter came up to Jerusalem, [a]those who were circumcised took
issue with him, ³ saying, "You [b]went to uncircumcised men and ate
with them." ⁴ But Peter began *speaking* [c]and *proceeded* to explain
to them in orderly sequence, saying, ⁵ "I was in the city of Joppa
praying; and in a trance I saw a vision, an [d]object coming down like
a great sheet lowered by four corners from [e]the sky; and it came
right down to me, ⁶ and when I had fixed my gaze on it and was
observing it [f]I saw the four-footed animals of the earth and the wild
beasts and the [g]crawling creatures and the birds of the [h]air. ⁷ I also
heard a voice saying to me, 'Get up, Peter; [i]kill and eat.' ⁸ But I

229

said, 'By no means, Lord, for nothing [i]unholy or unclean has ever entered my mouth.' [9] But a voice from heaven answered a second time, 'What God has cleansed, no longer [k]consider unholy.' [10] This happened three times, and everything was drawn back up into [l]the sky. [11] And behold, at that moment three men appeared at the house in which we were *staying*, having been sent to me from Caesarea. [12] The Spirit told me to go with them [m]without misgivings. These six brethren also went with me and we entered the man's house. [13] And he reported to us how he had seen the angel [n]standing in his house, and saying, 'Send to Joppa and have Simon, who is also called Peter, brought here; [14] and he will speak words to you by which you will be saved, you and all your household.' [15] And as I began to speak, the Holy Spirit fell upon them just as *He did* upon us at the beginning. [16] And I remembered the word of the Lord, how He used to say, 'John baptized with water, but you will be baptized [o]with the Holy Spirit.' [17] Therefore if God gave to them the same gift as *He gave* to us also after believing in the Lord Jesus Christ, who was I that I could [p]stand in God's way?" [18] When they heard this, they [q]quieted down and glorified God, saying, "Well then, God has granted to the Gentiles also the repentance *that leads* to life."

[19] So then those who were scattered because of the [r]persecution that occurred in connection with Stephen made their way [s]to Phoenicia and Cyprus and Antioch, speaking the word to no one except to Jews alone. [20] But there were some of them, men of Cyprus and Cyrene, who came to Antioch and *began* speaking to the [t]Greeks also, [u]preaching the Lord Jesus. [21] And the hand of the Lord was with them, and a large number who believed turned to the Lord. [22] The [v]news about them [w]reached the ears of the church at Jerusalem, and they sent Barnabas off [x]to Antioch. [23] Then when he arrived and [y]witnessed the grace of God, he rejoiced and *began* to encourage them all with [z]resolute heart to remain *true* to the Lord; [24] for he was a good man, and full of the Holy Spirit and of faith. And considerable [aa]numbers were [ab]brought to the Lord. [25] And he left for Tarsus to look for Saul; [26] and when he had found him, he brought him to Antioch. And for an entire year they [ac]met with the church and taught considerable [ad]numbers; and the disciples were first called Christians in Antioch.

²⁷ Now ^[ae]at this time some prophets came down from Jerusalem to Antioch. ²⁸ One of them named Agabus stood up and *began* to indicate ^[af]by the Spirit that there would certainly be a great famine all over the ^[ag]world. ^[ah]And this took place in the *reign* of Claudius. ²⁹ And in the proportion that any of the disciples had means, each of them determined to send *a contribution* for the ^[ai]relief of the brethren living in Judea. ³⁰ And this they did, sending it ^[aj]in charge of Barnabas and Saul to the elders. (Acts 11)
https://www.biblegateway.com/passage/?search=Acts+11&version=NASB

We should probably take a closer look at the city of Joppa. This is where Peter was when he saw the great sheet coming down. The sheet with the animals was teaching Peter that eating particular animals doesn't make you unholy or unclean. The unclean animals were all omnivores, like humans. The dietary Law was intended to teach us that we are sinners, unclean in the heart, there is no one righteous, not even one (Romans 3:10). The gentiles didn't have dietary Laws. Gentiles were on their way to get Peter to come to their gentile city, Caesarea. God was showing Peter that it was okay to go with them, to enter their house and to eat with them. Don't forget either that the whole purpose for Circumcision was to point to the coming Christ Child.

Joppa means beautiful. We saw a beautiful thing last chapter, Jews and gentiles united in one flock. So you have Peter being sent out from Joppa to the gentiles at Caesarea. In the Old Testament Book of Jonah, written over 700 years before the physical birth of Christ, we see Jonah sailing from Joppa. He was not listening to the command of God to go preach to the gentiles. But God got him to Nineveh regardless. 120,000 gentiles turned to God adding to His flock. This was the largest heart revival in all Bible history. Note as well that much of the building materials for the Temple came through the port at Joppa from the gentile countries of Tyre and Lebanon. So you have gentile and Jewish building supplies used in building the Temple (picture of Jews and gentiles building the church). Note also that the outer Gate of the Temple leading into

231

the Court of Women was called Beautiful. Remember that the name, Court of Women, is better translated Court of the Bride, being us. The inner Gate was Nicanor, which means Man of Victory. So you have a picture of the beautiful bride (us) walking through the Court of the Bride, then walking up the Temple stairs to our Groom, the Man of Victory. The Holy of Holies Veil has been torn from Top to bottom. The Holy Place with the Light, Incense and Bread, along with the Bronze Altar and Basin, all were fulfilled by our Groom, the Man of Victory; Jesus Christ!!!

Notice below in John 10:16 the term "other sheep", these are the gentiles. Also notice that Jesus addresses some of the Jews saying that they are not of His sheep, John 10:24-26. Also note that there is one flock.

I am the good shepherd, and I know My own and My own know Me, [15] even as the Father knows Me and I know the Father; and I lay down My life for the sheep. [16] I have other sheep, which are not of this fold; I must bring them also, and they will hear My voice; and they will become one flock *with* one shepherd. [17] For this reason the Father loves Me, because I lay down My life so that I may take it again. [18] No one has taken it away from Me, but I lay it down on My own initiative. I have authority to lay it down, and I have authority to take it up again. This commandment I received from My Father."

[19] A division occurred again among the Jews because of these words. [20] Many of them were saying, "He has a demon and is insane. Why do you listen to Him?" [21] Others were saying, "These are not the sayings of one demon-possessed. A demon cannot open the eyes of the blind, can he?"

[22] At that time the Feast of the Dedication took place at Jerusalem; [23] it was winter, and Jesus was walking in the temple in the portico of Solomon. [24] The Jews then gathered around Him, and were saying to Him, "How long [b]will You keep us in suspense? If You are [c]the Christ, tell us plainly." [25] Jesus answered them, "I told you, and you do not believe; the works that I do in My Father's name, these testify of Me. [26] But you do not believe because you are not of My sheep.

²⁷ My sheep hear My voice, and I know them, and they follow Me; ²⁸ and I give eternal life to them, and they will never perish; and no one will snatch them out of My hand. ²⁹ [d]My Father, who has given *them* to Me, is greater than all; and no one is able to snatch *them* out of the Father's hand. ³⁰ I and the Father are [c]one." (John 10:14-30)

Here is a link to Jonah 1, just page through with arrows at right of page to go through the four short chapters:
https://www.biblegateway.com/passage/?search=jonah+1&version=NASB

Jesus mentions Jonah in Matthew 12:

Then some of the scribes and Pharisees said to Him, "Teacher, we want to see a [ak]sign from You." ³⁹ But He answered and said to them, "An evil and adulterous generation craves for a [al]sign; and *yet* no [am]sign will be given to it but the [an]sign of Jonah the prophet; ⁴⁰ for just as JONAH WAS THREE DAYS AND THREE NIGHTS IN THE BELLY OF THE SEA MONSTER, so will the Son of Man be three days and three nights in the heart of the earth. ⁴¹ The men of Nineveh will stand up with this generation at the judgment, and will condemn it because they repented at the preaching of Jonah; and behold, something greater than Jonah is here. ⁴² *The* Queen of *the* South will rise up with this generation at the judgment and will condemn it, because she came from the ends of the earth to hear the wisdom of Solomon; and behold, something greater than Solomon is here. (Matthew 12:38-42)

Acts 12

Now about that time [a]Herod the king laid hands on some who belonged to the church in order to mistreat them. ² And he had James the brother of John put to death with a sword. ³ When he saw that it pleased the Jews, he proceeded to arrest Peter also. Now [b]it was during the days of Unleavened Bread. [4] When he had seized him, he put him in prison, delivering him to four [c]squads of soldiers to guard him, intending after the Passover to bring him out before the people. [5] So Peter was kept in the prison, but prayer for him was being made fervently by the church to God.

[6] On [d]the very night when Herod was about to bring him forward, Peter was sleeping between two soldiers, bound with two chains, and guards in front of the door were watching over the prison. [7] And behold, an angel of the Lord suddenly appeared and a light shone in the cell; and he struck Peter's side and woke him up, saying, "Get up quickly." And his chains fell off his hands. [8] And the angel said to him, "Gird yourself and [e]put on your sandals." And he did so. And he *said to him, "Wrap your cloak around you and follow me." [9] And he went out and continued to follow, and he did not know that what was being done by the angel was real, but thought he was seeing a vision. [10] When they had passed the first and second guard, they came to the iron gate that leads into the city, which opened for them by itself; and they went out and went along one street, and immediately the angel departed from him. [11] When Peter came [f]to himself, he said, "Now I know for sure that the Lord has sent forth His angel and rescued me from the hand of Herod and from all [g]that the Jewish people were expecting." [12] And when he realized *this*, he went to the house of Mary, the mother of John who was also called Mark, where many were gathered together and were praying. [13] When he knocked at the door of the gate, a servant-girl named Rhoda came to answer. [14] When she recognized Peter's voice, because of her joy she did not open the gate, but ran in and announced that Peter was standing in front of the gate. [15] They said to her, "You are out of your mind!" But she kept insisting that it was so. They kept saying, "It is his angel." [16] But Peter continued knocking; and when they had opened *the door*, they saw him and were amazed. [17] But motioning to them with his hand to be silent, he described to them how the Lord had led him out of the prison. And he said, "Report these things to [h]James and the brethren." Then he left and went to another place.

¹⁸ Now when day came, there was no small disturbance among the soldiers *as to* [i]what could have become of Peter. ¹⁹ When Herod had searched for him and had not found him, he examined the guards and ordered that they be led away *to execution*. Then he went down from Judea to Caesarea and was spending time there.

²⁰ Now he was very angry with the people of Tyre and Sidon; and with one accord they came to him, and having won over Blastus the king's chamberlain, they were asking for peace, because their country was fed by the king's country. ²¹ On an appointed day Herod, having put on his royal apparel, took his seat on the [j]rostrum and *began* delivering an address to them. ²² The people kept crying out, "The voice of a god and not of a man!" ²³ And immediately an angel of the Lord struck him because he did not give God the glory, and he was eaten by worms and [k]died.

²⁴ But the word of the Lord continued to grow and to be multiplied.

²⁵ And Barnabas and Saul returned [l]from Jerusalem when they had fulfilled their [m]mission, taking along with *them* John, who was also called Mark. (Acts 12)
https://www.biblegateway.com/passage/?search=acts+12&version=NASB

We are still in Jerusalem. We are seeing persecution, which is actually making the church grow outward from Jerusalem. Herod arrests some of the believers and has James put to death. This is the only recorded death of an apostle in the Bible. Remember James is the Greek form of Jacob. So it is interesting that the only recorded apostle death is "Jacob". In the Old Testament Jacob was given the name Israel. Israel is synonymous with a heart wrestling match i.e. the flesh vs. the Spirit. It is a daily battle to die to self, to die to "Jacob". Oddly enough as well is that Herod is a direct descendent of Esau. Remember Jacob and Esau were twin brothers from Isaac and Rebekah. Through Abraham, Isaac and Jacob came the Promised One, Jesus. Hebrews 12:16 says that Esau was godless. Here is a link showing Herod coming from Esau.

There are quite a few Herod's in the Bible. The first one was Herod
the great who rebuilt the Temple. He was also the one who had all
the male children that were under two executed in Bethlehem after
the birth of Jesus. Then his son would have been the Herod during
the execution of Jesus. The Herod in this chapter is the grandson of
Herod the great.

James/Jacob means supplanter, or heel catcher. James was one of
the inner three of Jesus; Peter, James and John. These three
witnessed a few things that the other disciples did not, one being
the Transfiguration with Jesus, Moses (Law) and Elijah (Prophets).
Jesus was the fulfillment of the Law and Prophets. Remember the
Law and Prophets are the two witnesses against us in Revelation 11.
But Jesus is born, Revelation 12, and comes to our defense as our
Advocate i.e. Intercessor. So when you look at the name meanings
of Peter (Stone), James (Supplanter) and John (Grace) you get the
Stone (Law i.e. Stone Tablets/Ten Commandments) supplanted
(fulfilled) by Grace i.e. Jesus. Through Jesus the Stone Tablets of
our heart become living stones. Peter writes about the living stones
in 1 Peter 2. These living stones, being us, are the building blocks of
Heaven. Jesus is the Chief Cornerstone, the apostles are the
foundations, and the twelve tribes are the gates (Revelation 21).

"Do not think that I came to abolish the Law or the Prophets; I did
not come to abolish but to fulfill. (Matthew 5:17)

So we know what actually happened to Peter. An angel of the Lord
came and freed him from prison. But looking a little deeper we see
this all happening during Passover and the Unleavened Bread
Week. Remember Unleavened Bread is one of the Three Required
Feast Weeks required by all Jewish males to attend. So Jerusalem is
again packed with people from all over the occupied world. Herod
intended on bringing Peter out after the Passover, during the
Unleavened Bread Week.

Jesus was in the Tomb (and in the Bosom of Abraham, "setting the captives free", Ephesians 4) during the first part of the Week of Unleavened Bread, 3 Days and 3 Nights. In the midst of that Week is First Fruits, Resurrection Day. Death could not hold Jesus captive. We seem to have a picture of this with Peter. I believe he was led out of prison on First Fruits, the "captive was set free". Peter's chains fell off. He'd been set free, in the very same timeframe as Jesus.

And coming to Him as to a living stone which has been rejected by men, but is [i]choice and precious in the sight of God, 5 you also, as living stones, [j]are being built up as a spiritual house for a holy priesthood, to offer up spiritual sacrifices acceptable to God through Jesus Christ. 6 For *this* is contained in [k]Scripture:

"BEHOLD, I LAY IN ZION A CHOICE STONE, A PRECIOUS CORNER *stone*, AND HE WHO BELIEVES IN [l]HIM WILL NOT BE [m]DISAPPOINTED."

7 This precious value, then, is for you who believe; but for those who disbelieve,

"THE STONE WHICH THE BUILDERS REJECTED, THIS BECAME THE VERY CORNER *stone*,"

8 and,

"A STONE OF STUMBLING AND A ROCK OF OFFENSE";

for they stumble because they are disobedient to the word, and to this *doom* they were also appointed.

9 But you are A CHOSEN RACE, A royal PRIESTHOOD, A HOLY NATION, A PEOPLE FOR *God's* OWN POSSESSION, so that you may proclaim the excellencies of Him who has called you out of darkness into His marvelous light; 10 for you once were NOT A PEOPLE, but now you are THE PEOPLE OF GOD; you had NOT RECEIVED MERCY, but now you have RECEIVED MERCY.

[11] Beloved, I urge you as aliens and strangers to abstain from fleshly lusts which wage war against the soul. [12] Keep your behavior excellent among the Gentiles, so that in the thing in which they slander you as evildoers, they may [n]because of your good deeds, as they observe *them*, glorify God in the day of [o]visitation. (1 Peter 2:4-12)

Then I will sprinkle clean water on you, and you will be clean; I will cleanse you from all your filthiness and from all your idols. [26] Moreover, I will give you a new heart and put a new spirit within you; and I will remove the heart of stone from your flesh and give you a heart of flesh. [27] I will put My Spirit within you and cause you to walk in My statutes, and you will be careful to observe My ordinances. [28] You will live in the land that I gave to your forefathers; so you will be My people, and I will be your God. (Ezekiel 36:25-28)

I affirm, brethren, by the boasting in you which I have in Christ Jesus our Lord, I die daily. (1 Corinthians 15:31)

Acts 13

Now there were at Antioch, in the church that was *there*, prophets and teachers: Barnabas, and Simeon who was called Niger, and Lucius of Cyrene, and Manaen who had been brought up with Herod the tetrarch, and Saul. [2] While they were ministering to the Lord and fasting, the Holy Spirit said, "Set apart for Me Barnabas and Saul for the work to which I have called them." [3] Then, when they had fasted and prayed and laid their hands on them, they sent them away.

[4] So, being sent out by the Holy Spirit, they went down to Seleucia and from there they sailed to Cyprus. [5] When they reached Salamis, they *began* to proclaim the word of God in the synagogues of the Jews; and they also had John as their helper. [6] When they had gone

through the whole island as far as Paphos, they found a magician, a Jewish false prophet whose name was Bar-Jesus, [7] who was with the proconsul, Sergius Paulus, a man of intelligence. This man summoned Barnabas and Saul and sought to hear the word of God. [8] But Elymas the magician (for so his name is translated) was opposing them, seeking to turn the proconsul away from the faith. [9] But Saul, who was also *known as* Paul, [a]filled with the Holy Spirit, fixed his gaze on him, [10] and said, "You who are full of all deceit and fraud, you son of the devil, you enemy of all righteousness, will you not cease to make crooked the straight ways of the Lord? [11] Now, behold, the hand of the Lord is upon you, and you will be blind and not see the sun for a time." And immediately a mist and a darkness fell upon him, and he went about seeking those who would lead him by the hand. [12] Then the proconsul believed when he saw what had happened, being amazed at the teaching of the Lord.

[13] Now Paul and his companions put out to sea from Paphos and came to Perga in Pamphylia; but John left them and returned to Jerusalem. [14] But going on from Perga, they arrived at Pisidian Antioch, and on the Sabbath day they went into the synagogue and sat down. [15] After the reading of the Law and the Prophets the synagogue officials sent to them, saying, "Brethren, if you have any word of exhortation for the people, say it." [16] Paul stood up, and motioning with his hand said,

"Men of Israel, and you who fear God, listen: [17] The God of this people Israel chose our fathers and [b]made the people great during their stay in the land of Egypt, and with an uplifted arm He led them out from it. [18] For a period of about forty years He put up with them in the wilderness. [19] When He had destroyed seven nations in the land of Canaan, He distributed their land as an inheritance—*all of which took* about four hundred and fifty years. [20] After these things He gave *them* judges until Samuel the prophet. [21] Then they asked for a king, and God gave them Saul the son of Kish, a man of the tribe of Benjamin, for forty years. [22] After He had removed him, He raised up David to be their king, concerning whom He also testified and said, 'I HAVE FOUND DAVID the son of Jesse, A MAN AFTER MY HEART, who will do all My [c]will.' [23] From the descendants of this man, according to promise, God has brought to Israel a Savior,

Jesus, [24] after John had proclaimed before [d]His coming a baptism of repentance to all the people of Israel. [25] And while John was completing his course, he kept saying, 'What do you suppose that I am? I am not *He*. But behold, one is coming after me the sandals of whose feet I am not worthy to untie.'

[26] "Brethren, sons of Abraham's family, and those among you who fear God, to us the message of this salvation has been sent. [27] For those who live in Jerusalem, and their rulers, recognizing neither Him nor the [e]utterances of the prophets which are read every Sabbath, fulfilled *these* by condemning *Him*. [28] And though they found no ground for *putting Him to* death, they asked Pilate that He be [f]executed. [29] When they had carried out all that was written concerning Him, they took Him down from the [g]cross and laid Him in a tomb. [30] But God raised Him from the dead; [31] and for many days He appeared to those who came up with Him from Galilee to Jerusalem, the very ones who are now His witnesses to the people. [32] And we preach to you the good news of the promise made to the fathers, [33] that God has fulfilled this *promise* [h]to our children in that He raised up Jesus, as it is also written in the second Psalm, 'YOU ARE MY SON; TODAY I HAVE BEGOTTEN YOU.' [34] *As for the fact* that He raised Him up from the dead, no longer to return to decay, He has spoken in this way: 'I WILL GIVE YOU THE HOLY *and* [i]SURE *blessings* OF DAVID.' [35] Therefore He also says in another *Psalm*, 'YOU WILL NOT [j]ALLOW YOUR [k]HOLY ONE TO [l]UNDERGO DECAY.' [36] For David, after he had [m]served the purpose of God in his own generation, fell asleep, and was laid among his fathers and [n]underwent decay; [37] but He whom God raised did not [o]undergo decay. [38] Therefore let it be known to you, brethren, that through [p]Him forgiveness of sins is proclaimed to you, [39] and [q]through Him everyone who believes is [r]freed [s]from all things, from which you could not be [t]freed [u]through the Law of Moses. [40] Therefore take heed, so that the thing spoken of in the Prophets may not come upon *you*:

[41] 'BEHOLD, YOU SCOFFERS, AND MARVEL, AND [v]PERISH;
FOR I AM ACCOMPLISHING A WORK IN YOUR DAYS,
A WORK WHICH YOU WILL NEVER BELIEVE, THOUGH SOMEONE
SHOULD DESCRIBE IT TO YOU.'"

[42] As [w]Paul and Barnabas were going out, the people kept begging that these [x]things might be spoken to them the next Sabbath. [43] Now when *the meeting of* the synagogue had broken up, many of the Jews and of the God-fearing [y]proselytes followed Paul and Barnabas, who, speaking to them, were urging them to continue in the grace of God.

[44] The next Sabbath nearly the whole city assembled to hear the word of [z]the Lord. [45] But when the Jews saw the crowds, they were filled with jealousy and *began* contradicting the things spoken by Paul, and were [aa]blaspheming. [46] Paul and Barnabas spoke out boldly and said, "It was necessary that the word of God be spoken to you first; since you repudiate it and judge yourselves unworthy of eternal life, behold, we are turning to the Gentiles. [47] For so the Lord has commanded us,

'I HAVE PLACED YOU AS A LIGHT FOR THE GENTILES,
THAT YOU MAY [ab]BRING SALVATION TO THE END OF THE EARTH.'"

[48] When the Gentiles heard this, they *began* rejoicing and glorifying the word of [ac]the Lord; and as many as had been appointed to eternal life believed. [49] And the word of the Lord was being spread through the whole region. [50] But the Jews incited the [ad]devout women of prominence and the leading men of the city, and instigated a persecution against Paul and Barnabas, and drove them out of their [ae]district. [51] But they shook off the dust of their feet *in protest* against them and went to Iconium. [52] And the disciples were continually filled with joy and with the Holy Spirit. (Acts 13) https://www.biblegateway.com/passage/?search=Acts+13&version=NASB

History says that the Herod that was eaten by worms at end of the last chapter died in 44 A.D. So we are looking at the church being about ten years old at this point. Also, Acts 12 is the last mention of the apostle/disciple John. If you believe in a pre-70 A.D. writing of the Book of Revelation this timeframe of his "disappearance" from the early church fits. The John you see in this chapter is John Mark, he being the one that wrote the Book of Mark.

241

It is important to note how much the early church depended on the Holy Spirit. Here is a quote from A.W. Tozer about the Holy Spirit:

"If the Holy Spirit was withdrawn from the church today, 95 percent of what we do would go on and no one would know the difference. If the Holy Spirit had been withdrawn from the New Testament church, 95 percent of what they did would stop, and everybody would know the difference."

All throughout the civilized world wherever there were Jews, there were synagogues. We had Jews and converted gentiles (God-fearers i.e. proselytes) all throughout civilization. Having these synagogues was very useful in the spread of the Gospel. People from these synagogues would make the three trips to Jerusalem every year. All the roadways that the Romans built were also very useful. Now we have Barnabas and Saul being sent out on a missionary journey. Notice in this chapter that Saul will now always be referred to as Paul. They are first being sent to Cyprus. We recently studied the dove in relation to the Holy Spirit. We tied Noah and the dove with the olive branch to the Romans 11 olive tree. In Romans 11 the gentiles are mentioned as wild olive branches being grafted in, taking part (partakers as in Communion) in the Rich Root of the olive tree. The "Root of Jesse", is Jesus Christ. On this first major missionary journey they are first sent to the island Cyprus, which is known for their olive production, even today: https://www.oliveoiltimes.com/olive-oil-basics/cyprus-beyond-bulk/30226

But if some of the branches were broken off, and you, being a wild olive, were grafted in among them and became partaker with them of the [h]rich root of the olive tree, [18] do not be arrogant toward the branches; but if you are arrogant, *remember that* it is not you who supports the root, but the root *supports* you. (Romans 11:17, 18)

Note that Paul is now also focusing on the gentiles; this could be why he uses his gentile name, Paul, instead of his Jewish name Saul. In 1 Corinthians 9 we see this as a strategy so to speak:

For though I am free from all *men*, I have made myself a slave to all, so that I may win more. [20] To the Jews I became as a Jew, so that I might win Jews; to those who are under [h]the Law, as under [i]the Law though not being myself under [j]the Law, so that I might win those who are under [k]the Law; [21] to those who are without law, as without law, though not being without the law of God but under the law of Christ, so that I might win those who are without law. [22] To the weak I became weak, that I might win the weak; I have become all things to all men, so that I may by all means save some. [23] I do all things for the sake of the gospel, so that I may become a fellow partaker of it. (1 Corinthians 9:19-23)

On Cyprus a gentile Roman proconsul, named Sergius Paulus, seeks Paul and Barnabas out. It is interesting that Sergius Paulus means "humble servant" in Latin. We have a Jewish false prophet that tries to interfere but Paul rebukes him, and God blinds the man. The Roman gentile believes. Paul and Barnabas then sail back to the mainland to Perga. John Mark goes back to Jerusalem.

From Perga, Paul and Barnabas travel to Pisidian Antioch. This Antioch is different from the Antioch that they were initially sent out from. Here is a map of their journey:
http://www.biblestudy.org/maps/pauls-first-journey-map.html

We have Paul giving an awesome history and thorough Gospel Message. The Gospel is beautifully spoken very plainly. Many believe, Jews and God Fearers. Paul and Barnabas were requested to speak at the next Sabbath as well. At the next Sabbath some Jews, who didn't believe, filled with jealousy, started blaspheming. Trouble ensued and Paul and Barnabas headed to Iconium. Above in Acts 13:47, Paul and Barnabas quote from Isaiah 49:

And now says the LORD, who formed Me from the womb to be His Servant,
To bring Jacob back to Him, so that Israel might be gathered to Him
(For I am honored in the sight of the LORD,
And My God is My strength),
[6] He says, "It is too [d]small a thing that You should be My Servant

To raise up the tribes of Jacob and to restore the preserved ones of
Israel;
I will also make You a light [e]of the nations
So that My salvation may [f]reach to the end of the earth."
(Isaiah 49:5, 6)

Isaiah was written about seven hundred years before Jesus walked
as a Man. The Scripture above starts with describing Jesus in the
womb. God Himself, in Love and Humility, became a Man to teach
all men the Way. His Salvation goes out to the entire earth!!! Jesus
quotes from Isaiah quite a bit. Below are some of the most popular
Isaiah Scriptures:

Isaiah 7:14, "Therefore the Lord Himself will give you a sign: The
virgin will be with Child and will give birth to a Son, and will call
Him Immanuel."

Isaiah 9:6, "For to us a Child is born, to us a Son is given, and the
government will be on His shoulders. And He will be called
Wonderful Counselor, Mighty God, Everlasting Father, Prince of
Peace."

Isaiah 53:5-6, "But He was pierced for our transgressions, He was
crushed for our iniquities; the punishment that brought us peace was
upon Him, and by His wounds we are healed. We all, like sheep,
have gone astray, each of us has turned to his own way; and the
LORD has laid on Him the iniquity of us all."

Acts 14

In Iconium they entered the synagogue of the Jews together, and
spoke in such a manner that a large number of people believed, both
of Jews and of Greeks. 2 But the Jews who [a]disbelieved stirred up

the [b]minds of the Gentiles and embittered them against the brethren. [3] Therefore they spent a long time *there* speaking boldly *with reliance* upon the Lord, who was testifying to the word of His grace, granting that [c]signs and wonders be done by their hands. [4] But the [d]people of the city were divided; and some [e]sided with the Jews, and some with the apostles. [5] And when an attempt was made by both the Gentiles and the Jews with their rulers, to mistreat and to stone them, [6] they became aware of it and fled to the cities of Lycaonia, Lystra and Derbe, and the surrounding region; [7] and there they continued to preach the gospel.

[8] At Lystra a man was sitting who had no strength in his feet, lame from his mother's womb, who had never walked. [9] This man was listening to Paul as he spoke, who, when he had fixed his gaze on him and had seen that he had faith to be [f]made well, [10] said with a loud voice, "Stand upright on your feet." And he leaped up and *began* to walk. [11] When the crowds saw what Paul had done, they raised their voice, saying in the Lycaonian language, "The gods have become like men and have come down to us." [12] And they *began* calling Barnabas, [g]Zeus, and Paul, [h]Hermes, because he was [i]the chief speaker. [13] The priest of Zeus, whose *temple* was [j]just outside the city, brought oxen and garlands to the gates, and wanted to offer sacrifice with the crowds. [14] But when the apostles Barnabas and Paul heard of it, they tore their [k]robes and rushed out into the crowd, crying out [15] and saying, "Men, why are you doing these things? We are also men of the same nature as you, and preach the gospel to you that you should turn from these [l]vain things to a living God, WHO MADE THE HEAVEN AND THE EARTH AND THE SEA AND ALL THAT IS IN THEM. [16] [m]In the generations gone by He permitted all the [n]nations to go their own ways; [17] and yet He did not leave Himself without witness, in that He did good and gave you rains from heaven and fruitful seasons, [o]satisfying your hearts with food and gladness." [18] *Even* saying these things, with difficulty they restrained the crowds from offering sacrifice to them.

[19] But Jews came from Antioch and Iconium, and having won over the crowds, they stoned Paul and dragged him out of the city, supposing him to be dead. [20] But while the disciples stood around him, he got up and entered the city. The next day he went away with

Barnabas to Derbe. [21] After they had preached the gospel to that city and had made many disciples, they returned to Lystra and to Iconium and to Antioch, [22] strengthening the souls of the disciples, encouraging them to continue in the faith, and *saying*, "Through many tribulations we must enter the kingdom of God." [23] When they had appointed elders for them in every church, having prayed with fasting, they commended them to the Lord in whom they had believed.

[24] They passed through Pisidia and came into Pamphylia. [25] When they had spoken the word in Perga, they went down to Attalia. [26] From there they sailed to Antioch, from which they had been commended to the grace of God for the work that they had [p]accomplished. [27] When they had arrived and gathered the church together, they *began* to report all things that God had done with them and [q]how He had opened a door of faith to the Gentiles. [28] And they spent [r]a long time with the disciples. (Acts 14) https://www.biblegateway.com/passage/?search=acts+14&version=NASB

Isn't that amazing how synagogues were all over the known world? The gentiles would see the Jews going to synagogue every Saturday (but they wouldn't know that the 7th Day Sabbath and Eternal Rest is Jesus Christ, His Work=our Rest). They would know about how on the eighth day the Jewish males were circumcised (they wouldn't know that this was pointing to the coming Christ/Messiah). They would know about their dietary Laws (although they would not make the connection of the physical unclean/unholy to the need of a Spiritual Savior making us Clean/Holy). The Jews went to synagogue to hear the Word, which Jesus is "the Word became Flesh" (John 1). They would also sing Psalms, which so many are centered on the Christ. Isn't it amazing to think that all the males from all these outlying synagogues were in Jerusalem for the Crucifixion? Deuteronomy 16 states that all males must be in attendance for the Three Annual Feast Weeks.

Paul (means humble) and Barnabas (means prophet=to build up, to stir up and to cheer up) first went to Cyprus. Remember Barnabas was actually from Cyprus (Acts 4). Now they are in Asia Minor. We see Jews and gentiles coming to Christ. The terms God fearers and proselytes are the gentiles that over the years have seen the hearts of loving Jews, like Barnabas. Just like when the children of Israel came out of Egypt on their way to the Promised Land, they were to love the "stranger" (Leviticus 19:34). Many gentiles already had an established faith in God.

Notice in verse 15, the gentiles try and worship Paul and Barnabas. They mention the God, Who created the Heaven and the earth and the sea and all that is in them. Just like Romans 1, these particular gentiles would not be familiar with the Bible, but they are familiar with nature. A good chapter to share with people who have no Bible background is Psalm 19:

The heavens are telling of the glory of God;
And their expanse is declaring the work of His hands.
[2] Day to day pours forth speech,
And night to night reveals knowledge.
[3] There is no speech, nor are there words;
Their voice is not heard.
[4] Their [a]line has gone out through all the earth,
And their utterances to the end of the world.
In them He has placed a tent for the sun,
[5] Which is as a bridegroom coming out of his chamber;
It rejoices as a strong man to run his course.
[6] Its rising is from [b]one end of the heavens,
And its circuit to the [c]other end of them;
And there is nothing hidden from its heat.

[7] The law of the LORD is [d]perfect, restoring the soul;
The testimony of the LORD is sure, making wise the simple.
[8] The precepts of the LORD are right, rejoicing the heart;
The commandment of the LORD is pure, enlightening the eyes.
[9] The fear of the LORD is clean, enduring forever;
The judgments of the LORD are true; they are righteous altogether.
[10] They are more desirable than gold, yes, than much fine gold;
Sweeter also than honey and the drippings of the honeycomb.

[11] Moreover, by them Your servant is warned;
In keeping them there is great reward.
[12] Who can discern *his* errors? Acquit me of hidden *faults*.
[13] Also keep back Your servant from presumptuous *sins*;
Let them not rule over me;
Then I will be [c]blameless,
And I shall be acquitted of great transgression.
[14] Let the words of my mouth and the meditation of my heart
Be acceptable in Your sight,
O LORD, my rock and my Redeemer. (Psalm 19)

Notice how Paul and Barnabas backtrack to cities they were already in. They appoint elders, pray, and fast. Paul was just stoned to apparent death, but he lives, and continues to preach:

After they had preached the gospel to that city and had made many disciples, they returned to Lystra and to Iconium and to Antioch, [22] strengthening the souls of the disciples, encouraging them to continue in the faith, and *saying*, "Through many tribulations we must enter the kingdom of God." [23] When they had appointed elders for them in every church, having prayed with fasting, they commended them to the Lord in whom they had believed. (Acts 14:21-23)

Throughout history there has always been a "window of opportunity" to come to God in faith for all people, Jews and gentiles. Now in this chapter, verse 27, the window becomes a Door.

"Truly, truly, I say to you, he who does not enter by the door into the fold of the sheep, but climbs up some other way, he is a thief and a robber. [2] But he who enters by the door is a shepherd of the sheep. [3] To him the doorkeeper opens, and the sheep hear his voice, and he calls his own sheep by name and leads them out. [4] When he puts forth all his own, he goes ahead of them, and the sheep follow him because they know his voice. [5] A stranger they simply will not follow, but will flee from him, because they do not know the voice of strangers." [6] This figure of speech Jesus spoke to them, but they did not understand what those things were which He had been saying to them.

[7] So Jesus said to them again, "Truly, truly, I say to you, I am the door of the sheep. [8] All who came before Me are thieves and robbers, but the sheep did not hear them. [9] I am the door; if anyone enters through Me, he will be saved, and will go in and out and find pasture. [10] The thief comes only to steal and kill and destroy; I came that they may have life, and [a]have *it* abundantly.

[11] "I am the good shepherd; the good shepherd lays down His life for the sheep. [12] He who is a hired hand, and not a shepherd, who is not the owner of the sheep, sees the wolf coming, and leaves the sheep and flees, and the wolf snatches them and scatters *them*. [13] *He flees* because he is a hired hand and is not concerned about the sheep. [14] I am the good shepherd, and I know My own and My own know Me, [15] even as the Father knows Me and I know the Father; and I lay down My life for the sheep. [16] I have other sheep, which are not of this fold; I must bring them also, and they will hear My voice; and they will become one flock *with* one shepherd. [17] For this reason the Father loves Me, because I lay down My life so that I may take it again. [18] No one has taken it away from Me, but I lay it down on My own initiative. I have authority to lay it down, and I have authority to take it up again. This commandment I received from My Father." (John 10:1-18)

Imagine this; in Acts 14 we are at around 45 A.D., in 70 A.D. the physical Temple in Jerusalem is utterly destroyed, not one brick left upon another. Now we as believers become those bricks, living bricks to the Spiritual House for a Holy Priesthood (1 Peter 2), not built with human hands. Jesus Christ is the Total Fulfillment of the Law and Prophets. One Flock, with Jesus being the Good Shepherd. One Olive Tree, with Jesus being the Root.

So Jesus said to them again, "Truly, truly, I say to you, I am the Door of the sheep. (John 10:7)

Acts 15

Some men came down from Judea and *began* teaching the brethren, "Unless you are circumcised according to the custom of Moses, you cannot be saved." 2 And when Paul and Barnabas had [a]great dissension and debate with them, *the brethren* determined that Paul and Barnabas and some others of them should go up to Jerusalem to the apostles and elders concerning this issue. 3 Therefore, being sent on their way by the church, they were passing through both Phoenicia and Samaria, describing in detail the conversion of the Gentiles, and were bringing great joy to all the brethren. 4 When they arrived at Jerusalem, they were received by the church and the apostles and the elders, and they reported all that God had done with them. 5 But some of the sect of the Pharisees who had believed stood up, saying, "It is necessary to circumcise them and to direct them to observe the Law of Moses."

6 The apostles and the elders came together to [b]look into this [c]matter. 7 After there had been much debate, Peter stood up and said to them, "Brethren, you know that [d]in the early days God made a choice among you, that by my mouth the Gentiles would hear the word of the gospel and believe. 8 And God, who knows the heart, testified to them giving them the Holy Spirit, just as He also did to us; 9 and He made no distinction between us and them, cleansing their hearts by faith. 10 Now therefore why do you put God to the test by placing upon the neck of the disciples a yoke which neither our fathers nor we have been able to bear? 11 But we believe that we are

saved through the grace of the Lord Jesus, in the same way as they also are."

¹² All the people kept silent, and they were listening to Barnabas and Paul as they were relating what signs and wonders God had done through them among the Gentiles.

¹³ After they had stopped speaking, [e]James answered, saying, "Brethren, listen to me. ¹⁴ Simeon has related how God first concerned Himself about taking from among the Gentiles a people for His name. ¹⁵ With this the words of the Prophets agree, just as it is written,

¹⁶ 'AFTER THESE THINGS I will return,
AND I WILL REBUILD THE [f]TABERNACLE OF DAVID WHICH HAS FALLEN,
AND I WILL REBUILD ITS RUINS,
AND I WILL RESTORE IT,
¹⁷ SO THAT THE REST OF [g]MANKIND MAY SEEK THE LORD,
AND ALL THE GENTILES [h]WHO ARE CALLED BY MY NAME,'
¹⁸ SAYS THE LORD, WHO [i]MAKES THESE THINGS KNOWN FROM LONG AGO.

¹⁹ Therefore it is my judgment that we do not trouble those who are turning to God from among the Gentiles, ²⁰ but that we write to them that they abstain from [j]things contaminated by idols and from fornication and from what is strangled and from blood. ²¹ For Moses from ancient generations has in every city those who preach him, since [k]he is read in the synagogues every Sabbath."

²² Then it seemed good to the apostles and the elders, with the whole church, to choose men from among them to send to Antioch with Paul and Barnabas—Judas called Barsabbas, and Silas, leading men among the brethren, ²³ and they [l]sent this letter by them,

"The apostles and the brethren who are elders, to the brethren in Antioch and Syria and Cilicia who are from the Gentiles, greetings.

²⁴ "Since we have heard that some [m]of our number to whom we gave no instruction have disturbed you with *their* words, unsettling your souls, ²⁵ it seemed good to us, having [n]become of one mind, to select men to send to you with our beloved Barnabas and Paul, ²⁶ men who have [o]risked their lives for the name of our Lord Jesus Christ. ²⁷ "Therefore we have sent Judas and Silas, who themselves will also report the same things by word *of mouth*. ²⁸ "For it seemed good to the Holy Spirit and to us to lay upon you no greater burden than these essentials: ²⁹ that you abstain from things sacrificed to idols and from blood and from things strangled and from fornication; [p]if you keep yourselves free from such things, you will do well. Farewell."

³⁰ So when they were sent away, they went down to Antioch; and having gathered the [q]congregation together, they delivered the letter. ³¹ When they had read it, they rejoiced because of its [r]encouragement. ³² Judas and Silas, also being prophets themselves, [s]encouraged and strengthened the brethren with a lengthy message. ³³ After they had spent time *there*, they were sent away from the brethren in peace to those who had sent them out. ³⁴ [[t]But it seemed good to Silas to remain there.] ³⁵ But Paul and Barnabas stayed in Antioch, teaching and preaching with many others also, the word of the Lord.

³⁶ After some days Paul said to Barnabas, "Let us return and visit the brethren in every city in which we proclaimed the word of the Lord, *and see* how they are." ³⁷ Barnabas wanted to take John, called Mark, along with them also. ³⁸ But Paul kept insisting that they should not take him along who had deserted them [u]in Pamphylia and had not gone with them to the work. ³⁹ And there occurred such a sharp disagreement that they separated from one another, and Barnabas took Mark with him and sailed away to Cyprus. ⁴⁰ But Paul chose Silas and left, being committed by the brethren to the grace of the Lord. ⁴¹ And he was traveling through Syria and Cilicia, strengthening the churches. (Acts 15)
https://www.biblegateway.com/passage/?search=Acts+15&version=NASB

We have some very serious arguing going on about Circumcision. Remember this Covenant of Circumcision started with Abraham. Remember Abraham was given the Promise that the future Messiah/Christ would come through his loins. God even had Abraham travel, with his son that was in the Bloodline of the Messiah, to Mount Moriah. Mount Moriah is one in the same as Golgotha i.e. the exact location of the future Cross. Once Abraham and his son were on Mount Moriah, Isaac asked, "where is the lamb?" Abraham responded, "God will provide Himself the Lamb." Shortly after that there was a Ram with His head caught in the thorns (Genesis 22). Jesus Christ would wear our crown of thorns. Jesus Christ was the last required Circumcision. Matthew chapter 1 contains the genealogy of the Christ starting at Abraham (Luke 3 starts at Adam). Remember as well that the first Armor of God in Ephesians 6 is the Loins of Truth.

The [a]record of the genealogy of [b]Jesus [c]the Messiah, the son of David, the son of Abraham:

2 Abraham [d]was the father of Isaac, [e]Isaac the father of Jacob, and Jacob the father of [f]Judah and his brothers. 3 Judah was the father of Perez and Zerah by Tamar, Perez was the father of Hezron, and Hezron the father of [g]Ram. 4 Ram was the father of Amminadab, Amminadab the father of Nahshon, and Nahshon the father of Salmon. 5 Salmon was the father of Boaz by Rahab, Boaz was the father of Obed by Ruth, and Obed the father of Jesse. 6 Jesse was the father of David the king.

David was the father of Solomon by [h]Bathsheba who had been the wife of Uriah. 7 Solomon was the father of Rehoboam, Rehoboam the father of Abijah, and Abijah the father of [i]Asa. 8 Asa was the father of Jehoshaphat, Jehoshaphat the father of [j]Joram, and Joram the father of Uzziah. 9 Uzziah was the father of [k]Jotham, Jotham the father of Ahaz, and Ahaz the father of Hezekiah. 10 Hezekiah was the father of Manasseh, Manasseh the father of [l]Amon, and Amon the father of Josiah. [11] Josiah became the father of [m]Jeconiah and his brothers, at the time of the deportation to Babylon.

[12] After the deportation to Babylon: Jeconiah became the father of [n]Shealtiel, and Shealtiel the father of Zerubbabel. [13] Zerubbabel was the father of [o]Abihud, Abihud the father of Eliakim, and Eliakim the father of Azor. [14] Azor was the father of Zadok, Zadok the father of Achim, and Achim the father of Eliud. [15] Eliud was the father of Eleazar, Eleazar the father of Matthan, and Matthan the father of Jacob. [16] Jacob was the father of Joseph the husband of Mary, by whom Jesus was born, who is called [p]the Messiah.

[17] So all the generations from Abraham to David are fourteen generations; from David to the deportation to Babylon, fourteen generations; and from the deportation to Babylon to [q]the Messiah, fourteen generations. (Matthew 1:1-17)

Always remember that God chooses based on one thing, the heart. Consider this verse from Romans 2:

For he is not a Jew who is one outwardly, nor is circumcision that which is outward in the flesh. [29] But he is a Jew who is one inwardly; and circumcision is that which is of the heart, by the Spirit, not by the letter; and his praise is not from men, but from God. (Romans 2:28, 29)

Notice in the above Bloodline, that there is Bathsheba, who is a gentile. Notice Ruth the Moabite, being a gentile. Also notice Rahab, the gentile prostitute. Notice in this very chapter these Words:

And God, who knows the heart, testified to them giving them the Holy Spirit, just as He also did to us; [9] and He made no distinction between us and them, cleansing their hearts by faith. (Acts 15:8, 9)

The Book of Acts shows us how the Jews and gentiles began to understand what God was staying all along; it is all about the heart.

In verse 16 we see some awesome prophecies about the Christ. These are from Amos, Jeremiah, and Deuteronomy:

'AFTER THESE THINGS I will return,
AND I WILL REBUILD THE [f]TABERNACLE OF DAVID WHICH HAS FALLEN,
AND I WILL REBUILD ITS RUINS,
AND I WILL RESTORE IT,
[17] SO THAT THE REST OF [g]MANKIND MAY SEEK THE LORD,
AND ALL THE GENTILES [h]WHO ARE CALLED BY MY NAME,'
[18] SAYS THE LORD, WHO [i]MAKES THESE THINGS KNOWN FROM LONG AGO.

The above prophecies from Amos, Jeremiah and Deuteronomy are about the Christ, NOT about rebuilding some future Temple in Jerusalem. Jesus Christ in the Flesh was the Tabernacle of David. "God Himself Tabernacled amongst us." (John 1)

And I, if I am lifted up from the earth, will draw all men to Myself." [33] But He was saying this to indicate the kind of death by which He was to die. [34] The crowd then answered Him, "We have heard out of the Law that [l]the Christ is to remain forever; and how can You say, 'The Son of Man must be lifted up'? Who is this Son of Man?" [35] So Jesus said to them, "For a little while longer the Light is among you. Walk while you have the Light, so that darkness will not overtake you; he who walks in the darkness does not know where he goes. [36] While you have the Light, believe in the Light, so that you may become sons of Light."

These things Jesus spoke, and He went away and [m]hid Himself from them. [37] But though He had performed so many [n]signs before them, *yet* they were not believing in Him. [38] *This was* to fulfill the word of Isaiah the prophet which he spoke: "LORD, WHO HAS BELIEVED OUR REPORT? AND TO WHOM HAS THE ARM OF THE LORD BEEN REVEALED?" [39] For this reason they could not believe, for Isaiah said again, [40] "HE HAS BLINDED THEIR EYES AND HE HARDENED THEIR HEART, SO THAT THEY WOULD NOT SEE WITH THEIR EYES AND PERCEIVE WITH THEIR HEART, AND [o]BE CONVERTED AND I

HEAL THEM." [41] These things Isaiah said because he saw His glory, and he spoke of Him. [42] Nevertheless many even of the rulers believed in Him, but because of the Pharisees they were not confessing *Him*, for fear that they would be [p]put out of the synagogue; [43] for they loved the [q]approval of men rather than the [r]approval of God. (John 12:32-43)

An agreement is made on what they, as believers, should abstain from:

 that you abstain from things sacrificed to idols and from blood and from things strangled and from fornication; (Acts 15:29)

Not only were the above four things heavily associated with pagan worship of that day, but they are all in heavy opposition to the Message of Salvation. Of course satan knew that, and that's why he put them at the forefront of his pagan religions of that day. Sacrifice of Jesus vs. sacrifice to an idol, drinking blood vs. His Blood i.e. Communion, strangling creature with blood (life) still in them vs. Shedding of Blood for sin prior to death on a Cross, fornication i.e. whoring around vs. as the bride of Christ staying pure undefiled in Him. Ezekiel 22 deals with this issue: https://www.biblegateway.com/passage/?search=Ezekiel+22&version=NASB. Hebrews 9 expounds greatly on the Blood: https://www.biblegateway.com/passage/?search=Hebrews+9&version=NASB.

Acts 16

Paul came also to Derbe and to Lystra. And a disciple was there, named Timothy, the son of a Jewish woman who was a believer, but his father was a Greek, [2] and he was well spoken of by the brethren who were in Lystra and Iconium. ³ Paul wanted this man to [a]go with him; and he took him and circumcised him because of the Jews who were in those parts, for they all knew that his father was a Greek. ⁴ Now while they were passing through the cities, they were delivering the decrees which had been decided upon by the apostles and elders who were in Jerusalem, for them to observe. ⁵ So the churches were being strengthened [b]in the faith, and were increasing in number daily.

⁶ They passed through the [c]Phrygian and Galatian region, having been forbidden by the Holy Spirit to speak the word in [d]Asia; ⁷ and after they came to Mysia, they were trying to go into Bithynia, and the Spirit of Jesus did not permit them; ⁸ and passing by Mysia, they came down to Troas. ⁹ A vision appeared to Paul in the night: a man of Macedonia was standing and appealing to him, and saying, "Come over to Macedonia and help us." ¹⁰ When he had seen the vision, immediately we sought to [e]go into Macedonia, concluding that God had called us to preach the gospel to them.

¹¹ So putting out to sea from Troas, we ran a straight course to Samothrace, and on the day following to Neapolis; ¹² and from there to Philippi, which is a leading city of the district of Macedonia, a *Roman* colony; and we were staying in this city for some days. ¹³ And on the Sabbath day we went outside the gate to a riverside, where we were supposing that there would be a place of prayer; and we sat down and began speaking to the women who had assembled.

¹⁴ A woman named Lydia, from the city of Thyatira, a seller of purple fabrics, a worshiper of God, was listening; [f]and the Lord opened her heart to respond to the things spoken by Paul. ¹⁵ And when she and her household had been baptized, she urged us, saying, "If you have judged me to be faithful to the Lord, come into my house and stay." And she prevailed upon us.

¹⁶ It happened that as we were going to the place of prayer, a slave-girl having a spirit of divination met us, who was bringing her masters much profit by fortune-telling. ¹⁷ Following after Paul and us, she kept crying out, saying, "These men are bond-servants of the Most High God, who are proclaiming to you [g]the way of salvation."

¹⁸ She continued doing this for many days. But Paul was greatly annoyed, and turned and said to the spirit, "I command you in the name of Jesus Christ to come out of her!" And it came out at that very [h]moment.

¹⁹ But when her masters saw that their hope of profit was [i]gone, they seized Paul and Silas and dragged them into the market place before the authorities, ²⁰ and when they had brought them to the chief magistrates, they said, "These men are throwing our city into confusion, being Jews, ²¹ and are proclaiming customs which it is not lawful for us to accept or to observe, being Romans."

²² The crowd rose up together against them, and the chief magistrates tore their [j]robes off them and proceeded to order [k]*them* to be beaten with rods. ²³ When they had struck them with many blows, they threw them into prison, commanding the jailer to guard them securely; ²⁴ [l]and he, having received such a command, threw them into the inner prison and fastened their feet in the [m]stocks.

²⁵ But about midnight Paul and Silas were praying and singing hymns of praise to God, and the prisoners were listening to them; ²⁶ and suddenly there came a great earthquake, so that the foundations of the prison house were shaken; and immediately all the doors were opened and everyone's chains were unfastened. ²⁷ When the jailer awoke and saw the prison doors opened, he drew his sword and was about to kill himself, supposing that the prisoners had escaped. ²⁸ But Paul cried out with a loud voice, saying, "Do not harm yourself, for we are all here!" ²⁹ And he called for lights and rushed in, and trembling with fear he fell down before Paul and Silas, ³⁰ and after he brought them out, he said, "Sirs, what must I do to be saved?"

³¹ They said, "Believe in the Lord Jesus, and you will be saved, you and your household." ³² And they spoke the word of [n]the Lord to him together with all who were in his house. ³³ And he took them that *very* hour of the night and washed their wounds, and immediately he was baptized, he and all his *household*. ³⁴ And he brought them into his house and set [o]food before them, and rejoiced [p]greatly, having believed in God with his whole household.

³⁵ Now when day came, the chief magistrates sent their policemen, saying, "Release those men." ³⁶ And the jailer reported these words to Paul, *saying*, "The chief magistrates have sent to release you. Therefore come out now and go in peace." ³⁷ But Paul said to them, "They have beaten us in public without trial, men who are Romans, and have thrown us into prison; and now are they sending us away secretly? No indeed! But let them come themselves and bring us out." ³⁸ The policemen reported these words to the chief magistrates. They were afraid when they heard that they were Romans, ³⁹ and they came and appealed to them, and when they had brought them out, they kept begging them to leave the city. ⁴⁰ They went out of the prison and entered *the house of* Lydia, and when they saw the brethren, they [q]encouraged them and departed. (Acts 16) https://www.biblegateway.com/passage/?search=Acts+16&version= NASB

At the end of the previous chapter we had a sharp disagreement between Paul and Barnabas, so sharp in fact that they separated. Barnabas goes with John Mark and Paul goes with Silas. I believe the disagreement dealt with Circumcision since a major part of the previous chapter was about that, and this chapter opens with that. Remember the mindset of Paul; he would do anything to save people from hell.

For though I am free from all *men*, I have made myself a slave to all, so that I may win more. ²⁰ To the Jews I became as a Jew, so that I might win Jews; to those who are under [a]the Law, as under [b]the Law though not being myself under [c]the Law, so that I might win those who are under [d]the Law; ²¹ to those who are without law, as without law, though not being without the law of God but under the law of Christ, so that I might win those who are without law. ²² To the weak I became weak, that I might win the weak; I have become all things to all men, so that I may by all means save some. ²³ I do all things for the sake of the gospel, so that I may become a fellow partaker of it. (1 Corinthians 9:19-23)

So Paul thought he was going into Asia Minor to focus strongly on the Jews. So what does he do? He actually has a grown man

circumcised to win Jews. Yes, Paul circumcises Timothy. If I was
Timothy I would be saying, you know Paul, I think God is telling me,
to not be circumcised. Looking at Timothy, his mom is a Jew and his
dad is a Greek. This is a beautiful picture of the Jews and gentiles
becoming one church in Jesus Christ, but Paul goes through with
the circumcision, and lo and behold, they end up not initially going
to Jews but to Macedonia (Greece) to the Greeks, to the gentiles. It
is interesting that verse 7 uses "the Spirit of Jesus" did not permit
them to go into Asia Minor to the Jews. This reminds us of the road
to Damascus where Jesus meets Paul on the road. As far as
direction, usually the Holy Spirit leads them, in this case we have
Jesus stepping in. Here is a link to a map/info of their journey:
http://www.bible-history.com/new-testament/pauls-second-
missionary-journey.html

Paul, Silas, and Timothy end up in Greece instead of Asia Minor.
They usually go into the local synagogue on the Sabbath,
proclaiming Jesus as the fulfillment of the Law and Prophets. In this
case, there is no synagogue, so on the Sabbath they "go down to
the river to pray" i.e. "go down in the River to pray".
https://www.youtube.com/watch?v=zSif77IVQdY

People then and now still see God in nature. If you are true to your
heart, how could you not? Could we take all the individual parts to
a car and toss them up in the air, and as they fall they magically
become perfectly assembled into a car just by chance? The earth
i.e. nature, has much, much, more detail and order than any car.

On the Sabbath Paul, Silas, and Timothy meet Lydia at the river in
Philippi, Macedonia (Greece). She is from Thyatira, which is actually
in Asia Minor. (Thyatira means Hill Graveyard and it is one of the 7
churches the apostle John writes to in Revelation.) She is a seller of
purple, so she is probably away from home on business. Back then
people got the purple dye from clams. At the throat of a clam are
just a couple drops of deep purple dye. It takes a lot of clams to get

the color needed for purple, which gave it great value. Purple became the color of royalty.

Remember our study of the rainbow, which is made up of 7 colors (Red Orange Yellow Green Blue Indigo Purple). Remember the Rainbow Covenant with Noah. The Rainbow is actually a full circle (Promise Ring) if viewed from 42 degrees. Here is a full circle rainbow video: https://www.youtube.com/watch?v=6GGzvikbJOA. The outer color is Red. Red has the largest wavelength in the Light spectrum, meaning the most Coverage. We are Covered by the Blood. Remember the most inner color is Purple, having the tightest wavelength, and Most Power. The Ten Commandments were Sapphire Blue. A dead human heart is also blue. With the Blood of Jesus fulfilling the Sapphire Blue Ten Commandments we get Purple (Red + Blue=Purple). Physically a healthy human heart is purple. Spiritually a healthy human heart is also Purple. Purple is the color of Royalty, is Jesus the King of your heart? We receive a "Purple Heart" for His battle wounds.

"Believe in the Lord Jesus, and you will be saved, you and your household."

Acts 17

Now when they had traveled through Amphipolis and Apollonia, they came to Thessalonica, where there was a synagogue of the Jews. [2] And according to Paul's custom, he went to them, and for three Sabbaths reasoned with them from the Scriptures,
[3] [a]explaining and [b]giving evidence that the [c]Christ had to suffer

and rise again from the dead, and *saying*, "This Jesus whom I am proclaiming to you is the [d]Christ." 4 And some of them were persuaded and joined Paul and Silas, [e]along with a large number of the God-fearing Greeks and [f]a number of the leading women. 5 But the Jews, becoming jealous and taking along some wicked men from the market place, formed a mob and set the city in an uproar; and attacking the house of Jason, they were seeking to bring them out to the people. 6 When they did not find them, they *began* dragging Jason and some brethren before the city authorities, shouting, "These men who have upset [g]the world have come here also; 7 [h]and Jason has welcomed them, and they all act contrary to the decrees of Caesar, saying that there is another king, Jesus." 8 They stirred up the crowd and the city authorities who heard these things. 9 And when they had received a [i]pledge from Jason and the others, they released them.

10 The brethren immediately sent Paul and Silas away by night to Berea, [j]and when they arrived, they went into the synagogue of the Jews. 11 Now these were more noble-minded than those in Thessalonica, [k]for they received the word with [l]great eagerness, examining the Scriptures daily *to see* whether these things were so. 12 Therefore many of them believed, [m]along with a number of prominent Greek women and men. 13 But when the Jews of Thessalonica found out that the word of God had been proclaimed by Paul in Berea also, they came there as well, agitating and stirring up the crowds. 14 Then immediately the brethren sent Paul out to go as far as the sea; and Silas and Timothy remained there. 15 Now those who escorted Paul brought him as far as Athens; and receiving a command for Silas and Timothy to come to him as soon as possible, they left.

16 Now while Paul was waiting for them at Athens, his spirit was being provoked within him as he was observing the city full of idols. 17 So he was reasoning in the synagogue with the Jews and the God-fearing *Gentiles*, and in the market place every day with those who happened to be present. 18 And also some of the Epicurean and Stoic philosophers were [n]conversing with him. Some were saying, "What would this [o]idle babbler wish to say?" Others, "He seems to be a proclaimer of strange deities,"—because he was preaching Jesus and

the resurrection. [19] And they took him and brought him [p]to the [q]Areopagus, saying, "May we know what this new teaching is [r]which you are proclaiming? [20] For you are bringing some strange things to our ears; so we want to know what these things mean." [21] (Now all the Athenians and the strangers visiting there used to spend their time in nothing other than telling or hearing something new.)

[22] So Paul stood in the midst of the [s]Areopagus and said, "Men of Athens, I observe that you are very religious in all respects. [23] For while I was passing through and examining the objects of your worship, I also found an altar with this inscription, 'TO AN UNKNOWN GOD.' Therefore what you worship in ignorance, this I proclaim to you. [24] The God who made the world and all things in it, since He is Lord of heaven and earth, does not dwell in temples made with hands; [25] nor is He served by human hands, as though He needed anything, since He Himself gives to all *people* life and breath and all things; [26] and He made from one *man* every nation of mankind to live on all the face of the earth, having determined *their* appointed times and the boundaries of their habitation, [27] that they would seek God, if perhaps they might grope for Him and find Him, though He is not far from each one of us; [28] for in Him we live and move and [t]exist, as even some of your own poets have said, 'For we also are His children.' [29] Being then the children of God, we ought not to think that the Divine Nature is like gold or silver or stone, an image formed by the art and thought of man. [30] Therefore having overlooked the times of ignorance, God is now declaring to men that all *people* everywhere should repent, [31] because He has fixed a day in which He will judge [u]the world in righteousness [v]through a Man whom He has appointed, having furnished proof to all men [w]by raising Him from the dead."

[32] Now when they heard of the resurrection of the dead, some *began* to sneer, but others said, "We shall hear you [x]again concerning this." [33] So Paul went out of their midst. [34] But some men joined him and believed, among whom also were Dionysius the Areopagite and a woman named Damaris and others with them. (Acts 17)
https://www.biblegateway.com/passage/?search=acts+17&version=NASB

We are still in Greece, which is Europe. So the Gospel continues to spread outward from Jerusalem after Pentecost. When there is a synagogue, Paul will always begin there. At the synagogue, every Saturday, the Sabbath, the Word of God is read. Paul shows in Scripture that Jesus is the Word of God that became Flesh and dwelt amongst us, conquering sin and death. Jesus is the Christ i.e. the Messiah. Many believe at Thessalonica. Some Jews are jealous and they spark an uproar. Why are they jealous? They believed that God was their God and their God alone. Didn't God create all of us? What God did do, is give the Oracles of God to the children of Israel. With the Oracles of God, they were to let their Light shine to the world. And many did of course, hence the term God-fearers and proselytes.

Let's take a look at some Oracles of God Scriptures. The Acts 7 verse below refers to Moses. Moses, through God, wrote the first five Books of the Bible; Genesis, Exodus, Leviticus, Numbers and Deuteronomy. The Message of Circumcision i.e. the coming Christ i.e. Messiah was 100% Spiritual, for the heart of man, as shown below in Romans. That was a big problem back then (and even actually today); people thought that God was going to establish a physical world kingdom with the Christ. Jesus Christ is King of a 100% Spiritual Kingdom, a Heart Kingdom, leading to an Eternal Sabbath Rest Heavenly Kingdom.

This is the one who was in the [x]congregation in the wilderness together with the angel who was speaking to him on Mount Sinai, and *who was* with our fathers; and he received living oracles to pass on to you. (Acts 7:38)

For he is not a Jew who is one outwardly, nor is circumcision that which is outward in the flesh. [29] But he is a Jew who is one inwardly; and circumcision is that which is of the heart, by the Spirit, not by the letter; and his praise is not from men, but from God. Then what [a]advantage has the Jew? Or what is the benefit of circumcision? [2] Great in every respect. First of all, that they were entrusted with the oracles of God. [3] What then? If some [b]did not believe, their

[c]unbelief will not nullify the faithfulness of God, will it? [4] May it never be! (Romans 2:28-3:4a)

Again, remember that three times a year all Jewish males had to be in Jerusalem for the Three Feast Weeks (Deuteronomy 16). They had to ask themselves, why are having to make these trips every year? The required Three Feasts were Tabernacles (God in the Flesh Tabernacling amongst us), Unleavened Bread (Jesus the God Man living sinless amongst us, dying for our sin, in our place), and Weeks (not only conquering sin, but also death, rising from the dead and appearing for over forty days as proof, then on Day 50, Pentecost, the Holy Spirit was given).

From Thessalonica, Paul and the others go to Berea. It is a whole different story in Berea. It seems like all the Jews here believed, along with many Greeks. On a whole, why were they different? They eagerly searched the Scriptures to see if what Paul was saying was true. They were eager, they were alert, they were watchful for the Christ. They knew the Word spoke of the coming Christ, the Messiah of the heart. Romans 10:17 says faith comes by hearing and hearing by the Word of Christ. Then the jealous Jews end up showing up from Thessalonica. Paul leaves, getting on a boat for Athens (three days by boat or 12 days by foot).

In Athens, Paul goes to the synagogue; preaching Christ and the Resurrection. His audience grows from Jews and God-fearers to actually getting a platform at Mars Hill. Mars Hill was an open air concert setting. Many people would gather to hear what was being presented. Paul is given an open mic. The Greeks have many gods, they are full aware that there is a Higher Power. To make sure they have all god possibilities accounted for, they have One called, the Unknown God. Here again is Acts 17:22-31 with some Words in bold:

So Paul stood in the midst of the [s]Areopagus and said, "Men of Athens, I observe that you are very religious in all respects. 23 For while I was passing through and examining the objects of your worship, I also found an altar with this inscription, 'TO AN UNKNOWN GOD.' Therefore what you worship in ignorance, this I proclaim to you. 24 **The God who made the world and all things in it, since He is Lord of heaven and earth, does not dwell in temples made with hands; 25 nor is He served by human hands, as though He needed anything, since He Himself gives to all *people* life and breath and all things; 26 and He made from one *man* every nation of mankind to live on all the face of the earth, having determined *their* appointed times and the boundaries of their habitation, 27 that they would seek God, if perhaps they might grope for Him and find Him, though He is not far from each one of us; 28 for in Him we live and move and [t]exist, as even some of your own poets have said, 'For we also are His children.' 29 Being then the children of God, we ought not to think that the Divine Nature is like gold or silver or stone, an image formed by the art and thought of man. 30 Therefore having overlooked the times of ignorance, God is now declaring to men that all *people* everywhere should repent, 31 because He has fixed a day in which He will judge [u]the world in righteousness [v]through a Man whom He has appointed, having furnished proof to all men [w]by raising Him from the dead."**

Here is a link to the full chapter of Romans 3: https://www.biblegateway.com/passage/?search=Romans+3&version=NASB

Acts 18

After these things he left Athens and went to Corinth. 2 And he found a Jew named Aquila, a native of Pontus, having recently come from Italy with his wife Priscilla, because Claudius had commanded all the Jews to leave Rome. He came to them, 3 and because he was of the same trade, he stayed with them and they were working, for by trade they were tent-makers. ⁴ And he was reasoning in the synagogue every Sabbath and trying to persuade Jews and Greeks.

⁵ But when Silas and Timothy came down from Macedonia, Paul *began* devoting himself completely to the word, solemnly testifying to the Jews that Jesus was the [a]Christ. ⁶ But when they resisted and blasphemed, he shook out his garments and said to them, "Your blood *be* on your own heads! I am clean. From now on I will go to the Gentiles." ⁷ Then he left there and went to the house of a man named [b]Titius Justus, a worshiper of God, whose house was next to the synagogue. ⁸ Crispus, the leader of the synagogue, believed in the Lord with all his household, and many of the Corinthians when they heard were believing and being baptized. ⁹ And the Lord said to Paul in the night by a vision, "Do not be afraid *any longer*, but go on speaking and do not be silent; ¹⁰ for I am with you, and no man will attack you in order to harm you, for I have many people in this city." ¹¹ And he settled *there* a year and six months, teaching the word of God among them.

¹² But while Gallio was proconsul of Achaia, the Jews with one accord rose up against Paul and brought him before the judgment seat, ¹³ saying, "This man persuades men to worship God contrary to the law." ¹⁴ But when Paul was about to open his mouth, Gallio said to the Jews, "If it were a matter of wrong or of vicious crime, O Jews, it would be reasonable for me to put up with you; ¹⁵ but if there are questions about words and names and your own law, look after it yourselves; I am unwilling to be a judge of these matters." ¹⁶ And he drove them away from the judgment seat. ¹⁷ And they all took hold of Sosthenes, the leader of the synagogue, and *began* beating him in front of the judgment seat. But Gallio was not concerned about any of these things.

¹⁸ Paul, having remained many days longer, took leave of the brethren and put out to sea for Syria, and with him were Priscilla and Aquila. In Cenchrea [c]he had his hair cut, for he was keeping a vow. ¹⁹ They came to Ephesus, and he left them there. Now he himself entered the synagogue and reasoned with the Jews. ²⁰ When they asked him to stay for a longer time, he did not consent, ²¹ but taking

leave of them and saying, "I will return to you again if God wills," he set sail from Ephesus.

²² When he had landed at Caesarea, he went up and greeted the church, and went down to Antioch.

²³ And having spent some time *there*, he left and passed successively through the Galatian region and Phrygia, strengthening all the disciples.

²⁴ Now a Jew named Apollos, an Alexandrian by birth, [d]an eloquent man, came to Ephesus; and he was mighty in the Scriptures. ²⁵ This man had been instructed in the way of the Lord; and being fervent in spirit, he was speaking and teaching accurately the things concerning Jesus, being acquainted only with the baptism of John; ²⁶ and [e]he began to speak out boldly in the synagogue. But when Priscilla and Aquila heard him, they took him aside and explained to him the way of God more accurately. ²⁷ And when he wanted to go across to Achaia, the brethren encouraged him and wrote to the disciples to welcome him; and when he had arrived, he greatly [f]helped those who had believed through grace, ²⁸ for he powerfully refuted the Jews in public, demonstrating by the Scriptures that Jesus was the [g]Christ. (Acts 18)
https://www.biblegateway.com/passage/?search=Acts+18&version=NASB

Here is a link to a very nice map of the Roman Empire:
http://www.bible-history.com/maps/romanempire/

Paul is now in Corinth, which is west of Athens, still in modern day Greece. Paul had taken a boat to Athens. Silas and Timothy took the land route, so Paul is still waiting to meet up with them. In the meantime Paul meets Priscilla and Aquila. Aquila, who is a Jew, is from Pontus, which is northwest of Israel, in Asia Minor. Aquila and Priscilla just came from Rome, which is west of Greece, in Italy. We see some real turmoil beginning with the Roman Emperor, Claudius, kicking all the Jews out of Rome. This is no doubt related to the Christian/Jew conflicts that are arising across the Roman Empire.

Before the Temple destruction in 70 A.D. Paul and Peter are executed by the Roman Empire. Right now we are at around 52 A.D. Paul ends up staying at Corinth for a year and a half. This is a very busy metropolis, with people from many countries in and out. This is probably why the Corinthians had issues with the gift of tongues. God used tongues heavily here, but they obviously over emphasized that one gift, and lacked love at times. During Paul's stay at Corinth he writes to the Romans and Thessalonians. Paul probably received a lot of info on the church at Rome from Priscilla and Aquila. The couple are tentmakers, just like Paul. Paul is able to make some money while he waits for Silas and Timothy to arrive. This is an awesome trade, being that we as believers are now the Tent/Temple of the Holy Spirit. So Paul by sharing the Gospel is making Spiritual Tents. The Tent is also related to the Feast of Tabernacles. The Temporary Tent/Tabernacle that God Himself dwelt in as Jesus is related to us as we temporarily dwell in these bodies/tents, until the Last Trumpet.

Now that Silas and Timothy arrive with funds, Paul is able to go 100% into Spiritual Tent making. Paul gets upset with the Jews and leaves the synagogue. Notice where he goes, right next door, to the house of a Roman citizen named Titius Justus, a worshiper of God, no doubt brought into faith by Jews who shared the Oracles of God. Notice that the leader of the synagogue, Crispus, and many others gets saved.

The new leader of the synagogue, Sosthenes, does not get saved and he ends up trying, along with Jews not keen on sharing the Oracles of God, to get Paul in trouble with the Romans. The plan backfires and Sosthenes is beaten. The Roman leader i.e. proconsul, Gallio, doesn't want to take part in these "religious law" conflicts.

In verse 24 we are introduced to a Jew named Apollos from Alexandria. Remember the Greeks ruled prior to the Romans. Alexandria was actually in Africa. Remember when Stephen was

stoned in Acts 6 some of those that stoned him were from here. In Greek mythology Apollos (Greek sun god) is the son of Zeus (highest Greek god), and the brother of Artemis (Greek moon goddess). Zeus is mentioned in Acts 14:12 when people were calling Paul Hermes (chief speaker of god) and Barnabas Zeus. Apollos knew the Scriptures up until the baptism of repentance. Being a Jewish male he would have made those Three Feast journeys to Jerusalem each year. He no doubt went out to see John the Baptist who was baptizing "beyond the Jordon". Priscilla and Aquila fill him in on the full Gospel. He is mentioned quite a bit in 1 Corinthians 3. "Paul planted the Gospel Seed and Apollos watered, but God causes the growth." Here is 1 Corinthians 3:
https://www.biblegateway.com/passage/?search=1+Corinthians+3&version=NASB

Acts 19

It happened that while Apollos was at Corinth, Paul passed through the upper country and came to Ephesus, and found some disciples. [2] He said to them, "Did you receive the Holy Spirit when you believed?" And they *said* to him, "No, we have not even heard whether [a]there is a Holy Spirit." [3] And he said, "Into what then were you baptized?" And they said, "Into John's baptism." [4] Paul said, "John baptized with the baptism of repentance, telling the people to believe in Him who was coming after him, that is, in Jesus." [5] When they heard this, they were baptized [b]in the name of the Lord Jesus. [6] And when Paul had laid his hands upon them, the Holy Spirit came on them, and they *began* speaking with tongues and prophesying. [7] There were in all about twelve men.

[8] And he entered the synagogue and continued speaking out boldly for three months, reasoning and persuading *them* about the kingdom

of God. [9] But when some were becoming hardened and disobedient, speaking evil of the Way before the [c]people, he withdrew from them and took away the disciples, reasoning daily in the school of Tyrannus. [10] This took place for two years, so that all who lived in [d]Asia heard the word of the Lord, both Jews and Greeks.

[11] God was performing extraordinary [e]miracles by the hands of Paul, [12] so that handkerchiefs or aprons were even carried from his body to the sick, and the diseases left them and the evil spirits went out. [13] But also some of the Jewish exorcists, who went from place to place, attempted to name over those who had the evil spirits the name of the Lord Jesus, saying, "I adjure you by Jesus whom Paul preaches." [14] Seven sons of one Sceva, a Jewish chief priest, were doing this. [15] And the evil spirit answered and said to them, "I recognize Jesus, and I know about Paul, but who are you?" [16] And the man, in whom was the evil spirit, leaped on them and subdued all of them and overpowered them, so that they fled out of that house naked and wounded. [17] This became known to all, both Jews and Greeks, who lived in Ephesus; and fear fell upon them all and the name of the Lord Jesus was being magnified. [18] Many also of those who had believed kept coming, confessing and disclosing their practices. [19] And many of those who practiced magic brought their books together and *began* burning them in the sight of everyone; and they counted up the price of them and found it [f]fifty thousand pieces of silver. [20] So [g]the word of the Lord was growing mightily and prevailing.

[21] Now after these things were finished, Paul purposed in the [h]Spirit to go to Jerusalem after he had passed through Macedonia and Achaia, saying, "After I have been there, I must also see Rome." [22] And having sent into Macedonia two of those who ministered to him, Timothy and Erastus, he himself stayed in [i]Asia for a while.

[23] About that time there occurred no small disturbance concerning the Way. [24] For a man named Demetrius, a silversmith, who made silver shrines of [j]Artemis, was bringing no little [k]business to the craftsmen; [25] these he gathered together with the workmen of similar *trades*, and said, "Men, you know that our prosperity [l]depends upon this business. [26] You see and hear that not only in Ephesus, but in

almost all of [m]Asia, this Paul has persuaded and turned away a considerable number of people, saying that [n]gods made with hands are no gods *at all*. [27] Not only is there danger that this trade of ours fall into disrepute, but also that the temple of the great goddess [o]Artemis be regarded as worthless and that she whom all of [p]Asia and the [q]world worship will even be dethroned from her magnificence."

[28] When they heard *this* and were filled with rage, they *began* crying out, saying, "Great is [r]Artemis of the Ephesians!" [29] The city was filled with the confusion, and they rushed [s]with one accord into the theater, dragging along Gaius and Aristarchus, Paul's traveling companions from Macedonia. [30] And when Paul wanted to go into the [t]assembly, the disciples would not let him. [31] Also some of the [u]Asiarchs who were friends of his sent to him and repeatedly urged him not to [v]venture into the theater. [32] So then, some were shouting one thing and some another, for the [w]assembly was in confusion and the majority did not know [x]for what reason they had come together. [33] Some of the crowd [y]concluded *it was* Alexander, since the Jews had put him forward; and having motioned with his hand, Alexander was intending to make a defense to the [z]assembly. [34] But when they recognized that he was a Jew, a *single* outcry arose from them all as they shouted for about two hours, "Great is [aa]Artemis of the Ephesians!" [35] After quieting the crowd, the town clerk *said, "Men of Ephesus, what man is there after all who does not know that the city of the Ephesians is guardian of the temple of the great [ab]Artemis and of the *image* which fell down from [ac]heaven? [36] So, since these are undeniable facts, you ought to keep calm and to do nothing rash. [37] For you have brought these men *here* who are neither robbers of temples nor blasphemers of our goddess. [38] So then, if Demetrius and the craftsmen who are with him have a complaint against any man, the courts are in session and [ad]proconsuls are *available*; let them bring charges against one another. [39] But if you want anything beyond this, it shall be settled in the [ae]lawful [af]assembly. [40] For indeed we are in danger of being accused of a riot in connection with today's events, since there is no *real* cause *for it*, and in this connection we will be unable to account for this disorderly gathering." [41] After saying this he dismissed the [ag]assembly. (Acts 19)

https://www.biblegateway.com/passage/?search=Acts+19&version=NASB

Here is the Roman Empire map link again: http://www.bible-history.com/maps/romanempire/

So in the last chapter Paul had left Priscilla and Aquila in Ephesus. They met up with Apollos and gave him the full Gospel. Apollos then leaves Ephesus (Asia Minor) and goes to Corinth (Southern Greece in Europe). Paul comes back and teaches in the synagogue in Ephesus for three months. Things get heated at the synagogue and Paul moves to the school of Tyrannus in Ephesus. Paul teaches there for two years. Many Jews and Greeks come to Christ and receive the Holy Spirit.

Many miracles occur via the Holy Spirit through Paul. Some Jewish exorcists try and copy Paul and end up getting beat up, the counterfeit gospel has no Power of God.

The Greek goddess of Ephesus was Artemis i.e. Diana. She was the said daughter of Zeus, goddess of the moon. Sales of silver Artemis products were plummeting. The local silversmiths weren't too happy with Paul. Apparently in years past a meteor, possibly silver, had fallen from heaven that took on the name Artemis. The crowd settles down and Demetrius and the craftsmen are encouraged to use the Roman court system if they want to charge Paul.

An astounding fact is that the magic books, that people who came to Christ burned, equaled 50,000 pieces of silver! One piece of silver was a day's wages. We know from earlier studies that silver is the metal representing Redemption. Artemis was the silver moon goddess. The Jewish calendar uses the moon to appoint the New Year's Day, the first day of the 7th month. The entire year's calendar is based off of this day. The two day Feast is called Trumpets. There were two silver trumpets blown. Below is the first part of Numbers 10:

The LORD spoke further to Moses, saying, [2] "Make yourself two trumpets of silver, of hammered work you shall make them; and you shall use them for summoning the congregation and for having the camps set out. [3] When both are blown, all the congregation shall gather themselves to you at the doorway of the tent of meeting. [4] Yet if *only* one is blown, then the leaders, the heads of the [a]divisions of Israel, shall assemble before you. [5] But when you blow an alarm, the camps that are pitched on the east side shall set out. [6] When you blow an alarm the second time, the camps that are pitched on the south side shall set out; an alarm is to be blown for them to set out. [7] When convening the assembly, however, you shall blow without sounding an alarm. [8] The priestly sons of Aaron, moreover, shall blow the trumpets; and [b]this shall be for you a perpetual statute throughout your generations. [9] When you go to war in your land against the adversary who attacks you, then you shall sound an alarm with the trumpets, that you may be remembered before the LORD your God, and be saved from your enemies. [10] Also in the day of your gladness and in your appointed [c]feasts, and on the first *days* of your months, you shall blow the trumpets over your burnt offerings, and over the sacrifices of your peace offerings; and they shall be as a reminder of you before your God. I am the LORD your God." (Numbers 10:1-10)

Notice that when both Trumpets are blown that the entire congregation gathers. I believe the First (Alpha) Trumpet was at the birth of Christ. I believe the Last (Omega) Trumpet to be the Rapture when His entire congregation gathers to meet Him in the air.

Now I say this, brethren, that flesh and blood cannot inherit the kingdom of God; nor does [p]the perishable inherit [q]the imperishable. [51] Behold, I tell you a mystery; we will not all sleep, but we will all be changed, [52] in a moment, in the twinkling of an eye, at the last trumpet; for the trumpet will sound, and the dead will be raised [r]imperishable, and we will be changed. [53] For this [s]perishable must put on [t]the imperishable, and this mortal must put on immortality. [54] But when this [u]perishable will have put on [v]the imperishable, and this mortal will have put on immortality, then will come about the saying that is written, "DEATH IS SWALLOWED UP in victory. ⁵⁵ O DEATH, WHERE IS YOUR VICTORY? O DEATH, WHERE IS YOUR STING?" ⁵⁶ The sting of death is sin, and the power of sin is the law; ⁵⁷ but thanks be to God, who gives us the victory through our Lord Jesus Christ.

⁵⁸ Therefore, my beloved brethren, be steadfast, immovable, always abounding in the work of the Lord, knowing that your toil is not *in* vain in the Lord. (1 Corinthians 15:50-58)

"Behold, I am coming quickly, and My reward *is* with Me, to render to every man [g]according to what he has done. ¹³ I am the Alpha and the Omega, the first and the last, the beginning and the end." (Revelation 22:12-13)

Acts 20

After the uproar had ceased, Paul sent for the disciples, and when he had exhorted them and taken his leave of them, he left to go to Macedonia. ² When he had gone through those districts and had given them much exhortation, he came to Greece. ³ And *there* he spent three months, and when a plot was formed against him by the Jews as he was about to set sail for Syria, he decided to return through Macedonia. ⁴ And [a]he was accompanied by Sopater of Berea, *the son* of Pyrrhus, and by Aristarchus and Secundus of the Thessalonians, and Gaius of Derbe, and Timothy, and Tychicus and Trophimus of [b]Asia. ⁵ But these had gone on ahead and were waiting for us at Troas. ⁶ We sailed from Philippi after the days of Unleavened Bread, and came to them at Troas within five days; and there we stayed seven days.

⁷ On the first day of the week, when we were gathered together to break bread, Paul *began* talking to them, intending to leave the next

day, and he prolonged his [c]message until midnight. [8] There were many lamps in the upper room where we were gathered together. [9] And there was a young man named [d]Eutychus sitting [e]on the window sill, sinking into a deep sleep; and as Paul kept on talking, he was overcome by sleep and fell down from the third floor and was picked up dead. [10] But Paul went down and fell upon him, and after embracing him, he said, "[f]Do not be troubled, for his life is in him." [11] When he had gone *back* up and had broken the bread and [g]eaten, he talked with them a long while until daybreak, and then left. [12] They took away the boy alive, and were [h]greatly comforted.

[13] But we, going ahead to the ship, set sail for Assos, intending from there to take Paul on board; for so he had arranged it, intending himself to go [i]by land. [14] And when he met us at Assos, we took him on board and came to Mitylene. [15] Sailing from there, we arrived the following day opposite Chios; and the next day we crossed over to Samos; and the day following we came to Miletus. [16] For Paul had decided to sail past Ephesus so that he would not have to spend time in [j]Asia; for he was hurrying to be in Jerusalem, if possible, on the day of Pentecost.

[17] From Miletus he sent to Ephesus and called to him the elders of the church. [18] And when they had come to him, he said to them,

"You yourselves know, from the first day that I set foot in [k]Asia, how I was with you the whole time, [19] serving the Lord with all humility and with tears and with trials which came upon me [l]through the plots of the Jews; [20] how I did not shrink from declaring to you anything that was profitable, and teaching you publicly and [m]from house to house, [21] solemnly testifying to both Jews and Greeks of repentance toward God and faith in our Lord Jesus Christ. [22] And now, behold, bound by the [n]Spirit, I am on my way to Jerusalem, not knowing what will happen to me there, [23] except that the Holy Spirit solemnly testifies to me in every city, saying that bonds and afflictions await me. [24] But I do not consider my life of any account as dear to myself, so that I may finish my course and the ministry which I received from the Lord Jesus, to testify solemnly of the gospel of the grace of God.

25 "And now, behold, I know that all of you, among whom I went about preaching the kingdom, will no longer see my face. 26 Therefore, I [o]testify to you this day that I am [p]innocent of the blood of all men. 27 For I did not shrink from declaring to you the whole purpose of God. 28 Be on guard for yourselves and for all the flock, among which the Holy Spirit has made you [q]overseers, to shepherd the church of God which He [r]purchased [s]with His own blood. 29 I know that after my departure savage wolves will come in among you, not sparing the flock; 30 and from among your own selves men will arise, speaking perverse things, to draw away the disciples after them. 31 Therefore be on the alert, remembering that night and day for a period of three years I did not cease to admonish each one with tears. 32 And now I commend you to God and to the word of His grace, which is able to build *you* up and to give *you* the inheritance among all those who are sanctified. 33 I have coveted no one's silver or gold or clothes. 34 You yourselves know that these hands ministered to my *own* needs and to the men who were with me. 35 In everything I showed you that by working hard in this manner you must help the weak and remember the words of the Lord Jesus, that He Himself said, 'It is more blessed to give than to receive.'"

36 When he had said these things, he knelt down and prayed with them all. 37 And [t]they *began* to weep aloud and [u]embraced Paul, and repeatedly kissed him, 38 [v]grieving especially over the word which he had spoken, that they would not see his face again. And they were accompanying him to the ship. (Acts 20)
https://www.biblegateway.com/passage/?search=acts+20&version=NASB

Here is the Roman Empire map link, note as well that you can click on city names and it will lead you to a detailed description: http://www.bible-history.com/maps/romanempire/

We see the terms exhorted and exhortation. This is one of the Spiritual Gifts given by the Holy Spirit. Here is a link to a nice definition: https://gotquestions.org/definition-exhortation.html

We see an interesting name grouping of seven names. Being that the number is seven, let's take a look at their name meanings; we will use this link for all the names: http://biblehub.com/topical/

Sopater means the father who saves. Aristarchus means the best prince. Secundus means second. Gaius means Lord; an earthly man. Timothy means honoring God. Tychicus means fortuitous, which combines fortunate and fateful. Trophimus means well educated; well brought up; well nourished; foster child. Together we have the Father, Who sends His Prince, the Second Perfect Man, yet Better in that He remains Perfect, Honoring God all the Way to His fateful death, which makes us fortunate, in that He rose from the dead, making us His foster children, nourishing and teaching us by His Holy Spirit. These seven names also remind me of the Scripture from 1 Corinthians 15 where Paul refers to Jesus as a "Last Adam and Second Man".

So also it is written, "The first man, Adam, became a living soul." The last Adam *became* a life-giving spirit. [46] However, the spiritual is not first, but the natural; then the spiritual. [47] The first man is from the earth, [n]earthy; the second man is from heaven. [48] As is the earthy, so also are those who are earthy; and as is the heavenly, so also are those who are heavenly. [49] Just as we have borne the image of the earthy, [o]we will also bear the image of the heavenly. (1 Corinthians 15:45-49)

Name meanings are nothing to argue about. They do show the depth of God's Word. Some people believe that sometimes the Bible does have hidden meanings in name groupings etc. in case the letter was intercepted by anti-Christian Romans or anti-Christian Jews. Another excellent site for name meanings is: http://www.abarim-publications.com/Meaning/#.WCzyBclzWUm The Abarim site focuses mainly on the Jewish/Hebrew names of the Bible, so we used the Bible hub website this time.

It appears that Paul is trying to set sail to Syria, which is where the Christian home base of Antioch was, probably to go south from there to Jerusalem for one of the Three Required Feast Weeks, this Feast being Unleavened Bread. It was big business in getting all the Jews back to Jerusalem for the Three Feast Weeks. Every year people in the boating business would gear up those three times. This is another way that God reached out to the world. Jews travelled from Africa (remember Simon the Cyrene that carried the Cross of Jesus), from Europe, from Asia, and from all over the known world for those Three Feast Weeks. This no doubt got people curious about their God. In this case it looks like some Jews heading from Greece towards Jerusalem via Syria formed a plot against Paul. So Paul goes up towards Macedonia, to Philippi. The seven go ahead to Troas. After Unleavened Bread, Paul heads to Troas. So it appears Paul missed this required Feast.

Eventually the early church realizes that Christ was the total fulfillment of these Feasts. Most of today's churches only recognize four Feasts as having been fulfilled. This is puzzling to me, in that one that they don't recognize as having been fulfilled is the Day of Atonement. The final fulfillment of the Day of Atonement occurred at the tearing of the Veil to the Holy of Holies. Mind you as well that the Day of Atonement is for the atoning of sin. Without His Atonement we cannot go to Heaven. They also realized back then that the Covenant of Circumcision given to Abraham was also fulfilled in Christ. Jesus was Circumcised on the Day of Atonement (Luke 2:21). His Birth was at Trumpets (Luke 1 and 1 Chronicles 24). He lived 33 Perfect years without sin becoming our Perfect and Final Passover Lamb. We are at about the mid 50 A.D. timeframe at this point. In 70 A.D. the Temple and all of Jerusalem is completely destroyed. The point being is that in Christ we no longer have to abide by these Feasts. And after 70 A.D. and even to this very day there is no Temple to start the Feast process over again. Why should we anyway? Christ fulfilled all the Feasts. We now abide in Him.

Here is a nice timeline for the Book of Acts from the Bible hub website (note Jesus was born at about 4 B.C.):
http://biblehub.com/timeline/acts/1.htm

We see Paul, if possible, wants to make it to Jerusalem for the last Week of the Feast of Weeks which ends with Pentecost. In the next chapter we see he does make it, but anti-Christian Jews from Asia are also there, and they are enemies of the Gospel of Christ. The chapter ends with Paul giving a farewell speech to the elders of the church at Ephesus.

Acts 21

When we had parted from them and had set sail, we ran a straight course to Cos and the next day to Rhodes and from there to Patara; ² and having found a ship crossing over to Phoenicia, we went aboard and set sail. ³ When we came in sight of Cyprus, leaving it on the left, we kept sailing to Syria and landed at Tyre; for there the ship was to unload its cargo. ⁴ After looking up the disciples, we stayed there seven days; and they kept telling Paul [a]through the Spirit not to set foot in Jerusalem. ⁵ When [b]our days there were ended, we left and started on our journey, while they all, with wives and children, escorted us until *we were* out of the city. After kneeling down on the beach and praying, we said farewell to one another. ⁶ Then we went on board the ship, and they returned home again.

⁷ When we had finished the voyage from Tyre, we arrived at Ptolemais, and after greeting the brethren, we stayed with them for a day. ⁸ On the next day we left and came to Caesarea, and entering the house of Philip the evangelist, who was one of the seven, we stayed with him. ⁹ Now this man had four virgin daughters who were prophetesses. ¹⁰ As we were staying there for some days, a prophet named Agabus came down from Judea. ¹¹ And coming to us, he took

Paul's belt and bound his own feet and hands, and said, "This is what the Holy Spirit says: 'In this way the Jews at Jerusalem will bind the man who owns this belt and deliver him into the hands of the Gentiles.'" ¹² When we had heard this, we as well as the local residents *began* begging him not to go up to Jerusalem. ¹³ Then Paul answered, "What are you doing, weeping and breaking my heart? For I am ready not only to be bound, but even to die at Jerusalem for the name of the Lord Jesus." ¹⁴ And since he would not be persuaded, we fell silent, remarking, "The will of the Lord be done!"

¹⁵ After these days we got ready and started on our way up to Jerusalem. ¹⁶ *Some* of the disciples from Caesarea also came with us, taking us to Mnason of Cyprus, a disciple of long standing with whom we were to lodge.

¹⁷ After we arrived in Jerusalem, the brethren received us gladly. ¹⁸ And the following day Paul went in with us to ^[c]James, and all the elders were present. ¹⁹ After he had greeted them, he *began* to relate one by one the things which God had done among the Gentiles through his ministry. ²⁰ And when they heard it they *began* glorifying God; and they said to him, "You see, brother, how many ^[d]thousands there are among the Jews of those who have believed, and they are all zealous for the Law; ²¹ and they have been told about you, that you are teaching all the Jews who are among the Gentiles to forsake Moses, telling them not to circumcise their children nor to ^[e]walk according to the customs. ²² What, then, is *to be done*? They will certainly hear that you have come. ²³ Therefore do this that we tell you. We have four men who ^[f]are under a vow; ²⁴ take them and purify yourself along with them, and ^[g]pay their expenses so that they may shave their ^[h]heads; and all will know that there is nothing to the things which they have been told about you, but that you yourself also walk orderly, keeping the Law. ²⁵ But concerning the Gentiles who have believed, we wrote, having decided that they should abstain from ^[i]meat sacrificed to idols and from blood and from what is strangled and from fornication." ²⁶ Then Paul ^[j]took the men, and the next day, purifying himself along with them, went into the temple giving notice of the completion of the days of purification, until the sacrifice was offered for each one of them.

27 When the seven days were almost over, the Jews from [k]Asia, upon seeing him in the temple, *began* to stir up all the crowd and laid hands on him, 28 crying out, "Men of Israel, come to our aid! This is the man who preaches to all men everywhere against our people and the Law and this place; and besides he has even brought Greeks into the temple and has defiled this holy place." 29 For they had previously seen Trophimus the Ephesian in the city with him, and they supposed that Paul had brought him into the temple. 30 Then all the city was provoked, and [l]the people rushed together, and taking hold of Paul they dragged him out of the temple, and immediately the doors were shut. 31 While they were seeking to kill him, a report came up to the [m]commander of the *Roman* [n]cohort that all Jerusalem was in confusion. 32 At once he took along *some* soldiers and centurions and ran down to them; and when they saw the [o]commander and the soldiers, they stopped beating Paul. 33 Then the [p]commander came up and took hold of him, and ordered him to be bound with two chains; and he *began* asking who he was and what he had done. 34 But among the crowd some were shouting one thing *and* some another, and when he could not find out the [q]facts because of the uproar, he ordered him to be brought into the barracks. 35 When he got to the stairs, he was carried by the soldiers because of the violence of the [r]mob; 36 for the multitude of the people kept following them, shouting, "Away with him!"

37 As Paul was about to be brought into the barracks, he said to the [s]commander, "May I say something to you?" And he *said, "Do you know Greek? 38 Then you are not the Egyptian who some [t]time ago stirred up a revolt and led the four thousand men of the Assassins out into the wilderness?" 39 But Paul said, "I am a Jew of Tarsus in Cilicia, a citizen of no insignificant city; and I beg you, allow me to speak to the people." 40 When he had given him permission, Paul, standing on the stairs, motioned to the people with his hand; and when there [u]was a great hush, he spoke to them in the [v]Hebrew dialect, saying, (Acts 21)
https://www.biblegateway.com/passage/?search=Acts+21&version=NASB

282

Interactive Roman Empire map link (remember you can click on the names of the cities to get a ton of more info): http://www.bible-history.com/maps/romanempire/

We see Paul receiving several warnings to not go to Jerusalem. He is told he will be bound and given to the gentiles, in this case to the Romans. We see the Spiritual Gifts from the Holy Spirit via early believers warning Paul. Remember the church is empowered by the Holy Spirit. This is a big difference from just prior to the Crucifixion of Christ. Remember even tough guy Peter wimped out on Jesus, three times, once to a little girl. Why? He had not yet received Power from on High. Remember Jesus said to wait in Jerusalem for Pentecost. Pentecost signified that all the 7 Feasts (more properly named Holy Convocations i.e. Trumpets and Day of Atonement and Tabernacles and Passover and Unleavened Bread and First Fruits and Weeks) of Leviticus 23 were fulfilled. Pentecost, Day 50, Jubilee Day, in a Jubilee Year meant that the chains of sin and death were broken. Jesus Christ now has the keys to death and Hades. satan no longer has the keys.

Even given this information Paul still goes to Jerusalem. This is part of God's plan for Paul. He being a Roman citizen will be able to appeal all the way to Rome, to caesar. Paul has been an instrument of precision church planting and church watering, with God causing an abundant growth.

When Paul arrives at Jerusalem, he meets James. James is the leader of the church at Jerusalem. James is the half-brother of Jesus. Paul is advised to take four men who had taken a vow and complete a purification process with them. This is probably the vow of the Nazarite from Numbers 6: https://www.biblegateway.com/passage/?search=Numbers+6&version=NASB

We know Paul does all he can to win souls for Christ as per 1 Corinthians 9:

For though I am free from all *men*, I have made myself a slave to all, so that I may win more. ²⁰ To the Jews I became as a Jew, so that I might win Jews; to those who are under [h]the Law, as under [i]the Law though not being myself under [j]the Law, so that I might win those who are under [k]the Law; ²¹ to those who are without law, as without law, though not being without the law of God but under the law of Christ, so that I might win those who are without law. ²² To the weak I became weak, that I might win the weak; I have become all things to all men, so that I may by all means save some. ²³ I do all things for the sake of the gospel, so that I may become a fellow partaker of it. (1 Corinthians 9:19-23)

We are coming up on one of the three required Feast Weeks, that being the last week of Weeks ending with Pentecost. So the anti-Christian Jews from Asia are beginning to show up in Jerusalem. Paul is accused of preaching against the Law and Temple, which he never did, he preached Christ as the fulfillment of the Law and Temple. He is also accused of bringing a gentile/Greek into the Temple, which he didn't. In verse 36, the "Away with him!", sounds so very familiar with the words of the mob on Good Friday, the Day our Lord Jesus became the Unblemished Lamb of God that takes away the sin of the world.

Now it was the day of preparation for the Passover; it was about the [h]sixth hour. And he *said to the Jews, "Behold, your King!" ¹⁵ So they cried out, "Away with *Him*, away with *Him*, crucify Him!" Pilate *said to them, "Shall I crucify your King?" The chief priests answered, "We have no king but Caesar." (John 19:14-15)

In the uproar the Romans take Paul into custody. Paul surprises the Roman Commander in that he knows Greek. Paul requests to be able to speak to the Jews. Paul is given permission. This chapter ends on a comma. In the next chapter we will hear what Paul says. Note also that Luke, the author via the Holy Spirit, of the Book of Acts and Luke seems to actually be with Paul from possibly Acts chapter 16, which is when we start seeing "we" being used. Luke is the only gentile who is an instrument of the Holy Spirit in writing

His Word. Here is a link to some info on Luke:
https://gotquestions.org/Luke-in-the-Bible.html

Acts 22

"Brethren and fathers, hear my defense which I now *offer* to you."

[2] And when they heard that he was addressing them in the [a]Hebrew dialect, they became even more quiet; and he *said,

[3] "I am a Jew, born in Tarsus of Cilicia, but brought up in this city, educated [b]under Gamaliel, [c]strictly according to the law of our fathers, being zealous for God just as you all are today. [4] I persecuted this Way to the death, binding and putting both men and women into prisons, [5] as also the high priest and all the Council of the elders [d]can testify. From them I also received letters to the brethren, and started off for Damascus in order to bring even those who were there to Jerusalem [e]as prisoners to be punished.

[6] "But it happened that as I was on my way, approaching Damascus about noontime, a very bright light suddenly flashed from heaven all around me, [7] and I fell to the ground and heard a voice saying to me, 'Saul, Saul, why are you persecuting Me?' [8] And I answered, 'Who are You, Lord?' And He said to me, 'I am Jesus the Nazarene, whom you are persecuting.' [9] And those who were with me saw the light, to be sure, but did not [f]understand the voice of the One who was speaking to me. [10] And I said, 'What shall I do, Lord?' And the Lord said to me, 'Get up and go on into Damascus, and there you will be told of all that has been appointed for you to do.' [11] But since I could not see because of the [g]brightness of that light, I was led by the hand by those who were with me and came into Damascus.

[12] "A certain Ananias, a man who was devout by the standard of the Law, *and* well spoken of by all the Jews who lived there, [13] came to me, and standing near said to me, 'Brother Saul, receive your sight!' And [h]at that very time I looked up at him. [14] And he said, 'The God of our fathers has appointed you to know His will and to see the Righteous One and to hear an [i]utterance from His mouth. [15] For you will be a witness for Him to all men of what you have seen and heard. [16] Now why do you delay? Get up and be baptized, and wash away your sins, calling on His name.'

[17] "It happened when I returned to Jerusalem and was praying in the temple, that I fell into a trance, [18] and I saw Him saying to me, 'Make haste, and get out of Jerusalem quickly, because they will not accept your testimony about Me.' [19] And I said, 'Lord, they themselves understand that in one synagogue after another I used to imprison and beat those who believed in You. [20] And when the blood of Your witness Stephen was being shed, I also was standing by approving, and watching out for the coats of those who were slaying him.' [21] And He said to me, 'Go! For I will send you far away to the Gentiles.'"

[22] They listened to him up to this statement, and *then* they raised their voices and said, "Away with such a fellow from the earth, for he should not be allowed to live!" [23] And as they were crying out and throwing off their cloaks and tossing dust into the air, [24] the [j]commander ordered him to be brought into the barracks, stating that he should be examined by scourging so that he might find out the reason why they were shouting against him that way. [25] But when they stretched him out [k]with thongs, Paul said to the centurion who was standing by, "Is it [l]lawful for you to scourge a man who is a Roman and uncondemned?" [26] When the centurion heard *this*, he went to the [m]commander and told him, saying, "What are you about to do? For this man is a Roman." [27] The [n]commander came and said to him, "Tell me, are you a Roman?" And he said, "Yes." [28] The [o]commander answered, "I acquired this citizenship with a large sum of money." And Paul said, "But I was actually born *a citizen*." [29] Therefore those who were about to examine him immediately [p]let go of him; and the [q]commander also was afraid when he found out that he was a Roman, and because he had [r]put him in chains.

[30] But on the next day, wishing to know for certain why he had been accused by the Jews, he released him and ordered the chief priests and all the [s]Council to assemble, and brought Paul down and set him before them. (Acts 22)
https://www.biblegateway.com/passage/?search=Acts+22&version=NASB

Interactive Roman Empire Map link: http://www.bible-history.com/maps/romanempire/

Paul, in Roman protection, is given a platform to speak to Jewish men from all over the world. We are at the very end of one of the three required Feast Weeks for all Jewish men, this being Weeks, which ends with Pentecost. Remember in Acts 20:16 that Paul was hurrying if possible to make it to Jerusalem for Pentecost. Then in the last chapter we had:

When the seven days were almost over, the Jews from [k]Asia, upon seeing him in the temple, *began* to stir up all the crowd and laid hands on him, [28] crying out, "Men of Israel, come to our aid! This is the man who preaches to all men everywhere against our people and the Law and this place; and besides he has even brought Greeks into the temple and has defiled this holy place." (Acts 21:27-28)

Paul says that he is a Jew, born in Tarsus (Q7 on interactive map). He was raised in Jerusalem. He is educated under Gamaliel, a Pharisee, who was also one of the Council i.e. the Sanhedrin. We heard from Gamaliel in Acts 5 when Peter and John were close to being killed for preaching Christ:

But when they heard this, they were cut [t]to the quick and intended to kill them. [34] But a Pharisee named Gamaliel, a teacher of the Law, respected by all the people, stood up in the Council and gave orders to put the men outside for a short time. [35] And he said to them, "Men of Israel, take care what you propose to do with these men. [36] For some time ago Theudas rose up, claiming to be somebody, and a group of about four hundred men joined up with him. [u]But he was killed, and all who [v]followed him were dispersed and came to nothing. [37] After this man, Judas of Galilee rose up in the days of the census and drew away *some* people after him; he too perished, and all those who [w]followed him were scattered. [38] So in the present case, I say to you, stay away from these men and let them alone, for if this plan or [x]action is of men, it will be overthrown; [39] but if it is of God, you will not be able to overthrow them; or else you may even be found fighting against God."

[40] They [y]took his advice; and after calling the apostles in, they flogged them and ordered them not to [z]speak in the name of Jesus, and *then* released them. [41] So they went on their way from the presence of the [aa]Council, rejoicing that they had been considered worthy to suffer shame for *His* name. [42] And every day, in the temple and [ab]from house to house, they [ac]kept right on teaching and [ad]preaching Jesus *as* the [ae]Christ. (Acts 5:33-42)

Notice above in verse 39: but if it is of God, you will not be able to overthrow them; or else you may even be found fighting against God."

At the very end of Paul's testimony, in Acts 22:21, Jesus appearing to Paul says:

And He said to me, 'Go! For I will send you far away to the Gentiles.'

Some Jews were very well accepting of the Gospel. Some were not. Some Jews had no problem with gentiles coming into the family of God, into the flock, being grafted into the One Olive Tree having the One Root of Jesse i.e. the Root of Jesus Christ. The Christ was nothing new; the Jews were to be watchful and alert for the coming Christ, the fulfiller of the entire Old Testament. "The Old Testament is Christ concealed, the New Testament is Christ revealed." Notice the verses below from Psalms:

He also chose David His servant
And took him from the sheepfolds;
[71] From [am]the care of the [an]ewes with suckling lambs He brought

him
To shepherd Jacob His people,
And Israel His inheritance.
[72] So he shepherded them according to the integrity of his heart,
And guided them with his skillful hands. (Psalms 78:70-72)

Some Jews remain "Jacob", stopping at having only a physical genealogy. Some Jews are changed from "Jacob" to "Israel", transcending the physical genealogy, obtaining the Eternal Genealogy through Jesus the Christ, the Savior of all men. God came in the Flesh and won the heart wrestling match for us, in our place, through Him all humans can be Israel. We are now at over two thousand years since the Temple was utterly destroyed, which Jesus said would happen. But we still have "Jacob" Jews, who say the Christ has not yet come. We do have many "Israel" Jews as well, groups like "Jews for Jesus" and "Life in Messiah" are thriving.

Most of us won't have the opportunity to witness to non-Christ believing Jew. But if you do, be ready. I advise to not use any New Testament Scripture. There is an Entire Old Testament overflowing with Jesus Christ. I will paste a couple YouTube links below. One shows a pastor losing badly to an Orthodox Jew is Jerusalem. Another is a show with a panel of Jews, Completed Jews, and Christians. It is interesting to see and hear the different attitudes.

https://www.youtube.com/watch?v=o6IYvP07LG4

https://www.youtube.com/watch?v=A1eE8IuInNo

Acts 23

Paul, looking intently at the [a]Council, said, "Brethren, I have [b]lived my life with a perfectly good conscience before God up to this day." ² The high priest Ananias commanded those standing beside him to strike him on the mouth. ³ Then Paul said to him, "God is going to strike you, you whitewashed wall! Do you sit to try me according to the Law, and in violation of the Law order me to be struck?" ⁴ But the bystanders said, "Do you revile God's high priest?" ⁵ And Paul said, "I was not aware, brethren, that he was high priest; for it is written, 'YOU SHALL NOT SPEAK EVIL OF A RULER OF YOUR PEOPLE.'"

⁶ But perceiving that one group were Sadducees and the other Pharisees, Paul *began* crying out in the [c]Council, "Brethren, I am a Pharisee, a son of Pharisees; I am on trial for the hope and resurrection of the dead!" ⁷ As he said this, there occurred a dissension between the Pharisees and Sadducees, and the assembly was divided. ⁸ For the Sadducees say that there is no resurrection, nor an angel, nor a spirit, but the Pharisees acknowledge them all. ⁹ And there occurred a great uproar; and some of the scribes of the Pharisaic party stood up and *began* to argue heatedly, saying, "We find nothing wrong with this man; suppose a spirit or an angel has spoken to him?" ¹⁰ And as a great dissension was developing, the [d]commander was afraid Paul would be torn to pieces by them and ordered the troops to go down and take him away from them by force, and bring him into the barracks.

¹¹ But on the night *immediately* following, the Lord stood at his side and said, "Take courage; for as you have solemnly witnessed to My cause at Jerusalem, so you must witness at Rome also."

¹² When it was day, the Jews formed a [e]conspiracy and bound themselves under an oath, saying that they would neither eat nor drink until they had killed Paul. ¹³ There were more than forty who formed this plot. ¹⁴ They came to the chief priests and the elders and said, "We have bound ourselves under a solemn oath to taste nothing until we have killed Paul. ¹⁵ Now therefore, you [f]and the [g]Council notify the [h]commander to bring him down to you, as though you were going to determine his case by a more thorough investigation; and we for our part are ready to slay him before he comes near *the place*."

[16] But the son of Paul's sister heard of their ambush, [i]and he came and entered the barracks and told Paul. [17] Paul called one of the centurions to him and said, "Lead this young man to the [j]commander, for he has something to report to him." [18] So he took him and led him to the [k]commander and *said, "Paul the prisoner called me to him and asked me to lead this young man to you since he has something to tell you." [19] The [l]commander took him by the hand and stepping aside, *began* to inquire of him privately, "What is it that you have to report to me?" [20] And he said, "The Jews have agreed to ask you to bring Paul down tomorrow to the [m]Council, as though they were going to inquire somewhat more thoroughly about him. [21] So do not [n]listen to them, for more than forty of them are lying in wait for him who have bound themselves under a curse not to eat or drink until they slay him; and now they are ready and waiting for the promise from you." [22] So the [o]commander let the young man go, instructing him, "Tell no one that you have notified me of these things."

[23] And he called to him two of the centurions and said, "Get two hundred soldiers ready by [p]the third hour of the night to proceed to Caesarea, [q]with seventy horsemen and two hundred [r]spearmen." [24] *They were* also to provide mounts to put Paul on and bring him safely to Felix the governor. [25] And he wrote a letter having this form:

[26] "Claudius Lysias, to the most excellent governor Felix, greetings.

[27] "When this man was arrested by the Jews and was about to be slain by them, I came up to them with the troops and rescued him, having learned that he was a Roman. [28] "And wanting to ascertain the charge for which they were accusing him, I brought him down to their [s]Council; [29] and I found him to be accused over questions about their Law, but [t]under no accusation deserving death or [u]imprisonment.

[30] "When I was informed that there would be a plot against the man, I sent him to you at once, also instructing his accusers to [v]bring charges against him before you."

³¹ So the soldiers, in accordance with their orders, took Paul and brought him by night to Antipatris. ³² But the next day, leaving the horsemen to go on with him, they returned to the barracks. ³³ When these had come to Caesarea and delivered the letter to the governor, they also presented Paul to him. ³⁴ When he had read it, he asked from what province he was, and when he learned that he was from Cilicia, ³⁵ he said, "I will give you a hearing after your accusers arrive also," giving orders for him to be kept in Herod's ^[w]Praetorium. (Acts 23)
https://www.biblegateway.com/passage/?search=Acts+23&version=NASB

In the previous chapter Paul was given a platform to speak to the Jews by the Roman commander. Remember many Jews have already come to Christ. These Jews are the ones who have hardened their hearts to God's love for all people. In the last chapter, when Paul mentioned that Jesus told him to go to the gentiles they wanted to kill Paul. When you see gentiles in the Bible notice it is capitalized. Gentiles is also translated Nations. The Bible goes much deeper than terms like Jews or Gentiles. The heart is what counts. The condition of your heart determines your eternal life or eternal death. Jesus never used the term Jew. Even just before the Cross when asked by Pilate, "Are you King of the Jews?" Jesus said, "**You** (emphasis on Pilate) have said so." (Mark 15:2) The entire Old Testament pointed to the need of the Christ, the Savior of the heart. Matthew 5:17 says that Christ came to fulfill the Law and the Prophets. The focus should be on Him and on hearts, not on terms like Jews or Gentiles.

Paul makes the claim that he has a perfectly good conscience before God; he has been washed of his sin and filled with God's Holy Spirit. The high priest, Ananias, has Paul punched in the mouth. Paul says to Ananias that God is going to strike him, calling him a whitewashed wall. Remember the Words of Jesus in Matthew 23:

"Woe to you, scribes and Pharisees, hypocrites! For you are like whitewashed tombs which on the outside appear beautiful, but inside they are full of dead men's bones and all uncleanness. [28] So you, too, outwardly appear righteous to men, but inwardly you are full of hypocrisy and lawlessness. (Matthew 23:27, 28)

Before major Holydays in Jerusalem, the tombs would be whitewashed, so people would notice them and not come in contact with them, making themselves "unclean". They were also whitewashed for show, meaning the hypocritical Jews (Matthew 23) in Jerusalem wanted to show the visiting Jews how much they honored the tombs of the dead prophets, although in reality their ancestors murdered them, because they exposed their dirty sinful hearts that needed a Savior. Whitewash was a chalky lime/water mix. Once you painted the tombs they looked brand new on the outside, but on the inside were dead men's bones and uncleanness. It is interesting that lime is actually used to speed up decomposition i.e. rot or death.

The situation starts to get heated and Paul brings up the Resurrection, knowing that this would change the focus off of him and cause a stir between the Sadducees and the Pharisees. Verse 8 says, "For the Sadducees say that there is no resurrection, nor an angel, nor a spirit, but the Pharisees acknowledge them all." The Roman commander has Paul brought back into the barracks fearing that Paul will be torn to pieces.

Notice in verse 11 that Jesus Himself appears to Paul. Jesus tells Paul that he will go to Rome. Remember that after the Crucifixion, on First Fruits i.e. Resurrection Day, which was Day 1 of the 49 Days of Weeks, that during these 49 Days that Jesus appeared to the disciples and to many others, up to five hundred at one time (1 Corinthians 15:6). Then Jesus went to the Right Hand of the Father. Then on Day 50, Pentecost, the Father sent the Helper i.e. the Holy Spirit. Jesus Himself is making multiple special visits to Paul, the first being the Road to Damascus. By Jesus Himself visiting Paul, Paul was assured that He was going to make it to Rome. Here is a link to the Interactive Roman Empire map, notice the huge distance between Jerusalem and Rome: http://www.bible-history.com/maps/romanempire/

Being a Roman citizen is great benefit for Paul, he gets the protection he needs, and later he can appeal to Caesar, to Rome. A plot is formed by forty men, swearing to not eat or drink until they kill Paul, learning of this plot, the commander has Paul moved a two days journey to Caesarea, about 65 miles. Paul's accusers could go there to make their case against him. Paul would not get a fair trial in Jerusalem. Remember thousands of Jews have already come to Christ. The ones that have not come to Christ have missed the point of the "heart" of the matter. It is very interesting that the phrase the "heart of the matter" comes from the phrase "the crux of the matter". Crux is Latin for Cross. At the end of this physical life, all that matters is Jesus. Faith in Him, in His Work, cleans us from the inside out.

"Woe to you, scribes and Pharisees, hypocrites! For you clean the outside of the cup and of the dish, but inside they are full [w]of robbery and self-indulgence. 26 You blind Pharisee, first clean the inside of the cup and of the dish, so that the outside of it may become clean also. (Matthew 23:25, 26)

Here is link to an awesome song:
https://www.youtube.com/watch?v=X-afZJ9_TIM

Acts 24

After five days the high priest Ananias came down with some elders, [a]with an [b]attorney *named* Tertullus, and they [c]brought charges to the governor against Paul. ² After *Paul* had been summoned, Tertullus began to accuse him, saying *to the governor,*

"Since we have through you attained much peace, and since by your providence reforms are being carried out for this nation, ³ we acknowledge *this* in every way and everywhere, most excellent Felix, with all thankfulness. ⁴ But, that I may not weary you any further, I beg you [d]to grant us, by your kindness, a brief hearing. ⁵ For we have found this man a real pest and a fellow who stirs up dissension among all the Jews throughout [e]the world, and a ringleader of the sect of the Nazarenes. ⁶ And he even tried to desecrate the temple; and [f]then we arrested him. [[g]We wanted to judge him according to our own Law. ⁷ But Lysias the commander came along, and with much violence took him out of our hands, ⁸ ordering his accusers to come before you.] By examining him yourself concerning all these matters you will be able to ascertain the things of which we accuse him." ⁹ The Jews also joined in the attack, asserting that these things were so.

¹⁰ When the governor had nodded for him to speak, Paul responded:

"Knowing that for many years you have been a judge to this nation, I cheerfully make my defense, ¹¹ since you can take note of the fact that no more than twelve days ago I went up to Jerusalem to worship. ¹² Neither in the temple, nor in the synagogues, nor in the city *itself* did they find me carrying on a discussion with anyone or causing [h]a riot. ¹³ Nor can they prove to you *the charges* of which they now accuse me. ¹⁴ But this I admit to you, that according to the Way which they call a sect I do serve [i]the God of our fathers, believing everything that is in accordance with the Law and that is written in the Prophets; ¹⁵ having a hope in God, which these men cherish themselves, that there shall certainly be a resurrection of both the righteous and the wicked. ¹⁶ In view of this, I also [j]do my best to maintain always a blameless conscience *both* before God and before men. ¹⁷ Now after several years I came to bring [k]alms to my nation and to present offerings; ¹⁸ in which they found me *occupied* in the temple, having been purified, without *any* crowd or uproar. But *there were* some Jews from [l]Asia— ¹⁹ who ought to have been present before you and to make accusation, if they should have anything against me. [20] Or else let these men themselves tell what misdeed they found when I stood before the [m]Council, [21] other than for this one statement which I shouted out while standing among them, 'For the resurrection of the dead I am on trial before you today.'"

[22] But Felix, [n]having a more exact knowledge about the Way, put them off, saying, "When Lysias the [o]commander comes down, I will decide your case." [23] Then he gave orders to the centurion for him to be kept in custody and *yet* have *some* freedom, and not to prevent any of his friends from ministering to him.

[24] But some days later Felix arrived with Drusilla, his [p]wife who was a Jewess, and sent for Paul and heard him *speak* about faith in Christ Jesus. [25] But as he was discussing righteousness, self-control and the judgment to come, Felix became frightened and said, "Go away for the present, and when I find time I will summon you." [26] At the same time too, he was hoping that money would be given him by Paul; therefore he also used to send for him quite often and converse with him. [27] But after two years had passed, Felix [q]was succeeded by Porcius Festus, and wishing to do the Jews a favor, Felix left Paul imprisoned. (Acts 24)
https://www.biblegateway.com/passage/?search=acts+24&version=NASB

In the last chapter Paul was moved to Caesarea, due to the plot to kill him, and for a fair trial. We have the high priest and some elders, along with a Roman lawyer now in Caesarea bringing charges against Paul. The Roman lawyer, Tertullus, really kisses up to the Roman Governor, Felix, as he begins to state the charges. Paul does an excellent job responding. Here are verses 14-16 again:

But this I admit to you, that according to the Way which they call a sect I do serve [i]the God of our fathers, believing everything that is in accordance with the Law and that is written in the Prophets; [15] having a hope in God, which these men cherish themselves, that there shall certainly be a resurrection of both the righteous and the wicked. ^{16} In view of this, I also $^{[i]}$do my best to maintain always a blameless conscience *both* before God and before men.

The charges don't stick and Felix puts off the high priest, elders and the lawyer. He says he will decide the case when the commander shows up. The high priest, elders and lawyer probably leave at this point, going back to Jerusalem. Some days later, Felix, he being Roman gentile, with his wife, she being a Jew, send for Paul to hear him speak about faith in Christ, along with discussing righteousness, self-control and the judgement to come. Felix becomes frightened. Notice that Paul is kept in custody for two years in Caesarea, but not tight custody; verse 23 says, "to be kept in custody and *yet* have *some* freedom, and not to prevent any of his friends from ministering to him." Part of Felix wanted a bribe; part of him was "frightened" by the preaching of Paul.

We see in the next chapter that two years changed nothing as far as the hatred and wanting to kill Paul by the chief priests and elders. So we know that Paul was very active in sharing his faith in the two years at Caesarea. Caesarea was the capital of the province of Judea. So we can assume he was perfectly placed here, having an open door to witness to the highest leaders of this area of the world, along with anyone else put in his path there. He will soon be taken to the capital of the entire known world, Rome. It is possible that he may have written some letters to churches from here. For instance, Philippians doesn't have any clues to where it was written from. Nothing to argue about though, we know Paul did not lie idle. Here is a nice timeline of Paul's entire life from the blue letter Bible: https://www.blueletterbible.org/study/paul/timeline.cfm

Acts 25

Festus then, having arrived in the province, three days later went up to Jerusalem from Caesarea. [2] And the chief priests and the leading men of the Jews brought charges against Paul, and they were urging him, [3] requesting a [a]concession against [b]Paul, that he might [c]have him brought to Jerusalem (*at the same time*, setting an ambush to kill him on the way). [4] Festus then answered that Paul was being kept in custody at Caesarea and that he himself was about to leave shortly. [5] "Therefore," he *said, "let the influential men among you [d]go there with me, and if there is anything wrong [e]about the man, let them [f]prosecute him."

[6] After he had spent not more than eight or ten days among them, he went down to Caesarea, and on the next day he took his seat on the tribunal and ordered Paul to be brought. [7] After Paul arrived, the Jews who had come down from Jerusalem stood around him, bringing many and serious charges against him which they could not prove, [8] while Paul said in his own defense, "I have committed no offense either against the Law of the Jews or against the temple or against Caesar." [9] But Festus, wishing to do the Jews a favor, answered Paul and said, "Are you willing to go up to Jerusalem and [g]stand trial before me on these *charges*?" [10] But Paul said, "I am standing before Caesar's tribunal, where I ought to be tried. I have done no wrong to *the* Jews, as you also very well know. [11] If, then, I am a wrongdoer and have committed anything worthy of death, I do not refuse to die; but if none of those things is *true* of which these men accuse me, no one can hand me over to them. I appeal to Caesar." [12] Then when Festus had conferred with [h]his council, he answered, "You have appealed to Caesar, to Caesar you shall go."

[13] Now when several days had elapsed, King Agrippa and Bernice arrived at Caesarea [i]and paid their respects to Festus. [14] While they were spending many days there, Festus laid Paul's case before the king, saying, "There is a man who was left as a prisoner by Felix; [15] and when I was at Jerusalem, the chief priests and the elders of the

Jews brought charges against him, asking for a sentence of condemnation against him. [16] I answered them that it is not the custom of the Romans to hand over any man before the accused meets his accusers face to face and has an opportunity to make his defense against the charges. [17] So after they had assembled here, I did not delay, but on the next day took my seat on the tribunal and ordered the man to be brought before me. [18] When the accusers stood up, they *began* bringing charges against him not of such crimes as I was expecting, [19] but they *simply* had some points of disagreement with him about their own [i]religion and about a dead man, Jesus, whom Paul asserted to be alive. [20] Being at a loss how to investigate [k]such matters, I asked whether he was willing to go to Jerusalem and there stand trial on these matters. [21] But when Paul appealed to be held in custody for [l]the Emperor's decision, I ordered him to be kept in custody until I send him to Caesar." [22] Then Agrippa *said* to Festus, "I also would like to hear the man myself." "Tomorrow," he *said, "you shall hear him."

[23] So, on the next day when Agrippa came [m]together with Bernice amid great pomp, and entered the auditorium [n]accompanied by the [o]commanders and the prominent men of the city, at the command of Festus, Paul was brought in. [24] Festus *said, "King Agrippa, and all you gentlemen here present with us, you see this man about whom all the people of the Jews appealed to me, both at Jerusalem and here, loudly declaring that he ought not to live any longer. [25] But I found that he had committed nothing worthy of death; and since he himself appealed to [p]the Emperor, I decided to send him. [26] [q]Yet I have nothing definite about him to write to my lord. Therefore I have brought him before you *all* and especially before you, King Agrippa, so that after the investigation has taken place, I may have something to write. [27] For it seems absurd to me in sending a prisoner, not to indicate also the charges against him." (Acts 25)
https://www.biblegateway.com/passage/?search=Acts+25&version=NASB

We have the new governor, Porcius Festus, which oddly enough means pork festival. The governor of the Judean province, which contains the Most Holy City in the world i.e. Jerusalem, gets assigned a governor with the name meaning of pork festival. The pig is one of the unclean animals in Leviticus 11 and Deuteronomy 14. We had studied earlier that a dominate feature of the unclean animals was that they were omnivores. They ate from both kingdoms (plant and animal), on a spiritual level, they served two masters. I believe humans were to see that we ourselves are omnivores, that we are unclean i.e. sinners.

Notice in verse 1 that Festus goes "up" to Jerusalem. In the Bible we always see going "up" to Jerusalem, or going "down" from Jerusalem, no matter which direction you were approaching or leaving from. The hidden meaning is that another name for Heaven is New Jerusalem, always being above. Verse 1 says "three days later" went up to Jerusalem; this seems to me to be one of those hidden Christ references.   After three days Jesus rose from the grave, going up to Heaven, up to New Jerusalem. Then in verse 7, you have the accusing Jews "coming down" from Jerusalem. These are just fun observations.

So even after two years these particular Jews want Paul dead. They try and get Paul brought to Jerusalem, but actually they just want to ambush and kill him, as he comes to Jerusalem. Festus has another idea; you all come with me to Caesarea and prosecute Paul there, which they do. The Jews bring charges, Paul defends himself. Festus then asks Paul if he is willing to go Jerusalem for another trial. This is when Paul appeals to Caesar.

Several days pass and King Agrippa and Bernice pay a visit to Festus. Remember that King Agrippa, a Herod, can actually be traced all the way back to Esau. Remember Isaac (the son of Abraham) and Rebekah. They had twin sons, Jacob and Esau. Remember the Bible says, Jacob I loved and Esau I hated (Malachi 1:1-3 and Romans 9:13). Similar to the two kingdoms with the omnivores, Jacob represents the Eternal Spiritual Kingdom i.e. New Jerusalem/Heaven. Esau is the worldly kingdom, this life i.e. wealth (mammon).

"No one can serve two masters; for either he will hate the one and love the other, or he will be devoted to one and despise the other. You cannot serve God and [m]wealth. (Matthew 6:24)

Notice how Agrippa and Bernice entered, "amid great pomp". They were all about this world. They brought the commanders and prominent men of the city, which gives Paul the open door once again to preach the Gospel to several more people. Festus would really like to have charges go with Paul to Rome. Festus sending Paul to Caesar without him being charged would probably not sit well with Nero Caesar; he is hoping Agrippa will help him figure out a charge.

Acts 26

Agrippa said to Paul, "You are permitted to speak for yourself." Then Paul stretched out his hand and *proceeded* to make his defense:

2 "In regard to all the things of which I am accused by the Jews, I consider myself fortunate, King Agrippa, that I am about to make my defense before you today; 3 [a]especially because you are an expert in all customs and [b]questions among *the* Jews; therefore I beg you to listen to me patiently.

4 "So then, all Jews know my manner of life from my youth up, which from the beginning was spent among my *own* nation and at Jerusalem; 5 since they have known about me for a long time, if they are willing to testify, that I lived *as* a Pharisee according to the strictest sect of our religion. 6 And now I am [c]standing trial for the hope of the promise made by God to our fathers; 7 *the promise* to which our twelve tribes hope to attain, as they earnestly serve *God* night and day. And for this hope, O King, I am being accused by

301

Jews. [8] Why is it considered incredible among you *people* if God does raise the dead?

[9] "So then, I thought to myself that I had to do many things hostile to the name of Jesus of Nazareth. [10] And this is [d]just what I did in Jerusalem; not only did I lock up many of the [e]saints in prisons, having received authority from the chief priests, but also when they were being put to death I cast my vote against them. [11] And as I punished them often in all the synagogues, I tried to force them to blaspheme; and being furiously enraged at them, I kept pursuing them even to [f]foreign cities.

[12] "[g]While so engaged as I was journeying to Damascus with the authority and commission of the chief priests, [13] at midday, O King, I saw on the way a light from heaven, [h]brighter than the sun, shining all around me and those who were journeying with me. [14] And when we had all fallen to the ground, I heard a voice saying to me in the [i]Hebrew dialect, 'Saul, Saul, why are you persecuting Me? [j]It is hard for you to kick against the goads.' [15] And I said, 'Who are You, Lord?' And the Lord said, 'I am Jesus whom you are persecuting. [16] But get up and stand on your feet; for this purpose I have appeared to you, to appoint you a minister and a witness not only to the things which you have [k]seen, but also to the things in which I will appear to you; [17] rescuing you from the *Jewish* people and from the Gentiles, to whom I am sending you, [18] to open their eyes so that they may turn from darkness to light and from the dominion of Satan to God, that they may receive forgiveness of sins and an inheritance among those who have been sanctified by faith in Me.'

[19] "So, King Agrippa, I did not prove disobedient to the heavenly vision, [20] but *kept* declaring both to those of Damascus first, and *also* at Jerusalem and *then* throughout all the region of Judea, and *even* to the Gentiles, that they should repent and turn to God, performing deeds appropriate to repentance. [21] For this reason *some* Jews seized me in the temple and tried to put me to death. [22] So, having obtained help from God, I stand to this day testifying both to small and great, stating nothing but what the Prophets and Moses said was going to take place; [23] [l]that [m]the Christ was [n]to suffer, *and* [o]that by reason

of *His* resurrection from the dead He would be the first to proclaim light both to the *Jewish* people and to the Gentiles."

24 While *Paul* was saying this in his defense, Festus *said in a loud voice, "Paul, you are out of your mind! [p]*Your* great learning is [q]driving you mad." 25 But Paul *said, "I am not out of my mind, most excellent Festus, but I utter words [r]of sober truth. 26 For the king [s]knows about these matters, and I speak to him also with confidence, since I am persuaded that none of these things escape his notice; for this has not been done in a [t]corner. 27 King Agrippa, do you believe the Prophets? I know that you [u]do." 28 Agrippa *replied* to Paul, "[v]In a short time you [w]will persuade me to [x]become a Christian." 29 And Paul *said*, "[y]I would wish to God, that whether [z]in a short or long time, not only you, but also all who hear me this day, might become such as I am, except for these chains."

30 The king stood up and the governor and Bernice, and those who were sitting with them, 31 and when they had gone aside, they *began* talking to one another, saying, "This man is not doing anything worthy of death or [aa]imprisonment." 32 And Agrippa said to Festus, "This man might have been set free if he had not appealed to Caesar." (Acts 26)
https://www.biblegateway.com/passage/?search=Acts+26&version=NASB

Paul is given the opportunity to share his testimony with King Herod Agrippa, Bernice, Governor Festus, commanders, and prominent men of the city. Paul says he is on trial "for the hope of the Promise made by God to our fathers". The Promise was in reference to the Messiah i.e. the Christ. This Promise was given to Abraham in Genesis. Paul also makes reference to the Resurrection in verse 8. The Pharisees believed in the Resurrection, the Sadducees did not. Here are a couple Old Testament Resurrection Scriptures:

Therefore my heart is glad and my glory rejoices;
My flesh also will dwell securely.
10 For You will not abandon my soul to [i]Sheol;
Nor will You [j]allow Your [k]Holy One to [l]undergo decay.

[11] You will make known to me the path of life;
In Your presence is fullness of joy;
In Your right hand there are pleasures forever. (Psalm 16:9-11)

Your dead will live;
[m]Their corpses will rise.
You who lie in the dust, awake and shout for joy,
For your dew *is as* the dew of the [n]dawn,
And the earth will [o]give birth to the [p]departed spirits. (Isaiah 26:19)

In verse 14 Paul is addressed by Jesus in the Hebrew dialect. In Genesis 14, Abraham is the first to be called a Hebrew. Abraham lives at the Oak of Mamre, which is in Hebron. Doing a quick earth history we had Adam, then a while later came Noah, one of Noah's sons was Shem (then we have the Great Flood occurring), a short while later we have Eber. Eber is also sometimes Heber in the Bible. Heber or Eber is where the Hebrew term came from. Right after Eber was Peleg, in which Genesis 10 says, that during his time is when the earth was divided from being one people. How did that happen?

Now the whole earth [a]used the same language and [b]the same words. [2] It came about as they journeyed east, that they found a plain in the land of Shinar and [c]settled there. [3] They said to one another, "Come, let us make bricks and burn *them* thoroughly." And they used brick for stone, and they used tar for mortar. [4] They said, "Come, let us build for ourselves a city, and a tower whose top *will reach* into heaven, and let us make for ourselves a name, otherwise we will be scattered abroad over the face of the whole earth." [5] The LORD came down to see the city and the tower which the sons of men had built. [6] The LORD said, "Behold, they are one people, and they all have [d]the same language. And this is what they began to do, and now nothing which they purpose to do will be [e]impossible for them. [7] Come, let Us go down and there confuse their [f]language, so that they will not understand one another's [g]speech." [8] So the LORD scattered them abroad from there over the face of the whole earth; and they stopped building the city. [9] Therefore its name was called

[h]Babel, because there the LORD confused the [i]language of the whole earth; and from there the LORD scattered them abroad over the face of the whole earth. (Genesis 11:1-9)

(Did you notice the Trinity "Us" reference in verse 7?) Now you know where the phrase, "quit your babbling" came from. I personally believe that they were building the tower just in case the world got flooded again. They didn't believe the Rainbow Promise God gave Noah, no faith. So in a sense the normal teaching of this Scripture is correct in that they were "working/building their way to Heaven." You have the old "Faith (in the Righteous One) verses works righteousness" debate. One of the languages after Babel was Hebrew. So that is how we got the name Hebrew, from Eber/Heber. Heber is in the genealogy of the Messiah as well in Luke 3. You could even make the argument that all humans spoke Hebrew prior to Babel.

Note that the Promise given to Abraham is given at Hebron. So Abraham is a Hebrew living at Hebron. Hebron means to join together. Later in history after the Hebrew people are freed from Egypt, only two of the original adult men of the 600,000 (Exodus 12:37) that were freed from Egypt, live to make it into the Promised Land (Numbers 14:28-30, 26:63-65 and 32:11, 12). The two originals are Joshua, meaning savior, and Caleb, meaning whole heart. So with the two names you have Savior of the whole heart; the Gospel. I mention this because Caleb inherited Hebron. Joshua inherited Timnath-serah in the hill country of Ephraim. Timnath means manna and serah means abundant, together we have Abundant Manna. We know Jesus to be the Manna from Heaven, the Bread of Life; He joins our divided hearts together as One in Him. Later in history David is anointed king in Hebron, serving 7 years there. David joins together the two kingdoms (divided kingdom) of Israel i.e. the divided heart of Israel. David was born at Bethlehem, meaning House of Bread. Mary when visiting Elizabeth is overshadowed by the Holy Spirit, in Hebron. Jesus was born in Bethlehem.

So Paul is trying to get people to look past the whole Jew/Gentile division issue. The Promise has always been for all humans. The Hebrews were entrusted to tell the world, to be the priests to the world.

In the third month after the sons of Israel had gone out of the land of Egypt, [a]on that very day they came into the wilderness of Sinai. [2] When they set out from Rephidim, they came to the wilderness of Sinai and camped in the wilderness; and there Israel camped in front of the mountain. [3] Moses went up to God, and the LORD called to him from the mountain, saying, "Thus you shall say to the house of Jacob and tell the sons of Israel: [4] 'You yourselves have seen what I did to the Egyptians, and *how* I bore you on eagles' wings, and brought you to Myself. [5] Now then, if you will indeed obey My voice and keep My covenant, then you shall be My [b]own possession among all the peoples, for all the earth is Mine; [6] and you shall be to Me a kingdom of priests and a holy nation.' These are the words that you shall speak to the sons of Israel." (Exodus 19:1-6)

But you are A CHOSEN RACE, A royal PRIESTHOOD, A HOLY NATION, A PEOPLE FOR *God's* OWN POSSESSION, so that you may proclaim the excellencies of Him who has called you out of darkness into His marvelous light; (1 Peter 2:9)

"Worthy are You to take the [i]book and to break its seals; for You were slain, and purchased for God with Your blood *men* from every tribe and tongue and people and nation.

[10] "You have made them *to be* a kingdom and priests to our God; and they will reign upon the earth." (Revelation 5:8-10)

Hebrew meaning:

To us moderns the name Hebrew has a unique and exclusive (and even religious) ring to it, but it should be noted with some stress that this is not at all the case in the narrative of the Bible. The "name" Hebrew isn't an abstract label but much rather an ordinary word used as an appellative, like a nickname or even a signature quality. It means **Passed Over** or **Passer Over** or **Transition** or **One Who Transits** or **One From The Other [Dry] Side** or even **Flower Forth** or **Deducer** or **He Who Looks At Something From All Sides**.

In the Bible the name Hebrew obviously does not denote a particular religion or language or nationality, but rather the intrinsic human need to cut through all the legalizing and restricting, all the deceit and ballyhoo, and arrive at something timeless and natural; something as natural as we ourselves are: the natural laws upon which we were designed to operate, the same truth that famously sets us free (John 8:32), that existed before everything else (John 1:1) and in which everything holds together (Colossians 1:17); the same truth that purposes to hand over His kingdom to the God and Father, when He has abolished all rule and all authority and power (1 Corinthians 15:24). http://www.abarim-publications.com/Meaning/Hebrew.html#.WEBzZMIzWUl

With all this in mind and heart try reading Hebrews!!!

Acts 27

When it was decided that we would sail for Italy, they proceeded to deliver Paul and some other prisoners to a centurion of the Augustan [a]cohort named Julius. ² And embarking in an Adramyttian ship, which was about to sail to the regions along the coast of [b]Asia, we put out to sea accompanied by Aristarchus, a Macedonian of Thessalonica. ³ The next day we put in at Sidon; and Julius treated Paul with consideration and allowed him to go to his friends and receive care. ⁴ From there we put out to sea and sailed under the shelter of Cyprus because the winds were contrary. ⁵ When we had sailed through the sea along the coast of Cilicia and Pamphylia, we landed at Myra in Lycia. ⁶ There the centurion found an Alexandrian ship sailing for Italy, and he put us aboard it. ⁷ When we had sailed slowly for a good many days, and with difficulty had arrived off Cnidus, since the wind did not permit us *to go* farther, we sailed under the shelter of Crete, off Salmone; ⁸ and with difficulty sailing past it we came to a place called Fair Havens, near which was the city of Lasea.

⁹ When considerable time had passed and the voyage was now dangerous, since even the [c]fast was already over, Paul *began* to admonish them, ¹⁰ and said to them, "Men, I perceive that the voyage will certainly be with damage and great loss, not only of the cargo and the ship, but also of our lives." ¹¹ But the centurion was more persuaded by the pilot and the [d]captain of the ship than by what was being said by Paul. ¹² Because the harbor was not suitable for wintering, the majority reached a decision to put out to sea from there, if somehow they could reach Phoenix, a harbor of Crete, facing southwest and northwest, and spend the winter *there*.

¹³ [e]When a moderate south wind came up, supposing that they had attained their purpose, they weighed anchor and *began* sailing along Crete, close *inshore*.

¹⁴ But before very long there rushed down from [f]the land a violent wind, called [g]Euraquilo; ¹⁵ and when the ship was caught *in it* and could not face the wind, we gave way *to it* and let ourselves be driven along. ¹⁶ Running under the shelter of a small island called Clauda, we were scarcely able to get the *ship's* [h]boat under control. ¹⁷ After they had hoisted it up, they used [i]supporting cables in undergirding the ship; and fearing that they might run aground on *the shallows* of Syrtis, they let down the [j]sea anchor and in this way let themselves be driven along. ¹⁸ The next day as we were being violently storm-tossed, [k]they began to jettison the cargo; ¹⁹ and on the third day they threw the ship's tackle overboard with their own hands. ²⁰ Since neither sun nor stars appeared for many days, and no small storm was assailing *us*, from then on all hope of our being saved was gradually abandoned.

^{21} [l]When they had gone a long time without food, then Paul stood up in their midst and said, "Men, you ought to have [m]followed my advice and not to have set sail from Crete and [n]incurred this damage and loss. ^{22} *Yet* now I urge you to keep up your courage, for there will be no loss of life among you, but *only* of the ship. ^{23} For this very night an angel of the God to whom I belong and whom I serve stood before me, ^{24} saying, 'Do not be afraid, Paul; you must stand before Caesar; and behold, God has granted you all those who are sailing with you.' ^{25} Therefore, keep up your courage, men, for I believe God that [o]it will turn out exactly as I have been told. ^{26} But we must run aground on a certain island."

^{27} But when the fourteenth night came, as we were being driven about in the Adriatic Sea, about midnight the sailors *began* to surmise that [p]they were approaching some land. ^{28} They took soundings and found *it to be* twenty fathoms; and a little farther on they took another sounding and found *it to be* fifteen fathoms. ^{29} Fearing that we might run aground somewhere on the [q]rocks, they cast four anchors from the stern and [r]wished for daybreak. ^{30} But as the sailors were trying to escape from the ship and had let down the *ship's* boat into the sea, on the pretense of intending to lay out anchors from the bow, ^{31} Paul said to the centurion and to the soldiers, "Unless these men remain in the ship, you yourselves cannot be saved." ^{32} Then the soldiers cut away the ropes of the *ship's* boat and let it fall away.

^{33} Until the day was about to dawn, Paul was encouraging them all to take some food, saying, "Today is the fourteenth day that you have been constantly watching and going without eating, having taken nothing. ^{34} Therefore I encourage you to take some food, for this is for your preservation, for not a hair from the head of any of you will perish." ^{35} Having said this, he took bread and gave thanks to God in the presence of all, and he broke it and began to eat. ^{36} All of them [s]were encouraged and they themselves also took food. ^{37} All of us in the ship were two hundred and seventy-six [t]persons. ^{38} When they had eaten enough, they *began* to lighten the ship by throwing out the wheat into the sea.

³⁹ When day came, they [u]could not recognize the land; but they did observe a bay with a beach, and they resolved to drive the ship onto it if they could. ⁴⁰ And casting off the anchors, they left them in the sea while at the same time they were loosening the ropes of the rudders; and hoisting the foresail to the wind, they were heading for the beach. ⁴¹ But striking a [v]reef where two seas met, they ran the vessel aground; and the prow stuck fast and remained immovable, but the stern *began* to be broken up by the force *of the waves*. ⁴² The soldiers' plan was to kill the prisoners, so that none *of them* would swim away and escape; ⁴³ but the centurion, wanting to bring Paul safely through, kept them from their intention, and commanded that those who could swim should [w]jump overboard first and get to land, ⁴⁴ and the rest *should follow*, some on planks, and others on various things from the ship. And so it happened that they all were brought safely to land. (Acts 27)
https://www.biblegateway.com/passage/?search=Acts+27&version=NASB

Paul, being a Roman citizen, is able to appeal to Caesar. Thousands and thousands of Jews and gentiles have come to Christ at this point. The Jews that have not yet come are very eager to kill Paul. God has given Paul several open platforms to share the Gospel. By appealing to Caesar, Paul is being sent to Rome. In Rome, being the capitol of the Roman Empire, Paul will be given yet another huge platform to share the Gospel. We know by history that sometime later a Roman Emperor (Constantine) actually becomes a Christian. History says that Christianity was made the "national religion". For one thousand years the Christian church was the Roman Catholic Church. The Roman Sun god holiday of December 25th was declared Christmas. The Roman spring fertility god (celebrated with the rabbit) holiday was changed to Easter Sunday. We know from our studies that Jesus was born in the fall (Trumpets), for the fall of man. Jesus rose from the dead on First Fruits (actually a Tuesday) in the midst of the Unleavened Bread Week.

Here is the map of the Roman Empire: http://www.bible-history.com/maps/romanempire/

The trip from Caesarea to Rome can take six months. We get a timestamp from verse 9. The annual fast was for the Day of Atonement. The Day of Atonement (Yom Kippur) is the tenth day of the 7th month. On our calendar this is in the fall, in the late September-October timeframe.

The first ship they sail on goes along the coast, probably not a huge ship. The next ship is an Alexandrian ship, carrying wheat, these ship are of good size. They end up in Fair Haven, and the decision, contrary to Paul's advice is to sail from there. We learn that winter travel is not a good idea. The voyage is not going well at all. Paul gets a visit from an angel of God. The angel says:

'Do not be afraid, Paul; you must stand before Caesar; and behold, God has granted you all those who are sailing with you.'

Paul shares this with the 276 onboard. They realize by taking fathoms (lowering a weighted rope with knots tied at measured increments) that they are coming to land. The sailors want to take the small boat to land and desert the ship. Paul warns that they need the crew to survive. The rope to the smaller boat is cut away. At Fair Haven, Paul was not listened to. Now Paul's advice is being taken. Paul encourages everyone to eat. They do come upon land. The soldiers want to kill the prisoners so none escape. The centurion wanting to save Paul, orders that none should be killed. If a prisoner escapes, the Roman soldier would lose his life for the escaped prisoner's life. The chapter ends with: And so it happened that they all were brought safely to land. It is interesting that they land safely at Malta, which means land of honey.

Remember our study of Revelation. Remember in Revelation 10, John eats the Book. It is Bitter in his stomach. Then it is Sweet like Honey in his mouth (the Gospel). Revelation 11 explains the bitter, the Two Witnesses, being the Law and Prophets. Revelation 12 goes on to the Sweet, the Honey, that being Jesus Christ. If you search the internet you won't find anywhere that can explain the Land of Milk and Honey, just many suggestions, and even the

Jewish Rabbis can't agree. Isn't that strange? The Promised Land is the Land of Milk and Honey. Why? I believe the Milk originates from the Almond. Almond milk is naturally bitter. The word Almond means "to be watchful". The Message of the Law and Prophets was to be watchful for the coming Messiah, the Christ. The best tasting Almond Milk is Sweetened with Honey. Earlier in this chapter we had the Day of Atonement mentioned. This was the One Day a year that the High Priest could go behind the Veil to the Holy of Holies. Within the Holy of Holies was the Ark of the Covenant. What was in the Ark of the Covenant? The Beautiful Sapphire Blue Stone Ten Commandments, the Golden Jar of Manna (being a Sweet Honey Bread), and the Almond Budded Rod of Aaron were in the Ark. Could the Land of Milk and Honey be referring to the Christ? Remember the Veil tore from Top to bottom when Jesus said, "it is finished!"

"Do not think that I came to abolish the Law or the Prophets; I did not come to abolish but to fulfill. (Matthew 5:17)

Acts 28

When they had been brought safely through, then we found out that the island was called [a]Malta. 2 The [b]natives showed us extraordinary kindness; for because of the rain that had set in and because of the cold, they kindled a fire and received us all. 3 But when Paul had gathered a bundle of sticks and laid them on the fire, a viper came out [c]because of the heat and fastened itself on his hand. 4 When the [d]natives saw the creature hanging from his hand, they *began* saying to one another, "Undoubtedly this man is a murderer, and though he has been saved from the sea, [e]justice has

312

not allowed him to live." ⁵ However he shook the creature off into the fire and suffered no harm. ⁶ But they were expecting that he was about to swell up or suddenly fall down dead. But after they had waited a long time and had seen nothing unusual happen to him, they changed their minds and *began* to say that he was a god.

⁷ Now in the neighborhood of that place were lands belonging to the leading man of the island, named Publius, who welcomed us and entertained us courteously three days. ⁸ And it happened that the father of Publius was lying *in bed* afflicted with *recurrent* fever and dysentery; and Paul went in *to see* him and after he had prayed, he laid his hands on him and healed him. ⁹ After this had happened, the rest of the people on the island who had diseases were coming to him and getting cured. ¹⁰ They also honored us with many [f]marks of respect; and when we were setting sail, they [g]supplied *us* with [h]all we needed.

¹¹ At the end of three months we set sail on an Alexandrian ship which had wintered at the island, and which had [i]the Twin Brothers for its figurehead. ¹² After we put in at Syracuse, we stayed there for three days. ¹³ From there we sailed around and arrived at Rhegium, and a day later a south wind sprang up, and on the second day we came to Puteoli. ¹⁴ [j]There we found *some* brethren, and were invited to stay with them for seven days; and thus we came to Rome. ¹⁵ And the brethren, when they heard about us, came from there as far as the [k]Market of Appius and [l]Three Inns to meet us; and when Paul saw them, he thanked God and took courage.

¹⁶ When we entered Rome, Paul was allowed to stay by himself, with the soldier who was guarding him.

¹⁷ After three days [m]Paul called together those who were the leading men of the Jews, and when they came together, he *began* saying to them, "Brethren, though I had done nothing against our people or the customs of our [n]fathers, yet I was delivered as a prisoner from Jerusalem into the hands of the Romans. ¹⁸ And when they had examined me, they were willing to release me because there was no ground [o]for putting me to death. ¹⁹ But when the Jews [p]objected, I was forced to appeal to Caesar, not that I had any accusation against

my nation. ²⁰ For this reason, therefore, I [q]requested to see you and to speak with you, for I am wearing this chain for the sake of the hope of Israel." ²¹ They said to him, "We have neither received letters from Judea concerning you, nor have any of the brethren come here and reported or spoken anything bad about you. ²² But we desire to hear from you what [r]your views are; for concerning this sect, it is known to us that it is spoken against everywhere."

²³ When they had set a day for Paul, they came to him at his lodging in large numbers; and he was explaining to them by solemnly testifying about the kingdom of God and trying to persuade them concerning Jesus, from both the Law of Moses and from the Prophets, from morning until evening. ²⁴ Some were being persuaded by the things spoken, but others would not believe. ²⁵ And when they did not agree with one another, they *began* leaving after Paul had spoken one *parting* word, "The Holy Spirit rightly spoke through Isaiah the prophet to your fathers, ²⁶ saying,

'GO TO THIS PEOPLE AND SAY,
"[s]YOU WILL KEEP ON HEARING, [t]BUT WILL NOT UNDERSTAND;
AND [u]YOU WILL KEEP ON SEEING, BUT WILL NOT PERCEIVE;
²⁷ FOR THE HEART OF THIS PEOPLE HAS BECOME DULL,
AND WITH THEIR EARS THEY SCARCELY HEAR,
AND THEY HAVE CLOSED THEIR EYES;
OTHERWISE THEY MIGHT SEE WITH THEIR EYES,
AND HEAR WITH THEIR EARS,
AND UNDERSTAND WITH THEIR HEART AND RETURN,
AND I WOULD HEAL THEM.""'

²⁸ Therefore let it be known to you that this salvation of God has been sent to the Gentiles; they will also listen." ²⁹ [[v]When he had spoken these words, the Jews departed, having a great dispute among themselves.]

³⁰ And he stayed two full years [w]in his own rented quarters and was welcoming all who came to him, ³¹ [x]preaching the kingdom of God and teaching concerning the Lord Jesus Christ with all openness, unhindered. (Acts 28)

https://www.biblegateway.com/passage/?search=Acts+28&version=NASB

Here is a map link that is numbered at each location, showing Paul's journey to Rome: http://www.bible-history.com/maps/maps/map_pauls_journey_to_rome.html

Paul makes it to Rome. The Bible makes a contrast between Rome and Jerusalem. Rome is a picture of the "world", the lust of the flesh and the lust of the eyes and the boastful pride of life (1 John 2:16). In Genesis 3:1-7, Adam and Eve give in to the lust of the flesh and the lust of their eyes and the boastful pride of life; they and we sin. In Matthew 4:1-11 and Luke 4:1-13, Jesus, God in the Flesh, was offered the same as us by satan; the lust of the flesh and the lust of the eyes and the boastful pride of life, yet without sin. Jerusalem is a picture of the Eternal Heavenly Kingdom. Unlike the "world" that might give us 80 years, Heaven i.e. New Jerusalem gives us "unlimited minutes". So do you want a plan with limited world minutes or unlimited Heavenly minutes? In this life of limited minutes, we have a limited time to confess from our mouth, from our heart, that Jesus is Lord (Romans 10). This confession requires faith. The definition of faith is believing in the unseen (Hebrews 11:1). But without faith it is impossible to see God (Hebrews 11:6). But we know faith comes by hearing and hearing by the Word of God (Romans 10:17). Thank God for the Law, thank God for the Prophets, and thank God for Jesus Christ!!! Here is Romans 10:

Brethren, my heart's desire and my prayer to God for them is for *their* salvation. [2] For I testify about them that they have a zeal for God, but not in accordance with knowledge. [3] For not knowing about God's righteousness and seeking to establish their own, they did not subject themselves to the righteousness of God. [4] For Christ is the [a]end of the law for righteousness to everyone who believes.

[5] For Moses writes that the man who practices the righteousness which is [b]based on law shall live [c]by that righteousness. [6] But the righteousness [d]based on faith speaks as follows: "DO NOT SAY IN

YOUR HEART, 'WHO WILL ASCEND INTO HEAVEN?' (that is, to bring Christ down), [7] or 'WHO WILL DESCEND INTO THE ABYSS?' (that is, to bring Christ up from the dead)." [8] But what does it say? "THE WORD IS NEAR YOU, IN YOUR MOUTH AND IN YOUR HEART"—that is, the word of faith which we are preaching, [9] [c]that if you confess with your mouth Jesus *as* Lord, and believe in your heart that God raised Him from the dead, you will be saved; [10] for with the heart a person believes, [f]resulting in righteousness, and with the mouth he confesses, [g]resulting in salvation. [11] For the Scripture says, "WHOEVER BELIEVES IN HIM WILL NOT BE [h]DISAPPOINTED." [12] For there is no distinction between Jew and Greek; for the same *Lord* is Lord of all, abounding in riches for all who call on Him; [13] for "WHOEVER WILL CALL ON THE NAME OF THE LORD WILL BE SAVED."

[14] How then will they call on Him in whom they have not believed? How will they believe in Him whom they have not heard? And how will they hear without a preacher? [15] How will they preach unless they are sent? Just as it is written, "HOW BEAUTIFUL ARE THE FEET OF THOSE WHO [i]BRING GOOD NEWS OF GOOD THINGS!"

[16] However, they did not all heed the [j]good news; for Isaiah says, "LORD, WHO HAS BELIEVED OUR REPORT?" [17] So faith *comes* from hearing, and hearing by the word [k]of Christ.

[18] But I say, surely they have never heard, have they? Indeed they have;

"THEIR VOICE HAS GONE OUT INTO ALL THE EARTH,
AND THEIR WORDS TO THE ENDS OF THE [l]WORLD."

[19] But I say, surely Israel did not know, did they? First Moses says,

"I WILL MAKE YOU JEALOUS BY THAT WHICH IS NOT A NATION,
BY A NATION WITHOUT UNDERSTANDING WILL I ANGER YOU."

[20] And Isaiah is very bold and says,

"I WAS FOUND BY THOSE WHO DID NOT SEEK ME,
I BECAME MANIFEST TO THOSE WHO DID NOT ASK FOR ME."

21 But as for Israel He says, "ALL THE DAY LONG I HAVE STRETCHED OUT MY HANDS TO A DISOBEDIENT AND OBSTINATE PEOPLE." (Romans 10)
https://www.biblegateway.com/passage/?search=Romans+10&version=NASB

Chapter 4: The Book of Hebrews

Hebrews 1

God, after He spoke long ago to the fathers in the prophets in many portions and in many ways, 2 [a]in these last days has spoken to us [b]in His Son, whom He appointed heir of all things, through whom also He made the [c]world. 3 [d]And He is the radiance of His glory and the exact representation of His nature, and [e]upholds all things by the word of His power. When He had made purification of sins, He sat down at the right hand of the Majesty on high, 4 having become as much better than the angels, as He has inherited a more excellent name than they.

5 For to which of the angels did He ever say,

"YOU ARE MY SON,
TODAY I HAVE BEGOTTEN YOU"?

And again,

"I WILL BE A FATHER TO HIM
AND HE SHALL BE A SON TO ME"?

6 And [f]when He again brings the firstborn into [g]the world, He says,

"And let all the angels of God worship Him."

[7] And of the angels He says,

"Who makes His angels winds,
And His ministers a flame of fire."

[8] But of the Son *He says*,

"Your throne, O God, is forever and ever,
And the righteous scepter is the scepter of [h]His kingdom.
[9] "You have loved righteousness and hated lawlessness;
Therefore God, Your God, has anointed You
With the oil of gladness above Your companions."

[10] And,

"You, Lord, in the beginning laid the foundation of the
earth,
And the heavens are the works of Your hands;
[11] They will perish, but You remain;
And they all will become old like a garment,
[12] And like a mantle You will roll them up;
Like a garment they will also be changed.
But You are the same,
And Your years will not come to an end."

[13] But to which of the angels has He ever said,

"Sit at My right hand,
Until I make Your enemies
A footstool for Your feet"?

[14] Are they not all ministering spirits, sent out to render service for the sake of those who will inherit salvation? (Hebrews 1) https://www.biblegateway.com/passage/?search=Hebrews+1&version=NASB

Nobody knows for sure who wrote this Book, which is fine with me, because the True Author of the entire Bible is the Holy Spirit. Why the name Hebrews? Most often it is obvious who/what church a certain Book is written to....to the churches of Galatia...to the saints at Ephesus... The opening Verse says, God, after He spoke long ago to the fathers in the prophets.... So we see the term "fathers" and "prophets" used. The Prophets are the Old Testament Books, the fathers being early Hebrews.

The first five Books of the Old Testament, written through Moses, are called the Law. Moses was raised up in Egypt, actually living in the house of pharaoh for forty years, then as a shepherd for forty years with the Midianites, his brother-in-law being a priest, then his last forty years he wandered in the wilderness of sin, as a shepherd/prophet to the Hebrews. God established the Priesthood through Moses in those first five Books and through some of the Psalms.

The entire camp of Israel was centered on the Priesthood, with the Tent of Meeting being center stage. The center of the Tent of Meeting was the Ark of the Covenant. The Ark of the Covenant contained the Gospel Message. We will see the contents of the Ark in Hebrews 9. But we know that we have the Law in the form of Two Beautiful Sapphire Stone Tablets, known as the Ten Commandments, which Jesus summed up as to love God and love your neighbor. We have the Almond Budded Rod of Aaron. Aaron, the brother of Moses, was the first high priest, Jesus being the Last and Final Great High Priest. The Almond Tree is a picture of the Cross. We also had the Golden Jar of Manna, which is a picture of Jesus, the Bread of Life. The Old Testament is Jesus concealed, and the New Testament is Jesus revealed. Jesus powerfully said, "Do not think that I came to abolish the Law or the Prophets; I did not come to abolish but to fulfill...." (Matthew 5:17) On the Cross, when Jesus said, "it is finished", the Veil to the Holy of Holies, which contained the Ark of the Covenant, was tore from Top to bottom. The curtain was 80 feet high and twelve inches thick!!! God tore it.

The first few Verses of this chapter are very rich and deep. They show the Deity of Jesus. When showing someone the Deity of Christ this chapter along with John 1 and Colossians 1 are very, very awesome.

https://www.biblegateway.com/passage/?search=John+1&version=NASB

https://www.biblegateway.com/passage/?search=Colossians+1&version=NASB

The rest of the chapter are Old Testament quotes about Jesus. The quotes are from: Psalm 2:7, 2 Samuel 7:14, Deuteronomy 32:43, Psalm 104:4, Psalm 45:6, Deuteronomy 33:27, Psalm 71:3, Psalm 45:7, Isaiah 61:1, 3 (John 10:17), Psalm 102:25, 26, Isaiah 51:6, Psalm 102:26, 27 (Hebrews 13:8), Psalm 110:1 (Matthew 22:44, Hebrews 1:3), and Joshua 10:24 (Hebrews 10:13).

The use of the above Scriptures shows us that these Hebrews were being told by someone that Jesus was an angel, just a messenger of God, not God. But we have all the above Verses showing that Jesus was no angel, He was God in the Flesh. The last quote is,

"SIT AT MY RIGHT HAND,
UNTIL I MAKE YOUR ENEMIES
A FOOTSTOOL FOR YOUR FEET"

The enemies are sin and death. Jesus conquered them both. This is the Gospel Message, this is the Good News. Jesus after fulfilling all 7 Feasts from Leviticus 23, after the last and final Feast of Weeks, which was 49 days, 7 weeks of 7, came Pentecost, Day 50, the day that Jesus sat down at the Right Hand of God the Father, and sent the Helper, the Holy Spirit. Mission of Jesus Accomplished!!!

Remember prior to the Tower of Babel we had one language, one people, Heber was before Babel, He being the originator of the word Hebrew, then after Babel we were separated by language. Now the whole earth [a]used the same language and [b]the same words. (Genesis 11:1) Yes, you can show that the entire earth spoke Hebrew prior to Babel. Then post Babel, we see Abram, later named Abraham, being the first to actually be called a Hebrew. Then [h]a fugitive came and told Abram the Hebrew. (Genesis 14:13) So after the Work of Christ, i.e. the 7 Feasts, the very next day, Pentecost, we have different languages uniting God's people. With Babel language divided, at Pentecost language united.

When the day of Pentecost [a]had come, they were all together in one place. [2] And suddenly there came from heaven a noise like a violent rushing wind, and it filled the whole house where they were sitting. [3] And there appeared to them tongues as of fire [b]distributing themselves, and [c]they [d]rested on each one of them. [4] And they were all filled with the Holy Spirit and began to speak with other [e]tongues, as the Spirit was giving them [f]utterance.

[5] Now there were Jews living in Jerusalem, devout men from every nation under heaven. [6] And when this sound occurred, the crowd came together, and were bewildered because each one of them was hearing them speak in his own [g]language. [7] They were amazed and astonished, saying, "[h]Why, are not all these who are speaking Galileans? [8] And how is it that we each hear *them* in our own [i]language [j]to which we were born? [9] Parthians and Medes and Elamites, and residents of Mesopotamia, Judea and Cappadocia, Pontus and [k]Asia, [10] Phrygia and Pamphylia, Egypt and the districts of Libya around Cyrene, and [l]visitors from Rome, both Jews and [m]proselytes, [11] Cretans and Arabs—we hear them in our *own* tongues speaking of the mighty deeds of God." [12] And they all continued in amazement and great perplexity, saying to one another, "What does this mean?" [13] But others were mocking and saying, "They are full of [n]sweet wine."

[14] But Peter, [o]taking his stand with the eleven, raised his voice and declared to them: "Men of Judea and all you who live in Jerusalem, let this be known to you and give heed to my words. [15] For these men are not drunk, as you suppose, for it is *only* the [p]third hour of the day; [16] but this is what was spoken of through the prophet Joel:

¹⁷ 'AND IT SHALL BE IN THE LAST DAYS,' God says,
'THAT I WILL POUR FORTH OF MY SPIRIT ON ALL ^[q]MANKIND;
AND YOUR SONS AND YOUR DAUGHTERS SHALL PROPHESY,
AND YOUR YOUNG MEN SHALL SEE VISIONS,
AND YOUR OLD MEN SHALL DREAM DREAMS;
¹⁸ EVEN ON MY BONDSLAVES, BOTH MEN AND WOMEN,
I WILL IN THOSE DAYS POUR FORTH OF MY SPIRIT
And they shall prophesy.
¹⁹ 'AND I WILL GRANT WONDERS IN THE SKY ABOVE
AND SIGNS ON THE EARTH BELOW,
BLOOD, AND FIRE, AND VAPOR OF SMOKE.
²⁰ 'THE SUN WILL BE TURNED INTO DARKNESS
AND THE MOON INTO BLOOD,
BEFORE THE GREAT AND GLORIOUS DAY OF THE LORD SHALL COME.
²¹ 'AND IT SHALL BE THAT EVERYONE WHO CALLS ON THE NAME OF
THE LORD WILL BE SAVED.'

²² "Men of Israel, listen to these words: Jesus the Nazarene, a man
^[r]attested to you by God with ^[s]miracles and wonders and ^[t]signs
which God performed through Him in your midst, just as you
yourselves know— ²³ this *Man*, delivered over by the predetermined
plan and foreknowledge of God, you nailed to a cross by the hands
of ^[u]godless men and put *Him* to death. ²⁴ ^[v]But God raised Him up
again, putting an end to the ^[w]agony of death, since it was
impossible for Him to be held ^[x]in its power. ²⁵ For David says of
Him,

'I SAW THE LORD ALWAYS IN MY PRESENCE;
FOR HE IS AT MY RIGHT HAND, SO THAT I WILL NOT BE SHAKEN.
²⁶ 'THEREFORE MY HEART WAS GLAD AND MY TONGUE EXULTED;
MOREOVER MY FLESH ALSO WILL LIVE IN HOPE;
²⁷ BECAUSE YOU WILL NOT ABANDON MY SOUL TO HADES,
NOR ^[y]ALLOW YOUR ^[z]HOLY ONE TO ^[aa]UNDERGO DECAY.
²⁸ 'YOU HAVE MADE KNOWN TO ME THE WAYS OF LIFE;
YOU WILL MAKE ME FULL OF GLADNESS WITH YOUR PRESENCE.'

²⁹ "^[ab]Brethren, I may confidently say to you regarding the patriarch
David that he both died and was buried, and his tomb is ^[ac]with us to
this day. ³⁰ And so, because he was a prophet and knew that GOD

HAD SWORN TO HIM WITH AN OATH TO SEAT *one* [ad]OF HIS DESCENDANTS ON HIS THRONE, ³¹ he looked ahead and spoke of the resurrection of [ae]the Christ, that HE WAS NEITHER ABANDONED TO HADES, NOR DID His flesh [af]SUFFER DECAY. ³² This Jesus God raised up again, to which we are all witnesses. ³³ Therefore having been exalted [ag]to the right hand of God, and having received from the Father the promise of the Holy Spirit, He has poured forth this which you both see and hear. ³⁴ For it was not David who ascended into [ah]heaven, but he himself says:

'THE LORD SAID TO MY LORD,
"SIT AT MY RIGHT HAND,
³⁵ UNTIL I MAKE YOUR ENEMIES A FOOTSTOOL FOR YOUR FEET."'

³⁶ Therefore let all the house of Israel know for certain that God has made Him both Lord and [ai]Christ—this Jesus whom you crucified."

³⁷ Now when they heard *this*, they were [aj]pierced to the heart, and said to Peter and the rest of the apostles, "[ak]Brethren, [al]what shall we do?" ³⁸ Peter *said* to them, "Repent, and each of you be baptized in the name of Jesus Christ for the forgiveness of your sins; and you will receive the gift of the Holy Spirit. ³⁹ For the promise is for you and your children and for all who are far off, as many as the Lord our God will call to Himself." ⁴⁰ And with many other words he solemnly testified and kept on exhorting them, saying, "[am]Be saved from this perverse generation!" ⁴¹ So then, those who had received his word were baptized; and that day there were added about three thousand [an]souls. ⁴² They were continually devoting themselves to the apostles' teaching and to fellowship, to the breaking of bread and [ao]to prayer.

⁴³ [ap]Everyone kept feeling a sense of awe; and many wonders and [aq]signs were taking place through the apostles. ⁴⁴ And all those who had believed [ar]were together and had all things in common; ⁴⁵ and they *began* selling their property and possessions and were sharing them with all, as anyone might have need. ⁴⁶ Day by day continuing with one mind in the temple, and breaking bread [as]from house to house, they were taking their [at]meals together with gladness and [au]sincerity of heart, ⁴⁷ praising God and having favor with all the

people. And the Lord was adding [av]to their number day by day those who were being saved. (Acts 2)
https://www.biblegateway.com/passage/?search=Acts+2&version=NASB

His Work equals our Rest,

Jesus being our 7th Day Sabbath Rest,

Rest in the Prince of Peace today and Forevermore

R.I.P.

Hebrews 2

For this reason we must pay much closer attention to [a]what we have heard, so that we do not drift away *from it*. [2] For if the word spoken through angels proved [b]unalterable, and every transgression and disobedience received a just [c]penalty, [3] how will we escape if we neglect so great a salvation? [d]After it was at the first spoken through the Lord, it was confirmed to us by those who heard, [4] God also testifying with them, both by signs and wonders and by various [e]miracles and by [f]gifts of the Holy Spirit according to His own will.

[5] For He did not subject to angels [g]the world to come, concerning which we are speaking. [6] But one has testified somewhere, saying,

"WHAT IS MAN, THAT YOU REMEMBER HIM?
OR THE SON OF MAN, THAT YOU ARE CONCERNED ABOUT HIM?
7 "YOU HAVE MADE HIM [h]FOR A LITTLE WHILE LOWER THAN THE
ANGELS;
YOU HAVE CROWNED HIM WITH GLORY AND HONOR,
[i]AND HAVE APPOINTED HIM OVER THE WORKS OF YOUR HANDS;
8 YOU HAVE PUT ALL THINGS IN SUBJECTION UNDER HIS FEET."

For in subjecting all things to him, He left nothing that is not subject
to him. But now we do not yet see all things subjected to him.

9 But we do see Him who was made [j]for a little while lower than the
angels, *namely*, Jesus, because of the suffering of death crowned
with glory and honor, so that by the grace of God He might taste
death for everyone.

10 For it was fitting for Him, for whom are all things, and through
whom are all things, in bringing many sons to glory, to perfect the
[k]author of their salvation through sufferings. 11 For both He who
sanctifies and those who are [l]sanctified are all from one *Father*; for
which reason He is not ashamed to call them brethren, 12 saying,

"I WILL PROCLAIM YOUR NAME TO MY BRETHREN,
IN THE MIDST OF THE CONGREGATION I WILL SING YOUR PRAISE."

13 And again,

"I WILL PUT MY TRUST IN HIM."

And again,

"BEHOLD, I AND THE CHILDREN WHOM GOD HAS GIVEN ME."

14 Therefore, since the children share in [m]flesh and blood, He
Himself likewise also partook of the same, that through death He
might render powerless him who had the power of death, that is, the
devil, 15 and might free those who through fear of death were subject
to slavery all their lives. 16 For assuredly He does not [n]give help to
angels, but He gives help to the [o]descendant of Abraham.

¹⁷ Therefore, He [p]had to be made like His brethren in all things, so that He might become a merciful and faithful high priest in things pertaining to God, to make propitiation for the sins of the people. ¹⁸ For since He Himself was tempted in that which He has suffered, He is able to come to the aid of those who are tempted. (Hebrews 2) https://www.biblegateway.com/passage/?search=Hebrews+2&version=NASB

As we learned in chapter one, Jesus was not and is not an angel. God actually became as one of us. When we study the Bible and see all caps, like in verses 6-8, we know that this is an Old Testament quote. We see a lot of Old Testament quotes in Hebrews. Why? God is showing the Hebrews and us that Jesus is the fulfillment of the entire Old Testament. This has been the Master's Plan all along. There was never a failure with a plan B put into action. Plan A has always been Plan A. The Old Testament quotes in this chapter are from Psalms 8, 22 and Isaiah 8.

Adam and Eve, Jesus, and we have all been tempted. But only One, Jesus Christ, is without sin. Picture a farmer looking out of a window on a colder than cold blizzard day. He sees a fragile shivering bird on a branch. He knows the bird will die in this blizzard. The farmer bundles up and goes outside and opens the barn door. He frantically waves to the bird, come here, into the barn lest you die. The bird does not respond. He does not understand. The farmer thinks to himself, if I could only become a bird, I could then communicate with this bird. He would understand and come into the barn and live.

Have this attitude [e]in yourselves which was also in Christ Jesus, ⁶ who, although He existed in the form of God, did not regard equality with God a thing to be [f]grasped, ⁷ but [g]emptied Himself, taking the form of a bond-servant, *and* being made in the likeness of men. ⁸ Being found in appearance as a man, He humbled Himself by becoming obedient to the point of death, even death [h]on a cross. For this reason also, God highly exalted Him, and bestowed on Him the name which is above every name, (Philippians 2:5-9)

The above Scripture has already occurred. The Scripture below is
going to happen.

so that at the name of Jesus EVERY KNEE WILL BOW, of those who are
in heaven and on earth and under the earth, [11] and that every tongue
will confess that Jesus Christ is Lord, to the glory of God the Father.
(Philippians 2:10, 11)

Every knee will bow and **every** tongue will confess that Jesus is
Lord. This applies to **all** humans, those that believe **and** those that
do not believe.

For all that is in the world, the lust of the flesh and the lust of the
eyes and the boastful pride of life, is not from the Father, but is from
the world. [17] The world is passing away, and *also* its lusts; but the
one who does the will of God lives forever. (1 John 2:16, 17)

temporary world lust or Everlasting Love

Hebrews 3

Therefore, holy brethren, partakers of a heavenly calling, consider
Jesus, the Apostle and High Priest of our confession; [2] [a]He was
faithful to Him who appointed Him, as Moses also was in all His
house. [3] For He has been counted worthy of more glory than Moses,
by just so much as the builder of the house has more honor than the
house. [4] For every house is built by someone, but the builder of all
things is God. [5] Now Moses was faithful in all His house as a
servant, for a testimony of those things which were to be spoken
later; [6] but Christ *was faithful* as a Son over His house—whose house
we are, if we hold fast our confidence and the boast of our hope firm
until the end.

⁷ Therefore, just as the Holy Spirit says,

"TODAY IF YOU HEAR HIS VOICE,
⁸ DO NOT HARDEN YOUR HEARTS AS [b]WHEN THEY PROVOKED ME,
AS IN THE DAY OF TRIAL IN THE WILDERNESS,
⁹ WHERE YOUR FATHERS TRIED *Me* BY TESTING *Me*,
AND SAW MY WORKS FOR FORTY YEARS.
¹⁰ "THEREFORE I WAS ANGRY WITH THIS GENERATION,
AND SAID, 'THEY ALWAYS GO ASTRAY IN THEIR HEART,
AND THEY DID NOT KNOW MY WAYS';
¹¹ AS I SWORE IN MY WRATH,
'THEY SHALL NOT ENTER MY REST.'"

¹² Take care, brethren, that there not be in any one of you an evil, unbelieving heart [c]that falls away from the living God. ¹³ But encourage one another day after day, as long as it is *still* called "Today," so that none of you will be hardened by the deceitfulness of sin. ¹⁴ For we have become partakers of Christ, if we hold fast the beginning of our assurance firm until the end, ¹⁵ while it is said,

"TODAY IF YOU HEAR HIS VOICE,
DO NOT HARDEN YOUR HEARTS, AS [d]WHEN THEY PROVOKED ME."

¹⁶ For who provoked *Him* when they had heard? Indeed, did not all those who came out of Egypt *led* by Moses? ¹⁷ And with whom was He angry for forty years? Was it not with those who sinned, whose bodies fell in the wilderness? ¹⁸ And to whom did He swear that they would not enter His rest, but to those who were disobedient? ¹⁹ *So* we see that they were not able to enter because of unbelief. (Hebrews 3)
https://www.biblegateway.com/passage/?search=hebrews+3&version=NASB

The first verse is very deep. The Author is writing to the Hebrews. He uses "holy brethren", meaning they are set apart. He uses "heavenly calling", they were a called people of God, called for what? They were called to share their faith, the Messiah i.e. the Christ would someday come through their loins (marked by

Circumcision). The Promised One i.e. Sent One, would come through Abraham. Jesus is called "Apostle", meaning Sent One.

So Jesus said to them again, "Peace *be* with you; as the Father has sent Me, I also send you." (John 20:21)

Jesus is then called High Priest. How can this be? Jesus was from Judah, not Levi (In Levitical Law priests came through Levi). Levi is a picture of the Law. The Law by Itself was not everlasting. The Law was a Tutor to Christ (Galatians 3).

"Do not think that I came to abolish the Law or the Prophets; I did not come to abolish but to fulfill. (Matthew 5:17)

Jesus fulfilled the Law. Jesus was from Judah, meaning Praise, Everlasting Praise. The Law alone does not last forever, Levi together with Judah, the Law with Praise, does last forever. In the last chapter we learned that although Jesus was tempted, He did not sin, He did not break the Law, He fulfilled the Law.

Unlike Levi, Jesus was called according to the order of Melchizedek, well before Moses wrote the Levitical Law. In chapter one Jesus is above angels, in chapter two He is above sin, in this chapter He is above Moses. (We will study Melchizedek more deeply in chapters 5-7.)

The "father" of the Hebrews was Abraham. Melchizedek first meets with Abram (later called Abraham) in Genesis 14. Notice how they partake in Communion (Bread/Body and Wine/Blood). We previously studied in depth that the enemies are sin and death. Salem means Peace. Melchizedek means King of Righteousness. Below in Genesis 14 and Psalm 110, you actually have the Gospel Message.

And Melchizedek king of Salem brought out bread and wine; now he was a priest of [s]God Most High. [19] He blessed him and said,

"Blessed be Abram of [t]God Most High,
[u]Possessor of heaven and earth;
[20] And blessed be [v]God Most High,
Who has delivered your enemies into your hand." (Genesis 14:18-20)

In Hebrews 1 we saw Psalm 110 quoted. This is a very important Messianic Psalm.

The LORD says to my Lord:
"Sit at My right hand
Until I make Your enemies a footstool for Your feet."
[2] The LORD will stretch forth Your strong scepter from Zion, *saying*,
"Rule in the midst of Your enemies."
[3] Your people [a]will volunteer freely in the day of Your [b]power;
In [c]holy array, from the womb of the dawn,
[d]Your youth are to You *as* the dew.

[4] The LORD has sworn and will not [e]change His mind,
"You are a priest forever
According to the order of Melchizedek."
[5] The Lord is at Your right hand;
He [f]will shatter kings in the day of His wrath.
[6] He will judge among the nations,
He [g]will fill *them* with corpses,
He [h]will shatter the [i]chief men over a broad country.
[7] He will drink from the brook by the wayside;
Therefore He will lift up *His* head. (Psalm 110)

Starting in Hebrew 3:7 we then see Psalm 95:7-11 quoted. This Scripture is speaking that out of the 600,000 Hebrew men that left Egypt that only two originals made it into the Promised Land. The two were Joshua (Savior) and Caleb (whole heart). The 599,998 died in the wilderness due to hard hearts, hearts hardened by sin. These did not enter His Rest. In the next chapter we will learn that the 7th Day Sabbath Rest is Jesus Christ, not a day of the week. Faith in the Work of Jesus equates to our Eternal Rest, His Work our Rest.

But before faith came, we were kept in custody under the law, being shut up to the faith which was later to be revealed. ²⁴ Therefore the Law has become our tutor *to lead us* to Christ, so that we may be justified by faith. ²⁵ But now that faith has come, we are no longer under a [ai]tutor. ²⁶ For you are all sons of God through faith in Christ Jesus. ²⁷ For all of you who were baptized into Christ have clothed yourselves with Christ. ²⁸ There is neither Jew nor Greek, there is neither slave nor free man, there is [aj]neither male nor female; for you are all one in Christ Jesus. ²⁹ And if you [ak]belong to Christ, then you are Abraham's [al]descendants, heirs according to promise. (Galatians 3:23-29)

An interesting fact is that the word Salvation occurs 7 times in the Book of Hebrews and a total of 49 (7X7) times in the New Testament.

We don't "fall" into sin, we walk into it

Hebrews 4

Therefore, let us fear if, while a promise remains of entering His rest, any one of you may seem to have come short of it. ² For indeed we have had good news preached to us, just as they also; but the word [a]they heard did not profit them, because [b]it was not united by faith in those who heard. ³ For we who have believed enter that rest, just as He has said,

"AS I SWORE IN MY WRATH,
THEY SHALL NOT ENTER MY REST,"

although His works were finished from the foundation of the world. ⁴ For He has said somewhere concerning the seventh *day*: "AND GOD RESTED ON THE SEVENTH DAY FROM ALL HIS WORKS"; ⁵ and again in this *passage*, "THEY SHALL NOT ENTER MY REST." ⁶ Therefore, since it remains for some to enter it, and those who formerly had good news preached to them failed to enter because of disobedience, ⁷ He again fixes a certain day, "Today," saying [c]through David after so long a time just as has been said before,

"TODAY IF YOU HEAR HIS VOICE,
DO NOT HARDEN YOUR HEARTS."

⁸ For if [d]Joshua had given them rest, He would not have spoken of another day after that. ⁹ So there remains a Sabbath rest for the people of God. ¹⁰ For the one who has entered His rest has himself also rested from his works, as God did from His. ¹¹ Therefore let us be diligent to enter that rest, so that no one will fall, through *following* the same example of disobedience. ¹² For the word of God is living and active and sharper than any two-edged sword, and piercing as far as the division of soul and spirit, of both joints and marrow, and able to judge the thoughts and intentions of the heart. ¹³ And there is no creature hidden from His sight, but all things are open and laid bare to the eyes of Him with whom we have to do.

¹⁴ Therefore, since we have a great high priest who has passed through the heavens, Jesus the Son of God, let us hold fast our confession. ¹⁵ For we do not have a high priest who cannot sympathize with our weaknesses, but One who has been tempted in all things as *we are, yet* without sin. ¹⁶ Therefore let us draw near with confidence to the throne of grace, so that we may receive mercy and find grace to help in time of need. (Hebrews 4)

https://www.biblegateway.com/passage/?search=Hebrews+4&version=NASB

We start off this chapter with a "therefore", which we have to look back at chapter 3 to see what this "therefore" is referring to. We ended chapter three with the "hard heart" topic. A hard heart is due to unbelief, no faith. Out of the 600,000 Hebrew men that left Egypt, 599,998 died of hard hearts. God teaches us the Spiritual with the physical. Even today, physically the biggest killer in the world is heart disease (hard heart). Spiritually the biggest killer in the world is also heart disease. Please pray for my youngest daughter, she is nineteen, and has a hard heart, a heart of unbelief.

The Gospel Message was in the Garden of Eden. God Rested on the Seventh Day. By the end of this paper we will see that Jesus is our 7th Day Rest, the Fourth Commandment. I believe that the Garden of Eden was in the same area as Jerusalem (Gihon Spring/River link). Due to sin in the heart, Adam and Eve exited east. The Hebrew people going east ended up in Babel (Iraq). After Babel, Abraham, a descendant of Heber who lived prior to Babel, moves back to the Jerusalem area. Before Babel we were all Hebrews. After Babel, Abraham continued the Hebrew people. Abraham is called by Melchizedek, King of Salem (King of Jerusalem), into priesthood. Abraham, with the Covenant of Circumcision, is told that through is loins, a Savior, the Promised King, the Messiah will be born. In Genesis 22, God actually has Abraham take Isaac to Mount Moriah (Golgotha), to offer his son as a sacrifice. God stops Abraham, and says, "God will provide Himself a Sacrifice." The Ram, with His Head caught in the thorns, is a picture of the future Christ with a Crown of Thorns.

Here is a very important article to read on Jerusalem:
http://www.abarim-publications.com/Meaning/Jerusalem.html#.WGVPdcIzWUk

Keep in mind that in Revelation 21 and 22, when Heaven comes down to earth that Heaven is called New Jerusalem. Remember in our study of John and Nehemiah how the walls of Jerusalem are the walls of our heart. Remember how Jesus took our sin upon Himself within the walls of Jerusalem. He was then led out of a gate (I believe the Dung Gate), to Mount Moriah i.e. Golgotha, to be crucified. He was led out with our sin (our dung) upon Himself. He removed the sin from our heart, making us whole again, a whole heart, at peace with God. Remember the only two that made it into the Promised Land of the 600,000 Hebrew men that left Egypt, were Joshua (means Savior, also Jesus is Greek equivalent for the Hebrew Joshua) and Caleb (means whole heart, at peace with God, Jerusalem).

When the children of Israel came into the Promised Land, Jerusalem was not important to them. We see this evidenced in Judges. In Judges 1:8, Jerusalem is burned. We read in Judges 1:21 that the Jebusites remain in Jerusalem. Remember as well that the Hebrews did not name Jerusalem; no one knows Who named Jerusalem. It is not until the time of King David (a picture Jesus) that Jerusalem actually becomes important. In 2 Samuel 24, David buys the Temple Mount area from a Jebusite. One thousand years after David, God in the Flesh, Jesus Christ purchases Jerusalem, a picture of the heart of the earth, with His Blood. The first high priest was Aaron; the Last Great High Priest was Jesus Christ. Jesus Christ, while on the Cross, said, "It is finished!" The price for sin was atoned for, the Day of Atonement ultimately fulfilled. The Veil to the Holy of Holies tore from Top to bottom, God tore it. The Work of Christ is the fulfillment of all 7 Feasts of Leviticus 23. Trumpets: His birth, Day of Atonement: His Circumcision, Tabernacles: Dwelling amongst us, Passover: the Lamb that was slain, Unleavened Bread: in the Tomb without sin, First Fruits: Resurrection Day, and Weeks: appearing to many for 49 Days giving evidence of the Resurrection. Day Fifty was Pentecost, the Giving of the Holy Spirit. In 70 A.D. the Temple is destroyed, no longer needed. The entire Old Testament is completely satisfied in the Work of Jesus Christ. His Work equals our Eternal Sabbath Rest. With a completed heart in Christ, a Spiritual rebirth (being born again), we are made whole again, no longer body and soul and dead spirit, but now body and soul and Living Spirit!!! You are now the Temple of the Holy Spirit!!!

Then I saw a new heaven and a new earth; for the first heaven and the first earth passed away, and there is no longer *any* sea. ² And I saw the holy city, new Jerusalem, coming down out of heaven from God, made ready as a bride adorned for her husband. ³ And I heard a loud voice from the throne, saying, "Behold, the tabernacle of God is among men, and He will [a]dwell among them, and they shall be His people, and God Himself will be among them[b], ⁴ and He will wipe away every tear from their eyes; and there will no longer be *any* death; there will no longer be *any* mourning, or crying, or pain; the first things have passed away."

⁵ And He who sits on the throne said, "Behold, I am making all things new." And He *said, "Write, for these words are faithful and true." ⁶ Then He said to me, "[c]It is done. I am the Alpha and the Omega, the beginning and the end. I will give to the one who thirsts from the spring of the water of life without cost. ⁷ He who overcomes will inherit these things, and I will be his God and he will be My son. ⁸ But for the cowardly and [d]unbelieving and abominable and murderers and immoral persons and sorcerers and idolaters and all liars, their part *will be* in the lake that burns with fire and [e]brimstone, which is the second death."

⁹ Then one of the seven angels who had the seven bowls [f]full of the seven last plagues came and spoke with me, saying, "Come here, I will show you the bride, the wife of the Lamb."

¹⁰ And he carried me away [g]in the Spirit to a great and high mountain, and showed me the holy city, Jerusalem, coming down out of heaven from God, ¹¹ having the glory of God. Her [h]brilliance was like a very costly stone, as a stone of crystal-clear jasper. ¹² [i]It had a great and high wall, [j]with twelve gates, and at the gates twelve angels; and names *were* written on them, which are *the names* of the twelve tribes of the sons of Israel. ¹³ *There were* three gates on the east and three gates on the north and three gates on the south and

three gates on the west. [14] And the wall of the city had twelve foundation stones, and on them *were* the twelve names of the twelve apostles of the Lamb.

[15] The one who spoke with me had a [k]gold measuring rod to measure the city, and its gates and its wall. [16] The city is laid out as a square, and its length is as great as the width; and he measured the city with the [l]rod, [m]fifteen hundred miles; its length and width and height are equal. [17] And he measured its wall, [n]seventy-two yards, *according to* human [o]measurements, which are *also* angelic *measurements*. [18] The material of the wall was jasper; and the city was pure gold, like [p]clear glass. [19] The foundation stones of the city wall were adorned with every kind of precious stone. The first foundation stone was jasper; the second, sapphire; the third, chalcedony; the fourth, emerald; [20] the fifth, sardonyx; the sixth, sardius; the seventh, chrysolite; the eighth, beryl; the ninth, topaz; the tenth, chrysoprase; the eleventh, jacinth; the twelfth, amethyst. [21] And the twelve gates were twelve pearls; each one of the gates was a single pearl. And the street of the city was pure gold, like transparent glass.

[22] I saw no [q]temple in it, for the Lord God the Almighty and the Lamb are its [r]temple. [23] And the city has no need of the sun or of the moon to shine on it, for the glory of God has illumined it, and its lamp *is* the Lamb. [24] The nations will walk by its light, and the kings of the earth [s]will bring their glory into it. [25] In the daytime (for there will be no night there) its gates will never be closed; [26] and they will bring the glory and the honor of the nations into it; [27] and nothing unclean, and no one who practices abomination and lying, shall ever come into it, but only those [t]whose names are written in the Lamb's book of life. (Revelation 21)
https://www.biblegateway.com/passage/?search=Revelation+21&version=NASB

So faith *comes* from hearing, and hearing by the Word of Christ. (Romans 10:17)

Hebrews 5

For every high priest taken from among men is appointed on behalf of men in things pertaining to God, in order to offer both gifts and sacrifices for sins; ² [a]he can deal gently with the ignorant and misguided, since he himself also is [b]beset with weakness; ³ and because of it he is obligated to offer *sacrifices* for sins, as for the people, so also for himself. ⁴ And no one takes the honor to himself, but *receives it* when he is called by God, even as Aaron was.

⁵ So also Christ did not glorify Himself so as to become a high priest, but He who said to Him,

"YOU ARE MY SON,
TODAY I HAVE BEGOTTEN YOU";

⁶ just as He says also in another *passage*,

"YOU ARE A PRIEST FOREVER
ACCORDING TO THE ORDER OF MELCHIZEDEK."

⁷ [c]In the days of His flesh, [d]He offered up both prayers and supplications with loud crying and tears to the One able to save Him [e]from death, and He [f]was heard because of His piety. ⁸ Although He was a Son, He learned obedience from the things which He suffered. ⁹ And having been made perfect, He became to all those who obey Him the source of eternal salvation, ¹⁰ being designated by God as a high priest according to the order of Melchizedek.

¹¹ Concerning [g]him we have much to say, and *it is* hard to explain, since you have become dull of hearing. ¹² For though [h]by this time you ought to be teachers, you have need again for someone to teach you the [i]elementary principles of the oracles of God, and you have come to need milk and not solid food. ¹³ For everyone who partakes *only* of milk is not accustomed to the word of righteousness, for he is an infant. ¹⁴ But solid food is for the mature, who because of practice

have their senses trained to discern good and evil. (Hebrews 5)
https://www.biblegateway.com/passage/?search=Hebrews+5&versio
n=NASB

The first four verses describe the Levitical priest, which began with
Aaron, the first high priest. He was from the tribe of Levi. The Book
of Hebrews is addressing Hebrews, so they are asking the question,
"How can Jesus be the Great High Priest, when He is from the tribe
of Judah?"

The Author of Hebrews is teaching them that Jesus was a Priest
forever by the order of Melchizedek. Melchizedek first appeared to
Abram/later Father Abraham back in Genesis 14, hundreds of years
before Aaron, before there was even a Levite tribe. Melchizedek is
King of Salem. He actually has Communion with Abram. In that
same chapter Abram is called a Hebrew.

In Genesis 17, 18 and 22 we learn that Abram, now Father Abraham
is to be the father of a multitude of nations. Notice that nations are
plural.

Now when Abram was ninety-nine years old, the LORD appeared to
Abram and said to him,

"I am [a]God Almighty;
Walk before Me, and be [b]blameless.
2 "I will [c]establish My covenant between Me and you,
And I will multiply you exceedingly."

3 Abram fell on his face, and God talked with him, saying,

4 "As for Me, behold, My covenant is with you,
And you will be the father of a multitude of nations.
5 "No longer shall your name be called [d]Abram,
But your name shall be [e]Abraham;
For I have made you the father of a multitude of nations.

338

⁶ I will make you exceedingly fruitful, and I will make nations of you, and kings will come forth from you. ⁷ I will establish My covenant between Me and you and your [f]descendants after you throughout their generations for an everlasting covenant, to be God to you and to your [g]descendants after you. ⁸ I will give to you and to your [h]descendants after you, the land of your sojournings, all the land of Canaan, for an everlasting possession; and I will be their God." (Genesis 17:1-8)

This Covenant is enacted with Circumcision. Remember the purpose of the Circumcision was to point to the Christ. Through the loins of Abraham all nations would be blessed. We see the genealogy from Father Abraham to Jesus in Matthew 1: https://www.biblegateway.com/passage/?search=Matthew+1&version=NASB

In Genesis 22, Father Abraham is tested by God. He is told to offer his only begotten son, the son in the coming Promised One genealogy, Isaac. (Recall that in Genesis 16, prior to being given the name Abraham that Abram had a son with his wife's maidservant.)

Then the angel of the LORD called to Abraham a second time from heaven, ¹⁶ and said, "By Myself I have sworn, declares the LORD, because you have done this thing and have not withheld your son, your only son, ¹⁷ indeed I will greatly bless you, and I will greatly multiply your [e]seed as the stars of the heavens and as the sand which is on the seashore; and your [f]seed shall possess the gate of [g]their enemies. ¹⁸ In your [h]seed all the nations of the earth shall [i]be blessed, because you have obeyed My voice." (Genesis 22:15-18)

Notice the plural nations above, "all the nations of the earth shall be blessed". So how do we put all this together? The Priest of God Most High, Melchizedek, anoints Abram the Hebrew. The Promised Messiah will now come through his loins. Here is a controversial statement, "Today and through the years we have been taught to believe that the Hebrews/Jews were God's chosen people. He is God and can choose who He wants. Do not ever question the

Sovereignty of God." I do not question God; I question the teaching of man. I whole heartedly believe that it is better said, "The Hebrews are God's chosen priesthood of people to reach all people for God." It started at Abraham when he was blessed by Melchizedek. Remember in Genesis 10, his ancestor Heber (where the name Hebrew comes from) was prior to the Tower of Babel. Everyone spoke Hebrew prior to Babel. At Babel God confused the languages. The world was divided by language. Remember what happened after the Messiah, Jesus Christ, came and fulfilled the 7 Feasts? The very next day was Pentecost. In that Upper Room, people from "many nations" heard the hillbilly Galileans speaking in their own language. Languages that once divided the world now united the world, because of the Completed Work of Christ; we now have a Helper, the Holy Spirit was given on Pentecost.

When the day of Pentecost [a]had come, they were all together in one place. 2 And suddenly there came from heaven a noise like a violent rushing wind, and it filled the whole house where they were sitting. 3 And there appeared to them tongues as of fire [b]distributing themselves, and [c]they [d]rested on each one of them. 4 And they were all filled with the Holy Spirit and began to speak with other [e]tongues, as the Spirit was giving them [f]utterance.

5 Now there were Jews living in Jerusalem, devout men from every nation under heaven. 6 And when this sound occurred, the crowd came together, and were bewildered because each one of them was hearing them speak in his own [g]language. 7 They were amazed and astonished, saying, "[h]Why, are not all these who are speaking Galileans? 8 And how is it that we each hear *them* in our own [i]language [j]to which we were born? 9 Parthians and Medes and Elamites, and residents of Mesopotamia, Judea and Cappadocia, Pontus and [k]Asia, 10 Phrygia and Pamphylia, Egypt and the districts of Libya around Cyrene, and [l]visitors from Rome, both Jews and [m]proselytes, 11 Cretans and Arabs—we hear them in our *own* tongues speaking of the mighty deeds of God." 12 And they all continued in amazement and great perplexity, saying to one another, "What does this mean?" (Acts 2:1-12)

"For God so loved the world, that He gave His [e]only begotten Son, that whoever believes in Him shall not perish, but have eternal life. [17] For God did not send the Son into the world to judge the world, but that the world might be saved through Him. [18] He who believes in Him is not judged; he who does not believe has been judged already, because he has not believed in the name of the [f]only begotten Son of God. [19] This is the judgment, that the Light has come into the world, and men loved the darkness rather than the Light, for their deeds were evil. [20] For everyone who does evil hates the Light, and does not come to the Light for fear that his deeds will be exposed. [21] But he who practices the truth comes to the Light, so that his deeds may be manifested as having been wrought in God." (John 3:16-21)

And I, if I am lifted up from the earth, will draw all men to Myself." (John 12:32)

Hebrews 6

Therefore leaving the [a]elementary teaching about the [b]Christ, let us press on to [c]maturity, not laying again a foundation of repentance from dead works and of faith toward God, [2] of instruction about washings and laying on of hands, and the resurrection of the dead and eternal judgment. [3] And this we will do, if God permits. [4] For in the case of those who have once been enlightened and have tasted of the heavenly gift and have been made partakers of the Holy Spirit, [5] and have tasted the good word of God and the powers of the age to come, [6] and *then* have fallen away, it is impossible to renew them again to repentance, [d]since they again crucify to themselves the Son of God and put Him to open shame. [7] For ground that drinks the rain which often [c]falls on it and brings forth vegetation useful to those for whose sake it is also tilled, receives a blessing from God; [8] but if it yields thorns and thistles, it is worthless and close [f]to being cursed, and [g]it ends up being burned.

[9] But, beloved, we are convinced of better things concerning you, and things that [h]accompany salvation, though we are speaking in this way. [10] For God is not unjust so as to forget your work and the love which you have shown toward His name, in having ministered and in still ministering to the [i]saints. [11] And we desire that each one of you show the same diligence [j]so as to realize the full assurance of hope until the end, [12] so that you will not be sluggish, but imitators of those who through faith and patience inherit the promises.

[13] For when God made the promise to Abraham, since He could swear by no one greater, He swore by Himself, [14] saying, "I WILL SURELY BLESS YOU AND I WILL SURELY MULTIPLY YOU." [15] And so, having patiently waited, he obtained the promise. [16] For men swear by [k]one greater *than themselves*, and with them an oath *given* as confirmation is an end of every dispute. [17] [l]In the same way God, desiring even more to show to the heirs of the promise the unchangeableness of His purpose, [m]interposed with an oath, [18] so that by two unchangeable things in which it is impossible for God to lie, we who have [n]taken refuge would have strong encouragement to take hold of the hope set before us. [19] [o]This hope we have as an anchor of the soul, a *hope* both sure and steadfast and one which enters [p]within the veil, [20] where Jesus has entered as a forerunner for us, having become a high priest forever according to the order of Melchizedek. (Hebrews 6)
https://www.biblegateway.com/passage/?search=Hebrews+6&version=NASB

There are all kinds of disagreements over the first eight verses of this chapter. Remember Hebrew believers are being addressed here. These verses are talking about a Hebrew who has come to realize that Jesus is the total fulfillment of the Old Testament, but knowing this, they go back to the Temple system that was already fulfilled in Christ. The Veil to the Holy of Holies was torn from Top to bottom, God tore it, "It is finished!" The verse below somehow has not set into the heart of many of today's believers.

Do not think that I came to abolish the Law or the Prophets; I did not come to abolish but to fulfill. (Matthew 5:17)

For some reason many today teach that God still has a special plan for His chosen Hebrews. They teach that there are two Covenants, two peoples of God, the Jews and the Gentiles. But like we discussed in the last chapter, this is not the case. Gentiles is actually better translated Nations. The Hebrews were a chosen people to be centered on a Priesthood that pointed all people to the coming Promised One, the Messiah, Jesus the Christ.

Through Father Abraham **many Nations** would be blessed. Was it coincidence that the building supplies for the Temple came from other Nations (1 Kings 5)? Was it coincidence that Solomon teamed up with Hiram from Tyre, another Nation, to build the Temple (1 Kings 5)? Hiram, half Hebrew and half Gentile (better said, half Hebrew and half other Nation) actually does the detailed inner work of the Temple (1 Kings 7). Solomon himself is half Hebrew (David) and half other Nation (Bathsheba). There is even a pillar in the Temple named Boaz (Hebrew), a patriarch who married the Gentile Ruth, whose child is actually in the genealogy of the Christ (Salmon and Rahab also in the same way). Also, why would God design a Court of the Gentiles next to the Temple (better translated the Court of the Nations) if the Hebrew Priesthood was to not be for ALL people?

I believe the modern day translation of the Book of Revelation has a lot to do with how doctrine got so twisted. Today's popular Revelation doctrine insists on another temple being built, actually a couple more temples. The Temple was fulfilled in Christ. The Temple was destroyed in 70 A.D. At Pentecost God sent us His Holy Spirit. We are now the Temple of the Holy Spirit.

Do not think that I came to abolish the Law or the Prophets; I did not come to abolish but to fulfill. (Matthew 5:17)

Hebrews 7

For this Melchizedek, king of Salem, priest of the Most High God, who met Abraham as he was returning from the slaughter of the kings and blessed him, ² to whom also Abraham apportioned a tenth part of all *the spoils*, was first of all, by the translation *of his name*, king of righteousness, and then also king of Salem, which is king of peace. ³ Without father, without mother, without genealogy, having neither beginning of days nor end of life, but made like the Son of God, he remains a priest perpetually.

⁴ Now observe how great this man was to whom Abraham, the patriarch, gave a tenth of the choicest spoils. ⁵ And those indeed of the sons of Levi who receive the priest's office have commandment [a]in the Law to collect [b]a tenth from the people, that is, from their brethren, although these [c]are descended from Abraham. ⁶ But the one whose genealogy is not traced from them collected [d]a tenth from Abraham and [e]blessed the one who had the promises. ⁷ But without any dispute the lesser is blessed by the greater. ⁸ In this case mortal men receive tithes, but in that case one *receives them*, of whom it is witnessed that he lives on. ⁹ And, so to speak, through Abraham even Levi, who received tithes, paid tithes, ¹⁰ for he was still in the loins of his father when Melchizedek met him.

¹¹ Now if perfection was through the Levitical priesthood (for on the basis of it the people received the Law), what further need *was there* for another priest to arise according to the order of Melchizedek, and

not be designated according to the order of Aaron? [12] For when the priesthood is changed, of necessity there takes place a change of law also. [13] For the one concerning whom these things are spoken belongs to another tribe, from which no one has officiated at the altar. [14] For it is evident that our Lord [f]was descended from Judah, a tribe with reference to which Moses spoke nothing concerning priests. [15] And this is clearer still, if another priest arises according to the likeness of Melchizedek, [16] who has become *such* not on the basis of a law of [g]physical requirement, but according to the power of an indestructible life. [17] For it is attested *of Him*,

"YOU ARE A PRIEST FOREVER
ACCORDING TO THE ORDER OF MELCHIZEDEK."

[18] For, on the one hand, there is a setting aside of a former commandment because of its weakness and uselessness [19] (for the Law made nothing perfect), and on the other hand there is a bringing in of a better hope, through which we draw near to God. [20] And inasmuch as *it was* not without an oath [21] (for they indeed became priests without an oath, but He with an oath through the One who said to Him,

"THE LORD HAS SWORN
AND WILL NOT CHANGE HIS MIND,
'YOU ARE A PRIEST FOREVER'");

[22] so much the more also Jesus has become the guarantee of a better covenant.

[23] [h]The *former* priests, on the one hand, existed in greater numbers because they were prevented by death from continuing, [24] but Jesus, on the other hand, because He continues forever, holds His priesthood permanently. [25] Therefore He is able also to save [i]forever those who draw near to God through Him, since He always lives to make intercession for them.

[26] For it was fitting for us to have such a high priest, holy, innocent, undefiled, separated from sinners and exalted above the heavens; [27] who does not need daily, like those high priests, to offer up

sacrifices, first for His own sins and then for the *sins* of the people, because this He did once for all when He offered up Himself. [28] For the Law appoints men as high priests who are weak, but the word of the oath, which came after the Law, *appoints* a Son, made perfect forever. (Hebrews 7)
https://www.biblegateway.com/passage/?search=Hebrews+7&version=NASB

This chapter continues on with the Levite priesthood and Melchizedek Priesthood comparison. The first being temporary, earthly; we learn in the next chapter a "shadow" of the Heavenly. The second being a Forever Priesthood, Heavenly, not a shadow, but the Substance of things hoped for. Jesus is the Light, not the shadow. Let's take one more look at the original Melchizedek Scripture from Genesis 14:

Then after his return from the [r]defeat of Chedorlaomer and the kings who were with him, the king of Sodom went out to meet him at the valley of Shaveh (that is, the King's Valley). [18] And Melchizedek king of Salem brought out bread and wine; now he was a priest of [s]God Most High. [19] He blessed him and said,

"Blessed be Abram of [t]God Most High,
[u]Possessor of heaven and earth;
[20] And blessed be [v]God Most High,
Who has delivered your enemies into your hand."

He gave him a tenth of all. [21] The king of Sodom said to Abram, "Give the [w]people to me and take the goods for yourself." [22] Abram said to the king of Sodom, "I have [x]sworn to the LORD [y]God Most High, [z]possessor of heaven and earth, [23] that I will not take a thread or a sandal thong or anything that is yours, for fear you would say, 'I have made Abram rich.' [24] [aa]I will take nothing except what the young men have eaten, and the share of the men who went with me, Aner, Eshcol, and Mamre; let them take their share." (Genesis 14:17-24)

We have the word "Chedorlaomer" which means sheaves, wheat sheaves (bundles of wheat). The sheaves of wheat were taken to the threshing floor to separate the wheat from the chaff. The wheat goes to Heaven, the chaff burns in hell. The Forever Priest named Melchizedek, having no father or mother or genealogy or beginning or ending blesses Abram. We also have the king of sodom, he being a picture of worldly temptation and evil. Abram's nephew chooses that area to dwell in when he and Abram separate. In Genesis 19 God destroys sodom and gomorrah. sodom and gomorrah are where the Dead Sea is today. No life dwells in this sea, even today, its shores are literally the lowest point on earth. We know from our Jordan River (means descending from Above) study that when Joseph went to bury his father Jacob/Israel and when the children of Israel went up into the Promised Land, that both times a detour was taken to go out of the way to cross the Jordan opposite Jericho (Remember that the waters were pushed back to the town of "Adam", Joshua 3:16), then back over to the Promised Land side. This is a picture of our sin being washed off and flowing south into the Dead Sea. Even John the Baptist baptized at a spot on the Jordan called Bethany "Beyond the Jordan", which was on the opposite side of the Jordan. Bethany means house of figs, which takes us back to the Garden of Eden, the tree of the knowledge of good and evil. The leaves that Adam and Eve covered themselves with were from the fig tree. Not only is the Gospel in geography but in nature as well. Check out this strangler fig tree video: https://www.youtube.com/watch?v=UCUtpmwacoE Abram takes nothing from the king of sodom. He does take the share of the three Amorites. Amorite means speaker/talker of Love. What do the names Aner, Eshcol and Mamre mean?

Aner: City of Manasseh given to the Levites (1 Chronicles 6:70). Manasseh means forgiveness. Also means flesh, male. Also means sprout, waterfall and answer.
http://www.biblestudytools.com/dictionary/aner/

Eshcol: cluster of grapes.
http://www.biblestudytools.com/encyclopedias/isbe/eshcol-1.html

Mamre: Oak, bitterness, rebellion i.e. sin.
http://www.biblestudytools.com/dictionary/mamre/

Jesus is the Waterfall i.e. the Living Water from Heaven. He is a Waterfall of Forgiveness. He took on Flesh (Bread of Life), being found in the likeness of a Man. Jesus is the Sprout, the Promised Seed. He is the Answer to the sin problem. Jesus is a Blood (Cluster of Grapes) Waterfall that washes our sin away!!! The Above Gospel is the Light, He was in the beginning. The Aaronic Levite Tent of Meeting/Temple priesthood is the shadow. Jesus is the Light.

In the beginning was the Word, and the Word was with God, and the Word was God. [2] [a]He was in the beginning with God. [3] All things came into being through Him, and apart from Him nothing came into being that has come into being. [4] In Him was life, and the life was the Light of men. [5] The Light shines in the darkness, and the darkness did not [b]comprehend it. (John 1:1-5)

And the Word became flesh, and [k]dwelt among us, and we saw His glory, glory as of [l]the only begotten from the Father, full of grace and truth. [15] John *testified about Him and cried out, saying, "This was He of whom I said, 'He who comes after me [m]has a higher rank than I, for He existed before me.'" [16] For of His fullness [n]we have all received, and [o]grace upon grace. [17] For the Law was given through Moses; grace and truth [p]were realized through Jesus Christ. (John 1:14-17)

Hebrews 8

Now the main point in what has been said *is this*: we have such a high priest, who has taken His seat at the right hand of the throne of the Majesty in the heavens, ² a minister [a]in the sanctuary and [b]in the true [c]tabernacle, which the Lord pitched, not man. ³ For every high priest is appointed to offer both gifts and sacrifices; so it is necessary that this *high priest* also have something to offer. ⁴ Now if He were on earth, He would not be a priest at all, since there are those who offer the gifts according to the Law; ⁵ who serve a copy and shadow of the heavenly things, just as Moses [d]was warned *by God* when he was about to erect the [e]tabernacle; for, "SEE," He says, "THAT YOU MAKE all things ACCORDING TO THE PATTERN WHICH WAS SHOWN YOU ON THE MOUNTAIN." ⁶ But now He has obtained a more excellent ministry, by as much as He is also the mediator of a better covenant, which has been enacted on better promises.

⁷ For if that first *covenant* had been faultless, there would have been no occasion sought for a second. ⁸ For finding fault with them, He says,

"BEHOLD, DAYS ARE COMING, SAYS THE LORD,
[f]WHEN I WILL EFFECT A NEW COVENANT
WITH THE HOUSE OF ISRAEL AND WITH THE HOUSE OF JUDAH;
⁹ NOT LIKE THE COVENANT WHICH I MADE WITH THEIR FATHERS
ON THE DAY WHEN I TOOK THEM BY THE HAND
TO LEAD THEM OUT OF THE LAND OF EGYPT;
FOR THEY DID NOT CONTINUE IN MY COVENANT,
AND I DID NOT CARE FOR THEM, SAYS THE LORD.
¹⁰ "FOR THIS IS THE COVENANT THAT I WILL MAKE WITH THE HOUSE OF ISRAEL
AFTER THOSE DAYS, SAYS THE LORD:
[g]I WILL PUT MY LAWS INTO THEIR MINDS,
AND I WILL WRITE THEM ON THEIR HEARTS.
AND I WILL BE THEIR GOD,

AND THEY SHALL BE MY PEOPLE.
[11] "AND THEY SHALL NOT TEACH EVERYONE HIS FELLOW CITIZEN,
AND EVERYONE HIS BROTHER, SAYING, 'KNOW THE LORD,'
FOR ALL WILL KNOW ME,
FROM [h]THE LEAST TO THE GREATEST OF THEM.
[12] "FOR I WILL BE MERCIFUL TO THEIR INIQUITIES,
AND I WILL REMEMBER THEIR SINS NO MORE."

[13] [i]When He said, "A new *covenant*," He has made the first obsolete. But whatever is becoming obsolete and growing old is [j]ready to disappear. (Hebrews 8)
https://www.biblegateway.com/passage/?search=Hebrews+8&version=NASB

This current earth and the current life we live are but a blink of an eye as compared to Forever. Moses was privy to seeing a copy and shadow of the Forever Heavenly Tabernacle. An earthly copy was built. Man would have to sacrifice over and over and over again. But one day the Son of God, the Promised One, as told to Abraham would come and Perfectly fulfill everything about this tabernacle, He being the Tabernacle Who dwelt amongst us. The earthly copy and shadow of the Heavenly is now **obsolete**.

In verse five, Exodus 25:40, is quoted. The children of Israel were free from Egypt, they were at Mount Sinai. Moses had already gone up once. He came back down and verbally gave the Ten Commandments, the Three Required Annual Feasts (Tabernacles and Unleavened Bread and Weeks, which is the Gospel: Jesus Tabernacled on earth conquering sin, being without leaven, and He conquered death, appearing for over forty days during Weeks proving His Resurrection), and about the Sabbath Rest (which due to the 7 Feast Work of Jesus we can now Sabbath Rest Forever, His Work=our Rest). They made a Covenant with God in Exodus 24. Then in Exodus 25-31, Moses goes back up to Mount Sinai. Moses was gone for a while and the people with Aaron decide to make an idol, a golden calf.

Sounds familiar? Today many Christians and Jews are looking for the perfect Red Heifer cow to restart the temple process again. WHAT??? Redo the system that Christ fulfilled. The one that in this chapter, in verse 13, says is **obsolete**. Yep, that's what they are doing. They teach that there is one way to Heaven for gentiles, with Jesus and another for His supposedly chosen Jews, the temple, which is the system that Christ fulfilled and made **obsolete**. This is false teaching but is extremely popular in today's church. The Hebrews were God's chosen priesthood centered people to reach all people for God.

Again here is Matthew 5:17:

Do not think that I came to abolish the Law or the Prophets; I did not come to abolish but to fulfill. (Matthew 5:17)

The second half of this chapter is a quote from Jeremiah 31. This is speaking of Heaven, the Forever. Below is the last half of that quote.

I WILL PUT MY LAWS INTO THEIR MINDS,
AND I WILL WRITE THEM ON THEIR HEARTS.
AND I WILL BE THEIR GOD,
AND THEY SHALL BE MY PEOPLE.
[11] "AND THEY SHALL NOT TEACH EVERYONE HIS FELLOW CITIZEN,
AND EVERYONE HIS BROTHER, SAYING, 'KNOW THE LORD,'
FOR ALL WILL KNOW ME,
FROM [h]THE LEAST TO THE GREATEST OF THEM.
[12] "FOR I WILL BE MERCIFUL TO THEIR INIQUITIES,
AND I WILL REMEMBER THEIR SINS NO MORE." (Jeremiah 31 and Hebrews 8)

Moses saw a copy and shadow of Heaven. Heaven will one day come down to earth. The current earth will one day burn with intense heat.

Then I saw a new heaven and a new earth; for the first heaven and the first earth passed away, and there is no longer *any* sea. ² And I saw the holy city, new Jerusalem, coming down out of heaven from God, made ready as a bride adorned for her husband. ³ And I heard a loud voice from the throne, saying, "Behold, the tabernacle of God is among men, and He will [a]dwell among them, and they shall be His people, and God Himself will be among them[b], ⁴ and He will wipe away every tear from their eyes; and there will no longer be *any* death; there will no longer be *any* mourning, or crying, or pain; the first things have passed away." (Revelation 21:1-4)

But do not let this one *fact* escape your notice, beloved, that with the Lord one day is like a thousand years, and a thousand years like one day. ⁹ The Lord is not slow about His promise, as some count slowness, but is patient toward you, not wishing for any to perish but for all to come to repentance.

¹⁰ But the day of the Lord will come like a thief, in which the heavens will pass away with a roar and the elements will be destroyed with intense heat, and the earth and [b]its works will be [c]burned up.

¹¹ Since all these things are to be destroyed in this way, what sort of people ought you to be in holy conduct and godliness, ¹² looking for and hastening the coming of the day of God, because of which the heavens will be destroyed by burning, and the elements will melt with intense heat! ¹³ But according to His promise we are looking for new heavens and a new earth, in which righteousness dwells. (2 Peter 3:8-13)

Don't buy into the millennium kingdom teaching either. There won't be a time that we believers can lay in the gold dust and do snow/gold angels. We won't have a time to be filthy rich with all the glitter and gold. Just simply study the two Resurrections in the "millennium" Revelation chapter 20, and you will quickly see that the first Resurrection was with Christ and the captives He set free from the Bosom of Abraham. But satan isn't locked up? It is all about the keys; Jesus now has the keys to death and hades, to sin and death, the Gospel.

This is the first resurrection. [6] Blessed and holy is the one who has a part in the first resurrection; over these the second death has no power, but they will be priests of God and of Christ and will reign with Him for a thousand years. (Revelation 20:5b, 6)

The second Resurrection is the Rapture; it will come like a thief in the night.

For the Lord Himself will descend from heaven with a [m]shout, with the voice of *the* archangel and with the trumpet of God, and the dead in Christ will rise first. [17] Then we who are alive [n]and remain will be caught up together with them in the clouds to meet the Lord in the air, and so we shall always be with the Lord. [18] Therefore comfort one another with these words. (1 Thessalonians 4:16-18)

Saints that died from Adam to before Christ, those that were in the Bosom of Abraham are currently reigning with Christ in Heaven. 1 Thessalonians 4 describes the rest that died after Christ to those that are living during His return.

Hebrews 9

Now even the first *covenant* had regulations of divine worship and the earthly sanctuary. [2] For there was a [a]tabernacle prepared, the [b]outer one, in which *were* the lampstand and the table and the [c]sacred bread; this is called the holy place. [3] Behind the second veil there was a [d]tabernacle which is called the Holy of Holies, [4] having a golden [e]altar of incense and the ark of the covenant covered on all sides with gold, in which was a golden jar holding the manna, and

Aaron's rod which budded, and the tables of the covenant; ⁵ and above it *were* the cherubim of glory overshadowing the mercy seat; but of these things we cannot now speak in detail.

⁶ Now when these things have been so prepared, the priests are continually entering the [f]outer [g]tabernacle performing the divine worship, ⁷ but into the second, only the high priest *enters* once a year, not without *taking* blood, which he offers for himself and for the [h]sins of the people committed in ignorance. ⁸ The Holy Spirit *is* signifying this, that the way into the holy place has not yet been disclosed while the [i]outer tabernacle is still standing, ⁹ which *is* a symbol for the present time. Accordingly both gifts and sacrifices are offered which cannot make the worshiper perfect in conscience, ¹⁰ since they *relate* only to food and drink and various washings, regulations for the [j]body imposed until a time of reformation.

¹¹ But when Christ appeared *as* a high priest of the good things [k]to come, *He entered* through the greater and more perfect [l]tabernacle, not made with hands, that is to say, not of this creation; ¹² and not through the blood of goats and calves, but through His own blood, He entered the holy place once for all, [m]having obtained eternal redemption. ¹³ For if the blood of goats and bulls and the ashes of a heifer sprinkling those who have been defiled sanctify for the [n]cleansing of the flesh, ¹⁴ how much more will the blood of Christ, who through [o]the eternal Spirit offered Himself without blemish to God, cleanse [p]your conscience from dead works to serve the living God?

¹⁵ For this reason He is the mediator of a new covenant, so that, since a death has taken place for the redemption of the transgressions that were *committed* under the first covenant, those who have been called may receive the promise of the eternal inheritance. ¹⁶ For where a [q]covenant is, there must of necessity [r]be the death of the one who made it. ¹⁷ For a [s]covenant is valid *only* when [t]men are dead, [u]for it is never in force while the one who made it lives. ¹⁸ Therefore even the first *covenant* was not inaugurated without blood. ¹⁹ For when every commandment had been spoken by Moses to all the people according to the Law, he took the blood of the calves and the goats, with water and scarlet wool and hyssop, and sprinkled both the book

itself and all the people, [20] saying, "THIS IS THE BLOOD OF THE COVENANT WHICH GOD COMMANDED YOU." [21] And in the same way he sprinkled both the [v]tabernacle and all the vessels of the ministry with the blood. [22] And according to the [w]Law, *one may* almost *say*, all things are cleansed with blood, and without shedding of blood there is no forgiveness.

[23] Therefore it was necessary for the copies of the things in the heavens to be cleansed with these, but the heavenly things themselves with better sacrifices than these. [24] For Christ did not enter a holy place made with hands, a *mere* copy of the true one, but into heaven itself, now to appear in the presence of God for us; [25] nor was it that He would offer Himself often, as the high priest enters the holy place year by year with blood that is not his own. [26] Otherwise, He would have needed to suffer often since the foundation of the world; but now once at the consummation of the ages He has been manifested to put away sin [x]by the sacrifice of Himself. [27] And inasmuch as it is [y]appointed for men to die once and after this *comes* judgment, [28] so Christ also, having been offered once to bear the sins of many, will appear a second time for salvation without *reference to* sin, to those who eagerly await Him. (Hebrews 9) https://www.biblegateway.com/passage/?search=Hebrews+9&version=NASB

Hebrews is so over the top rich. We learned that first Covenant or Testament (Old Testament, Leviticus etc.) was a shadow of the Heavenly. The Old Testament is Christ concealed. The New Testament is Christ revealed. We have previously studied the Ark within the Holy of Holies in depth. We learned that Jesus is the Bread of Life, the Golden Jar of Manna. In the wilderness God provided enough Manna in that the children of Israel had enough Good Friday Manna to enable the 7th Day Sabbath Saturday Rest i.e. the Eternal Sabbath Rest. On Friday, the sixth day, that being Good Friday, more Manna was provided, Manna that would last into Forever. Jesus on the Cross is the Manna from Heaven.

The Almond Budded Rod of Aaron is a picture of the Cross. The Word Almond means to be watchful. We previously traced the Tree of Life to the Almond Tree. The Almond, being a Seed, is actually the best physical food for one's heart, and sprouts after three days. Reading Ezekiel 33 we see the term "watchman". In the Garden of Eden after sin entered this world, cherubim guarded the Tree of Life. In the Holy of Holies the cherubim are above the Ark.

We then have the beautiful Sapphire Blue Stone Ten Commandments. We know the Ten Commandments are written on every human heart, the conscience. We know physically a dead human heart is blue. The Blood of Christ covering/fulfilling the Ten Commandments; Red over Blue equates to Purple. Purple is the color of a healthy human heart. When we studied the Rainbow Promise (Noah), we learned Red was the outer color, and Purple the inner. The Rainbow is actually a full circle when viewed from 42 degrees, a "Promise Ring". Notice also the Mercy Seat being part of the Ark. Remember "Mercy" in Titus 3.

But when the kindness of God our Savior and *His* love for mankind appeared, [5] He saved us, not on the basis of deeds which we have done in righteousness, but according to His mercy, by the washing of regeneration and renewing by the Holy Spirit, [6] whom He poured out upon us richly through Jesus Christ our Savior, [7] so that being justified by His grace we would be made heirs [a]according to *the* hope of eternal life. (Titus 3:4-7)

Recently I have tried to define, what the "chosen people" means. Ezekiel 34 does a much better job than me. Ezekiel uses the term shepherds; the Hebrews were the shepherds for all mankind. I have used the definition: the Hebrews were a chosen priesthood i.e. a chosen people centered on a priesthood, who were to point all people to the coming Messiah.

Then the word of the LORD came to me saying, [2] "Son of man, prophesy against the shepherds of Israel. Prophesy and say to [a]those shepherds, 'Thus says the Lord [b]GOD, "Woe, shepherds of Israel who have been [c]feeding themselves! Should not the shepherds [d]feed the flock? [3] You eat the fat and clothe yourselves with the

wool, you slaughter the fat *sheep* without [c]feeding the flock.
⁴ Those who are sickly you have not strengthened, the [f]diseased you
have not healed, the broken you have not bound up, the scattered you
have not brought back, nor have you sought for the lost; but with
force and with severity you have dominated them. ⁵ They were
scattered for lack of a shepherd, and they became food for every
beast of the field and were scattered. ⁶ My flock wandered through
all the mountains and on every high hill; My flock was scattered
over all the surface of the earth, and there was no one to search or
seek *for them.*"""" (Ezekiel 34:1-6)

Blood is very central to this chapter as well. We could study Blood
for a long time. Without Blood we would all die. There is Only One
Blood type, O negative, which is a Universal Donor. His Blood
moves through our dead hearts of sapphire stone. Blood gives the
heart life, Everlasting Life.

Then I will sprinkle clean water on you, and you will be clean; I will
cleanse you from all your filthiness and from all your idols.
²⁶ Moreover, I will give you a new heart and put a new spirit within
you; and I will remove the heart of stone from your flesh and give
you a heart of flesh. ²⁷ I will put My Spirit within you and cause you
to walk in My statutes, and you will be careful to observe My
ordinances. ²⁸ You will live in the land that I gave to your
forefathers; so you will be My people, and I will be your God.
(Ezekiel 36:25-28)

Jesus left Heaven, the Light came into the world. The Old
Testament shadow was made obsolete because of the Light. The
shadow is gone. Jesus fulfilled all 7 Feasts from Leviticus 23. Then
the day after the last Feast, the Feast of Weeks, being 7 Weeks of 7
i.e. 49 Days came Pentecost, Day 50, the Jubilee Day in thee Jubilee
Year. Ezekiel 36 fulfilled.

When the day of Pentecost [a]had come, they were all together in one
place. ² And suddenly there came from heaven a noise like a violent

rushing wind, and it filled the whole house where they were sitting.
[3] And there appeared to them tongues as of fire [b]distributing themselves, and [c]they [d]rested on each one of them. [4] And they were all filled with the Holy Spirit and began to speak with other [e]tongues, as the Spirit was giving them [f]utterance. (Acts 2:1-4)

The Holy Spirit changes everything. Never forget how the disciples ran scared prior to receiving the Holy Spirit. Even tough guy Peter denied Christ three times before the Spirit was given. Only after Christ completed His Work, conquering sin and death, did He return to the Right Hand of the Father, then He sent the Helper, the Holy Spirit.

Hebrews 10

For the Law, since it has *only* a shadow of the good things to come *and* not the very [a]form of things, [b]can never, by the same sacrifices which they offer continually year by year, make perfect those who draw near. [2] Otherwise, would they not have ceased to be offered, because the worshipers, having once been cleansed, would no longer have had consciousness of sins? [3] But in [c]those *sacrifices* there is a reminder of sins year by year. [4] For it is impossible for the blood of bulls and goats to take away sins. [5] Therefore, when He comes into the world, He says,

"SACRIFICE AND OFFERING YOU HAVE NOT DESIRED,
BUT A BODY YOU HAVE PREPARED FOR ME;
[6] IN WHOLE BURNT OFFERINGS AND *sacrifices* FOR SIN YOU HAVE TAKEN NO PLEASURE.
[7] "THEN I SAID, 'BEHOLD, I HAVE COME
(IN THE SCROLL OF THE BOOK IT IS WRITTEN OF ME)
TO DO YOUR WILL, O GOD.'"

8 After saying above, "SACRIFICES AND OFFERINGS AND WHOLE BURNT OFFERINGS AND *sacrifices* FOR SIN YOU HAVE NOT DESIRED, NOR HAVE YOU TAKEN PLEASURE *in them*" (which are offered according to the Law), 9 then He [d]said, "BEHOLD, I HAVE COME TO DO YOUR WILL." He takes away the first in order to establish the second. 10 By [e]this will we have been sanctified through the offering of the body of Jesus Christ once for all.

11 Every priest stands daily ministering and offering time after time the same sacrifices, which can never take away sins; 12 but He, having offered one sacrifice for [f]sins for all time, SAT DOWN AT THE RIGHT HAND OF GOD, 13 waiting from that time onward UNTIL HIS ENEMIES BE MADE A FOOTSTOOL FOR HIS FEET. 14 For by one offering He has perfected for all time those who are [g]sanctified. 15 And the Holy Spirit also testifies to us; for after saying,

16 "THIS IS THE COVENANT THAT I WILL MAKE WITH THEM
AFTER THOSE DAYS, SAYS THE LORD:
I WILL PUT MY LAWS UPON THEIR HEART,
AND ON THEIR MIND I WILL WRITE THEM,"

He then says,

17 "AND THEIR SINS AND THEIR LAWLESS DEEDS
I WILL REMEMBER NO MORE."

18 Now where there is forgiveness of these things, there is no longer *any* offering for sin.

19 Therefore, brethren, since we have confidence to enter the holy place by the blood of Jesus, 20 by a new and living way which He inaugurated for us through the veil, that is, His flesh, 21 and since *we have* a great priest over the house of God, 22 let us draw near with a [h]sincere heart in full assurance of faith, having our hearts sprinkled *clean* from an evil conscience and our bodies washed with pure water. 23 Let us hold fast the confession of our hope without wavering, for He who promised is faithful; 24 and let us consider how to stimulate one another to love and good deeds, 25 not forsaking our

own assembling together, as is the habit of some, but encouraging *one another*; and all the more as you see the day drawing near.

26 For if we go on sinning willfully after receiving the knowledge of the truth, there no longer remains a sacrifice for sins, 27 but a terrifying expectation of judgment and THE FURY OF A FIRE WHICH WILL CONSUME THE ADVERSARIES. 28 Anyone who has set aside the Law of Moses dies without mercy on *the testimony of* two or three witnesses. 29 How much severer punishment do you think he will deserve who has trampled under foot the Son of God, and has regarded as unclean the blood of the covenant by which he was sanctified, and has insulted the Spirit of grace? 30 For we know Him who said, "VENGEANCE IS MINE, I WILL REPAY." And again, "THE LORD WILL JUDGE HIS PEOPLE." 31 It is a terrifying thing to fall into the hands of the living God.

32 But remember the former days, [i]when, after being enlightened, you endured a great conflict of sufferings, 33 partly by being made a public spectacle through reproaches and tribulations, and partly by becoming sharers with those who were so treated. 34 For you showed sympathy to the prisoners and accepted joyfully the seizure of your property, knowing that you have for yourselves a better possession and a lasting one. 35 Therefore, do not throw away your confidence, which has a great reward. 36 For you have need of endurance, so that when you have done the will of God, you may receive [j]what was promised.

37 FOR YET IN A VERY LITTLE WHILE,
HE WHO IS COMING WILL COME, AND WILL NOT DELAY.
38 BUT MY RIGHTEOUS ONE SHALL LIVE BY FAITH;
AND IF HE SHRINKS BACK, MY SOUL HAS NO PLEASURE IN HIM.

39 But [k]we are not of those who shrink back to destruction, but of those who have faith to the [l]preserving of the soul. (Hebrews 10) https://www.biblegateway.com/passage/?search=Hebrews+10&version=NASB

In the last chapter we learned what was within the Holy of Holies, behind the Veil. Recall that there was only One Day a year that the high priest, and him only, could go behind the Veil. This Day is considered the Holiest Day of the Year, namely The Day of Atonement, also known as Yom Kippur. Here is a link to Leviticus 16, the Day of Atonement chapter:
https://www.biblegateway.com/passage/?search=Leviticus+16&version=NASB

We learned from Luke 1 and 2, with the timeslot of the priest Zacharias, who was the father of John the Baptist, who was of Abijah (1 Chronicles 24 has timeslots for the 24 priestly divisions, starting Nisan 1), would of performed his priestly two weeks of service and his one week of the last week of Weeks (Three Feast Weeks were required by all males, priests included) all together. Recall in Luke that an angel tells him that his wife Elizabeth will soon become pregnant with John the Baptist. By reading Luke we see that John the Baptist would have been born Nisan 1. Nisan is the number one month of the year. It is not the New Year's Day though. Oddly enough, not really, God picks the first Day of the 7th Month as New Year's Day. The Hebrew name for the 7th Month is Ethanim, which means Gift of God, which is the birthday of Jesus Christ (late September to early October). The first two days of the 7th Month are the Feast of Trumpets. What else would of terrified shepherds, lions? No; bears? No; wolves? No; Thousands of angels blowing on Trumpets? YES!!! Something very awesome as well is that if you backtrack nine months prior to Trumpets you end up at Hanukkah, the Holyday for the Light. The virgin Mary was actually overshadowed by the Holy Spirit on Hanukkah. The Light came into the world on the Holyday of the Light. Here is Luke 1 and 2 links:

https://www.biblegateway.com/passage/?search=Luke+1&version=NASB
https://www.biblegateway.com/passage/?search=Luke+2&version=NASB

With Jesus being born on Trumpets, which is a two day feast, He would have been circumcised eight days later (Luke 2:21), which is the Day of Atonement. The Promised One has arrived. The Circumcision Covenant is fulfilled. Matthew 1 shows the genealogy starting at Abraham and ending in Christ. The Once for all sin offering was in motion. Jesus would live sinless for 33 years. On the Cross Jesus would say, "It is finished!" God, Himself, knew that if He wanted Everlasting Life done Right, He would have to do it Himself. Imagine God Himself entering Human existence as a single cell within the uterus of the virgin Mary, you cannot get any more humble than this.

Have this attitude [e]in yourselves which was also in Christ Jesus, [6]who, although He existed in the form of God, did not regard equality with God a thing to be [f]grasped, [7]but [g]emptied Himself, taking the form of a bond-servant, *and* being made in the likeness of men. [8]Being found in appearance as a man, He humbled Himself by becoming obedient to the point of death, even death [h]on a cross. (Philippians 2:5-8)

We have several Old Testament Scriptures quoted in Hebrews 10: Psalm 40, Psalm 110, Jeremiah 31, Deuteronomy 32, Habakkuk 2, and Isaiah 26.

Sacrifice after sacrifice, offering after offering, over and over, **NOT** any more. **"Once for all"**, is one of the very strong messages in Hebrews. Then why do so many modern day believers say there will be more temples built? They say that they will be for the Jews to use, for their covenant. WRONG. This Book is directed to Jews, to Hebrews, hence the name Hebrews!!! The previous copy and shadow covenant is fulfilled in the Light of Jesus. Who wants to walk in the shadow i.e. darkness, when you can walk in the Marvelous Light!!!

For it is impossible for the blood of bulls and goats to take away sins.

By this will we have been sanctified through the offering of the body of Jesus Christ once for all.

Hebrews 11

Now faith is the [a]assurance of *things* [b]hoped for, the [c]conviction of things not seen. 2 For by it the men of old [d]gained approval.

3 By faith we understand that the [e]worlds were prepared by the word of God, so that what is seen was not made out of things which are visible. 4 By faith Abel offered to God a better sacrifice than Cain, through which he obtained the testimony that he was righteous, God testifying [f]about his gifts, and through [g]faith, though he is dead, he still speaks. 5 By faith Enoch was taken up so that he would not see death; AND HE WAS NOT FOUND BECAUSE GOD TOOK HIM UP; for he obtained the witness that before his being taken up he was pleasing to God. 6 And without faith it is impossible to please *Him*, for he who comes to God must believe that He is and *that* He is a rewarder of those who seek Him. 7 By faith Noah, being warned *by God* about things not yet seen, [h]in reverence prepared an ark for the salvation of his household, by which he condemned the world, and became an heir of the righteousness which is according to faith.

⁸ By faith Abraham, when he was called, obeyed [i]by going out to a place which he was to receive for an inheritance; and he went out, not knowing where he was going. ⁹ By faith he lived as an alien in the land of promise, as in a foreign *land*, dwelling in tents with Isaac and Jacob, fellow heirs of the same promise; ¹⁰ for he was looking for the city which has foundations, whose architect and builder is God. ¹¹ By faith even Sarah herself received [j]ability to conceive, even beyond the proper time of life, since she considered Him faithful who had promised. ¹² Therefore there was born even of one man, and him as good as dead [k]at that, *as many descendants* AS THE STARS OF HEAVEN IN NUMBER, AND INNUMERABLE AS THE SAND WHICH IS BY THE SEASHORE.

¹³ All these died in faith, without receiving the promises, but having seen them and having welcomed them from a distance, and having confessed that they were strangers and exiles on the earth. ¹⁴ For those who say such things make it clear that they are seeking a country of their own. ¹⁵ And indeed if they had been [l]thinking of that *country* from which they went out, they would have had opportunity to return. ¹⁶ But as it is, they desire a better *country*, that is, a heavenly one. Therefore God is not [m]ashamed to be called their God; for He has prepared a city for them.

¹⁷ By faith Abraham, when he was tested, offered up Isaac, and he who had received the promises was offering up his only begotten *son*; ¹⁸ *it was he* to whom it was said, "IN ISAAC YOUR [n]DESCENDANTS SHALL BE CALLED." ¹⁹ [o]He considered that God is able to raise *people* even from the dead, from which he also received him back [p]as a type. ²⁰ By faith Isaac blessed Jacob and Esau, even regarding things to come. ²¹ By faith Jacob, as he was dying, blessed each of the sons of Joseph, and worshiped, *leaning* on the top of his staff. ²² By faith Joseph, when he was dying, made mention of the exodus of the sons of Israel, and gave orders concerning his bones.

²³ By faith Moses, when he was born, was hidden for three months by his parents, because they saw he was a beautiful child; and they were not afraid of the king's edict. ²⁴ By faith Moses, when he had grown up, refused to be called the son of Pharaoh's daughter, ²⁵ choosing rather to endure ill-treatment with the people of God than

to enjoy the passing pleasures of sin, [26] considering the reproach of [q]Christ greater riches than the treasures of Egypt; for he was looking to the reward. [27] By faith he left Egypt, not fearing the wrath of the king; for he endured, as seeing Him who is unseen. [28] By faith he [r]kept the Passover and the sprinkling of the blood, so that he who destroyed the firstborn would not touch them. [29] By faith they passed through the Red Sea as though *they were passing* through dry land; and the Egyptians, when they attempted it, were [s]drowned.

[30] By faith the walls of Jericho fell down after they had been encircled for seven days. [31] By faith Rahab the harlot did not perish along with those who were disobedient, after she had welcomed the spies [t]in peace.

[32] And what more shall I say? For time will fail me if I tell of Gideon, Barak, Samson, Jephthah, of David and Samuel and the prophets, [33] who by faith conquered kingdoms, performed *acts of* righteousness, obtained promises, shut the mouths of lions, [34] quenched the power of fire, escaped the edge of the sword, from weakness were made strong, became mighty in war, put foreign armies to flight. [35] Women received *back* their dead by resurrection; and others were tortured, not accepting their [u]release, so that they might obtain a better resurrection; [36] and others [v]experienced mockings and scourgings, yes, also chains and imprisonment. [37] They were stoned, they were sawn in two, [w]they were tempted, they were put to death with the sword; they went about in sheepskins, in goatskins, being destitute, afflicted, ill-treated [38] (*men* of whom the world was not worthy), wandering in deserts and mountains and caves and holes [x]in the ground.

[39] And all these, having [y]gained approval through their faith, did not receive [z]what was promised, [40] because God had [aa]provided something better for us, so that apart from us they would not be made perfect. (Hebrews 11)
https://www.biblegateway.com/passage/?search=Hebrews+11&versi on=NASB

We learned some very deep doctrine in the last several chapters. Humans can be seen as the copy and shadow, being an earthly tent of meeting or temple. Sorry after sorry, sacrifice after sacrifice, offering after offering, but still just a shadow on earth. A shadow happens when we block the Light. The Father teaches us about the Son with the sun. But when the Light came down to earth, by faith we no longer block the Son, the Son shines through us. We are now the Tent of Meeting i.e. Temple of the Holy Spirit. Jesus was said to be a Carpenter and Paul a Tent Maker.

The Old Testament quotes from this chapter are in the order of Genesis 5, 15, 22, and 21. The very first Promise of the Son came soon after the fall of man in Genesis 3:15; Jesus will crush the head of sin, having proof with the bruises on His heels. His heels are now on the footstool; the footstool being the enemies of God i.e. sin and death. Jesus, the Promise, is Himself now at the Right Hand of the Father, us not to be left as orphans, sending us His Holy Spirit. The Son will come again.

This chapter is the famous faith chapter. If you ever want the definition of faith you just read verse 1:

Now faith is the [a]assurance of *things* [b]hoped for, the [c]conviction of things not seen.

Footnotes:

1. Hebrews 11:1 Or *substance* [a]
2. Hebrews 11:1 Or *expected* [b]
3. Hebrews 11:1 Or *evidence* [c]

Everyone is this chapter was saved by faith in the coming Promised One. They saw the Big Picture i.e. Heaven, Eternity, Forever. They didn't fall in worldly love i.e. lust with this world, a world that is a blink of an eye compared to Forever with Him. True Love, God is Love. A Love not forced. Love cannot be forced.

All these died in faith, without receiving the promises, but having seen them and having welcomed them from a distance, and having confessed that they were strangers and exiles on the earth. [14] For those who say such things make it clear that they are seeking a country of their own. [15] And indeed if they had been [l]thinking of that *country* from which they went out, they would have had opportunity to return. [16] But as it is, they desire a better *country*, that is, a heavenly one. Therefore God is not [m]ashamed to be called their God; for He has prepared a city for them.

So faith *comes* from hearing, and hearing by the word of Christ. (Romans 10:17)

Hebrews 12

Therefore, since we have so great a cloud of witnesses surrounding us, let us also lay aside every encumbrance and the sin which so easily entangles us, and let us run with endurance the race that is set before us, [2] [a]fixing our eyes on Jesus, the [b]author and perfecter of faith, who for the joy set before Him endured the cross, despising the shame, and has sat down at the right hand of the throne of God.

[3] For consider Him who has endured such hostility by sinners against Himself, so that you will not grow weary [c]and lose heart.

[4] You have not yet resisted [d]to the point of shedding blood in your striving against sin; [5] and you have forgotten the exhortation which is addressed to you as sons,

"My son, do not regard lightly the discipline of the Lord,
Nor faint when you are reproved by Him;
⁶ For those whom the Lord loves He disciplines,
And He scourges every son whom He receives."

⁷ It is for discipline that you endure; God deals with you as with sons; for what son is there whom *his* father does not discipline? ⁸ But if you are without discipline, of which all have become partakers, then you are illegitimate children and not sons. ⁹ Furthermore, we had [c]earthly fathers to discipline us, and we respected them; shall we not much rather be subject to the Father of [f]spirits, and live? ¹⁰ For they disciplined us for a short time as seemed best to them, but He *disciplines us* for *our* good, so that we may share His holiness. ¹¹ All discipline for the moment seems not to be joyful, but sorrowful; yet to those who have been trained by it, afterwards it yields the peaceful fruit of righteousness.

¹² Therefore, [g]strengthen the hands that are weak and the knees that are feeble, ¹³ and make straight paths for your feet, so that *the limb* which is lame may not be put out of joint, but rather be healed.

¹⁴ Pursue peace with all men, and the sanctification without which no one will see the Lord. ¹⁵ See to it that no one comes short of the grace of God; that no root of bitterness springing up causes trouble, and by it many be defiled; ¹⁶ that *there be* no immoral or godless person like Esau, who sold his own birthright for a *single* meal. ¹⁷ For you know that even afterwards, when he desired to inherit the blessing, he was rejected, for he found no place for repentance, though he sought for it with tears.

¹⁸ For you have not come to *a mountain* that can be touched and to a blazing fire, and to darkness and gloom and whirlwind, ¹⁹ and to the blast of a trumpet and the sound of words which *sound was such that* those who heard begged that no further word be spoken to them. ²⁰ For they could not bear the command, "If even a beast touches the mountain, it will be stoned." ²¹ And so terrible was the sight, *that* Moses said, "I am full of fear and trembling." ²² But you have come to Mount Zion and to the city of the living God, the heavenly Jerusalem, and to myriads of [h]angels, ²³ to the general assembly and

church of the firstborn who are enrolled in heaven, and to God, the Judge of all, and to the spirits of *the* righteous made perfect, ²⁴ and to Jesus, the mediator of a new covenant, and to the sprinkled blood, which speaks better than *the blood* of Abel.

²⁵ See to it that you do not refuse Him who is speaking. For if those did not escape when they refused him who warned *them* on earth, [i]much less *will* we *escape* who turn away from Him who *warns* from heaven. ²⁶ And His voice shook the earth then, but now He has promised, saying, "YET ONCE MORE I WILL SHAKE NOT ONLY THE EARTH, BUT ALSO THE HEAVEN." ²⁷ This *expression*, "Yet once more," denotes the removing of those things which can be shaken, as of created things, so that those things which cannot be shaken may remain. ²⁸ Therefore, since we receive a kingdom which cannot be shaken, let us [i]show gratitude, by which we may offer to God an acceptable service with reverence and awe; ²⁹ for our God is a consuming fire. (Hebrews 12)
https://www.biblegateway.com/passage/?search=Hebrews+12&version=NASB

Jesus is the Author and Perfecter of faith. A very strong emphasis in the Book of Hebrews is that there has always been One Covenant i.e. One Promise. The Old Testament contains the Covenant that is humanly impossible to attain/finish/fulfill, but God said in the Old Testament that He was sending His Son i.e. the Messiah to attain/finish/fulfill it for us. In this chapter we see that the children of Israel couldn't even touch the Mountain. Humans can't do it, but God in the Flesh, the Author and Perfecter, could and did.

If we look at the Garden of Eden we see this Promise; He (Jesus) will crush his (satan) head (Genesis 3:15). If we look at Noah, the Promise/Covenant was made with the Rainbow. The world was physically washed of sin, with Jesus we are spiritually washed of sin. The Rainbow is the Light. The Rainbow is 7 colors making up the Light, and is actually a full circle when viewed from 42 degrees, forming a Promise Ring i.e. Covenant in the clouds. We previously studied the Rainbow in depth, you have the Gospel Message in colors i.e. the outer color is Red, the Blood, we are covered….. This same Covenant was made to Abraham with Circumcision, which pointed to the coming Messiah/Promise/Light through his loins. Moses was given the 7 Feasts i.e. Holy Convocations. All 7 were fulfilled in Christ, the Covenant/Promise Fulfiller. A good way to understand is by this saying: The Old Testament is Christ concealed, the New Testament is Christ revealed.

You might ask yourself, well what about all the saints that died prior to Jesus? I assure you that they went to the Bosom of Abraham (Luke 16). Jesus went and preached to them (Ephesians 4 and 1 Peter 3). When Jesus said in John 14:6, "I am the Way, and the Truth, and the Life; **no one** comes to the Father except through Me." He was not lying. Notice at the Resurrection of Jesus (the **First Resurrection**) in Matthew 27, that there were saints who previously died seen in Jerusalem. These are the ones who are ruling with Christ in Heaven at this very moment i.e. the "millennium".

Jesus *said to him, "I am the way, and the truth, and the life; no one comes to the Father but through Me. (John 14:6)

"Now there was a rich man, and he habitually dressed in purple and fine linen, joyously living in splendor every day. [20] And a poor man named Lazarus was laid at his gate, covered with sores, [21] and longing to be fed with the *crumbs* which were falling from the rich man's table; besides, even the dogs were coming and licking his sores. [22] Now the poor man died and was carried away by the angels to Abraham's bosom; and the rich man also died and was buried. [23] In Hades he lifted up his eyes, being in torment, and *saw Abraham far away and Lazarus in his bosom. [24] And he cried out and said, 'Father Abraham, have mercy on me, and send Lazarus so that he may dip the tip of his finger in water and cool off my tongue, for I am in agony in this flame.' ²⁵ But Abraham said, 'Child, remember that during your life you received your good things, and likewise Lazarus bad things; but now he is being comforted here, and you are in agony. ²⁶ And [r]besides all this, between us and you there is a great chasm fixed, so that those who wish to come over from here to you will not be able, and *that* none may cross over from there to us.' ²⁷ And he said, 'Then I beg you, father, that you send him to my father's house— ²⁸ for I have five brothers—in order that he may warn them, so that they will not also come to this place of torment.' ²⁹ But Abraham *said, 'They have Moses and the Prophets; let them hear them.' ³⁰ But he said, 'No, father Abraham, but if someone goes to them from the dead, they will repent!' ³¹ But he said to him, 'If they do not listen to Moses and the Prophets, they will not be persuaded even if someone rises from the dead.'" (Luke 16:19-31)

But to each one of us grace was given according to the measure of Christ's gift. ⁸ Therefore [a]it says,

"WHEN HE ASCENDED ON HIGH,
HE LED CAPTIVE A HOST OF CAPTIVES,
AND HE GAVE GIFTS TO MEN."

⁹ (Now this *expression*, "He ascended," what [b]does it mean except that He also [c]had descended into the lower parts of the earth? ¹⁰ He who descended is Himself also He who ascended far above all the heavens, so that He might fill all things.) (Ephesians 4:7-10)

For Christ also died for sins once for all, *the* just for *the* unjust, so that He might bring us to God, having been put to death in the flesh, but made alive in the [n]spirit; ¹⁹ in [o]which also He went and made proclamation to the spirits *now* in prison, ²⁰ who once were disobedient, when the patience of God kept waiting in the days of Noah, during the construction of the ark, in which a few, that is, eight persons, were brought safely through *the* [p]water. ²¹ Corresponding to that, baptism now saves you—not the removal of dirt from the flesh, but an appeal to God [q]for a good conscience—through the resurrection of Jesus Christ, [22] who is at the right hand of God, having gone into heaven, after angels and authorities and powers had been subjected to Him. (1 Peter 3:18-22) (Notice above that in verse 19 that the *now* is italicized, meaning it was added by man, *now* is not in the original Greek. Noah and his family also heard the Gospel.)

And Jesus cried out again with a loud voice, and yielded up His spirit. [51] And behold, the [z]veil of the temple was torn in two from top to bottom; and the earth shook and the rocks were split. [52] The tombs were opened, and many bodies of the [aa]saints who had fallen asleep were raised; [53] and coming out of the tombs after His resurrection they entered the holy city and appeared to many. (Matthew 27:50-53)

This very chapter actually has all those currently in Heaven in detail:

But you have come to Mount Zion and to the city of the living God, the heavenly Jerusalem, and to myriads of [h]angels, [23] to the general assembly and church of the firstborn who are enrolled in heaven, and to God, the Judge of all, and to the spirits of *the* righteous made perfect, [24] and to Jesus, the mediator of a new covenant, and to the sprinkled blood, which speaks better than *the blood* of Abel. (Hebrews 12:22-24)

Notice the word **firstborn** in verse 23; these are those from the **First Resurrection**, the saints that were in the Bosom of Abraham, when Hades was two compartments: hell and the Bosom of Abraham. Notice they are currently **enrolled** in Heaven. The Rapture is the Second Resurrection. Notice at the end of verse 23, "the spirits of the righteous made perfect"; these are believers that die between the First Resurrection and Second Resurrection, only their spirit goes to Heaven until the Second Resurrection. Remember at the

Second Resurrection, at the Last Trumpet, that "the dead in Christ will rise first." In other words, if I die today, my spirit goes to Heaven, and then at the Last Trumpet I will receive my new body. Those who Jesus set free from the Bosom are currently in their new bodies in the "millennium" in Heaven.

For the Lord Himself will descend from heaven with a [m]shout, with the voice of *the* archangel and with the trumpet of God, and the dead in Christ will rise first. [17] Then we who are alive [n]and remain will be caught up together with them in the clouds to meet the Lord in the air, and so we shall always be with the Lord. [18] Therefore comfort one another with these words. (1 Thessalonians 4:16-18)

Behold, I tell you a mystery; we will not all sleep, but we will all be changed, [52] in a moment, in the twinkling of an eye, at the last trumpet; for the trumpet will sound, and the dead will be raised [r]imperishable, and we will be changed. (1 Corinthians 15:51, 52)

Here is some of Revelation 20 below, the "millennium" chapter.

Then I saw thrones, and they sat on them, and judgment was given to them. And I *saw* the souls of those who had been beheaded because of [b]their testimony of Jesus and because of the word of God, and those who had not worshiped the beast or his image, and had not received the mark on their forehead and on their hand; and they came to life and reigned with Christ for a thousand years. [5] The rest of the dead did not come to life until the thousand years were completed. This is the **first resurrection**. [6] Blessed and holy is the one who has a part in the **first resurrection**; over these the second death has no power, but they will be priests of God and of Christ and will reign with Him for a thousand years. (Revelation 20:4-6)

It is interesting how this chapter opens with "the cloud of witnesses", referring to those from the previous Faith chapter. Notice the end of Hebrews 11:

And all these, having [y]gained approval through their faith, **did not** receive [z]what was promised, 40 because God had [aa]provided something better for us, so that apart from us they would not be made perfect. (Hebrews 11:39, 40)

They died before the Promise/Covenant was fulfilled. They waited in the Bosom for the preaching of Christ. Then this chapter, referring to them, opens with calling them, "a great cloud of witnesses", which is interesting, because "clouds" are generally above, such as, caught up together with them in the **clouds** to meet the Lord in the air….(1 Thessalonians 4:17).

Therefore, since we have so great a cloud of witnesses surrounding us, let us also lay aside every encumbrance and the sin which so easily entangles us, and let us run with endurance the race that is set before us, 2 [a]fixing our eyes on Jesus, the [b]author and perfecter of faith, who for the joy set before Him endured the cross, despising the shame, and has sat down at the right hand of the throne of God. (Hebrews 12:1, 2)

Above Jesus is called the Author and Perfecter i.e. the Author of the Covenant and the Perfecter/Fulfiller of the Covenant. Jesus is the Author and Perfecter. Jesus is the Alpha and the Omega. Jesus is the First and the Last. Jesus is the Beginning and the End.

"I am the Alpha and the Omega," says the Lord God, "who is and who was and who [f]is to come, the Almighty." (Revelation 1:8)

Then He said to me, "[c]It is done. I am the Alpha and the Omega, the beginning and the end. I will give to the one who thirsts from the spring of the water of life without cost. (Revelation 21:6)

"Behold, I am coming quickly, and My reward *is* with Me, to render to every man [g]according to what he has done. 13 I am the Alpha and the Omega, the first and the last, the beginning and the end."

[14] Blessed are those who wash their robes, so that they may have the right to the tree of life, and may enter by the gates into the city. [15] Outside are the dogs and the sorcerers and the immoral persons and the murderers and the idolaters, and everyone who loves and practices lying.

[16] "I, Jesus, have sent My angel to testify to you these things [h]for the churches. I am the root and the descendant of David, the bright morning star." (Revelation 22:12-16)

Hebrews 13

Let love of the brethren continue. [2] Do not neglect to show hospitality to strangers, for by this some have entertained angels without knowing it. [3] Remember the prisoners, as though in prison with them, *and* those who are ill-treated, since you yourselves also are in the body. [4] Marriage *is to be held* in honor among all, and the *marriage* bed *is to be* undefiled; for fornicators and adulterers God will judge. [5] *Make sure that* your character is free from the love of money, being content with what you have; for He Himself has said, "I WILL NEVER DESERT YOU, NOR WILL I EVER FORSAKE YOU," [6] so that we confidently say,

"THE LORD IS MY HELPER, I WILL NOT BE AFRAID.
WHAT WILL MAN DO TO ME?"

[7] Remember those who led you, who spoke the word of God to you; and considering the [a]result of their conduct, imitate their faith. [8] Jesus Christ *is* the same yesterday and today and forever. [9] Do not be carried away by varied and strange teachings; for it is good for the heart to be strengthened by grace, not by foods, through which those who [b]were so occupied were not benefited. [10] We have an

altar from which those who serve the [c]tabernacle have no right to eat. [11] For the bodies of those animals whose blood is brought into the holy place by the high priest *as an offering* for sin, are burned outside the camp. [12] Therefore Jesus also, that He might sanctify the people through His own blood, suffered outside the gate. [13] So, let us go out to Him outside the camp, bearing His reproach. [14] For here we do not have a lasting city, but we are seeking *the city* which is to come.

[15] Through Him then, let us continually offer up a sacrifice of praise to God, that is, the fruit of lips that [d]give thanks to His name. [16] And do not neglect doing good and sharing, for with such sacrifices God is pleased.

[17] Obey your leaders and submit *to them*, for they keep watch over your souls as those who will give an account. [e]Let them do this with joy and not [f]with grief, for this would be unprofitable for you.

[18] Pray for us, for we are sure that we have a good conscience, desiring to conduct ourselves honorably in all things. [19] And I urge *you* all the more to do this, so that I may be restored to you the sooner.

[20] Now the God of peace, who brought up from the dead the great Shepherd of the sheep [g]through the blood of the eternal covenant, *even* Jesus our Lord, [21] equip you in every good thing to do His will, working in us that which is pleasing in His sight, through Jesus Christ, to whom *be* the glory forever and ever. Amen.

[22] But I urge you, brethren, [h]bear with [i]this word of exhortation, for I have written to you briefly. [23] [j]Take notice that our brother Timothy has been released, with whom, if he comes soon, I will see you. [24] Greet all of your leaders and all the [k]saints. Those from Italy greet you.

[25] Grace be with you all. (Hebrews 13)
https://www.biblegateway.com/passage/?search=Hebrews+13&version=NASB

Love God and love your neighbor, which are the first and second greatest Commandments. The first part of the Ten Commandments is about loving God; the second is about loving your neighbor. Avoid sinning; giving into the flesh is still unacceptable. Do not sin, thinking that you can always just ask for forgiveness. Remember part of the last chapter dealt with discipline. God is not mocked (Galatians 6:7). In the last chapter we read quotes from Proverbs 3, such as, "FOR THOSE WHOM THE LORD LOVES HE DISCIPLINES".

While still in these bodies we will continue to have to crucify the flesh, the battle between the flesh and the Spirit continues (Galatians 5 and Romans 7). Hebrews 13:5&6 quotes Psalm 118:6 and Deuteronomy 31:6. In other words we are not left as orphans; we have a Helper i.e. the Holy Spirit.

I will ask the Father, and He will give you another [b]Helper, that He may be with you forever; [17] *that is* the Spirit of truth, whom the world cannot receive, because it does not see Him or know Him, *but* you know Him because He abides with you and will be in you.

[18] "I will not leave you as orphans; I will come to you. [19] [c]After a little while the world will no longer see Me, but you *will* see Me; because I live, you will live also. [20] In that day you will know that I am in My Father, and you in Me, and I in you. [21] He who has My commandments and keeps them is the one who loves Me; and he who loves Me will be loved by My Father, and I will love him and will disclose Myself to him." (John 14:16-21)

We previously studied the clean and unclean animals. God was teaching the spiritual with the physical. The unclean animals ate from two kingdoms, the plant and the animal/flesh kingdoms. The clean animals ate from the plant kingdom only. This is a picture of the Tree of Life vs. the tree of knowledge of good and evil, which is also a picture of the Spirit vs. the flesh. Remember satan tempted Eve to eat from the tree of knowledge of good and evil with the lust of the flesh and the lust of the eyes and the boastful pride of life (1

John 2:16). Recall that satan used the exact same three to tempt Jesus. Remember Esau in the last chapter, Hebrews 12:

See to it that no one comes short of the grace of God; that no root of bitterness springing up causes trouble, and by it many be defiled; that *there be* no immoral or godless person like Esau, who sold his own birthright for a *single* meal. [17] For you know that even afterwards, when he desired to inherit the blessing, he was rejected, for he found no place for repentance, though he sought for it with tears. (Hebrews 12:16, 17)

Remember the Herod's were direct descendants of Esau, they were the Edomites. Esau is a picture of the worldly kingdom, the flesh, the tree of knowledge of good and evil. Through Jacob, the Promise i.e. the Covenant was fulfilled in Jesus Christ, the Cross being related to the Tree of Life. With this in mind and heart we can understand Romans 9:13, "Just as it is written, "Jacob I loved, but Esau I hated.""

Notice verses 11-14:

For the bodies of those animals whose blood is brought into the holy place by the high priest *as an offering* for sin, are burned outside the camp. [12] Therefore Jesus also, that He might sanctify the people through His own blood, suffered outside the gate. [13] So, let us go out to Him outside the camp, bearing His reproach. [14] For here we do not have a lasting city, but we are seeking *the city* which is to come.

We previously learned that the Jerusalem is a picture of the heart. Jesus took our sin upon Himself within the walls of Jerusalem, within the walls of our heart. He then exited the walls with our sin. He took our sin outside the gate, outside the camp to Golgotha to be crucified. Verse 14 above speaks of the New Jerusalem, which is to come.

Now the God of peace, who brought up from the dead the great Shepherd of the sheep through the blood of the **eternal covenant, Jesus our Lord**, [21] equip you in every good thing to do His will, working in us that which is pleasing in His sight, **through Jesus Christ, to whom** *be* **the glory forever and ever. Amen. (Hebrews 13:20, 21)**

90938335R00227

Made in the USA
Middletown, DE
27 September 2018